LAW AND MORALITY
IN ISRAEL'S WAR WITH THE PLO

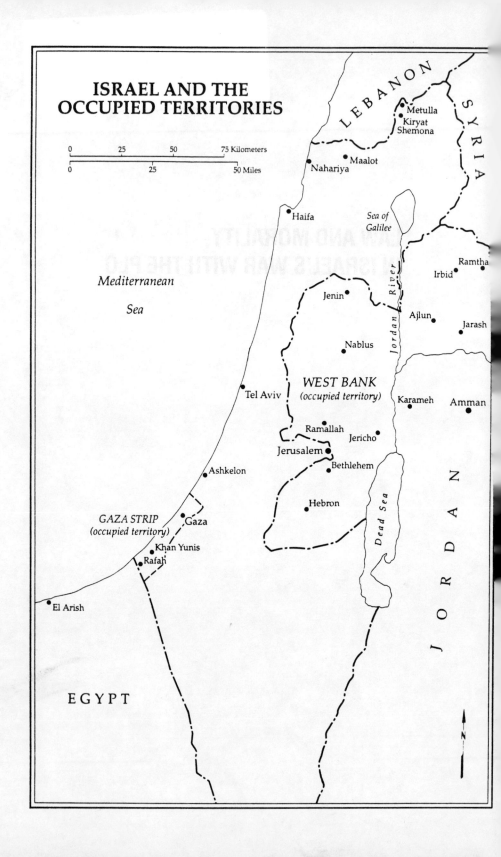

ISRAEL AND THE
OCCUPIED TERRITORIES

0   25   50   75 Kilometers
0   25   50 Miles

Mediterranean

Sea

LEBANON

SYRIA

Metulla

Kiryat
Shemona

Maalot

Nahariya

Haifa

*Sea of
Galilee*

Ramtha

Irbid

Jenin

Jordan River

Ajlun

Jarash

Nablus

WEST BANK
(occupied territory)

Tel Aviv

Karameh

Amman

Ramallah

Jericho

Jerusalem

Bethlehem

Ashkelon

Hebron

Dead Sea

GAZA STRIP
(occupied territory)

Gaza

Khan Yunis

Rafah

JORDAN

El Arish

EGYPT

N

LAW AND MORALITY
IN ISRAEL'S WAR WITH THE PLO
William V. O'Brien

Routledge   New York and London

This book is dedicated to my mentor, Professor Ernst H. Feilchenfeld, and my wife, Madge L. O'Brien

Published in 1991 by

Routledge
An imprint of Routledge, Chapman and Hall, Inc.
29 West 35 Street
New York, NY 10001

Published in Great Britain by

Routledge
11 New Fetter Lane
London EC4P 4EE

Printed in the United States of America

Credit: the maps in the text (on the frontispiece and opposite the opening page of chapter 5) were prepared by Bowring Cartographic.

Library of Congress Cataloging in Publication Data

O'Brien, William Vincent.
    Law and morality in Israel's war with the PLO / William
V. O'Brien.
        p.   cm.
    ISBN 0-415-90300-9 (HB). ISBN 0-415-90301-7 (PB)
    1. Jewish-Arab relations—Moral and ethical aspects. 2. Israel—
Military policy—Moral and ethical aspects. 3. Munaẓẓamat al
-Taḥrīr al-Filasṭīnīyah. 4. Just war doctrine. 5. War
(International law) I. Title.
DS119.7.O27   1991
956.04—dc20
                                                            90-23299

British Library Cataloguing in Publication Data also available.

Contents

Preface

I have received generous assistance in many forms from institutions and individuals over the years. A grant from the United States Institute of Peace, matched by Georgetown University, permitted me to take a leave of absence in fall 1989 to complete the first draft of the book. Summer Research Grants from the Graduate School (1984) and the Edmund A. Walsh School of Foreign Service (1989 and 1990) also sustained my research. I am grateful for the assistance of Gerald M. Mara, Associate Dean for Research, Graduate School, and Charles E. Pirtle, Associate Dean, School of Foreign Service, Georgetown University, in obtaining these grants.

I have had the cooperation of the government of Israel in the preparation of this book. So many Israeli diplomats, officials and military officers have been of assistance that it is somewhat arbitrary to name some of them here. However, in the Ministry of Foreign Affairs, I am especially grateful to Ambassadors Simcha Dinitz, Ephraim Evron, Meir Rosenne, Benjamin Netanyahu and Moshe Arad, as well as Amira Arnon, Moshe Fox, Patricia Friedman, Hemda Golan, Dan Kyram, Dan Meggido, David Peleg, Moshe Raviv, Robbie Sabel and Moshe Yeagar. Among the officers of the Israel Defense Forces I was assisted and instructed by Maj. Gen. Shlomo Gazit (Res.), Maj. Gen. Menachem Meron (Res.), Maj. Gen. Dov Shefi (Res.), Brig. Gen. (Res.) Amos Gilboa, Brig. Gen. Nahman Shai, Brig. Gen. Ephraim Sneh (Res.), Col. Shalom Harari, Col. (Res.) Yoel Singer, Col. David Yahav and Lt. Col. Arik Gordin.

My special thanks go to Yigal Carmon, Advisor to the Prime Minister for Countering Terrorism, who provided me with his insights based on vast experience and valuable materials.

I greatly profited from the advice of Maj. Gen. (Res.) Aharon Yariv, head of the Jafee Center for Strategic Studies, Tel Aviv University, and his colleagues, particularly Mark Heller and Maj. Gen. (Res.) Aryeh Shalev. Likewise, I am indebted to Professor Itamar Rabinovitch, former head of the Moshe Dayan Center for Middle East and African Studies, now dean of faculties, Tel Aviv University, and to his successor as head of the Dayan Center, Dr. Asher Susser and their colleagues for their valuable information and analyses.

Professors Ruth Lapidoth and Yoram Dinstein of the law faculties of the Hebrew University of Jerusalem and Tel Aviv, respectively, have given me the benefit of their deep understanding of international law and practical experience.

My colleagues who have participated in the Aaron and Cecile Visiting Israeli Professor Program in our Department of Government at Georgetown have encouraged, informed and corrected me over the years. My warm thanks to Dan Horowitz, Moshe Ma'Oz, Amnon Sella, Ehud Sprinzak of the Hebrew University of Jerusalem; Haggai Erlich, Yair Evron, Aharon Kleiman and Yaacov Ro'i of Tel Aviv University; and Avner Yaniv of Haifa University.

Professors James Turner Johnson of Rutgers University, Alan Dowty of the University of Notre Dame, Guenter Lewy of the University of Massachusetts-Amherst (emeritus) and Christopher Joyner of The George Washington University read my manuscript and provided helpful criticism. Lt. Col. Richard L. Winslow, Ph.D. Georgetown, 1989, now assigned to the U.S. Joint Staff as a Middle East specialist, also read the manuscript and made extremely useful comments.

Over the years W. Hays Parks has been a source of legal materials and realistic appraisals of law-of-war issues. From his vantage point in the International Affairs Division of the U.S. Army's Judge Advocate General's Office, Parks has become, in my view, the most informed and authoritative American expert on the law of war.

I gratefully recall that my friend and late colleague Professor Marver Bernstein read and commented at length on several of my chapters just before leaving for the Middle East, to die tragically with his wife Sheva in a hotel fire in Cairo. My colleagues Professors Robert Lieber and Anthony Arend gave me valuable critiques of the manuscript.

A group of my graduate students read my draft chapters and criticized them roundly in numerous meetings. I thank Mark Genest, Mark Lagon and Haleh Vaziri for their conscientious and spirited critiques.

My research assistants during the years that I have been working on this book have matched scholarly excellence with dedication to the project. Dr. Chong Pin Lin and Dr. Robert Beck helped me begin the long task of research necessary to lay the foundation for my analyses. For the last three years, Gary T. Armstrong has been my research assistant. He has contributed mightily to every aspect of the project, from organization to research to composition and editing. I thank him for his indispensable help and support.

Mr. Armstrong and I owe thanks to librarians of Georgetown's Lauinger Library, the United Nations Library in Washington and the Library of Congress for their prompt and friendly assistance.

I have dedicated this book, first, to Professor Ernst H. Feilchenfeld (1900–1956), my mentor who launched me as a student of the law of war and who aroused my interest in Israel. Finally, I have dedicated the book to my wife, Madge, who has inspired my scholarly work from the first days of our marriage, when we were living in Paris on a Fulbright scholarship while I wrote my Ph.D. dissertation, to the present.

William V. O'Brien
Washington, D.C.
November 1990

Introduction

Israel's war with the Palestine Liberation Organization (PLO) is one of the most enduring and bitter conflicts of our era. It has been waged under intense international scrutiny. This has been the result, in part, of the constant fears of escalation from low-intensity conflict to a conventional international war, fears that proved to be well founded in 1956, 1967, 1973 and 1982. However, the international scrutiny—by governments, by the United Nations, by the world media—has also been the consequence of the form of the hostilities. This has been a war waged almost entirely in a pattern of terrorist attacks and counterterror responses. Both forms of belligerent action are dramatic and readily depicted on television and in photographs. The pictures of masked terrorists brandishing their weapons during a highjacking, of devastated sites of terrorist bombings in market-places, of collapsed buildings and women weeping over the death of loved ones killed in Israeli counterterror attacks on PLO bases located in villages or towns, of the outraged mourners at funerals for victims of either terror or counterterror attacks—all appear prominently on television and in news-papers and magazines around the world.

These images of death and destruction elicit strong emotions. These emotions affect profoundly the attitudes that governmental decision-mak-ers, ordinary citizens, humanitarian organizations and the media take with respect to the political issues in the Arab-Israeli conflict. Thus, the way in which the war between the PLO and Israel is conducted greatly affects the attitudes of third parties with respect to the political and moral claims of the adversaries.

This is not a new problem for a state at war. However, the form of the PLO's war with Israel, waged in the context of the broader Arab-Israeli conflict, presents a particularly acute problem for Israel. The PLO's "armed struggle" in its war of national liberation with Israel takes the form of terrorist attacks in Israel, in the West Bank and Gaza, and throughout the world against Israeli or other Jewish persons and interests. Clearly, such a war by itself cannot defeat Israel. However, the PLO's terrorist war may accomplish several important things.

First, PLO terror attracts attention to the Palestinian cause, and this is apparently considered desirable despite the negative reactions that terrorist behavior elicits. Second, PLO terror provokes Israel into counterterror measures that are controversial and risky. Since the PLO operates mainly from sanctuary states bordering Israel, Israeli counterterror attacks have been carried out in those states, particularly, since 1970, in Lebanon. The PLO makes every effort to blend into the local population in these countries so that it is virtually impossible to attack its bases and personnel without harming the population.

This then is Israel's strategic problem in its war with the PLO. It is the problem of reconciling the requirements for effective counterterror operations with the restraints of the international law of war and with morality. This book undertakes to describe Israel's war with the PLO and to discuss the legal and moral issues raised by its conduct.

In this book I continue my effort in *The Conduct of Just and Limited War* (1981) to understand the proper use of the military instrument of foreign policy in the service of a state's vital interest and to relate true military utility to legal and moral restraint in the use of armed coercion. As I will demonstrate, the fundamental legal and moral requirement limiting use of the military instrument is that it must be justified by true military necessity and that it must be limited by the principle of humanity. Both the international law of war and modern just war doctrine which I will employ attempt to balance the fair demands of military necessity with considerations of humanity that serve to mitigate the suffering and destruction of war.

This book is divided into three parts. Part I outlines the basic objectives and strategies of the PLO and Israel as I understand them. As far as I am aware, the overview of the conflict from the PLO's organization in 1964 and the beginning of its war of national liberation against Israel in 1965 to the present has not been approximated in the literature on the Arab-Israeli conflict. It is important that the character and duration of this long war be understood. Much of the governmental, popular and media reaction to Israeli actions in this conflict have reflected a failure to recognize that the conflict is not a series of violent episodes, to be judged individually, but a continuous war that varies in intensity but never stops.

Given PLO Chairman Yasir Arafat's December 1988 claims to have recognized Israel and renounced terrorism, it has been necessary in these chapters and throughout the book to consider alternative versions of the PLO's objectives and strategies: (1) the original objective of regaining all of Palestine by "armed struggle"—which has meant mainly terrorism; (2) a revised objective of obtaining a Palestinian state in the West Bank and Gaza through negotiations, followed by peaceful coexistence with Israel; or (3) establishment of a Palestinian state in the West Bank and Gaza (Phase I), followed, when feasible, by resumption of "armed struggle" to "liberate" and reclaim all of Palestine.

As this book was written it was extremely difficult to evaluate the evidence of the PLO's ultimate intentions and current strategies. Opinions differed greatly over the question whether the PLO was firmly committed to a policy of reconciliation with Israel or to a continuation of its war with Israel. As of Fall 1990 the PLO was identified with the aggressive and oppressive policies of Iraq's Saddam Hussein. The PLO and many individual Palestinians vigorously supported Hussein's threats against Israel. This identification naturally suggests pessimism about the prospects for a peaceful settlement of the Palestinian-Israeli conflict. There is no way of predicting what the state of this question will be when this book appears. Consequently, the three versions suggested above will be retained in the legal and moral analyses.

Part II analyzes Israel's war with the PLO from the standpoint of international law. The international law of war consists of two main parts: (1) war-decision law governing recourse to armed force, traditionally known as the *jus ad bellum;* and (2) war-conduct law regulating the conduct of military operations, traditionally known as the *jus in bello.*

The PLO's "armed struggle" against Israel has been waged almost exclusively in the form of terrorist attacks in Israel and worldwide. During most of this long war Israel has responded with limited counterterror operations of short duration, usually in the form of ground or air attacks on PLO bases in sanctuary states bordering Israel from which the PLO has operated. In 1978 Israel conducted an incursion into Lebanon of several months duration, the Litani Operation. In 1982 Israel fought a conventional war with the PLO and Syria lasting almost three months.

In Part II, I devote five chapters to the international legal issues raised by Israel's counterterror strategies and tactics. Chapter 3 is an introduction to international law generally and to the law of war in particular. Chapters 4 and 5 deal with international war-decision law regarding Israeli counterterror operations generally and the 1982 Lebanon War. Chapters 6 and 7 evaluate the conduct of Israeli counterterror operations and the 1982 Lebanon War. Chapter 8 discusses the international law issues raised by Israel's prolonged occupation of the West Bank and Gaza, especially since the outbreak of the *intifada* in December 1987.

Part III of this book approaches the normative issues of Israel's war with the PLO from perspectives of modern just war doctrine. Some of these issues have already been discussed in the war-conduct chapters, 6 and 7, since both the international law of war and just war doctrine base the *jus in bello* on the principles of military necessity and humanity, of which the core elements are the requirements of proportionality and discrimination. In Part III emphasis is placed on the difference between the international law of war, in which the legal permissibility of a belligerent's recourse to armed force is strictly separated from its rights and duties in the conduct of hostilities, and just war doctrine, which intermingles issues of the ends, means and probable consequences of a war in a comprehensive moral analysis.

This book is concerned with the legal and moral issues confronted by Israel in its war with the PLO. It does not attempt a parallel analysis of the legal and moral issues raised by the PLO's war with Israel, with two important exceptions. First, the book takes the view that, no matter what the legal status or moral claims of the PLO's objectives, its principal means of "armed struggle" is terror, and terror is by definition illegal and immoral. There is no legally permissible terror, nor is there any just terror. Second, given the possibility that the PLO and others may be committed to the goal of destroying Israel and its Jewish society, it is necessary in Chapter 10 to raise issues of comparative justice between the adversaries and of the probable consequences of a definitive victory by the PLO and its Arab allies.

Unlike most books on the Arab-Israeli conflict, this one will not offer any political judgments, solutions or predictions. For me Israel's war with the PLO is the tragic consequence of two peoples claiming the same home-land and being prepared to fight for possession of it for generations. The international law of war and just war doctrine may offer some guidelines for the conduct of this intractable war and some bases for evaluating the legality and morality of Israeli actions in it. I believe that these legal and moral guidelines may often lead to prudent and effective use of the military instrument. Finally, both the law of war and just war doctrine end with the injunction that a belligerent should not take measures that will unnecessarily diminish the prospects for a just and lasting peace. In this conflict obser-vance of this precept is extremely difficult but extremely necessary.

Part I
Israel's War with the PLO

1

The Belligerents' Objectives, Strategies and Tactics

Since its creation in 1964 the Palestine Liberation Organization has been engaged in a war of national liberation against Israel. This war has its origins in the creation of the Jewish state and, beyond that, in Arab-Jewish clashes going back to the early days of the Zionist movement. The goals of the PLO, as mandated explicitly in the 1968 Palestinian Covenant, are:

(1) the dismantling of the state of Israel and the defeat of the "imperialist" Zionist movement, which is "racist and fanatic in its nature, aggressive, expansionist and colonial in its aims, and fascist in its methods";
(2) removal from Palestine of all Jews who had not "normally resided in Palestine" at the time of the "Zionist invasion";
(3) establishment of a Palestinian state as the homeland of the Arab Palestinians, "with the boundaries it had during the British mandate," "an indivisible territorial unit."

The means to achieve these goals are also clearly stated in the covenant: "Armed struggle is the only way to liberate Palestine."[1]

This armed struggle began on New Year's Eve 1965, when the PLO announced the launching of its first *fedayeen* attacks on Israel.[2] Since then, the PLO has been at war with Israel. There had been little question about the goals of this war from 1964 until November 1988, when the Palestine National Council (PNC) declared Palestine an independent state, agreed to negotiate a solution to the Arab-Israel conflict based on UN Security Council Resolutions 242 and 338, and condemned terrorism.[3] The main unanswered question had been—and remains—the implications of the resolution of the Twelfth PNC's 1974 Cairo meeting to establish a Palestinian state in whatever part of Palestine the PLO could control, a question to be discussed below. Neither Israel or the United States accepted the PNC's November 1988 statement as a sufficient renunciation of the PLO's covenant ends and

7

means. However, in December 1988 the PLO's chairman, Yasir Arafat, went through a series of declarations which finally satisfied the United States, leading to diplomatic talks with the PLO in Tunis. In a December 14 press conference in Geneva, Arafat accepted Security Council Resolutions 242 and 338 without the usual PLO qualifications and "renounced" rather than "condemned" terrorism.[4]

It is still an open question whether the goals of the Palestinian Covenant and the commitment to armed struggle remain the basis for the PLO's campaign for Palestinian self-determination. On May 2, 1989, Arafat, speaking on French television from Paris, stated that the covenant was "null and void" ("c'est caduque").[5]

Article 33 of the covenant states that it may not be amended except by a vote of the majority of two-thirds of the membership of the PNC at a special session convened for that purpose. Beyond the legal requirement, the political reality is that the PLO is a federation of Palestinian resistance groups of different sizes, influence within the organization, political/ideological orientations and relationships with Arab states. The covenant has been assumed to be the fundamental basis for the often contentious cooperation of these groups. It is not clear that Arafat, even as leader of Fatah, the largest and most important group, and chairman of the PLO, recognized universally as its leader, can change the goals of the covenant without the assent of the PNC.[6]

Moreover, the Israelis claim that Arafat has not renounced armed struggle against them. Arafat's December 14, 1988, Geneva statement indicated his willingness to accept the lesser goal of a Palestinian state in the West Bank and Gaza, coexisting with Israel. However, while renouncing terrorism, Arafat has continued to justify attacks on Israel across the Lebanon border, claiming that they are "military," not "terror," attacks. Arafat also has rejected requests to abate or end the use of violence in the *intifada* in the West Bank and Gaza.[7] To be sure, it is uncertain to what degree Arafat controls either form of resistance to Israel. The fifth congress of Fatah, August 3–9, 1989, adopted a program calling for "intensifying and escalating armed action and all forms of struggle to eliminate the Zionist Israeli occupation of our land." The United States branded this development "unhelpful," as Israel cited it as proof of Fatah's intention to continue terrorist activities.[8] Throughout the first half of 1990 the United States, which was conducting a dialogue with the PLO based on the assumption that terrorism had been renounced by Arafat, and Israel debated whether Arafat had lived up to his commitment. The debate was punctuated on May 30, 1990, when Palestine Liberation Front (PLF) *fedayeen* attempted to attack beaches in the Tel Aviv area. When Arafat failed satisfactorily to disavow the incident and discipline its perpetrators, the United States suspended talks with the PLO on June 20, 1990.[9] In any event, the PLO's war with Israel continues and the Israeli government continues to brand the PLO as a "terrorist organization" and refuses to deal with it.

To many outsiders, the obvious solution to the conflict is to create a Palestinian state in the West Bank and Gaza that would coexist peacefully with Israel. Some in Israel are willing to discuss this possibility, but there has been no sufficient political base for such an initiative. Moreover, even those Israelis who would consider accepting a Palestinian state tend to be apprehensive about it, especially if it were to be governed by a predominantly PLO leadership. There is the fear that the PLO might accept a West Bank/Gaza state without renouncing its covenant goal of an all-Palestine state. Many Israelis believe that creation of the West Bank/Gaza state would only be the first step toward total liberation of Palestine—no matter what the PLO and other Palestinians might say. This fear is expressed in terms of a "two-phase" plan which was apparently adopted by the PLO in 1974, although there was considerable disagreement over this within the organization.[10]

Under the "two-phase" plan the PLO would, first, establish a Palestinian state in any part of Palestine that it could obtain—phase one. Thereafter, this Palestinian state would serve as the base for a continued armed struggle, ultimately leading to the recovery of all of Palestine and the liquidation of Israel, as demanded by the covenant. While it is true that the Palestinians alone could not defeat Israel militarily, the fear has been that the West Bank and Gaza in the hands of Palestinians committed to continuation of the war of national liberation could be the launching pad for attacks by Arab states, such as Syria and Iraq, which would profit from the extreme vulnerability of Israel's pre–June 1967 borders. Israel would also be more vulnerable to terrorist incursions.[11]

Yehoshafat Harkabi has confronted Israel's dilemma of evaluating the prospects for a secure peace with the Palestinians and their Arab allies. As one of Israel's leading experts on the PLO, he knows the threat to Israel's existence that is implicit in the Palestinian Covenant. However, Harkabi distinguishes between goals that represent a "grand design"—aspirations, hopes—and "policy" that designates the practical goals which are judged to be attainable. Harkabi believes that continued Israeli occupation of the territories will bring disasters for all concerned. Accordingly, he pleads for Israeli policies that accept the possibility that the Palestinians and their Arab allies will operate on the basis of realistic policies rather than adamant commitment to the grand design of destroying Israel and reclaiming all of Palestine. He believes that, even if the Palestinians and/or other Arabs consider a West Bank/Gaza state as only phase one of the two-phase program, the benefits of phase one and the risks of phase two will in time be clarified, and phase one will become semipermanent. It should be emphasized that Harkabi's main goal is the preservation of the state of Israel, not the realization of Palestinian self-determination.[12]

Whatever the prospects for a realistic Palestinian/Arab policy as distinguished from unrelenting pursuit of the grand design of the Palestinian Covenant, the threat of a two-phase Palestinian war of national liberation is sufficiently plausible to warrant caution in declaring an end to Israel's war with the PLO even should there appear to be unprecedented progress toward peaceful coexistence between the adversaries. This threat need not originate entirely from the Palestinians. It is notorious that Arab states have often used the Palestinian cause for their own purposes. Even if a Palestinian leadership and population might be reconciled to a West Bank/Gaza state, Arab states might incite "phase two" for their own reasons. Beyond this, there are the incalculable possibilities that profound religious/ideological motivations might lead to Arab holy wars to drive the Jews from land sacred to Islam.

Israel's war with the PLO has already continued for over twenty-five years. The end is not in sight and, given the spectre of the two-phase threat to Israel, it may be difficult to recognize the true end if and when it comes. This war has elicited a number of debates over legal and moral issues. As will be seen in subsequent chapters, these issues have been difficult to clarify because of the unsettled state of international law and the lack of moral consensus in the international system. But beyond these obstacles to normative analysis, there is a lack of knowledge about and understanding of the belligerent interaction in Israel's war with the PLO. It has been difficult to obtain a reasonably objective picture of what the adversaries are doing and why they are doing it. There is no comprehensive history of Israel's war with the PLO. Accordingly, it is necessary to present an overview of the hostilities in this war as a basis for the succeeding normative chapters. This is the task of this and the following chapter.

This chapter describes the pattern of hostilities in this long war, viewed primarily from Israeli perspectives. First, however, the PLO's organization, strategies and tactics will be reviewed. Explanations for the motivations behind PLO policies will be suggested, but it remains for others to provide evidence of the reasons for these policies.

Following a section on the PLO, the organization, strategies and tactics of Israel will be described. In Chapter 2 the course of hostilities in this war will then be traced in discernible phases to the present. Together, these two chapters will provide the material bases for the normative analyses in succeeding chapters.

The PLO's Strategies and Tactics

The PLO is made up of a number of organizations. The list changes from time to time. Presently the PLO includes:

(1) Fatah, led by Yasir Arafat, based in Tunis after August 1982; forces estimated at 6,000, of which one-third are in Lebanon;

(2) Popular Front for the Liberation of Palestine (PFLP), led by George Habash, a neo-Marxist group of about 3,000, based in Syria and Lebanon, originally very militant, recently more moderate;

(3) Democratic Front for the Liberation of Palestine (DFLP), led by Nayif Hawatmeh, a Marxist-Leninist group of about 1,200 in Syria and 400 in South Yemen;

(4) Palestine Liberation Front (PLF), led by Mohammed Abbas, better known as Abul Abbas; about 500 members in Tunisia and Iraq;

(5) Arab Liberation Front (ALF), led by Abdel Rahim Amed, part of the Baath party based in Baghdad; about 450 members, controlled by Iraq;

(6) Palestine Communist party (PCP), led by Suleiman Najjab, did not participate in the Executive Committee until 1987 but has been active in all PLO institutions since then, has no militia.

These groups are generally loyal to Arafat, although they sometimes deviate sharply from his policies. Anti-Arafat groups include:

(1) Popular Front for the Liberation of Palestine—General Command (PFLP–GC), led by Ahmed Jebril; about 1,000 members; one of the active militant groups with headquarters in Damascus and bases in Lebanon;

(2) Fatah Uprising, led by Col. Saaed Mousa, known as Abu Musa; broke away from Arafat's Fatah in 1983 and with Syrian encouragement and active combat support drove Arafat's forces out of the Bekaa Valley and Tripoli; about 3,000 members in Syria and eastern Lebanon;

(3) Saiqa, led by Issam al Qadi, with headquarters in Damascus; is part of the Baath party; about 1,500 members;

(4) Popular Struggle Front (PSF), led by Samir Ghouseh; 350 members, mostly in Syria and eastern Lebanon;

(5) Fatah Revolutionary Council, led by Sabry al Banna, known worldwide as Abu Nidal, the most violent Palestinian group; membership
not known, relation to the PLO unclear.

In addition to the PLO groups, the Islamic Resistance Organization,
known in Arabic as Hamas, is a fundamentalist group in the West Bank
and Gaza which rejects compromise and urges *jihad* against Israel.[13]

The PLO is governed by an Executive Committee which elects a chairman.
Yasir Arafat has been chairman since 1969.[14] The Executive Committee is
elected by the Palestine National Council (PNC) which aims to meet annually
but in practice has not always been able to do so.[15] The members, who
represent constituent organizations of the PLO, are limited in the degree to
which they can transcend the policies of their organizations in order to
reach unified PLO positions. A Central Council of 60 to 90 members,
including the Executive Committee, serves as an advisory body that can
meet more frequently than the PNC.[16]

Historically, the PLO's grand strategy has been to achieve the goals of
the covenant, namely, the complete defeat and elimination of Israel and
establishment of a state in all of Palestine.[17] This original objective might
remain unaltered, particularly if one takes seriously the two-phase plan
concept. The 1988 Algiers PNC declaration of the establishment of the state
of Palestine does not clearly recognize the existence of the state of Israel.
It remained for Arafat to recognize Israel and propose Israeli-Palestinian
coexistence in his December 1988 statements. This position, supplemented
by Arafat's May 1988 announcement that the covenant was "caduque,"
would seem to mean that the PLO's grand strategy is now based on the goal
of creating a Palestinian state in the West Bank and Gaza which would live
peaceably side-by-side with Israel.

Accordingly, a study of Israel's war with the PLO must, first, analyze
that organization's strategies in pursuit of the covenant's goals, which
presumably remained unchanged from 1964 until 1988. To be sure, there
were many hints over the years that the PLO would settle for less than the
liberation of all of Palestine, but these never led to clear and reliable
undertakings. If one accepts Arafat's position from December 1988 on-
wards, it would seem that a new set of strategies would be discernible.
Chapter 2, summarizing the events of the recent period of the conflict, will
explore that possibility. The analysis that follows is valid for the period
1964–88 and would be of continuing validity if Arafat's assurances regarding peaceful coexistence with Israel prove misleading, as would be the case
if the two-phase plan turned out to be a grim reality.

The PLO's grand strategy in its war of national liberation with Israel has been two-fold. It has combined adroit diplomacy with terror. Politically, the PLO has worked unceasingly to become accepted as the sole representative of the Palestinian people and as a highly favored national liberation movement, at the head of the list of communist/Third World causes. Concomitantly, the PLO has sought recognition in the West. The major arenas for this campaign for international diplomatic/legal status have been in the United Nations and other international organizations, as well as in international conferences on any subject.

In its "armed struggle," the PLO's grand strategy has been to wage a war of national liberation against Israel, almost exclusively through the use of terror—in Israel, in the West Bank and Gaza and worldwide, wherever Israelis, their interests and supporters could be found. The purpose of this war of terror is to harass Israel and to provoke it to extreme reactions, notably attacks on states giving sanctuary to the PLO. This, in turn, could spark conventional wars between Arab states and Israel, as in 1956, 1967 and 1982. Important ancillary purposes of this war of terror have been to publicize the Palestinian cause and to maintain the morale of the Palestinians and their Arab and other supporters.

Moreover, PLO terror, provoking Israel to drastic countermeasures, serves the strategic purpose of stripping Israel of international recognition and respect at the same time that the PLO increases its international recognition and respect. The strategy of the PLO and its allies has been to cast Israel as a pariah, an outlaw state like South Africa, condemned by world opinion and isolated.

The PLO's success with its strategies, both of acquiring recognition and respect and of discrediting Israel, is well known. The political/diplomatic element in the PLO's strategy has succeeded in gaining unchallenged recognition as the sole representative of the Palestinian people and, since November 1988, numerous recognitions of the state of Palestine.[18] The PLO has participated in Security Council debates under rule 37 of the council's provisional rules of procedure. Rule 37 applies to any member of the UN which is not a member of the Security Council at the time of invitation to participate in its debates. The PLO, first invited to the council in December 1975, was neither a state nor a member of the UN at the time. The U.S. protested in vain that the only basis for inviting the PLO to participate in the council's proceedings would be rule 39, which applies broadly to "persons." Since the matter is procedural rather than substantive, the U.S. has no veto.[19]

Arafat was invited to address the General Assembly in November 1974 and the PLO has participated in that body's debates, as well as in the meetings of many other UN organs. The PLO cause has repeatedly been endorsed by international organizations and conferences.[20] The PLO has been accorded belligerent status under the law of war—without meeting the usual requirements for belligerency, as will be explained in Chapter 2—in Article 1 (4) of the 1977 Geneva Protocol I additional to the Geneva Conventions of 12 August 1949 and Relating to the Protection of Victims of International Armed Conflicts.[21]

"Armed struggle," primarily in the form of terror, the coercive element in the PLO's grand strategy, has had repercussions far beyond its immediate effects. Terror has forced Israel to take internal security measures that affect the quality of life in Israeli society. Since internal security precautions alone have not sufficed, the PLO's terror campaigns have elicited Israeli countermeasures against the sources of PLO terrorism in sanctuary states. These countermeasures have contributed to the outbreak of international conventional wars in 1956, 1967 and 1982 and have brought down near unanimous condemnations in the United Nations and in world opinion. Israeli counterterror attacks in sanctuary states and Israel's occupation of the territories captured in the 1967 June war have been condemned over twenty times in the Security Council. The PLO, on the other hand, has never been condemned by the council for its terror attacks on Israel. The most that the council has done is to "deplore" violence in the Arab-Israeli conflict without mentioning the PLO explicitly. Ironically, the PLO and its friends and sympathizers have turned the issue of terrorism on its head so that debates on Israeli reactions to PLO terrorism end with condemnations of Israeli "state terrorism."[22]

The political/diplomatic strategy employed by the PLO in carrying out its grand strategy has been highly successful. It has made an art form of acquiring political/legal status with nebulous content. The practical manifestations of "recognition" or "observer status" have often been obscure, but the sheer quantity of recognitions and grants of status have produced the appearance of an international person, notwithstanding the fact that for most of its existence the PLO has not even claimed to be a government-in-exile and, even after the proclamation of the state of Palestine, has possessed no territory and exercised sovereign powers over no population.[23]

As far as the substantive issues of the Arab-Israeli conflict are concerned, the PLO has kept alive its respectable side by zig-zag diplomacy that alternates obdurate insistence on its maximum covenant goals with intimations of moderation. Arafat excelled in this technique, never being pinned down until December 1988. Obviously, the evasive character of PLO diplomacy has resulted in large measure from the necessity of holding together a heterogeneous collection of resistance groups with varying views as to the proper ends of means of the PLO's war of national liberation. The PLO has also had to retain the support of Arab states with very different interests and positions on the conflict, as well as states such as the Soviet Union and other communist states which have supported it.

Concurrently, the PLO has maintained a military strategy of terror. This characterization is controversial since terror is not, properly speaking, a *military* strategy. Efforts to define terror have proliferated without consensus being reached.[24] However, by any definition the essence of terror is that it is almost entirely pure "countervalue" violence. That is to say, its targets are not military objectives but civilian persons and places. The military instrument of foreign policy is usually predominantly "counterforce" in nature. It targets military objectives and is guided by military necessity. To be sure, counterforce warfare, with modern weapons and used against mixed military/civilian targets, produces collateral damage. Disproportionate collateral damage, particularly if it appears to result from ineffective and/or indifferent efforts to limit it, is a violation of the legal/moral principle of discrimination or noncombatant immunity. Intentional infliction of civilian damage by conventional military means, pure countervalue warfare, sometimes called "terror bombing," is indeed terror. However, terror, the principal weapon of the PLO, is systematically, intentionally countervalue in purpose and execution. Terror attacks targets, not for their military value, but for the political/psychological purpose of terrorizing the target society, to disrupt ordinary life and reduce the population to a condition of perpetual fear and apprehension. No mundane act—shopping, waiting at a bus stop, driving to work, stopping at a bar—can be taken without the fear that a terrorist bomb or machine gun will kill and destroy at random.

The genius of terror is that it is so economical as a means of armed coercion. All it requires is a small number of terrorists—variously viewed as "martyrs," "fanatics," "criminals," "strugglers," according to one's perspective—to strike from time to time. For every terrorist attack there results, beyond the damage done, a ripple effect of fear, frustration and insecurity that erodes life in the target society. Beyond that, crucial to the terrorist enterprise, every terrorist attack breeds hatred and rage, a demand for vengeance. This is likely to drive the government of the target society into drastic countermeasures which will often be regretted and/or condemned by the outside world. Additionally, terror is "guerrilla theater" which focuses attention on the terrorists' cause in ways unachievable through other means, including ordinary military counterforce operations. For example, the PLO considered that the worldwide publicity attending the hostage taking and massacre of Israeli athletes at the 1972 Munich Olympic Games was well worth the price of moral revulsion against the actual terrorist acts. Significantly, only a U.S. veto prevented passage of a Security

Council resolution condemning Israeli attacks on PLO bases in Lebanon and Syria following the massacre, a resolution in which no mention was made of the massacre and/or the PLO's continued use of terror.[25]

To be consistent with the counterforce/countervalue distinction, one would have to distinguish a terrorist bomb thrown into a marketplace from a guerrilla ambush of an army patrol. The latter would be a counterforce act of war, not a countervalue act of terrorism. Unfortunately, this distinction may become blurred when, for example, people infiltrating on a terrorist mission to seize and threaten to kill hostages are intercepted and become engaged in a counterforce fight. Nevertheless, this distinction should be kept in mind. It is important in reviewing the record of Israel's war with the PLO because the overwhelming number of PLO attacks have been terrorist in intention and execution. The PLO has seldom engaged in counterforce attacks against Israeli military forces and installations. Of 353 terrorist attacks in Israel that caused casualties between June 1967 and October 1985, 25 involved Israeli Defense Forces (IDF) or security forces personnel and none were aimed at military installations. Many of the military personnel attacked were off duty, e.g., at a hitch-hiking post.[26] Of course, in the cases when the Israelis have attacked the PLO, as in the 1978 Litani Operation and the 1982 Lebanon War, the PLO has been forced to fight in the counterforce mode or retreat.

Some further dimensions of the PLO's terror strategy must be mentioned. This dimension is the value of claims to success in terrorist attacks on Israel within the PLO, in the Arab world and in countries and with individuals sympathetic to the Palestinian cause. Lacking the capability and occasion to win respect through conventional combat, except when the Israelis have attacked, as in the 1978 Litani Operation and the 1982 Lebanon War, the PLO is obliged to demonstrate its commitment to an "armed struggle" primarily through terrorist actions. It is important to the PLO to continue terrorist operations to show that the war of national liberation goes on.

However, the need for credit and publicity for terrorist actions carried out by a number of competing organizations has led to a somewhat confusing record. Sometimes several different PLO factions claim credit for the same action. Indeed, spurious claims have been made for actions that never occurred.[27] The very first PLO actions, claimed to have been launched on New Year's Eve 1965 and celebrated by terrorist attacks in succeeding years' end, were aborted.[28]

Another purpose of terror employed by the PLO or some of its factions has been to defend against what could be called "the threat of peace." There is evidence that the mainstream PLO has, from time to time, increased its terror campaign in order to poison the international environment while promising negotiations for peace or disengagement were in progress.[29] Nayif Hawatmeth of the DFLP stated that the purpose of the May 15, 1974, Maalot terrorist attack in which twenty Israeli high school student hostages were killed and seventy wounded was to disrupt Secretary of State Henry Kissinger's mission to secure a Syrian-Israeli disengagement agreement.[30]

It appears that most of the terrorist attacks on Israel since the October 1988 declaration of the state of Palestine and the December 1988 statements of Arafat recognizing Israel and renouncing terror have been the work of anti-Arafat rejectionist PLO elements, as well as of Lebanese Shiite radicals.[31] Nevertheless, there have been a substantial number of terrorist attacks from Lebanon, as well as the May 31, 1990, sea-borne attack launched from Libya, carried out by the PLF, PFLP and DFLP, all represented on the PLO's Executive Committee.[32]

Finally, the heterogeneous and often conflictual character of the PLO federation of resistance movements has sometimes resulted in the use of terror in intramural warfare which has taken the form of assassinations of rival leaders and intimidation.[33]

All of this leads to the question: What to call the PLO's warriors? The Israelis call them all "terrorists," in all circumstances, even when they have been forced to fight in a conventional counterforce mode. Indeed, the entire PLO is branded as a "terrorist organization." Newspapers such as the *New York Times* and *Washington Post* refer to them as "guerrillas" and "commandos." However, the best name, that employed by the Dayan Center in Tel Aviv University, is *fedayeen*. Professor Yehoshafat Harkabi of the Hebrew University of Jerusalem explains:

> *Fedayeen* is presently a name for Arab or Palestinian irregulars. Etymologically it comes from "sacrifice," i.e., those ready to sacrifice themselves. Historically this name was given in the twelfth century to those sent to assassinate the enemies of a Shiite sect popularly called "the assassins." Its meaning became diffused as a name for Arabs engaged in guerrilla warfare.[34]

Fedayeen is the term used to describe the Arabs who infiltrated into Israel in the 1950s and thereafter to carry out guerilla or terrorist attacks. The problem with calling the PLO forces "guerrillas" is that there are different kinds of guerrillas. Guerrillas vary as to the mix of counterforce and countervalue operations they conduct. They may employ a little, a great deal or no terror. The Viet Cong employed a great deal of terror but its operations were predominantly counterforce, military, in nature. Mosby's Rangers in the American Civil War were counterforce guerrillas who did not use terror. The main weapon of the PLO *fedayeen,* like their *fedayeen* predecessors before 1965, has been terror. With the understanding that this is so but that the PLO may also engage in guerrilla counterforce operations against the Israeli armed forces and even in conventional warfare, *fedayeen* will be the term used here for its warriors.

The PLO's tactics on the political/diplomatic front have been amply discussed elsewhere and need no further amplification here.[35] The PLO's tactics in its terror campaigns against Israel have included infiltration of *fedayeen* into Israel and the West Bank and Gaza by land, sea and air (gliders); explosion of bombs in public places and in public transportation; laying of mines in roads and fields; throwing of hand grenades at civilian targets; seizure of dwellings, schools, other public buildings and buses wherein hostages are held and often killed or wounded either by the *fedayeen* or in the course of rescue operations; indiscriminate bazooka, rocket and artillery fire against Israeli population centers; hijacking of aircraft wherein hostages are held and sometimes killed by the hijackers or in rescue operations; sabotage of public, farm and business facilities.[36]

We turn now to Israel's response to the PLO's strategies and tactics.

Israel's Counterterror Organization, Strategies and Tactics

Israel's national security is entrusted primarily to the Israel Defense Forces (IDF). The Shin Bet (General Security Service), an intelligence organization, operates within both Israel and the occupied territories of the West Bank and Gaza, identifying and repressing subversive activities. The Shin Bet and the IDF are assisted by civil defense reservists. Military intelligence, the Shin Bet and the Mossad, Israel's civilian overseas intelligence service, provide intelligence about terrorist preparations and activities abroad. The El Al airline has its own security service, supervised by the Mossad, as do many private corporations.[37]

Major terrorist attacks and Israeli responses are closely monitored and/ or supervised by responsible Cabinet members and the prime minister. A special advisor on terrorism is assigned to the prime minister. The ministers of defense and police will be directly involved, depending on the character and location of terrorist attacks and the force or agency called upon to deal with them.[38] Strikes against terrorist bases or areas from which terrorists operate may be approved by the prime minister with a variety of different Cabinet combinations. Except where an immediate decision is required, proposals for counterterror strikes are submitted to the Cabinet and the Ministerial Defense Committee. Full Cabinet concurrence would be required for an action of the magnitude of the 1978 Litani Operation and for any action that might lead to hostilities with an Arab state, as in the case of Syria in the 1982 Lebanon War. For a routine strike against PLO bases in Lebanon, the authority of the prime minister and defense minister would suffice during most of the period of Israel's war with the PLO.[39]

A major issue in Israel's defense decision process has been the lack of Cabinet checks and balances in situations where the prime minister was his own defense minister, e.g., David Ben-Gurion, May 1949–December 1953, July 1956–June 1963; Levi Eshkol, June 1963–May 1967; and Menachem Begin from Ezer Weizman's resignation in April 1979 until Ariel Sharon's appointment in August 1981.

An even more troublesome issue has been the alleged denial of full and candid briefings of planned operations to the prime minister and Cabinet. This was clearly the case in Sharon's maneuvering before and during the 1982 Lebanon invasion. There have been other instances, e.g., when Sharett was prime minister and Lavon defense minister.[40] On the whole, however, such gaps in confidence and communication have not been typical of Israeli security processes.

Naturally, all Israeli security operations are subject to the review of the legislative branch, the Knesset. The opposition parties may be expected to question and criticize such operations.[41] As a parliamentary democracy and free society, Israel cannot avoid wide knowledge of and discussions concerning its security measures. The fact that so many Israelis, of many diverse political persuasions, serve in the armed forces, active and reserve, increases the knowledge and interest of the citizenry in security policies. It is, accordingly, difficult for the government to persist in security policies that do not have substantial popular support.

Israel's first objective, of course, is to preserve the Jewish state founded in 1948. However, Israeli political opinion is divided on the issue of the extent and character of the state of Israel. There is disagreement as to whether the West Bank and Gaza should be included permanently either as integral parts of an enlarged Israel or as some sort of dependency, or whether these territories should ultimately become an independent Palestinian state or a quasi-sovereign component of some kind of confederation with Jordan or Israel. The objective of annexing what is referred to as Judea and Samaria, the biblical names for the West Bank, is held by some conservative elements in the Likud coalition. The objective of preserving Israeli sovereignty only over pre-1967 Israel plus Jerusalem and perhaps the Golan Heights while relinquishing control over the territories as part of a comprehensive peace settlement is generally held by the liberal elements centered around the Labor party. Of course, there are all sorts of variations on these options. A majority of Israelis probably would like to see autonomy for the West Bank and Gaza short of an independent Palestinian state, with security arrangements for Israel.

Arab and third party perceptions of Israel's objectives in its war with the PLO will be strongly influenced by estimates as to which approach will prevail in Israeli politics. If it is the Greater Israel (Eretz Israel) approach, the stakes in the conflict become greater since this approach denies any prospect of a Palestinian sovereign state. If it is the so-called land for peace approach of Israeli liberals, there is more hope for Palestinian self-determination and, perhaps, some incentive to eschew terrorist violence and try to advance the Palestinian cause by peaceful means.

Israel's grand strategy in its war with the PLO has followed classic counterinsurgency lines. The political/psychological element in this strategy has been dedicated to denying the PLO the recognition and respectability it sought. As is usual with a counterinsurgent party, Israel has branded the PLO as terrorists, epitomized by the evil, bloodthirsty Arab terrorists of the kind that gained notoriety in the 1972 massacre of Israeli athletes at Munich. Israel's counterinsurgency strategy has also had an important economic component in the form of economic development in the occupied territories since 1967. Economic measures contributed to maintenance of order in the territories for most of the period up to the outbreak of the Palestinian uprising, the *intifada,* in December 1987. Since then the economic element in counterinsurgency has generally been more coercive than developmental and, of course, the Palestinians have employed tactics such as strikes and boycotts that have undone much of the economic achievements of Israel's policies in the territories.

Israel's military grand strategy has been to deter, prevent and preempt PLO terrorist attacks and to contain them promptly and efficiently when they occur. Above all, from the early days of *fedayeen* incursions and continuing throughout the war with the PLO, Israel's grand strategy has been to strike the sources of terrorism, not relying on passive defense alone. The purpose of these strikes has been to make the terrorists insecure as well to inflict material damage on their personnel and facilities.

Israel's political/psychological strategy has been to contest the political/legal gains of the PLO in international organizations, conferences, bilateral relations with states and world opinion. Generally this strategy has failed, even in the West where there is considerable sympathy for Israel. However, Israel's political/psychological strategy has been successful in the United States, which is, of course, of critical importance. Israel and her American supporters obtained a firm US policy of nonintercourse with the PLO until Arafat's December 1988 statements recognizing Israel and renouncing terrorism—obtained only by American pressure. Occasional exceptions were made for humanitarian and security reasons, e.g., PLO assistance to the U.S. in Lebanon, but no discussion of the great issues of the conflict took place between the US and the PLO until December 1988.[42]

Israel's military counterterror strategies include elements of deterrence, preventive/attrition, preemption and passive defense. These elements are intermingled. To begin with the last, Israel has secured its land borders with security fences and electronic warning systems, patrolled by special forces as well as IDF units. Towns, settlements, kibbutzim all have their own counterterror defenses. The Israeli Navy patrols the Israeli coast, much of the Lebanon coast, and far out into the Mediterranean as necessary, interdicting infiltration by sea. Israeli citizens are trained to be security conscious, e.g., not to leave briefcases, baggage and packages unattended in public places. El Al, has the most effective counterterror policies and personnel of any airline. All of these measures make terrorist infiltration and attacks difficult.[43]

If these passive defense measures were the sum total of Israel's counterterror strategy, most of the normative issues discussed in this book would not arise. Interdiction of terrorist infiltrators on the high seas and by air outside of Israeli airspace would remain controversial, but the main normative issues would concern human rights and due process questions within Israel and the occupied territories. However, from the early days of *fedayeen* infiltrations and terrorist attacks in the 1950s, Israel's counterterror strategy has emphasized offensive attacks on the sources of terrorist activity. Since the PLO has seldom been able to maintain significant bases in Israel, the West Bank or Gaza, it has had to operate from sanctuary states such as Jordan, Egypt, Syria and Lebanon. Attacks on the sources of PLO terror, therefore, had to be attacks on the sovereign territory of those states. Since the PLO typically colocated its bases with civilian areas, offensive actions against it necessarily involved collateral damage to the nationals of the sanctuary states.

Aside from passive defense, then, the main elements in Israel's counterterror strategy have been (1) deterrence, (2) preventive/attrition, (3) preemption, and (4) retaliation.

As already observed, these strategies are not mutually exclusive; on the contrary, the same operation may be conceived as performing several functions simultaneously, e.g., deterrence, preventive/attrition and retaliation. Accordingly, the official rationale given by the Israeli government for a counterterror action may emphasize one of the strategic elements but the operation may also be based on others.

Counterterror deterrence is served by all of the other strategies. They are all necessary to it because counterterror deterrence requires offensive actions that impose damage, ideally unacceptable damage, on the terrorists and those who support them. Counterterror deterrence differs from nuclear and conventional deterrence. Nuclear and conventional deterrence are effective when they are based on a military posture projecting the capability and will to inflict unacceptable damage in the event of aggression. This capability and will need not be demonstrated in actual hostilities in the case of nuclear deterrence and in most cases of conventional deterrence. However, there is no counterterror deterrent posture that can deter all terrorist attacks, as well as deterring support for terrorists in the form of territorial sanctuaries and material assistance. Counterterror deterrence must be maintained by active responses to terrorism, by concrete—painful—demonstration of capability and will to inflict unacceptable damage on the terrorists and their supporters.

Israel has a *strategy of counterforce deterrence by demonstration* that targets three distinct although interrelated sources of terrorism: the PLO, the sanctuary states, the local populations in areas in which the PLO maintains bases and launches its terrorist operations. Israeli counterterror measures intended to have a deterrent effect are always aimed at a PLO military target or at the sanctuary state's military forces supporting the PLO. The damage done to the PLO may deter their operations although more likely rationales are preventive/attrition and preemption. Preventive/attrition attacks inflict damage on PLO bases and facilities, produce PLO casualties, and put the PLO on the defensive. More important in terms of deterrence is the effect that attacks on PLO bases may, over time, discourage continued support or acquiescence by the sanctuary states from which terrorist attacks are emanating.[44] Finally, since the PLO usually deliberately locates its bases in populated areas, counterterror attacks may again, over time, discourage continued support, cooperation or toleration of its activities by the local population.

Particularly during the period of Dayan's leadership as chief of staff, when Israeli counterterror strategy was established, the element that was aimed at sanctuary states took the form of coercive diplomacy.[45] Initially, the strategy was designed to compel states from which *fedayeen* infiltrated into Israel to control their borders, prevent infiltration and even punish those found returning from raids. This strategy was also intended to convey to neighboring Arab states that Israel was strong, able and willing to take up arms to defend its security. It was hoped that this posture would encourage the Arab states to choose peaceful coexistence over dangerous hostilities.[46]

Eventually, *fedayeen* attacks were organized by Arab governments as instruments of their own policies. This was particularly the case with Egypt before the 1956 Suez war. Increasingly the Israelis deliberately attacked the military forces of the sanctuary states that were using the *fedayeen* as surrogates. The message was that Israel would not tolerate endless low-intensity hostilities with *fedayeen* raiders. Rather, it would escalate, involving the sanctuary state's own armed forces directly. The "unacceptable damage" inflicted and threatened by the Israeli counterterror raids, then, was not only the actual damage caused in the raids but the risk of escalation.[47]

The threefold Israeli counterterror deterrence strategy was authoritatively explained by then Chief of Staff Moshe Dayan in a November 1955 lecture to IDF officers:

> We cannot guard every water pipeline from explosion and every tree from uprooting. We cannot prevent every murder of a worker in an orchard or a family in their beds.
>
> But it is in our power to set a high price on our blood, a price too high for the Arab community, the Arab army, or the Arab governments to think it worth paying.
>
> We can see to it that the Arab villages oppose the raiding bands that pass through them, rather than give them assistance. It is in our power to see that Arab military commanders prefer a strict performance of their obligation to police the frontiers rather than suffer defeat in clashes with our units.
>
> We can cause the Arab governments to renounce a "policy of strength" towards Israel by turning it into a demonstration of weakness.
>
> The decision not to get into quarrels with Israel will come only if the Arabs have reason to suppose that otherwise they will have to reckon with sharp reactions from our side and be dragged into a conflict in which they would be the losers.[48]

This strategic doctrine was reiterated by Chief of Staff Yitzhak Rabin in April 1966, when terrorist attacks elicited Israeli raids on two Jordanian villages from which the terrorists were operating. Fourteen houses used by the terrorists were blown up. Rabin stated:

> The operation was intended to make it clear to Jordan, and to the population which is collaborating with Fatah, and to Fatah members themselves, that as long as this side of the border will not be quiet, no quiet will prevail on the other side.[49]

This last component in the deterrence target is obviously controversial. In some cases the population that suffers collateral damage from counterforce attacks on PLO targets may be PLO sympathizers who voluntarily reside in areas from which terrorist operations are launched. This would be the case if the Israelis attacked the PLO in one of the fortified Palestinian refugee camps wherein military targets are intermingled with civilian dwellings. In other cases the PLO target might be in or near a village whose inhabitants were unsympathetic or even hostile to the PLO but were constrained to tolerate its presence because of PLO intimidation. In some cases the local population might be able to secure the intervention of the national government, e.g., in Jordan in 1970, to curb or terminate the PLO's activities. In other cases, e.g., Lebanon, this might not be possible.

All of these contingencies must be kept in mind, although none of them would relieve Israel from the obligation to limit its counterterror strikes to discriminate, counterforce attacks in which serious efforts were made to avoid civilian damage. This issue will be discussed in Chapter 6. One point should be emphasized here, however. Israel's counterterror deterrence strategies have not included pure countervalue attacks on civilian targets of any kind. They have always been based on counterforce targeting of PLO or sanctuary state military bases and personnel. Because of the PLO's policy of merging with the local population these counterterror strikes on the PLO predictably have often caused collateral damage to civilians and their property. Even though Israel claims that it limits collateral damage as far as possible, it still considers this a kind of "unacceptable damage" to the civilians living in areas from which the PLO prepares and launches terrorist attacks on Israeli civilian targets. It is believed that this unacceptable damage may deter continued cooperation with the PLO.

Preventive/attrition attacks, as indicated, may often be the principal means employed to deter the PLO. Beyond that, however, they inflict substantial damage that decreases the PLO's capabilities and will. Destruction of weapons, ammunition dumps, vehicles, boats, training facilities, barracks, political and military headquarters, and casualties to PLO personnel, particularly leaders, all may contribute to the reduction of the PLO's military and terrorist capabilities. Over time, such attacks may have an attrition effect in the psychological as well as material sense.

Preemptive attacks on PLO units would be based on intelligence predicting imminent operations. These units would be hit as they deployed from their bases or in their bases. Often the Israelis will announce that a preemptive strike was executed in anticipation of a series of operations known to be planned by the PLO.

Finally, there is the element of *retaliation* in Israeli counterterror strategy. It is important to understand this element because of legal/moral debates over "reprisals" to be discussed in Chapters 4 and 10. Preventive/attrition and preemptive attacks may be carried out without reference to specific past terrorist attacks on Israel, Preventive/attrition attacks occur at times and against targets chosen with a view to the long term. Preemptive attacks are aimed at nipping imminent terrorist operations in the bud. The element of retaliation comes in when a particularly shocking terrorist action has taken place and/or in response to a major build-up of terrorist operations. The Israeli public expects and demands a clear, hard response to major terrorist attacks or campaigns. The *timing* of Israeli counterterror measures is, therefore, often clearly tied to some recent terrorist attack or series of attacks.[50] However, the *purpose* or *function* of the Israeli retaliatory measures is not simply to punish the terrorists and their supporters but to deter them and reduce their capabilities and will (preventive/attrition).

When PLO terrorists take Israelis as hostages and kill them, as in the 1972 Munich Olympics or at Maalot in 1974 or in the bus seized on the Haifa–Tel Aviv highway in the 1978 Country Club raid, the public demands that Israel strike back at the sources of such terrorist attacks. Accordingly, the pattern of PLO terrorist actions followed quickly by Israeli counterterror strikes dominates the pattern of hostilities in Israel's war with the PLO. However, it is not accurate to portray Israel's counterterror strategy as purely retaliatory and reactive.

The Israeli armed forces do not wait for particularly outrageous terrorist attacks to plan and prepare for counterterror operations. They have contingency plans that could be implemented at times and in ways that have little or nothing to do with some recent terrorist acts. Indeed, at times Israel has announced and proceeded to carry out preventive/attrition strategies, sometimes called "preemptive," that were claimed to be independent of the occurrence of recent terrorist attacks.[51] These initiatives will be noted in the overview of hostilities that follows in Chapter 2. In any event, the limited relevance of the retaliation rationale to the operational issue of targeting is indicated by the fact that the IDF may attack forces or locales believed to be directly related to recent terrorist attacks, but it may also attack other PLO targets, thought to be important, that have nothing to do with the terrorist actions recently experienced.

Underlying all of these forms of counterterror operations is the fact that Israel is at war with the PLO because the PLO's raison d'être is to fight a war of national liberation with Israel. This is reflected from time to time in official Israeli statements emphasizing that, despite its discontinuous pattern of hostilities, the PLO-Israeli conflict is a war.[52]

Israeli tactics in carrying out these counterterror strategies include:

(1) brief patrols and ground raids into sanctuary states to attack PLO personnel and bases;
(2) more extended comprehensive ground force sweeps with air support, lasting for several days, during which PLO forces are engaged, their bases destroyed, houses from which they have operated blown up, and PLO suspects and supporters detained, interrogated and sometimes returned to Israeli detention camps;
(3) artillery bombardments of PLO positions;
(4) air raids on PLO targets
(5) naval bombardments of PLO targets and amphibious raids;
(6) commando attacks on PLO political and military headquarters; assassination of political/military leaders;
(7) rescue missions such as Entebbe in 1976.

In addition to the counterterror strategies and tactics described, Israel has employed an ally in its war with the PLO. The South Lebanon Army (SLA), originally commanded by Major Saad Haddad, now by General Antoine Lahd, controls an Israeli security zone along the border. Since 1978, a substantial part of the war with the PLO has taken the form of IDF direct combat support, mainly artillery, first to Haddad's Christian militia and since 1983 to the reorganized SLA, which is entirely equipped and maintained by Israel.[53]

In Chapter 2 I will present an overview of the hostile interaction between Israel and the PLO in which of their respective strategies and tactics will be illustrated. These two chapters will serve as the material bases for the normative analysis in the succeeding chapters.

Notes

1. See the Palestinian National Charter of 1968, reproduced in translation in Leila Kidd, ed. *Basic Political Documents of the Armed Palestinian Liberation Organization Research Center* (Palestine Books No. 27, Palestine Liberation Organization Research Center, 1969), pp. 137–42; reprinted in John Norton Moore, ed., *The Arab-Israeli Conflict* (3 vols.; Princeton, N.J.: Princeton University Press, 1974), 3 (*Documents*): 706–11, especially Articles 8, 9, 15, 18, 19, 20, 22, 23, 26.
    See Y. Harkabi, *The Palestinian Covenant and Its Meaning* (Totowa, N.Y.: Valentine, Mitchell, 1979).

2. See Helena Cobban, *The Palestinian Liberation Organisation* (Cambridge: Cambridge University Press, 1984), p. 32; David Hirst, *The Gun and the Olive Branch* (2d ed.; London: Faber & Faber, 1984), pp. 276–7.

3. "PLO Proclaims Palestinian State," *Washington Post* [hereinafter, *WP*], November 15, 1988, A1, cols. 1–3; A27, cols. 1–4; "PLO Proclaims Palestine to Be an Independent State; Hints at Recognizing Israel," *New York Times* [hereinafter, *NYT*], November 15,

1988, A1, col. 6; A6, cols. 1–4; "Excerpts from Palestine Statement," ibid., A8, cols. 1–3.

4. "Arafat in Geneva, Calls on Israelis to Join in Talks," *NYT*, December 14, 1988, A1, col. 6; A12, cols. 5–6; "Shamir Calls Remarks by Arafat 'Double Talk'," ibid., A12, cols. 5–6; "U.S. in Shift, Agrees to "Substantive Dialogue" with PLO," *WP*, December 15, 1988, A1, cols. 1–2; 4–5; A44, cols. 1–3; "Secretary Shultz's Statement," ibid., A40, cols. 5–6; "Arafat, Again Spelling out PLO Positions, Says 'Enough Is Enough . . . We Want Peace,' " ibid., A40, cols. 1–4; "U.S. and PLO Conclude First Meetings in Tunis," ibid., December 17, 1988, A1, col. 2; A15, cols. 4–6.

5. "Arafat Calls PLO Charter Inoperative," *WP*, May 3, 1989, A1, col. 1; A20, cols. 1–3; "Rival [George Habash, PFLP] Challenges Arafat on Charter," ibid., May 6, 1989, A16, col. 1; "Arafat to Israel: Pardon My French," *Newsweek,* May 15, 1989, p. 48, col. 1–4.

6. See Article 33 of the 1968 Palestinian Covenant in Kadi's translation, reproduced in Moore, ed., *The Arab-Israeli Conflict* 3: 711.
    Arafat's biographer, Alan Hart, claims that Arafat is committed to peaceful Palestinian-Israeli coexistence but that it is Israel that has balked at accepting a Palestinian state. *Arafat* (Bloomington, Ind.: Indiana University Press, 1989), pp. 552–53.

7. "U.S. to Hold Arafat Accountable for Seeing That Terrorism Ends," *WP*, December 17, 1988, A15, cols. 1–6; "Arafat Vows to 'Do Best' Against Terrorism," ibid., December 18, 1988, cols. 1–4; "Arafat Presses Conflict," ibid., January 20, 1989, cols. 5–6; "The PLO's Many Faces," editorial, *Jerusalem Post* International Edition [hereinafter *JPI*], January 21, 1989, p. 23, cols. 1–2; "Israelis Say PLO Broke Antiterrorism Pledge," *WP*, February 7, 1989, A20, cols. 1–3; "U.S. Chides PLO Over Border Fray," ibid., February 12, 1989, A1, col. 1; A37, cols. 1–5; "Israel Urges U.S. to End PLO Talks: After Terror Attack Is Foiled," *JPI*, February 18, 1989, p. 1, cols. 1–2; "U.S. Again Says PLO Violating Vow," *WP*, March 1, 1989, A19, cols. 1–4; "Arafat Declines to Rule out Raids," ibid., March 4, 1989, A14, col. 1; A19, col. 1; "U.S. Voices 'Concern' over PLO Raids," ibid., March 4, 1989, A19, cols. 4–6; editorial, "First, End PLO Terrorism," ibid., March 8, 1989, A22, cols. 1–2; "PLO Aides Rebuff U.S. on Uprising," ibid., March 23, 1989, A1, col. 6; A32, cols. 1–27.

8. "Palestinian Affairs," *Keesings* (July/August 1989), p. 36860.

9. See the discussion of the debate over Arafat's renunciation of terrorism, the May 30, 1990, PLF raid and its consequences, Chapter 2 below.

10. See Moshe Gammer, "The PLO in the Arab-Israeli Conflict: Positions, Strategies and Tactics," *Middle East Contemporary Survey* [hereinafter *MECS*] 1 (1976–77): 186–89; Elaine Ruth Fletcher, "PLO Still Speaks of "a Phased Liberation," *JPI*, December 31, 1988, p. 7, cols. 1–4.
    The Twelfth PNC Cairo meeting, June/July 1974, adopted the following provision:

> 2. The PLO will struggle by every means, the foremost of which is armed struggle, to liberate Palestinian land and to establish the people's national, independent and fighting sovereignty *on every part of Palestinian land to be liberated.* This requires the creation of further changes in the balance of power in favor of our people and their struggle. [Cobban's emphasis]

International Documents on Palestine, 1974, p. 449, quoted in Helena Cobban, *The*

Palestine Liberation Organisation, p. 62. See Jillian Becker, *The PLO: The Rise and Fall of the Palestine Liberation Organization* (London: Weidenfeld & Nicolson), p. 82.

In an interview with *Newsweek*, Prime Minister Yitzhak Shamir was asked: *"If the PLO began with two goals, first to destroy Israel and second to establish a Palestinian state, can't you seem them eventually giving up their first goal in order to achieve the second?"* [original emphasis] Shamir replied:

> It's not two goals, it's one goal. The establishment of a Palestinian state for them is a means, a stage, in their goal of destruction of the state of Israel. You can notice when they speak of a Palestinian state, they don't even mention its borders. What they need is a base, a base for the continuation of their attacks against Israel. Abu Iyad [an Arafat deputy] said this week that they need a Palestinian state in a part of Palestine in order to get all of Palestine. *Voilà:* they say it openly.

The official Arafat line denies that there is a two-phase strategy envisaging the elimination of Israel. Arafat's special adviser Bassam Abu Sharif has stated that the PLO seeks "a package deal in the Middle East based on the principles of the initiative put forward by Yasser Arafat to the U.N. General Assembly on Dec. 13." He continued: "The substance of this package is the two-state solution. The state of Israel will live in peace side-by-side with the state of Palestine, which will be confederated with Jordan. An internationally guaranteed peace agreement will protect the interests of all parties including the Palestinians and the Israelis." Bassam Abu Sharif, "The PLO's Election Plan," *WP*, "Outlook," May 21, 1989, C1, cols. 4–5; C2, cols. 1–5.

11. The Israelis insisted that Palestinian statements and behavior continued to provide evidence of the intention of carrying out the "phased plan"; see *The PLO: Has It Complied with Its Commitments?* (Jerusalem: Ministry of Foreign Affairs, May 1990), pp. 20–22

12. Yehoshafat Harkabi, *Israel's Fateful Hour* (New York: Harper & Row, 1988).

13. See Aaron David Miller, *The PLO and the Politics of Survival* (The Washington Papers No. 99; New York: Praeger/Georgetown Center for Strategic and International Studies, 1983), pp. 127–27; "Through the Palestinian Labyrinth," *NYT*, January 22, 1989, IV, 5, cols. 1–4; *Background Brief: Palestine Liberation Organisation* (London: Foreign and Commonwealth Office, September 1989) [hereinafter, UK, *Background Brief: PLO*]; Neil C. Livingstone and David Halevy, *Inside the PLO* (New York: Morrow, 1990), pp. 72–79.

On Hamas, see Ze'ev Schiff and Ehud Ya'ari, *Intifada*, edited and translated by Ina Friedman (New York: Simon & Schuster, 1989), pp. 220–39; Don Peretz, *Intifada* (Boulder, Colo.: Westview Press, 1990), pp. 104–06.

14. As of September 1989 the PLO's Executive Committee consisted of Yasir Arafat (Abu Ammar), chairman, al-Fatah; Faruq Qaddoumi (Abu Lutf), al-Fatah; Mahmud Abbas (Abu Mazen), al-Fatah; Abd ar-Rahim Ahmade, ALF; Muhammed Abbas (Abu'l Abbas), PLF; Abu Ali Mustafa, PFLP; Yasser Abd Rabbuh, DFLP; Suleiman Najjab, PCP; and the independents: Jawid Ghossein, Jamal Sourani, Bishop Elia Khoury, Brig. Abd al-Rassaq Yahya, Muhammad Milhem, Abdullah Hourani, Mahmoud Darwish.

UK, *Background Brief: PLO*, pp. 9–10. See Livingstone and Halevy, *Inside the PLO*, Appendix 2, pp. 303–04.

15. The PNC is a "parliament-in-exile" and the primary policy-making body of the PLO. It has over 400 members "elected or selected from the political/military organisations, Palestinian communities in the diaspora and the refugee camps, professional bodies and trade

unions, Palestinian notables and from the army, drawn from throughout the region and further afield. There are also some 180 members from the Occupied Territories whose names are withheld and who are unable to attend PNC sessions." UK, *Background Brief–PLO*, p. 9.

See Livingstone and Halevy, *Inside the PLO*, p. 70–71 and Appendix 1 for list of all PNC meetings as of January 1989, pp. 299–301.

16. Livingstone and Halevy, *Inside the PLO*, p. 70–71; UK, *Background Brief*, p. 9.

17. See Shaul Mishal, *The PLO under Arafat: Between Olive Branch and Gun* (New Haven: Yale University Press, 1986), pp. 8, 56–60.

18. By 1984 the PLO had been granted full diplomatic status by over 60 states and about 50 more recognized the PLO without authorizing of PLO embassies. William V. O'Brien, "The PLO in International Law," *Boston University International Law Journal* 3 (1984): 379; A.F. Kassim, "The Palestine Liberation Organization's Claim to Status: A Juridical Analysis Under International Law," *Denver Journal of International Law and Policy* 9 (1980); 19–20.

    By February 1989 the state of Palestine was recognized by 91 states. "List of countries That Have Recognized the Palestinian State, *WAFA*, Washington, D.C., 2 February 1989," *Journal of Palestine Studies* 18 (1989): 175–76.

19. See William V. O'Brien, "The PLO in International Law," *Boston University International Law Journal* 3 (1984): 349, 389–90. For the US position, see Moynihan (U.S.A.), 30 U.N. SCOR (1859th mtg.), pp. 7–10.

20. See Avi Beker, *The United Nations and Israel* (Lexington, Mass.: Lexington Books, 1988); Harris A. Schoenberg, *A Mandate for Terror* (New York: Shapolsky, 1989).

21. UN Doc. A/32/144 (1977); *International Legal Materials* 16 (1977): 1391–1441.

22. E.g., Malik (Soviet Union), 27 U.N. SCOR (1650th mtg.), p. 7; Abdulla (Sudan), 28 U.N. SCOR (1650th mtg.), pp. 68–71; Kelani (Syria), 29 U.N. SCOR (1766th mtg.), p. 31; Abel Meguid (Egypt), 30 U.N. SCOR (1859th mtg.), pp. 56–57.

23. See O'Brien, "The PLO in International Law," 375–79.

24. See, e.g., Walter Laqueur, *Terrorism* (London: Abacus, 1978); Brian M. Jenkins, R–3302-AF, *International Terrorism* (Santa Monica, Calif.: RAND Project Air Force, November 1985); Ariel Merari and Shlomi Elad, *The International Dimension of Palestinian Terrorism* (Boulder, Colo.: Westview Press; Jafee Center For Strategic Studies Study no. 6, 1986), pp. 5–6.

25. See Bush (U.S.A.), 27 U.N. SCOR (1662d mtg.), p. 7; "U.S. Casts a Veto on Mideast, Citing Terror," *NYT*, September 11, 1972, p. 1, col. 8, p. 10, cols. 4–6.

26. IDF Spokesman, *Terrorist Attacks in Israel With Casualties, June 1967–October 1985 (1985)*.

27. See Moshe Gammer, "Armed Operations: Situations Along the Borders," *MECS* I (1977–78): 98–99.

28. See Cobban, *The Palestine Liberation Organisation* and Hirst, *The Gun and the Olive Branch*, cited in note 2 above.

29. For example, the March 11, 1978, Country Club attack that led to the Litani operation delayed a visit by Begin to Washington as Egyptian-Israeli-US negotiations continued. Fatah claimed credit for the attack. "Fatah Admits Raids," *NYT*, March 12, 1978, p. 1, col. 6.

30. "Israeli Jets, in Reprisal, Raid Palestinian Areas of Lebanon; Kissinger Presses Peace Drive," *NYT*, May 17, 1974, p. 1, col. 4.

31. While the Israelis charged that the PLO created an underground popular army in the West Bank and Gaza, "in mid-January the *New York Times* reported that the Israeli Army chief of staff, Lt. Gen. Dan Shomron, had told a Knesset committee that Fatah had not planned or carried out any guerrilla acts since November." "Arafat Faction of PLO Linked to Terrorism, Israelis Charge," *WP*, February 2, 1989, A30, cols. 4–6.

    Defense Minister Rabin told the Knesset on March 28, 1989, that the IDF refrained from attacking Fatah because Fatah had not launched attacks against Israel for five months. Rabin said that Israel had thwarted efforts by radical factions attempting to undermine Arafat's diplomatic initiatives. "Israelis, Arafat Forces Avoid Clashes: Rabin Says Fatah Wing of PLO Has Refrained from Attacks," *WP*, March 29, 1989, A20, cols. 4–6.

    See also: "Arafat Rivals Behind Terror," *JPI*, March 25, 1989 p. 1, cols. 4–5; p. 2, cols. 1–3

    Reported terrorist operations from Lebanon, December 1988–July 1989, almost all frustrated by the Israelis, involved forces of the PFLP-General Command, DFLP, PFLP, PLF and Abu Musa's Fatah Uprising. However, the Israelis accused Arafat of organizing terror operations, including attacks on those who collaborated with Israel, in the territories. "Arafat's Fatah Using Terror, Despite Vow," *JPI*, July 22, 1989, p. 2, cols. 1–2.

32. Ministry of Foreign Affairs, Israel, *The PLO: Has It Complied with Its Commitments?*, pp. 28–9.

33. Dr. Isam Sarwati, a highly influential PLO dove, was assassinated on April 10, 1983, in Albuferia, Portugal. He was described as the "most prominent of many moderates" who were killed. "In PLO Moderate's Death, Forbodings of Terror," *WP*, April 11, 1983, A18, cols. 1–4; Beker, *The PLO*, p. 175.

34. Yehoshafat Harkabi, *Arab Strategies and Israel's Response* (New York: Free Press, 1977), no. 6, p. 171.

35. See n. 20 above.

36. All of these tactics and others are reported in IDF Spokesman, *Major Terrorist Activities in Which Israeli Civilians Were Casualties (12 June 1967–15 September 1985)*.

37. Hanan Alon, *Countering Palestinian Terrorism in Israel: Toward a Policy Analysis of Countermeasures* (Santa Monica, Calif.: RAND, August 1980), pp. 72–87.

38. Ibid., p. 86.

39. On the decision process within the Israeli Cabinet concerning security decisions, see Yehuda Ben Meir, *National Decision-Making: The Israeli Case* (Boulder, Colo.: Westview/Jafee Center for Strategic Studies, Tel Aviv University, 1986). Aaron S. Kleiman, *Israel and the World after Forty Years* (Washington, D.C.: Pergamon-Brassy's, 1990), pp. 131–51.

40. On Sharon's relations with Begin and the Cabinet, see Schiff and Ya'ari, *Israel's Lebanon War*, passim.

    On Defense Minister Pinhas Lavon's independent attitude and policies regarding retaliation raids placing him at odds with Prime Minister Moshe Sharett, see Michael Bar-Zohar, *Ben-Gurion: A Biography*, trans. Peretz Kidron (New York: Delacorte Press, 1978), pp. 203–08.

41. For examples of questioning and crticism of Israeli security policies and practice in the

Knesset, see, e.g., the reaction to the Qibya raid of October 14–15, 1953, described in Dan Kurzman, *Ben-Gurion* (New York: Simon & Schuster, 1983), pp. 359–61; Gideon Rafael, *Destination Peace* (New York: Stein & Day, 1981), pp. 32–34.

See Sachar's account of then-Foreign Minister Moshe Sharett's opposition to Prime Minister Ben-Gurion's policy of large-scale retaliatory strikes in answer to Nasser's *fedayeen* infiltration strategy in the spring of 1956. Howard M. Sachar, *A History of Israel* (2 vols.; Vol. I, New York: Knopf, 1976; Vol. II, New York: Oxford University Press, 1987), I, 488–89.

See descriptions of internal Cabinet and Knesset debates over Israeli policy toward the PLO, July 1981–September 1982, in Schiff and Ya'ari, *Israeli's Lebanon War*, pp. 102–06; 164–66; 186–88; 198–99; 212–13; 226–27.

Systematic analyses of security debates by the public, the Knesset and the IDF are presented in Avner Yaniv, *Dilemmas of Security* (New York: Oxford University Press, 1987).

42. On US contacts with the PLO prior to December 1988, see David Ignatius, "The Secret History of U.S./PLO Terror Talks," WP, "Outlook," L1, cols. 1–5. On UN Ambassador Andrew Young's abortive initiative with the PLO, see Steven L. Speigel, *The Other Arab-Israeli Conflict* (Chicago: University of Chicago Press, 1985), p. 375.

On initiation of U.S.-PLO talks in Tunis, December 1988, see n. 3 above.

43. Alon, *Countering Palestinian Terrorism in Israel,* pp. 76–77, 83–87.

44. Early in Israel's war with the PLO, *fedayeen* attempted to blow up a grain silo in Kfar Hess. Israel retaliated with a raid on Jenin where a flour mill was blown up. Explaining the rationale for this and other raids into the West Bank, then Chief of Staff Yitzhak Rabin stated: "The purpose [of the raids] was to send Jordan a clear warning and to express that we will not accept her activity and lack of control over her sovereign area, nor her not preventing its transformation into a base of sabotage operations against Israel." Alon, *Countering Palestinian Terrorism in Israel*, p. 37, quoting *Skira Hodsheet [Monthly Survey, A Journal for IDF Officers]* (Hebrew), XII (1965), no. 5, p. 3.

45. Avner Yaniv, *Deterrence without the Bomb* (Lexington, Mass.: Lexington Books, 1987), pp. 42, 60; Barry M. Blechman, "The Impact of Israel's Reprisals on Behavior of the Bordering Arab Nations Directed at Israel," *Journal of Conflict Resolution* 16 (1972): 156–60; Jonathan Shimshoni, *Israel and Conventional Deterrence: Border Warfare from 1953 to 1970* (Ithaca, N.Y.: Cornell University Press, 1988).

46. Brig. Moshe Dayan, "Why Israel Strikes Back," in Donald Robinson, ed., *Under Fire: Israel's 20-Year Struggle for Survival* (New York: Norton, 1968), pp. 120–23 [from lecture to officers of the Israel Defense Forces, November 1955].

Blechman calls this strategy "positive compellence." *The impact of Israel's reprisals,* pp. 157–9

47. Blechman calls this strategy "negative compellence." Ibid., pp. 159–60. See Yaniv, *Deterrence without the Bomb*, pp. 60–61.

48. Dayan, "Why Israel Strikes Back," pp. 122–23.

49. *Skira Hodsheet [Monthly Survey, A Journal for IDF Officers]* (Hebrew), XIII, no. 4, 1966, p. 91, quoted in Alon, *Countering Palestinian Terrorism in Israel,* p. 38.

50. Yair Evron, *War and Intervention in Lebanon* (Baltimore: Johns Hopkins University Press, 1987), p. 74.

51. See Yaniv, *Dilemmas of Security,* pp. 68–70, who distinguishes "sustained operations" from "tit-for-tat" retaliatory attacks.

52. For example, General Elazar, justifying intense Israeli attacks on targets in Lebanon and Syria after the 1972 Munich massacre, stated that they were a response not only to the massacre but to a rising tide of terrorist attacks from those countries and "part of a continuous war." Top Israeli General Calls Raids Only 'Part of a Continuous War,' *NYT*, September 11, 1972, p. 12, cols. 2–3.

53. Beate Hamizrachi, *The Emergence of the South Lebanon Security Zone* (New York: Praeger, 1988): Moshe Gersovich, "Armed Operations," *MECS* 8 (1983–84): 98–100.

2

The Process of
Belligerent Interaction

The origins of Israel's war with the PLO go back to the earliest Arab-Jewish clashes as the Zionist movement developed in Palestine. These clashes were particularly violent in 1921 and 1929, and from 1936 to 1939.[1] Shortly after the end of Israel's War of Independence, *fedayeen* infiltrators began to commit terrorist acts in Israel, usually with the support and/or at the behest of the Arab states bordering on Israel. Israel's basic counterterror strategies, described in Chapter 1, were developed in the 1950s. The *fedayeen* threat was taken very seriously. Indeed, counterterror attacks on Egyptian-sponsored *fedayeen* bases in Gaza culminated in the 1956 Suez War, which, from Israel's standpoint, included elimination of the *fedayeen* threat in the south as a major objective.[2] Following Nasser's defeat by the Israelis, the Egyptian front became quiet and remained so well into the 1960s. Indeed, there was a general lull in *fedayeen* activity, Israel's main security problem being defense against Syrian shelling of settlements, farms and fishing boats in the Sea of Galilee.

Israel's war with the PLO began slowly in 1965. At that time Fatah was operating mainly from Syria and had not achieved the ascendancy it was to have later in the decade. The history of this war is not well known. I will offer an overview of the war, interspersed with examples of the kinds of counterterror strategies and tactics previously described.

The PLO's Early Operations

Early PLO operations, in contrast with PLO rhetoric, were not very effective. As indicated above, the 1964 New Year's Eve raids that were announced never took place.[3] From January 1965 to the outbreak of the 1967 June War, the PLO carried out 113 operations, 108 by Fatah and the rest by the Heroes of the Return. Fatah operated out of Syria, its place of origin, while Nasser shut down Fatah's terrorist activities from Gaza after three operations. In this period Israeli casualties from PLO terrorist attacks and Israeli counter raids were four civilians killed and seven wounded, and eight soldiers killed and twenty-four wounded. Much of the PLO's activity took the form of sabotage of water works and agricultural warehouses and laying mines and other explosives.[4]

During the early phase of the war a substantial part of the Israeli strategy emphasized defense of the borders to prevent infiltration by *fedayeen*. There were only six counterterror attacks against PLO bases, four in Jordan and one each in Syria and Lebanon.[5]

Although PLO terrorist operations at this time were not very productive, they were to play an important role in the events leading up to the 1967 June War. While Nassar had been restraining the PLO, its *fedayeen* were operating freely from Syria and Jordan. Nasser's Arab critics subjected him to ridicule, contrasting his pretensions to be the great Arab leader with his unwillingness to support the Palestinians' war of national liberation. Meanwhile, Syrian encouragement of Fatah and provocations by the Syrian military led to heightened Israeli reactions, including artillery exchanges and air battles over Syria. In this context the Soviet Union warned Nasser that Israel was planning a major attack on Syria. This sparked aggressive moves by Nasser including forcing the departure of United Nations Emergency Force (UNEF) peacekeepers at the border, massing troops on the border, closing the Straits of Tiran and launching a propaganda campaign in which Egypt and other Arab states threatened the destruction of Israel.[6] In all of this the PLO acted as a catalyst for a general Arab-Israeli war.

Revolutionary Warfare
June 1967–September 1970

When Israel took Arab threats and actions seriously and struck first on June 5, 1967, it achieved a staggering victory that dashed any hopes of the PLO that Palestine would be liberated by the Arab states. Moreover, the West Bank and Gaza were now under Israeli occupation. The PLO, with Arafat playing an increasingly important role, reacted to the June War debacle by declaring a war of national liberation on the model of the Algerian Front de libération nationale (FLN) and the Viet Cong, to be waged in Israel and the occupied territories.[7]

This PLO effort was a failure. Palestine's geography provides no natural sanctuaries or redoubts for revolutionary forces. The Palestinian people at the time did not respond with whole-hearted support of the PLO. Successful Israeli counterinsurgency policies combined effective security measures with programs that improved the standard of living in the occupied territories. By the end of 1968 the PLO was pushed back to the neighboring Arab states from which it continued the war.

In the period roughly from June 1967, when Arafat proclaimed his revolutionary strategy, to the end of 1968, the PLO fought what could be termed a guerrilla as well as a terrorist war. During this period about half of the Israeli casualties were military.[8] However, once forced back to the sanctuary states, the PLO returned to terrorism as its principal weapon. This includes what Alon calls "firing assaults," attacks across the Jordanian-Israeli border with bazookas, small arms, rockets and artillery, sometimes supported by Jordanian artillery fire. Often the fire was directed at civilian targets. In his 1980 RAND study, *Countering Palestinian Terrorism in Israel*, Hanan Alon puts overall PLO operations from 1967 to 1970 at 4,941; 189 civilians were killed and 1,136 wounded, and 118 military personnel were killed and 575 wounded in terrorist operations during this period. The large number of military casualties was a result of the PLO's effort to wage guerrilla war in the occupied territories. In subsequent periods military casualties were rare, PLO operations being almost exclusively countervalue terrorist attacks on civilian targets.[9]

One of the better-known Israeli attacks on the PLO in this phase of the war was carried out on March 21, 1968, against the Jordanian town of Karameh and adjoining villages. Karameh was the site of much of the PLO's command structure. Warned by Jordan that an attack was imminent, the PLO chose to stand and fight a large Israeli force which included armor and helicopter-lifted troops. Supported by Jordanian artillery and armor, the PLO forces put up a good fight, losing over a third of their 300-man force in casualties, while the Jordanian Army lost 100 dead and 90 wounded. The Israelis lost 28 dead and 90 wounded and left four damaged tanks and four armored vehicles on the field. As a result of the PLO's stand at Karameh, its prestige rose, recruiting improved and King Hussein became more supportive.[10]

Concurrently with the PLO's terror attacks in Israel and the occupied territories, international terrorism against Israel gained worldwide attention. Starting with the hijacking of an El Al aircraft en route from Rome to Lod Airport in Israel, July 23, 1968, the PLO hijacked aircraft of various nations, holding the passengers and crews hostage and demanding the release of PLO and other prisoners. There were also a number of attacks on Israeli airport facilities and personnel around the world. The PFLP initiated the PLO's international terror campaign, believing it to be a more effective way not only of fighting Israel but of bringing the Palestinian cause to the world's attention. The threat of international terror soon revolutionized international travel, forcing burdensome security precautions and introducing an element of risk which produced untold apprehension.[11]

Hijacking posed a difficult challenge to Israel. The strategic concept of attacking the source of terrorism was not as appropriate as in the case of cross-border terrorist attacks from sanctuary states. One possibility was to attack states that cooperated with international terrorism by permitting hijacked aircraft to land in their territory and the hijackers to continue to hold and threaten hostages, as was the case with Libya and Algeria. This was not attempted, however. Another option was to attack the sanctuary states in which the PLO planned and initiated international terrorist operations. This was done in the case of the raid on Beirut Airport, December 12, 1968.

PFLP terrorists attacked an El Al plane in Athens on December 10, 1968, killing one passenger. On December 12, Israeli helicopters attacked Beirut Airport and destroyed thirteen Arab aircraft. The rationale for the attack was that Beirut, an Arab capital, was the haven for the PFLP and other PLO organizations that waged war against Israel through international terrorism as well as through terrorist attacks in Israel and the occupied territories. Dramatic as it was, the raid does not appear to have had much effect because the Lebanese government was too weak and divided to hamper continued PLO planning and execution of terrorist operations.[12]

Certainly the PLO's international terror campaign attracted more world attention than its terrorist and guerrilla attacks in Israel and the occupied territories. Whether this publicity advanced the Palestinian cause is unclear. In retrospect, the number of aerial hijackings that were the main element in the international terror campaign is astonishingly low. Highjacking of aircraft flying to and from Israel were: 1 in 1968, 3 in 1969, 5 in 1970, 0 in 1971, 1 in 1972 and 1 in 1976. Additionally, there were PLO highjackings of aircraft not flying to or from Israel, most of them presumably intended to contribute to the war against Israel (e.g., by demanding release of PLO prisoners in exchange for release of hostages) or to punish Arab states for their failure sufficiently to support the PLO. There was one such highjacking in each year between 1971 and 1974, and one in 1976.[13] Besides the hijackings there were numerous attacks on Israeli-related targets in airports as well as other international terrorist incidents.[14] Once again it was demonstrated that raw terror is a very economical form of armed coercion and a source of publicity—or notoriety, depending on one's viewpoint. Merari and Elad conclude:

> Although the Palestinian organizations advanced their political struggle by means of international terrorism, the biggest boost to their status undoubtedly took place immediately after the drastic reduction in these

activities that occurred in 1974: in other words, terrorism benefited its perpetrators not only through the continuity of terrorist acts themselves, but also by the perpetrators' decision to refrain from these acts.[15]

In any event, a multiple hijacking brought to a head a long series of confrontations between the PLO and King Hussein's regime. By September 1970 this conflict arose from two sources. First, the PLO in Jordan had increasingly challenged Hussein's authority, intimidated the population and brought the country to the brink of civil war. Second, by making Jordan's East Bank a battleground that suffered heavily from Israeli counterterror attacks on the PLO, both the local population and Jordan as a sovereign state had suffered unacceptable damage, as envisaged by Israeli strategy. The specific events that brought this confrontation to a head began on September 6, 1970, when PFLP terrorists made four hijack attempts. One was foiled by El Al in London. A Pan American plane was forced to land in Cairo, where it was blown up by the terrorists after the crew disembarked. The other two aircraft, TWA and Swissair, were forced to land in the desert in Jordan near Zerka. As the terrorists negotiated with the Swiss, West German, British, American and Israeli governments, demanding release of prisoners, the passengers of the two hijacked planes plus those of a BOAC plane subsequently hijacked suffered a lengthy, painful and dangerous captivity in which Jewish hostages were singled out for special mistreatment.

Israel persuaded the Swiss and Germans not to submit to the terrorists' demands. On September 12, 1970, the terrorists evacuated and then blew up the planes. Forty of the hostages were held as "prisoners of war" until released when the Jordanian Army defeated the PLO elements holding them.[16]

Civil war broke out in Jordan and Hussein determinedly broke the PLO's power. Some PLO resistance continued, but by January 1971 the PLO had been decisively defeated and driven out of Jordan, although some resistance persisted until July 1971. Most of the PLO elements found refuge in Lebanon.[17] When Syria attempted to intervene on behalf of the PLO in September 1970, the threat of Israeli and U.S. intervention sealed Hussein's victory.[18]

Granted that there were many reasons for the PLO's defeat and ejection from Jordan, Dayan was surely right when he credited Hussein's action in large measure to the pressures of Israel's counterterror strategy.[19]

The Lebanon Front
September 1970–July 1976

The PLO regrouped in Lebanon in 1971. By 1972 it had resumed active terrorist operations against Israel. The succeeding four years demonstrated the efficacy of Israel's counterterror deterrence/defense strategy insofar as Syria was concerned, but its failure in the case of Lebanon. Syria was Israel's bitter enemy, but under the iron-fisted leadership of Hafez Assad, Syrian security took definite precedence over the PLO's aspirations to continue the armed struggle with Israel. Syria allowed PLO elements to train in its territory and provided them with assistance. Indeed, some of the PLO elements were controlled, entirely or partially by Syria, e.g., Saiqa. However, Syria did not permit the PLO to launch terrorist attacks from its territory because the predictable Israeli response would inflict unacceptable damage, as had been amply demonstrated in Jordan's experience and on the occasions when PLO incursions from Syria brought Israeli responses against PLO targets in Syria. Syria, therefore, shunted the PLO's fighting forces over to Lebanon, particularly in the southeast corner adjacent to the Syrian border soon known as "Fatahland."

Lebanon, the least hostile of Israel's Arab adversaries, was also the weakest. The Christian Lebanese in the government and army attempted to curb the PLO's terrorist operations. The Muslim elements, however, were either unwilling or unable to support these efforts. During this phase of Israel's war with the PLO the situation in Lebanon deteriorated, finally collapsing in the 1975–76 civil war.

The Lebanese government's policies toward the PLO were ambivalent to the point of being internally contradictory throughout this period. Earlier efforts to reconcile control of the PLO's activities with support of its war of national liberation had produced the Cairo Accord of November 3, 1969, which served to legitimize the PLO's "presence" in Lebanon and to control its activities. Operations against Israel were to be confined to certain localities and secretly "coordinated" with the Lebanese Army. However, the November 3, 1969, Cairo Accord, negotiated under Nasser's auspices, specifically pledged official Lebanese support of the PLO's war with Israel.[20]

In the early years of this period the Lebanese government and army tried repeatedly to limit PLO operations launched from south Lebanon. Periodic crisis meetings between Lebanese officials and Arafat followed cycles of hostilities wherein terrorist attacks triggered Israeli counterterror land incursions as well as air and sea attacks on PLO targets in Lebanon. Each time the parties would profess to be in complete agreement, the Lebanese pledging continued support of the PLO while Arafat promised to limit his operations. From time to time the Lebanese Army would attempt to enforce these agreements and there would be armed clashes, sometimes of long duration. However, in the end the PLO continued to do terrorist business as usual. By the end of this period it was evident that the Lebanese government was too weak and divided to control the PLO. Indeed, the PLO had built a state-within-a-state in much of south Lebanon. The Israeli deterrent would not work against the state of Lebanon because its government was no longer exercising sovereign power.[21]

Deterring the local population around PLO bases was another matter. The Israelis were successful, through their counterterror attacks, in motivating some of the south Lebanese to resist the PLO's presence and activities. Ultimately Christian militias were formed in the south and they fought the PLO. From these militias emerged the South Lebanon Army under Major Saad Haddad in 1983.[22]

Throughout this period Israeli strategy followed both the lines of retaliation and of preventive/attrition. A typical example of retaliation after an accumulation of terrorist attacks which also served a deterrent function was the operation launched on February 25, 1972. A battalion-strength force, supported by artillery and air cover, attacked four Lebanese villages and destroyed many homes which had served the PLO. The Israeli Air Force (IAF) bombed two villages. The operation continued until February 28. This incursion followed a series of PLO terrorist attacks and Israeli warnings to the Lebanese authorities that Israel would be compelled to attack the areas from which the terrorists were operating with impunity.[23]

Israeli incursions and air attacks of this kind, varying in magnitude and duration, continued throughout this period. Moreover, during this phase of the war the Israelis repeatedly announced preventive/attrition strategies, sometimes called "preemptive," emphasizing that they would strike at times and places of their own choosing in this continuing war, even when Israeli operations immediately followed major terrorist incidents such as the April 11, 1974, terrorist attack on an apartment building in Kiryat Shemona.[24]

Following the massacre of eleven members of the Israeli Olympic team who had been taken hostage in Munich on September 5, 1972, Israel unleashed a series of land and air attacks against PLO bases in Lebanon and Syria, lasting from September 7 to 17. As noted above, General Elazar stressed that these were not simply retaliatory attacks but part of a "continuing war" in the face of a rising wave of attacks from Lebanon and Syria.[25] To reiterate, the timing of Israeli counterterror measures is often linked to some particularly horrendous terrorist action, but the function of these measures is deterrence and preventive/attrition as well as retaliation.

The Yom Kippur War of October 6–25, 1973, did not seem to change the dynamics of the PLO-Israeli hostilities. However, the negotiations for disengagement agreements between Israel, Egypt and Syria elicited PLO efforts to frustrate them. Moreover, the Syrians, bitter after their bad defeat in the war, carried on low-level hostilities with Israel right up to the conclusion of the disengagement agreement of May 29, 1974. When the press revealed that Prime Minister Meir was insisting that, as part of the disengagement agreement, Syria promise to prevent PLO terrorist attacks from being initiated in her territory, Assad balked. However, on May 31 the *New York Times* reported that Assad had conveyed the required assurances to Israel through Henry Kissinger. The reason for Assad's promise appeared to be the threat of severe Israeli measures against sanctuary states and a U.S. undertaking henceforth to veto any Security Council condemnations of such measures.[26] It should be observed that Syria had long had a policy of preventing PLO terrorist attacks from originating within its territory. It is fair to conclude that the Israeli counterterror deterrence/defense strategy, successful against Jordan, had again succeeded.

A comparative lull in hostilities in the fall of 1974 may be explained by the PLO's successful drive for recognition and respectability, notably at the September 1974 Rabat Arab summit, which declared the PLO the sole representative of the Palestinian people, and in November when Arafat was hailed by the UN General Assembly. On November 23, 1974, the General Assembly passed resolutions declaring the right of the Palestinians to independence and granting the PLO observer status in UN affairs.[27]

The pattern of PLO-Israeli hostilities continued in the first part of 1975 but was broken by the outbreak of the Lebanese Civil War on April 13, 1975. The PLO was a major participant in the war from the outset. The war was sparked when, after unknown assailants fired at a church gathering attended by Pierre Gemayel, Christian Phalangists fired on a bus filled with Palestinian militants returning from a rally to celebrate the first anniversary of the PLO attack on Kiryat Shemona. It is significant that, for the Palestinians, a terrorist action in which women and children were brutally slaughtered was a great victory to be celebrated.[28]

Although the PLO and the leftist Muslim forces gained the upper hand in the Lebanon Civil War in 1975, Syria intervened on the side of the Christians and substantially defeated the leftist coalition forces by July 1976. Thereafter, a Syrian occupation camouflaged as an Arab peacekeeping force pushed the PLO back into its state within a state in southern Lebanon. This situation was in part a consequence of a tacit Syrian-Israeli "Red Line" agreement limiting Syrian movement south, deployment of missiles and prohibiting use of its air power against the Christians. While the PLO was barred from the immediate border areas by the Haddad south Lebanon forces, it still had a large territorial base in south Lebanon, free from Lebanese government or Syrian control.[29]

PLO preoccupation with the Lebanese civil war as well as effective Israeli counterterror measures reduced PLO attacks on Israel in the latter part of 1975 and throughout 1976.[30] However, the summer of 1976 saw the hijacking that led to the Israeli Entebbe raid, the first event to be discussed in the next phase of the conflict.

Entebbe, Litani, and a Cease-fire
July 1976–August 1979

An Air France plane departing Athens for Tel Aviv was hijacked by PFLP terrorists on June 27, 1976. Landing in Entebbe, Uganda, the terrorists were reinforced and given the support of Idi Amin's troops. The passengers were held hostage and the terrorists demanded release of prisoners held by Israel and four other states. An Israeli rescue mission on July 4 was successful, with few casualties among the hostages and the death of only one Israeli, the commander, Lt. Col. Yonatan Netanyahu. A number of terrorists and Ugandan soldiers and police were killed or wounded. An elderly Jewish woman, Dora Bloch, who had been put in a hospital, was murdered after the Israelis had evacuated the other hostages.

At this point there was a lull in Israel's war with the PLO, lasting well into 1977. However, the fighting in south Lebanon escalated in September 1977 and Israel's participation in it, sometimes unclear and denied in the past, became overt. The Israeli towns of Safad, Ramat Alma and Kiryat Shemona were hit by rocket fire from Lebanon. Eventually, U.S. mediators arranged a ceasefire that went into effect on September 26, 1977. The PLO—once again—agreed to withdraw from the border area and the Israelis discontinued patrols in Lebanon.[31] Artillery exchanges broke the cease fire on October 5, 1977, and fighting resumed with each side blaming the other. Terrorist attacks continued in Israel. Katyusha rockets killed two in Nahariya on November 6, 1977. Israel, which had already been shelling PLO positions, retaliated for the Nahariya attack with air raids on PLO targets in south Lebanon. Two villages were leveled and at least 70 civilians killed in raids in and around Tyre.[32]

Following Sadat's initiative of November 19, 1977, the pattern of PLO rocketing of Israeli population centers and Israeli air raids on the PLO in Lebanon continued. Israeli Ambassador to the UN Chaim Herzog wrote to UN Secretary General Waldheim explaining that the Israeli air raids were aimed solely at terrorist bases and were ordered on the basis of intelligence reports that the PLO was going to increase terrorist attacks.[33]

When Sadat made his historic trip to Jerusalem on November 19, 1977, the PLO desisted from terrorist activity, apparently because of Syrian and Lebanese pressures. Thereafter the PLO seemed more intent on punishing Egypt than on attacking Israel, as in the assassination of Yousef el-Sebal, editor-in-chief of Egypt's *Al Ahram* newspaper in Nicosia, Cyprus, on

February 18, 1978; the hostage taking at the Nicosia Airport that led to a botched Egyptian rescue mission in which fifteen Egyptian commandos died. Although Arafat denied responsibility, Egypt withdrew privileges previously enjoyed by the PLO, while Syria now encouraged the PLO to upset peace negotiations, permitting it to reopen bases and to operate a radio station in Syria.[34]

One of the PLO's most spectacular and bloody operations took place on March 11, 1978. Thirteen *fedayeen,* including two women, landed on a beach between Haifa and Tel Aviv. After killing an American Jewish woman photographer, they seized a bus and engaged in a running gun battle with security forces to the neighborhood of the Country Club resort north of Tel Aviv. Thirty-two civilians, including women and children, were killed before nine *fedayeen* were killed and the others captured.[35] The attack delayed a visit by Begin to Washington. Al Fatah claimed credit for the attack.[36] The Lebanese government disclaimed any responsibility for the raid, which was launched by small boat from Damour.[37]

The IDF invaded Lebanon with 10,000–12,000 troops supported by tanks on March 14–15, 1978 and attacked major PLO camps in south Lebanon. Israeli Navy gunboats shelled PLO targets in Tyre and Said, and the IAF hit PLO targets in both cities as well as in Beirut. Chief of Staff Lt. Gen. Mordechai Gur announced the establishment of a "security belt" ten kilometers deep in Lebanon, and a number of border PLO strongholds were occupied.[38]

When PLO rockets continued to fall on Israel, the Israelis resumed their advance to the Litani River. One reason for the extension of the operation to the Litani was to drive the PLO forces further away from the border. A second reason was to create a larger zone for the U.S.-inspired United Nations Interim Force in Lebanon (UNIFIL) to occupy, thus keeping the PLO at a distance over the long term.[39] Israel announced a ceasefire on March 21, 1978. Meanwhile, UNIFIL was being formed. Israel delayed its withdrawal until UNIFIL was in place, beginning a phased withdrawal on or about March 28 which continued until June 13, 1978.[40]

The Litani Operation pushed the PLO back and resulted in the introduction of UNIFIL, which barred the *fedayeen* from infiltrating into Israel to some extent. It also produced the security zone and further institutionalized Israel's use of the Christian militia under Major Haddad. In the following years there were clashes between UNIFIL forces and Haddad's troops. The PLO also clashed with UNIFIL but seemed to coexist better than did the Haddad militia. PLO hostilities with Haddad's forces resumed and continued intermittently until the 1982 war.

After Israel's withdrawal from Lebanon in June 1978, PLO attacks on

Israel virtually ceased until January 1979. Israeli action against the PLO was largely limited to support of the Haddad's militia.[41] A terrorist explosion in Jerusalem on January 18, 1979, provoked an IDF raid on PLO staff headquarters and artillery positions in South Lebanon, destroying the targets and killing approximately forty *fedayeen* and a civilian without Israeli losses.[42] This raid triggered four days of artillery and rocket exchanges, January 20–24, 1979, before a UN-sponsored cease-fire. Twenty thousand people reportedly fled the area, but many returned after the cease-fire.[43] Artillery exchanges between the PLO and Haddad's militia, sometimes reinforced by the IDF, continued throughout the early months of 1979. As the time approached for signature of the Egyptian-Israeli peace treaty in Washington, March 26, 1979, PLO terrorist activity picked up, but was consistently frustrated by the Israelis.

The PLO attempted to overcome, with little success, the disadvantage of having no direct access to the Israeli-Lebanese border by sea-borne raids and the use of gliders and balloons. More ominous was a build-up of conventional weapons systems, transport and material which would give the PLO the capability of firing with long-range artillery and rocket launchers over the UNIFIL areas and the security zone into northern Israel. It appears that this build-up and concomitant training absorbed the PLO's efforts to a great extent at this time.[44]

However, PLO terrorism again made headlines on April 22, 1979. The Palestinian Liberation Front (PLF), a dissident group that had broken off from the PFLP-GC, landed four *fedayeen* in Nahariya. In a series of fire-fights while taking hostages, the *fedayeen* killed a man and his five-year-old daughter.[45] Israel responded with four days of fighting in south Lebanon, this time with an emphasis on Israeli naval bombardments of PLO targets.[46]

This was the occasion for Begin to announce that Israel would adopt a new "preemptive" policy in lieu of a policy of retaliation.[47] Begin reiterated the preemptive policy in a Knesset statement on May 7, 1979.[48] As previously observed, this was not an entirely new policy, but it is true that escalation of Israeli preventive/attrition attacks on the PLO had generally followed particular terrorist incidents or a pattern of increased terrorist activity.

The more aggressive Israeli policy resulted in more attacks in Lebanon. These attacks—but even more, the bitter fighting between the PLO and the Haddad forces—produced more refugees, an estimated 60,000 in May 1979.[49]

Begin once again reiterated his preemptive policy in a speech at Kiryat Shemona on June 25, 1979.[50] Two days later the IAF and the Syrian air force engaged in aerial combat in which five Syrian MiG–21s were shot down. The clash apparently resulted from IAF bombing of PLO targets near Tyre and Sidon, close to Syrian positions.[51]

On July 5, 1979, the IDF and Haddad's forces initiated a series of raids on PLO positions within the UNIFIL areas.[52] Israeli naval vessels shelled PLO targets in Adlun on July 17, 1979, setting off two weeks of fighting, mainly in the form of artillery duels.[53] In these duels the PLO used 160 mm. long-range artillery for the first time—a major threshold in the course of events leading to the 1982 war.[54]

More ground fighting in late July 1979 was followed by a major series of IAF strikes on July 22, 1979. The United States condemned these raids and stated that it would check to determine whether U.S.-supplied weapons had been used in ways violating Israeli-U.S. agreements.[55] Hostilities featuring heavy artillery exchanges continued July 24–28, with UNIFIL at times involved and taking casualties.[56] Meanwhile, PLO *fedayeen* carried out terrorist bombing attacks in smaller Israeli towns to give an impression of ubiquity.[57]

Throughout August 1979 hostilities in south Lebanon continued to be heavy, with artillery exchanges between the PLO, the Haddad militia and the IDF, and IAF raids on PLO targets. Month-long UN efforts to arrange a cease-fire finally succeeded on August 27, 1979.[58]

Escalation
August 27, 1979–July 10, 1981

The August 27, 1979, cease-fire held substantially until April 1980. There were a few PLO terrorist operations in Israel and abroad but most of them were minor and/or unsuccessful. There were a number of possible explanations for this lull. Israel's inactivity may have resulted from U.S. pressure. The PLO's relative inactivity had multiple explanations: preoccupation with the continuing hostilities with Haddad's forces and with Shiite factions in south Lebanon, the restraining effects of UNIFIL, the effort to improve the PLO's international image. Undoubtedly, the effectiveness of Israeli preventive/attrition attacks was part of the explanation. Last, and possibly most important, the PLO was continuing its conventional build-up which would permit a new strategy of attacks on Israeli population centers with long-range artillery and rockets, a development that was soon to be demonstrated.[59]

The lull ended on April 6–7, 1980, when five Arab Liberation Front (ALF) *fedayeen* seized the children's house in the Misgav Am kibbutz on the Lebanese border. When the IDF stormed the house, all five *fedayeen*, the kibbutz secretary and an Israeli baby were killed. Four children and eleven soldiers were wounded. The Misgav Am terrorist attack coincided with Sadat's departure for the United States to discuss talks on Palestinian self-determination under the terms of the 1979 Egyptian-Israeli peace treaty.[60]

Israel now resumed sustained preventive/attrition attacks, which continued to April 1981. There was a notable concern about minimizing collateral damage. Air raids and shelling were held to the minimum and there was an emphasis on commando ground ambushes and assaults on PLO personnel and bases in south Lebanon. These tactics forced the PLO to concentrate more on their own defense.[61]

An example of the new Israeli tactics occurred on the night of May 7–8, 1980, when two sea-borne IDF detachments landed in Lebanon and ambushed *fedayeen* vehicles and patrols at Saksakiyya and Ra's al-Sa'diyyat, killing at least three *fedayeen* and wounding several.[62] The preventive/attrition operations continued throughout the summer of 1980, slackening somewhat in the fall but continuing the same tactical emphasis into April 1981.

Meanwhile, Major Haddad's hostilities with the PLO had been heavy. There were over 120 clashes between the PLO and the Christian militia from July 1980 to June 1981, mostly in the form of artillery exchanges in which the IDF frequently participated.[63]

Throughout the year of preventive/attrition attacks that began in April 1980, Israel concentrated on the smaller, more radical PLO elements such as the ALF, PFLP-GC, PLF and Saiqa, which had specialized in the traditional *fedayeen* small terrorist operations.[64] Now, however, growing concern over the PLO's conventional build-up and its implications for a new terrorist strategy of countervalue attacks on Israeli population centers led to more preventive/attrition attacks on the mainstream Fatah forces that had deployed long-range artillery and rocket launchers.[65]

This new phase of the hostilities began with a raid on a Fatah base near Arab Salim, near Nabitiya where tanks, anti-aircraft guns and ammunition were stored on the night of April 9–10, 1981. The PLO retaliated on April 10 with rocket attacks on the Galilee panhandle, to which the Israelis responded with heavy shelling and an air raid on PLO bases near Damur.[66] There followed a number of Israeli air raids on PLO bases, which were usually followed with PLO katyusha and artillery countervalue attacks on north Israeli population centers.[67] Israeli attacks continued until early June. There was an IDF ambush operation against PLO vehicles on the Sidon-Beirut highway on May 29. The Israeli Navy shelled a regional PFLP headquarters north of Tripoli on June 3, 1981, in the last Israeli action before the fighting escalated on July 10, 1981.[68]

At the same time the Syrian missile crisis developed. From April 1, 1981, the Syrian Army attacked Christian Phalangist forces in Zahle and elsewhere in the Bekaa Valley as well as in East Beirut. The Syrians used helicopters to land troops on the key Mount Sanin position and allegedly strafed Phalangist troops. Israel considered this to be a violation of the 1976 tacit "Red Line" agreement whereby Syria was not to use air power against the Christians. By the end of April the Christians were in desperate straits. On April 28 the IAF shot down two Syrian helicopters resupplying Syrian forces on Mount Sanin. Syria then installed SAM–3 ground-to-air missiles near Zahle in positions that had been prepared for several weeks.[69]

Israel considered the installation of the missiles to be a second and critical violation of the "Red Line" agreement.[70] The Syrian action challenged Israel. Failure to react would be interpreted as a humiliating defeat and a major change in the strategic balance. Moreover, the Syrian missiles could jeopardize Israel's ability to overfly Lebanon and to carry out reconnaissance and preventive/attrition attacks on the PLO. Additionally, the challenge damaged Begin's chances for reelection on June 30. Only bad weather prevented Begin from attacking the missiles immediately.[71] The United States then dispatched Special Envoy Philip Habib, who tried unsuccessfully to arrange a settlement. Meanwhile, the spectacular June 7, 1981, Israeli attack on the Iraqi Osirak nuclear reactor improved Israeli morale and Begin's political fortunes.[72]

Intensive Hostilities
July 10–21, 1981

Following Begin's electoral victory in late June 1981, the IDF resumed its preventive/attrition attacks on the PLO, concentrating on its conventional weapons systems and supporting infrastructure. These attacks, between July 10 and 16, elicited prompt PLO responses with artillery and rocket fire on population centers in northern Israel. Although there were few casualties, the effects on these daily indiscriminate bombardments caused a mass exodus and brought normal life to a halt.[73] Israel intensified its efforts with air attacks that destroyed bridges over the Zahrani and Litani rivers on July 16 and 17. The IAF then delivered a major raid on the Beirut headquarters of Fatah and the DFLP. Since the headquarters were in a civilian area, collateral damage was heavy, estimates running from 90 to 175 dead and 480 to 600 wounded.[74] In protest, the United States postponed lifting the suspension of deliveries of F16 fighter bombers to Israel.[75]

The PLO subjected Kiryat Shemona, Nahariya and northern Israeli villages and settlements to massive bombardments daily from July 17 to 24.

Israel hit the PLO hard with artillery, air strikes and ambushes in Lebanon.[76] On July 21, 1981, Habib announced a cease-fire negotiated through the Saudis and other Arab intermediaries.[77]

The Precarious Habib Cease-fire
July 24, 1981–June 6, 1982

There was no written document containing the terms of the Habib cease-fire. Israel claimed that it prohibited all PLO terrorist and military action anywhere, including attacks on Haddad's forces in south Lebanon and terrorist attacks around the world. The PLO insisted that it only prohibited attacks across the Lebanon border. From July 24, 1981, until April 1982 there were virtually no cross-border PLO attacks, but there were continued fighting between the PLO and Haddad's militia and continued PLO international terrorist activity.[78]

Moreover, the PLO's conventional build-up, the potential of which for indiscriminate attacks on Israeli population centers had been demonstrated in the July 1981 fighting, continued. Israel reported in August 1981 that the PLO had over one hundred artillery pieces including dozens of 130 mm. canon with a range of over seventeen miles, dozens of BM–21 and BM–11 multiple-rocket launchers capable of firing rapid salvos of up to forty katyusha rockets at targets over thirteen miles distant, dozens of Korean 107 mm. rocket launchers, undetermined numbers of BM–17 rocket launchers and heavy mortars, seventy to eighty tanks, including heavy T–54 and T–55 models, plus numerous T–34 tanks, dozens of armored personnel carriers and new anti-aircraft batteries including SAM–9 missiles and 23 mm.ZSU–4 radar-guided anti-aircraft canon, as well as SAM–7 shoulder-launched missiles.[79]

Israel was insisting to the United States that the cease fire had been broken repeatedly by the PLO, and the U.S. was restraining the Israelis from invading Lebanon as early as February 1982.[80] Meanwhile, Defense Minister Sharon had completed plans for a major invasion of Lebanon to deal the PLO a knock-out blow, force the Syrians out and establish a friendly Christian-led Lebanese government.

Following the deaths of Yacov Barsimantov, an Israeli diplomat in Paris, and of an IDF soldier from a mine in the Security Zone, Israel renewed air attacks on the PLO in Lebanon on April 21 and May 9, 1982.[81] Arafat restricted the PLO response to some shelling that was obviously intended to fall harmlessly.[82] Finally, the *casus belli* for the long-planned Israeli invasion was furnished by the assassination attempt by Abu Nidal terrorists against Israeli diplomat Sholom Argov in London on June 3, 1982.[83] The

IAF hit PLO targets in Beirut and south Lebanon on June 4. The PLO responded with artillery attacks on northern Israel, described by Evron as either "deliberately or inadvertently" "very scattered and ineffective."[84]

The 1982 Lebanon War

The 1982 Lebanon War will be discussed in greater detail in Chapters 6 and 7. In this overview of Israel's War with the PLO, it will suffice to outline the general development of the war. The war went through four phases:

(1) June 6–9, in which Israel overran southern Lebanon;
(2) June 10–13, in which Beirut was encircled;
(3) June 14–26, in which Israel gained control of the mountains overlooking Beirut;
(4) June 27–August 12, the siege of Beirut.[85]

The IDF attacked on June 6 in three sectors: western, along the coastal road; central, from Marjayoun toward Jezzine, aimed at the Beirut-Damascus highway; eastern, directed at Hasbaiya, Rachaiya and the center of the Bekaa Valley at Joub Jannine. On the 6th, the western elements advanced past Tyre and crossed the Litani River, by-passing and sealing off PLO strong points around Tyre. In the center, the IDF bypassed Nabitiya and forced the PLO to retreat to Jezzine. In the east the IDF moved to outflank the Syrian forces in the Bekaa Valley.[86]

On June 7 the IAF bombed PLO strong points in Beirut and along the line of advance, shooting down one Syrian aircraft over Beirut.[87] Otherwise, there was no engagement with the Syrians. In the west the IDF attacked the Rachidiya camp in difficult fighting. PLO camps such as this are usually described as "refugee camps," but they are also well-prepared military bases and strong points. The Israelis chose to use slow, arduous tactics rather than more indiscriminate means that would have brought earlier victory.[88] Units from the coast linked up with units from the center at Zaharani Junction. IDF troops from Tyre linked up at Jouaiya with troops coming from the Security Zone. The PLO's "Iron Triangle" was broken and the IDF began mopping up and destroying the PLO's infrastructure. Meanwhile, in the east the Crusader Beaufort castle, a PLO stronghold, was captured. The IDF controlled Hasbaiya and Koukaba and continued to outflank the Syrians by advancing on Rachaiya. Israeli artillery was now well within range of the Syrian missile sites and further Israeli advances would reach the main Syrian lines.[89]

The Israelis also launched an amphibious landing north of Sidon on June

6–7 near the mouth of the Awali River.[90] Caught between this force and troops coming up the coast and from the central region, the PLO sought to defend Sidon and Ein Hilwe camp. As forces in the center moved against Jezzine, light resistance included Syrian troops, but there was still no clear state of hostilities with Syria.[91]

On June 8, the western sector forces continued to fight for Rachidiya and Ein Hilwe camps. As the IDF advanced on Damour, the IAF engaged Syrian aircraft over Beirut and southern Lebanon, shooting down six.[92] The Israelis did not attack the Syrian missile sites, while the Syrians tracked Israeli aircraft with their radar but did not fire missiles.[93] After defeating PLO and Syrian forces around Jezzine, the central-sector IDF forces pressed on to Ain Zhalta commanding the Beirut-Damascus highway, where they encountered strong Syrian resistance.[94] To the east the IDF reached positions around Masghara and Lake Qaraoun. IDF units at Hasbaiya and Koukaba remained halted as the Syrians moved more missiles and troops into position opposite the Israelis.[95]

The IDF battled for Damour on June 9 as it continued the siege of the Ein Hilwe camp.[96] Israeli armor reached Beit a Din and the main road to Beirut through the Shouf Mountains.[97] A major battle developed with the Syrians around Ain Zhalta, stopping the Israeli advance and permitting Syrian redeployments along the highway and in the Shouf.[98] In the east, the IDF moved along the Barouk mountains and toward Rachaiya as the main IDF central force remained halted.[99]

Sharon now obtained authority from Begin and the Cabinet to take out the Syrian missiles, while receiving considerably less clear authority to engage the Syrian ground forces—which he had already been engaging.[100] The IAF attacked and destroyed fourteen of nineteen Syrian missile batteries and severely damaged three. This provoked a major air battle in which ninety Syrian Air Force (SAF) planes were shot down with no IAF losses.[101] The IDF central forces now attacked toward the Bekaa Valley and in two days reached all of their objectives. The campaign in Southern Lebanon was essentially over.[102]

On June 10 the IDF began to cut off the PLO in Beirut. In the west, as the Israelis mopped up in Tyre and Sidon, Syrian and PLO forces halted the Israelis in Beirut's southern suburbs. In the center sector, the IDF captured Ain Zhalta and the heights overlooking Ain Dara, even closer to the Beirut-Damascus highway.[103] The Israelis in the eastern sector drove toward Joub Jannine, captured Rachaiya and reached the outskirts of Yanta, twenty-four kilometers from Damascus.[104] In a major air battle in the eastern sector, the IAF shot down sixty-five SAF planes while losing one to ground fire.[105]

Syria and Israel announced a cease-fire for June 11, but it did not include the PLO. Syrian efforts to reinforce their troops before the cease-fire were thwarted by an Israeli ambush from the Barouk ridge.[106] In the west Khalde finally fell to the Israelis on June 11, although fighting around it continued.[107] Another major air battle resulted in the destruction of eighteen more Syrian MiGs.[108]

The cease fire was extended to the PLO on June 12, but it broke down on June 13 when heavy fighting resumed around Khalde, six miles south of Beirut.[109] A Syrian ambush frustrated Israeli flanking efforts toward Baabda where, after heavy fighting, the IDF broke through to the Lebanese presidential palace overlooking the airport, three major refugee camps and commanding the highway to Damascus. The PLO was now trapped in Beirut.[110]

Sharon had, unrealistically, expected the Christian Lebanese forces to take over at this point and finish off the PLO in Beirut. Failing this, Sharon faced a dilemma. He had gotten this far by a series of *faits accomplis* and subterfuges. He did not have a mandate to move promptly to attack the PLO in Beirut while they were defeated and off-balance. Instead, he had to mount a siege and discover means of intimidation and coercion sufficient to force the PLO to evacuate Beirut.[111]

In the next phase of the war, June 14–26, the Israelis demanded the withdrawal of Syrian troops from Lebanon. When the Syrians responded by reinforcing their Bekaa forces and keeping their brigade in Beirut, the Israelis launched a series of attacks with armor, artillery and air support on June 22.[112] The IDF cleared the Beirut-Damascus highway from Baabda to Sofar by June 25 and a new cease-fire went into effect.[113] Up to this time the Israelis had attacked the PLO positions in Beirut with artillery and air, but air attacks were discontinued—not to be resumed until July 22—on June 25. This was because U.S. envoy Habib had protested bitterly that the Israeli air raids made negotiations impossible.[114] Artillery and small-arms fire continued in limited combat until late July.

With a frequently broken cease-fire in effect, the Israelis conducted intensive psychological warfare operations in Beirut, with leaflets, loudspeakers and radio announcements and mock bombing runs, warning the inhabitants that they should leave the city to escape the fighting.[115] Following the six-day cease-fire, the siege of Beirut began on July 1.[116] Habib announced on July 2 that no progress had been made in negotiations. The PFLP's George Habash said that the PLO was playing for time.[117] On July 3, the IDF seized the "Green Line" dividing East and West Beirut.[118] The Israelis cut off war and electricity but restored them on July 7 at President Reagan's insistence.[119] Shipments of food and fuel into West Beirut were severely restricted at check points manned by Christian militia. Artillery, rocket and gunboat attacks on the PLO positions continued, leading to an intense duel on July 9 in which the PLO employed 130 mm. artillery and katyusha rockets.[120] Israeli probes around the airport on July 11 met with strong PLO resistance. On that day a cease-fire went into effect, holding until July 21.[121]

On July 21 the PLO and Syrians ignited an escalation of the hostilities. The Israelis were convinced that the PLO was stalling in the negotiations. They were, moreover, outraged that the PLO had been able to infiltrate from Syrian-controlled areas and attack the IDF in the rear, as well as defy the Israelis by katyusha rocket attacks on towns in northern Israel, something Operation Peace for Galilee was supposed to have made impossible. Moreover, the Syrians deployed three SA–8 batteries in the Bekaa Valley.[122]

The Israelis responded on July 22 to the stalemate and the new PLO attacks with what they termed "disproportionate force."[123] Air attacks, explicitly linked to the July 21 PLO attacks, were resumed against PLO positions in Beirut.[124] On the same day the Israelis attacked Syrian and PLO positions in the Syrian-controlled areas from which the PLO was infiltrating. This was the first major combat with the Syrians since June 25. On July 23 the Israelis destroyed the three SAM–8 missile batteries that the Syrians had moved into the Bekaa Valley.[125] At this time the Israelis, under intense American pressure, again allowed resumption of water supplies to West Beirut.[126]

On July 22 the Israelis began intensive air and artillery attacks on PLO positions in Beirut. These attacks continued with much collateral damage until July 30, when a cease-fire began. It lasted through July 31.[127] On August 1, PLO positions were subjected to fourteen straight hours of air, naval and artillery bombardment. On that day the IDF captured the airport and surrounding area.[128]

The IDF massed armor at the Beirut crossing on August 2, and on August 4 three armored columns penetrated West Beirut but soon bogged down, taking heavy casualties in city fighting. The three PLO camps were outflanked in these operations.[129] President Reagan considered that the thrusts into West Beirut violated Israeli promises and threatened negotiations, but the Israelis rejected Reagan's call for a return to the Green Line.[130]

During a lull, August 5–6, it was announced that negotiations had been completed for the PLO's evacuation.[131] On August 9 the IAF attacked the PLO positions in Beirut and behind Syrian lines inland.[132] On August 10 the Israeli government accepted the Habib plan in principle, while Israeli air, naval and artillery forces attacked the PLO camps south of Beirut.[133] On August 11, as negotiations continued, the Israelis continued air, sea and artillery attacks on PLO positions and moved an armored unit north of Beirut to block PLO reinforcements from Tripoli, where ten thousand PLO and Syrian troops were stationed.[134]

Israel unleashed a massive aerial bombardment against PLO targets in Beirut that lasted from 6 a.m. to 5:30 p.m. on August 12. Civilian casualties and damage were great.[135] Begin and his Cabinet were shocked at this operation, which was witnessed worldwide through television. President Reagan called Begin to express his rage at Israeli attacks on Beirut. Sharon's authority to direct the war without prior Cabinet authorization was rescinded.[136] Thereafter, Israeli military pressure was relaxed and the Israelis agreed to Habib's plan for the evacuation of the PLO and the introduction of a multinational force (MNF) on August 19.[137]

Israeli satisfaction with the defeat and evacuation of the PLO was short-lived. Bashir Gemayel, the Christian leader on whom the Israelis relied, was elected president on August 23, but on September 14 Gemayel and twenty-five others were killed when a bomb destroyed his party headquarters. Christian demands for vengeance coincided with an Israeli desire to root out remaining PLO elements. Christian forces perpetrated the Sabra and Shatilla massacres in Palestinian camps on September 14–15, unimpeded by the IDF forces in control of the area.[138]

Israel in Lebanon, the PLO in Disarray 1982–1985

Following its defeat in August 1982, the PLO's forces in Beirut were scattered in bases in Tunis, South Yemen, Syria, Sudan, Algeria and other Arab states.[139] However, some 8,000–9,000 PLO *fedayeen* remained in northern Lebanon in areas subject to Syrian control. The elements in Lebanon did not resume hostilities with Israel for a long time, in part because they became embroiled in a Palestinian civil war, beginning in May 1983.

Fatah elements led by Abu Musa, supported by the Syrian Army, began a civil war with elements loyal to Arafat in mid-May 1983. The rebels' motivation was twofold: resentment against corruption and favoritism in the *Fatah* leadership, and opposition to what they conceived to be Arafat's excessive moderation and propensity to compromise.[140] In early June there were armed clashes between the Fatah factions and the rebels, with Syrian support, proceeded to drive the loyalists out of the Bekaa Valley.[141] Concurrently, Arafat was declared persona non grata by Asad and expelled from Damascus.[142]

In the fall of 1983 the PLO forces loyal to Arafat were driven back to

Tripoli, where they were besieged by the rebels, again with Syrian support. Arafat's forces were defeated and forced to evacuate Tripoli on December 20, 1983.[143]

Despite this internecine PLO conflict, minor PLO terrorist and guerrilla attacks resumed in the spring of 1983. At this time the IDF remained deployed more or less as it had been since the end of the 1982 war, including positions in the Shouf mountains and south of the Beirut-Damascus highway in central Lebanon. Israeli reactions to terrorist and guerrilla attacks were complicated by the appearance of a Lebanese resistance group, the Lebanese National Resistance Front (LNRF). Both the PLO and the LNRF claimed credit for an ambush of IDF troops on June 10.[144]

The Israeli Cabinet voted to pull the IDF back to a position on the Awali River on July 20, 1983.[145] This move was delayed, in part because the Lebanese government and the United States feared that the Israeli withdrawal would leave a vacuum into which the rival Lebanese factions would move and clash, which is what eventuated. The IDF withdrawal began on September 4, as Begin prepared to turn over the post of prime minister to Shamir. Following the Israeli withdrawal to the Awali hostilities ensued between the Lebanese Army and Christian militia, on the one hand, and the Druze, Shiite and Muslim leftist elements supported by Syria, on the other.

The U.S. Marines, as well as the French and Italian troops in the multinational force that had been brought into the Beirut area after the Sabra and Shatilla massacres, were increasingly caught in the crossfires of Lebanese and Syrian hostilities and were frequently attacked directly. U.S. self-defense measures included naval bombardments of Druze and Syrian artillery positions, sources of attacks on the marines. Both the French and the Americans also launched retaliatory air raids. The violence peaked with the car bomb attack that killed 242 marines in their barracks on October 22, 1983.

Terrorist and guerrilla attacks against the Israelis in Lebanon increased in the fall of 1983. Demolition of houses used for attacks on the IDF in south Lebanon was instituted at this time. It became apparent that Shiite elements were becoming more of a threat to the Israelis in Lebanon than the PLO. However, despite its internecine travails, the PLO was still active. The Israeli estimate of the sources of resistance is reflected in its choice of targets for retaliatory and deterrent raids.

A suicide car bomb attack destroyed Israeli military intelligence headquarters in Tyre on November 4, 1983, killing at least twenty-nine Israeli soldiers and ten Arabs. The same day Israeli jets bombed Palestinian positions in the mountains overlooking Beirut in two raids.[146] On November

16 the IAF bombed a military stronghold of the pro-Iranian Shiite Muslim radicals, three miles from the Syrian border in eastern Lebanon. Israel announced that the raid was retaliation for terrorist attacks against U.S., French and Israeli forces in Lebanon.[147] The next day French planes bombed a military barracks of Shiite radicals in Syrian-controlled eastern Lebanon in a preemptive strike to prevent more terrorist attacks on French troops in the Multinational Force.[148] On November 20, 1983, the IAF attacked command posts and departure points for terrorist and guerrilla attacks of several PLO factions (Saiqa, PFLP-GC, DFLP) in Syrian-controlled territory near the Beirut-Damascus highway. The attacks were "a reaction against a long chain of terrorist attacks and attempted attacks against Israeli soldiers."[149] On December 21, as the IAF carried out another raid, Defense Minister Arens told the Knesset that Israel would continue to attack terrorist bases in Lebanon as long as Syria failed to restrain the terrorists.[150]

While the Israelis had withdrawn to the Awali line in the west, they still faced the Syrians in the Bekaa Valley. Within the Syrian areas PLO elements, mainly Musa Fatah rebels and radical factions such as the PFLP-GC, and radical Lebanese forces, mainly pro-Iranian Shiites, concentrated, occasionally striking out against the Israeli forces in Lebanon. Throughout 1984 the IAF frequently attacked the Lebanese Shiites.[151] In 1984 there were also a substantial number of Israeli air attacks on the bases of the Abu Musa PLO rebels.[152] On August 1, 1984, Israeli helicopters and gunboats twice attacked a PLO rebel naval base north of Tripoli to prevent sea-borne forays against Israel.[153]

An Israeli National Unity Government was formed on September 14, 1984. This government gradually accepted the fact that a negotiated withdrawal of Israeli forces from Lebanon was not possible and that withdrawal would have to be unilateral. Acceptance of this position increased in the early months of 1985 as Shiite and other Lebanese resistance groups escalated their attacks and IDF casualties in Lebanon increased.[154]

In the context of continuing Lebanese *fedayeen* attacks on the IDF and severe Israeli counterinsurgency measures, the Israeli forces evacuated all of Lebanon in three phases between February 14 and June 10, 1985.[155] Meanwhile, terrorist actions by Arafat's mainstream Fatah forces increased throughout 1985. This increase reflected Arafat's need to demonstrate his commitment to the "armed struggle" and the encouragement afforded the PLO *fedayeen* by the example of the south Lebanese resistance to Israeli occupation.[156]

Throughout 1985 there were a number of terrorist attacks in Israel— grenade throwing, explosion of bombs, stabbings, murder of people in isolated places.[157] Israel struck back with air raids against PLO—mainly PDFLP and PFLP-GC—elements, in the Bekaa Valley. The Israeli Navy was also active, intercepting PLO craft attempting to land infiltrators.[158]

The mainstream PLO also reemerged on the world scene in the fall of 1985. Members of the PLO's Force 17[159] were captured in September 1985 on a boat from Cyprus to Lebanon. On September 25, 1985, three PLO *fedayeen*, later identified as from Force 17, took control of an Israeli sailboat in the marina of Larnaca, Cyprus, and held three Israelis hostage, demanding the release of the Force 17 *fedayeen* captured earlier. Finally, the three *fedayeen* surrendered to the Cypriot authorities, after killing their Israeli hostages. Israel responded on October 1, 1985, with an air raid on PLO headquarters in a suburb of Tunis. The raid destroyed the Force 17 headquarters as well as the offices of the PLO's director of operations and Arafat's personal headquarters. Casualties reported by Tunisian authorities were: 73 killed, 61 of whom were PLO personnel and 12 Tunisian workers and police. Defense Minister Rabin justified the raid as a response to a rising tide of PLO terrorism as well as to the Larnaca terrorist incident.[160]

On October 7 the Italian cruise ship Achille Lauro was hijacked by *fedayeen* from the pro-Arafat faction of the PLF. They demanded release of a number of PLO *fedayeen* held by Israel and murdered an American Jewish tourist, Leon Klinghofer, and threw his body overboard. The original intention of the *fedayeen* was to wait until the ship reached the Israeli port of Ashdod before making their move, but when they were discovered with their weapons by crewmen, the highjacking was precipitated.

The leader of this PLF faction, Abul al-Abbas, held himself out as intervening by calling to the hijackers to go to Egypt and release this ship. However, Abul al-Abbas's complicity in the operation is clear. Egypt's Mubarak, after claiming that the hijackers had already left, permitted them, as well as Abul-Abbas and his aide, to leave secretly on a charter flight to Tunis. Their plane was intercepted by a U.S. Navy fighter plane which forced it to land in Sicily. The Italian authorities permitted Abul al-Abbas to escape with his aide but later charged them with kidnapping and murder.[161] Abul al-Abbas was tried in absentia by a court in Genoa, found guilty and sentenced to life imprisonment on July 10, 1986.[162] Judge Lino Monteverde ruled that the PLF's Achille Lauro operation had been intended to subvert Arafat's leadership of the PLO and his peace negotiations with King Hussein.[163]

Arafat declared in Cairo on November 7, 1985, that the PLO would henceforth limit its attacks to Israeli-held territory, and he professed to condemn terrorist attacks on unarmed civilians.[164] However, 1985 ended on a grim note when terrorists from the renegade Abu Nidal organization attacked the El Al ticket counters in Rome and Vienna on December 27, with automatic weapons, killing and wounding a number of people.[165]

During 1986 Israel's main counterinsurgency mission was to contain the attacks of radical Lebanese factions in the Security Zone. Attacks on IDF personnel were carried out by the Lebanese National Resistance and by the pro-Iranian Hezbollah. The PLO tried to take credit for much of this Lebanese *fedayeen* activity. During 1986 the PLO penetrated back into south Lebanon, mainly in the Sidon and Tyre areas. One result of this PLO return was an increase in katyusha attacks against northern Israel from 31 in 1985 to 62 in 1986. On the whole, however, the SLA and the IDF operations in the Security Zone were effective, although costly in terms of casualties.[166]

There was a significant decrease in PLO terrorist operations in Israel during 1986. The IDF's withdrawal from Lebanon made more troops available to guard the borders and control the territories. Israel also attributed the PLO's decline to the closing of their office in Amman in April 1986.[167] The PLO aspired to maintain its image as leader of the "armed struggle" by changing tactics. Although terrorist attacks with bombs, grenades and explosives declined, small bands of *fedayeen*, often local recruits, carried out numerous attacks with knives. In line with Arafat's Cairo declaration of November 1985, PLO worldwide terrorist operations were suspended, terrorist attacks being limited mainly to Israel and the occupied territories.[168] However, Arafat could not control pro-Syrian PLO elements who made an abortive attempt to plant a bomb on an El Al plane in London,[169] who attacked the El Al counter in Madrid, injuring 13,[170] and who attacked a newly refurbished synagogue in Istanbul as it reopened on September 6, killing 22 and wounding 3.[171]

The year 1987 opened with a major Hezbollah attack on SLA positions. Israel supported the SLA with helicopter gunship attacks on houses in two villages about six miles above the border from which Hezbollah forces were operating.[172] Israeli helicopters intervened frequently in January as the Hezbollah forces pressed the shaky SLA troops. In February Israel doubled its forces in south Lebanon to almost 3,000 in order to bolster the SLA.[173] The IDF increased the recruiting, equipping and training of SLA troops.[174] The Israeli forces interdicted reinforcements sailing from Cyprus for the PLO elements building up again in south Lebanon between Beirut and Tyre.[175] Meanwhile, PLO efforts to reestablish bases in refugee camps south of Beirut were resisted by Amal Shiites who fought and besieged the Palestinians until the Syrians intervened.[176]

The PLO's attempt to reestablish itself in Lebanon produced mixed results. Syria brought about an Amal-PLO truce in April, ending the fighting, and an accord in September 1987. The PLO relinquished mountain positions it had won in exchange for an end to Amal's siege of the Palestinian camps.[177] However, in April the Syrian Army moved into areas south of Beirut, preventing the PLO from strengthening its positions near the Sabra and Shatilla camps.[178]

Meanwhile, the Israelis carried out operations against the radical Lebanese and PLO forces. For example, at the end of March 1987 Israeli troops were landed from helicopters just north of the Security Zone and engaged Lebanese *fedayeen*.[179] Following artillery attacks on the SLA, Israeli helicopter gunships attacked a base of the Abu Nidal faction, in the Ain Helweh refugee camp and a Fatah base on April 9.[180] After two Israeli soldiers were killed in an ambush in the Security Zone, Israeli helicopters attacked villages at the edge of the zone on April 11.[181]

The first *fedayeen* attempt to infiltrate into Israel in more than a year and the first actually to enter Israel was thwarted by the Israelis on April 19, 1987, in a clash in which two Israeli soldiers and the three infiltrators were killed. The heavily armed PLO *fedayeen* were on a hostage-taking mission.[182] Such incursions as well as katyusha attacks on northern Israel moved Defense Minister Rabin to warn on April 21, 1987, that increased IDF activity in southern Lebanon would ensue if these attacks continued.[183]

Following a PLO conference in Algiers in which Arafat and some of his opponents were reconciled, infiltration attempts and rocket attacks on northern Israel increased.[184] In response, the IAF mounted a number of major attacks in May 1987 on PLO command posts and bases in refugee camps and training installations in Lebanon.[185] Syria's continued policy of blocking Arafat's PLO from restoring its position in Lebanon and its influence on the Lebanese was manifested on May 21, 1987, when the Lebanese parliament annulled the 1969 Cairo Accord on the grounds that it had never been properly implemented and had cost Lebanon disproportionate damage.[186]

Hezbollah and other radical Lebanese forces continued to attack the SLA throughout 1987 and the IDF was frequently involved in the hostilities.[187] By the end of 1987 the radical Shiites were attacking the SLA to demonstrate solidarity with the *intifada* in the occupied territories.[188]

Despite its disadvantaged position, the PLO continued to pose a terrorist threat to Israel. Israeli security forces arrested a group of West Bank Palestinians run by Fatah and a fundamentalist Islamic group who were planning suicide car bomb attacks.[189] Following a wave of terrorist attacks on civilian buses, the IAF hit PLO bases near Sidon on September 4, 1987, with the heaviest air raid since the 1982 war.[190] The Sabbath raid caught the Palestinians by surprise and a second raid hit as rescue operations were in progress. Collateral damage from both raids was heavy, with an estimated 40 dead.[191]

The PLO's continuing difficulties with different Lebanese factions were again illustrated in November 1987 by a pitched battle in Sidon with Sunni Muslim militia.[192] However, the PLO scored one of its greatest victories, albeit on a small scale, on November 26, 1987. A *fedayeen* from the PFLP-GC entered Israel in a motorized hang glider. After ambushing an IDF truck, killing an officer and wounding a woman soldier, he entered an IDF base near Kiryat Shemona, where he killed five soldiers and wounded seven others before he was killed. An official inquiry resulted in the disciplining of three responsible officers and a soldier.[193]

Throughout 1988 the PLO's "armed struggle" across the Lebanese border continued to be waged mainly by the radical hard-line elements who attempted repeatedly to infiltrate into Israel on terrorist missions. They were almost always intercepted, killed or captured, usually in the Security Zone. These *fedayeen* missions were attempted in order to demonstrate commitment to the struggle and to undermine any possible peace initiatives involving Fatah's mainstream organization.[194]

Notwithstanding the relative lull in hostilities with the mainline Fatah elements, Israel was still at war with the PLO. This was brought home forcibly on April 16, 1988, when Khalil El Wazir (*nom de guerre* Abu Jihad) was assassinated in his home in a Tunis suburb along with two body guards and a Tunisian gardener. Although Israel did not officially acknowledge responsibility, this was obviously an Israeli operation. The Israelis did point out that Khalil El Wazir/Abu Jihad was Fatah's military chief, responsible for a number of its terrorist operations including the 1978 Country Club raid that led to the Litani Operation and a number of recent PLO infiltration attempts, as well as chief PLO coordinator with the leaders of the *intifada*.[195] Israel had in the past assassinated PLO terrorists, notably those connected with the 1972 Munich massacre of Israeli Olympians.[196]

The IDF carried out a major two-day incursion into southern Lebanon on May 3–4, 1988, in an effort to clean out areas from which infiltration efforts were emanating. The Israeli troops swept the area and made house-to-house searches. On the second day of the operation the Israelis engaged Hezbollah forces, killing more than forty *fedayeen* and suffering three Israeli deaths. The tiny Shiite village of Maidun, which had been deserted by its inhabitants and taken over by Hezbollah, was destroyed by artillery fire and explosives set off by the SLA. Some Israelis questioned the necessity of the raid, claiming that it only enhanced the prestige of Hezbollah.[197] However, this, the first of several preemptive attacks on the Hezbollah and PLO forces in south Lebanon, together with efficient defense measures in the Security Zone by the SLA, protected the Lebanese border effectively.[198]

When infiltration attempts accumulated, the Israeli Air Force hit PLO bases and headquarters, usually those of the radical elements as well as those of Shiite elements active against the SLA and IDF in south Lebanon.[199] After a suicide car bomb killed seven Israelis in a convoy in the Security Zone on October 19, 1988, the IAF hit bases of the Islamic Resistance.[200]

Israeli naval, land and air forces raided PFLP-GC headquarters in a fortified complex in the Na'ima area about fifteen kilometers south of Beirut on December 9, 1988. The Israelis killed more than twenty PFLP-GC *fedayeen*, including Abu Jamil, commanding officer for the General Command in south Lebanon, responsible for armed activity in Israel. One IDF colonel and three enlisted men were killed in the raid that severely damaged the PFLP-GC's installations.[201]

In a typical operation at year's end, Israeli helicopter gunships rocketed a Shiite Amal base and wounded at least eight militiamen in retaliation for infiltration attempts the previous day.[202]

In the early months of 1989 it became apparent that Palestinian terrorist attacks from Lebanon against Israel and the territories were virtually all the work either of radical hardline PLO opponents of Arafat or of organizations such as PLF, PFLP and DFLP, which are represented on the PLO's Executive Council but often defy Arafat's policies.[203] Israeli sources claimed that although the mainstream Fatah PLO had discontinued cross-border terrorist operations, it had created an underground "Popular Army" to carry out terrorist attacks, including assassinations of Palestinians allegedly collaborating with the Israelis. In mid-January the IDF chief of staff, Lt. Gen. Dan Shomron, had told a Knesset committee that Fatah had not planned or carried out any guerrilla acts since November.[204] At the end of February 1989 the IAF bombed a DFLP headquarters about one hundred yards from an elementary school in the Druze village of Ainab, twelve miles southeast of Beirut. Two teachers and twenty-three students were wounded, five critically. The incident demonstrates the risks of collateral damage in air raids when the military target is located in a civilian area.[205]

After Israeli troops killed four PLO *fedayeen* infiltrators in Lebanon near the border on March 2, Nayef Hawatmeth, the DFLP leader, said in Damascus that his group would not be bound by Arafat's December 1988 renunciation of terrorism or concerned that the United States deemed terrorist operations a threat to dialogue with the PLO.[206] Throughout March 1989 the terrorist attempts of the radical PLO factions continued and the IDF continued to thwart them.[207]

In an extremely significant statement to the Knesset on March 28, 1989, Defense Minister Rabin said that Israel had not been attacking Fatah because Fatah was not launching attacks against Israel. Rabin observed that there was tension between the mainstream Fatah and the anti-Arafat PLO elements, and that the latter were attacking Israel to undermine Arafat's prestige and possible peace negotiations. Traditionally, Israeli statesmen and military commanders had refused to distinguish between different elements of the PLO, and Prime Minister Shamir and Foreign Minister Arens continued to insist that there was no difference between the various elements. Rabin's statement was, therefore, of great significance, given not only his position but the fact that he had been a leading counterterror policy-maker and practitioner throughout his career as a soldier and statesman.[208]

Throughout the spring of 1989 the elements of the PLO who refused to be limited by Arafat's stated policy of renouncing terrorism continued their attempts to infiltrate Israel on terrorist missions and to launch Katyusha rocket attacks on Israel. On May 31, 1989, the IAF reacted to these attacks with raids on radical PLO and pro-Iranian Lebanese positions in Lebanon. IDF sources continued to assert that the mainstream Fatah PLO was not attacking across the border although it supported the *intifada*.[209] As infiltration attempts and katyusha rocket attacks increased in June, with heavy participation by the Hezbollah *fedayeen*, Rabin gave the inhabitants of southern Lebanon the familiar Israeli warning that their lives would become a hell if they permitted these terrorist activities to continue. Rabin stated that there had been "innumerable" cases of Christian and Shiite Lebanese warning the Israelis of impending rocket attacks which were then prevented.[210] An IAF raid hit fortifications of the Palestine Liberation Front in a Druze-held village close to Beirut on June 14.[211]

Although the Israelis conceded that mainstream Fatah was not sending *fedayeen* across the border, they charged again in July 1989 that Fatah was training terrorist squads for attacks on civilian targets inside Israel and the territories. They claimed that ten such terrorist operations had been carried out inside Israel since Arafat's December 1988 renunciation of terrorism.[212]

The counterterror war against the radical Lebanese Shiite factions took a dramatic and controversial turn on July 28, 1989, when Israeli commandos kidnapped Sheik Abdul Karim Obeid in a helicopter raid on a Lebanese village. Sheik Obeid was said to have planned "a number of attacks against Israel."[213] It developed that the seizure of Sheik Obeid was intended to give Israel leverage in its attempts to effect a prisoner exchange in order to retrieve Israeli soldiers held by various Lebanese factions. The radical Lebanese responded by allegedly hanging U.S. Marine Lt. Col. William

R. Higgins, who had been taken hostage while serving with a UN peace-keeping team. A photograph of Colonel Higgins's hanged body failed to convince many that he had not been killed earlier. Radical Lebanese threatened other executions but relented. Ultimately, there was no general prisoner/hostage exchange as proposed by Israel, and Sheik Obeid told the Israelis that the three soldiers they sought were already dead.[214]

On August 8 a Jordanian in army uniform infiltrated a kibbutz in southern Israel, wounded an American woman visitor, took an Israeli woman hostage and was killed by soldiers.[215]

A suicide car bomb attack on an IDF convoy in the Security Zone wounded five Israeli and one SLA soldiers on August 9, 1989. Hezbollah claimed that the attack was made by a Shiite clergyman friend of Sheik Obeid. Hezbollah announced that the attack was dedicated to the memory of Imam Khomeini and was timed for a Shiite religious holiday.[216] In apparent retaliation, the IAF bombed Hezbollah offices near Sidon on August 27.[217]

In mid-September 1989 two IDF soldiers were slightly wounded by fire from across the Jordan River, the sixth incident on that border of the year. While the IDF warned Jordan in a statement that it would be held responsible for such incidents, the Israeli view was that Jordan was continuing to take measures to prevent them.[218] On September 14, 1989, Israeli helicopter gunships fired rockets at two Abu Nidal bases east of Sidon.[219]

The complexities of Israel's relations with the various factions in Lebanon was demonstrated in September 1989, when IDF Chief of Staff Dan Shomron said that the Shiite Amal group was helping to prevent terrorist attacks. Amal then issued a statement pledging to increase its terrorist attacks on the IDF and SLA in the Security Zone and to improve coordination with Hezbollah and other "religious and nationalist groups."[220]

In October three DFLP *fedayeen* on a terrorist mission were intercepted by the IDF in the Security Zone. One was killed, the others escaped.[221] On October 25 a report prepared by Yigal Carmon, Prime Minister Yitzhak Shamir's antiterrorism advisor, stated that Arafat's Fatah had ordered twelve attacks on Israeli civilians since Arafat promised in December 1988 to renounce terrorism. The report charged that groups affiliated with the PLO had carried out eighteen infiltrations or rocket attacks across Israel's borders since Arafat's December 1988 pledge. However, Anat Kurz, head of a terrorism research group at the Jafee Center for Strategic Studies, claimed that, on the contrary, Arafat had restrained militants in order to preserve his diplomatic initiative but that he had difficulty in controlling them. Kurz stated that "most of what we call terror activities have been conducted by locally affiliated elements and unorganized groups."[222]

In early November 1989 PFLP *fedayeen* in a fishing boat made a suicide attack on an Israeli patrol boat off the coast of southern Lebanon. The attacking craft was totally destroyed; the Israeli crew suffered only light injuries. Israeli patrol boats monitored and sometimes intercepted for questioning fishing boats from the Tyre area.[223]

A five-man *fedayeen* cell attempting to infiltrate from Egypt on the second anniversary of the *intifada* was intercepted, chased and wiped out by an IDF patrol in December 1989.[224] On December 26, 1989, Israeli air and ground attacks on Lebanese Communist party bases in central and southern Lebanon caused Lebanon to submit an urgent complaint to the UN Security Council, but there was no debate on the complaint.[225]

At the end of 1989 there were many indications that Israel expected to hold its Security Zone in southern Lebanon indefinitely. There was an impressive IDF headquarters in Marjayoun. Maj. Gen. Yossi Peled, commanding Israeli forces in the north, had recently said that the IDF expected to maintain the zone for an extended period. The SLA had continued to receive weapons and equipment and had strong fortifications. Israel spent about $3.5 million annually on aid to a civil government in the Security Zone that went into schools, roads and other public works. The Security Zone encompassed 325 square miles—8 percent of Lebanon's territory—and more than 200,000 Lebanese out of a total population of 2.7 million. As of late October 1989 the Israelis reported that the SLA had intercepted ten groups of *fedayeen*, killing more than sixty. The SLA had suffered heavy casualties: about two hundred killed and six hundred wounded. However, only two Israeli soldiers were killed along the border and there were no civilian casualties in northern Israel.[226]

Two major developments dominated the course of Israel's war with the PLO in the first half of 1990. Both had a strong impact on the prospects for negotiations leading to political resolution of the conflict. The first was the debate between the United States and Israel over the PLO's record of terrorist activity since Arafat's December 1988 renunciation of terrorism. The second was the May 30, 1990, seaborne attack on Israeli beaches by Abul Abbas's PLF *fedayeen*.

As indicated above, Israel, through Yigal Carmon, had been reporting on terrorist activities by PLO factions since December 1988. Carmon issued a special report in December 1989.[227] This and other reports accused the PLO of numerous terrorist attacks and even more numerous terrorist attempts that were thwarted by the Israelis. However, on March 19, 1990, the U.S. State Department submitted a report to the Senate Foreign Relations Committee, in compliance with the PLO Commitments Compliance Act of the Foreign Relations Authorization Act.[228]

The State Department's report minimized the role of the mainstream

PLO elements in terrorist activity against Israel since December 1988. It concluded that "the PLO has adhered to it commitment undertaken in 1988 to renounce terrorism."[229] Israel responded that the report wrongly excluded some failed terrorist operations, found the targets in many incidents "unclear" when they were manifestly clear, ignored PLO violence against fellow Palestinians, and took insufficient notice of numerous official PLO statements threatening continuation of the "armed struggle" by terrorist means and liberation by phases of all of Palestine.[230] The State Department report asserted that the U.S. was watching the PLO closely and was "disappointed that the PLO has not found a more authoritative way to distance or disassociate itself from activities undertaken by constituent groups acting independently without the organization's official sanction."[231]

The debate was resumed by Israel in earnest with the issuance in May 1990 of *The PLO: Has It Complied with Its Commitments?*[232] This report insisted that the PLO still held to its covenant goals and the two-phase plan for the liberation of Palestine, that PLO elements represented in the PNC and Executive Committee were identified as continuing terrorist attacks on Israel, that there was no evidence of Arafat and Fatah disavowing, condemning, restraining or punishing terrorist activity, that the PLO was inciting and organizing violence in the *intifada*, including violence against alleged Palestinian "collaborators" with Israel.

Despite these Israeli claims, the United States continued its dialogue with the PLO on the assumption that Arafat's December 1988 renunciation of terrorism was being substantially validated. This position, however, was gravely challenged on May 30, 1990, when PLF *fedayeen* attempted to raid beaches in the Tel Aviv area. The attack came on the Jewish holiday of Shabuoth, celebrating the handing down of the Ten Commandments to Moses. The PLF *fedayeen* departed from Libya in a Libyan ship which dropped them off in six speedboats about 120 miles off the coast of Tel Aviv. Only two of the speedboats got close to the Israeli coast. One was intercepted and surrendered north of Tel Aviv. The other landed at Nitsanim south of Ashdod in an unoccupied beach area where the *Fedayeen* engaged Israeli forces in a gun battle in which four *fedayeen* were killed and seven captured.[233]

One of the captured *fedayeen* stated on Israeli television that "the aim of the operation was to murder civilians" in the Tel Aviv hotel district.[234] On the basis of captured maps and interrogations, Chief of Staff Dan Shomron and other officers and officials asserted that this had been the mission of the operation.[235]

Arafat denied any PLO connection with or responsibility for the Shavuot raid and, after a meeting of the executive committee in Baghdad, announced no condemnation of the raid or disciplinary action against Abul Abbas, who did not attend the meeting. It was reported that Abul Abbas had not attended any executive committee meetings since the Achille Lauro highjacking in 1985.[236] Announcement that the PLO was going to conduct an inquiry into the raid to determine whether its targets were civilians failed to impress the U.S. government and President Bush announced suspension of U.S.-PLO talks on June 20, 1990.[237]

No matter what develops between the United States and the PLO, the dilemma epitomized by the PLF Shavuot raid and Arafat's response will presumably remain. This is the dilemma of Arafat as the leader and the mainstream PLO as the claimant to status as the representative of the Palestinian people: namely, either the PLO is responsible for the actions of its constituent elements and can require them to behave in accordance with commitments made by the organization, or it is not responsible for their actions and cannot control them, in which case its commitments are hollow. Of course, this dilemma would be mitigated if the overwhelming majority of the elements in the PLO accepted organizational discipline and honored its commitments. Those that did not could perhaps then be expelled from the organization. By Fall 1990, however, such a degree of unity and obedience appeared to be very far off.[238]

When Iraq invaded Kuwait on August 2, 1990, Arafat and the mainstream PLO had moved close to Saddam Hussein's regime. The PLO supported Iraq's conquest of Kuwait, although it attempted to temper its position by posing as a peace-making intermediary. There was widespread and highly vocal Palestinian support for Saddam Hussein and condemnation of the United States, Kuwait, Saudi Arabia and other members of the coalition against Iraq in Jordan, the Occupied Territories and other places. In the fall of 1990, therefore, the hopes that the PLO would hold to the conciliatory course implied by Arafat's December 1988 and May 1989 declarations— hopes long maintained by the United States but not Israel—appeared to be unrealistic. On the contrary, escalation of Palestinian violence in the *Intifada* appeared to reflect not only reactions to Israeli security measures but a profound animosity that threatened to thwart efforts to promote a peaceful settlement of the conflict. In Israel, moreover, attitudes toward the Arabs hardened virtually across the political spectrum after the Palestinians embraced Saddam Hussein's policies of conquest and oppression in Kuwait and continuing threats to Israel.

Notes

1. Howard M. Sachar, *A History of Israel* (2 vols.; Vol. I, New York: Knopf, 1976; Vol. II, Oxford University Press, 1987) I: 123, 125, 173–74, 199–201, 211–22.

2. Edward Luttwak and Dan Horowitz, *The Israeli Army* (London: Allen Lane, 1975), pp. 138–41; Jonathan Shimshoni, *Israel and Conventional Deterrence: Border Warfare from 1953 to 1970* (Ithaca, N.Y.: Cornell University Press, 1988), pp. 119–20.

3. See Chapter 1 above.

4. Hanan Alon, *Countering Palestinian Terrorism in Israel: Towards a Policy Analysis of Countermeasures* (Santa Monica, Calif.: RAND, August 1980), p. 36.

5. Ibid., pp. 37–40.

6. See Sachar, *History of Israel*, I, 617–38; Nadav Safran, *From War to War, 1948–1967* (New York: Pegasus, 1969), pp. 266–316.

7. See Helena Cobban, *The Palestinian Liberation Organisation*, (Cambridge: Cambridge University Press, 1984) pp. 36–38; Alon, *Countering Palestinian Terrorism in Israel*, pp. 41–47; Jilian Becker, *The PLO* (London: Weidenfeld & Nicolson, 1984), pp. 60–61.

8. Alon, *Countering Palestinian Terrorism in Israel*, p. 49.

9. Ibid., pp. 44 (Figure 2), 49–50. See IDF Spokesman, *Terrorist Attacks in Israel with Casualties: June 1967–October 1985*.

10. On the battle of Karameh and its effects, see William B. Quandt, "Political and Military Dimensions of Contemporary Palestinian Nationalism," in William B. Quandt, Fuad Jabber and Ann Mosely Lesch, *The Politics of Palestinian Nationalism* (Berkeley, Calif.: University of California Press, 1973), pp. 57, 79, 122; Becker, *The PLO*, pp. 62–64; Cobban, *The Palestinian Liberation Organisation*, pp. 41–42; Alan Hart, *Arafat* (Bloomington, Ind.: Indiana University Press, 1984), pp. 259–63.

11. See Alon, *Countering Palestinian Terrorism in Israel*, 49–55; Ariel Merari and Shlomi Elad, *The International Dimension of Palestinian Terrorism* (Boulder, Colo.: Westview; Jofee Center For Strategic Studies, Study no. 6).

12. Sachar, *History of Israel*, I, 699.

13. Merari and Elad, *The International Dimension of Palestinian Terrorism*, Appendix 3, "Chronology of Significant Terrorist Incidents Carried out by the Palestinian Organizations Outside of Israel, 1968–1985," pp. 130–42. Alon, *Countering Palestinian Terrorism in Israel*, pp. 51–53, gives slightly different figures and is not as comprehensive as Merari and Elad.

14. See Merari and Elad, *The International Dimension of Palestinian Terrorism*, Appendix 3, for a chronology of Palestinian international terrorism.

15. Ibid., p. 91.

16. Sachar, *History of Israel*, I, 700; Henry Kissinger, *White House Years* (Boston: Little, Brown, 1979), pp. 600–609.

17. Quandt, Jabber and Lesch, *The Politics of Palestinian Nationalism*, pp. 137–41.

18. Kissinger, *White House Years*, pp. 609–31.

19. Moshe Dayan, *Story of My Life* (New York: Morrow, 1976), p. 431.

20. On the November 3, 1969, Cairo Accord, see Walid Khalidi, *Conflict and Violence in Lebanon* (Cambridge, Mass.: Harvard Studies in International Affairs, no. 38, Harvard Center for International Affairs, 1975), p. 41, text on pp. 185–87; Cobban, *The Palestinian Liberation Organisation*, pp. 47–48; Wadi D. Haddad, *Lebanon: The Politics of*

Revolving Doors (New York: Praeger/Center for Strategic and International Studies, 1985), p. 42; Avner Yaniv, *Dilemmas of Security: Policies, Strategy and the Israeli Experience in Lebanon* (New York: Oxford University Press, 1987), pp. 44–45.

21. See Khalidi, *Conflict and Violence in Lebanon*, pp. 42–45; Itamar Rabinovitch, *The War in Lebanon, 1970–1983* (Ithaca, N.Y.: Cornell University Press, 1984), pp. 40–43.

22. Beate Hamizrachi, *The Emergence of the South Lebanon Security Belt* (New York: Praeger, 1988).

23. "Israeli Troops and Planes Raid Lebanon in Reprisal," the *New York Times* [hereinafter *NYT*], February 26, 1972, p. 1, cols. 5–6; p. 3, cols. 3–5; "Israel Reports Pullout from Lebanon," ibid., February 28, 1972, p. 3, col. 1.

24. Following the Kiryat Shemona attack in which 18 Israelis, including 8 children and 4 women, were killed, some of the children being thrown from upper-story windows, the IDF attacked several Lebanese villages from which the PLO terrorists had operated. Of this Israeli incursion on April 12–13, 1974, Defense Minister Dayan stated:

> It was not revenge. There can be no revenge for what took place in Kiryat Shemona. We did not try to match that disaster, not by the scale nor by the methods. . . .
>
> Our objectives this time were political, not military. . . . We are trying to explain that we are not the police of Lebanon. . . . Each government is responsible for what is taking place inside its territory. . . . The Government of Lebanon knows where to find [the headquarters of the Jibril group, PFLP-GC] . . . and it is their job to do it.
>
> We made all the villagers aware that . . . it is their business to go to their Government and tell them that they have to take care no terrorists cross the border into Israel, That was the message.

Quoted by Tekoah (Israel) in 29 U.N. SCOR (1766th mtg.), p. 22; "Dayan Says Raids Against Lebanon Will Be Continued," *NYT* April 14, 1974, p. 1, col. 8.

25. See Elazar's statement, Chapter 1, n. 52 above.

26. "Israel Counts on U.S. to Bar U.N. Sanctions," *NYT*, May 31, 1974, p. 8, cols. 7–8; "Excerpts from Mrs. Meir's Speech to Israeli Parliament on the Accord with Syria," ibid., p. 8, cols. 3–8; "Syria Reported to Pledge to Bar Guerrilla Raids," ibid., June 1, 1974, p. 1, col. 5; p. 8, cols. 2–4.

27. Resolution 3237, adopted November 22, 1974 (XXIX session), in *United Nations Resolutions on Palestine and the Arab-Israeli Conflict,* George Tomeh, ed. (Washington, D.C.: Institute for Palestine Studies, 1988), I:112.

28. On the outbreak of the Lebanese civil war, see W. Khalidi, *Conflict and Violence in Lebanon,* p. 47.

29. Avner Yaniv, *Dilemmas of Security,* pp. 60–61.

30. Total terrorist incidents in 1975 = 9: four with casualties: 18 killed, 79 wounded, of which none of the dead and 20 of the wounded were Israelis. Total terrorist incidents in 1976 = 14: one with casualties: 6 killed, 5 wounded, all Israelis. Alon, *Countering Palestinian Terrorism in Israel,* p. 51.

31. "New Fighting in South Lebanon," *NYT*, September 14, 1977, II, 13, col. 6; "PLO Site in Lebanon under Heavy Gunfire," ibid., September 23, 1977, p. 3, col. 2; "Israeli

Border Town Is Hit by 10 Rockets," ibid., September 24, 1977, p. 3., col. 4; "The Conflict in Southern Lebanon: Israel Seems on the Offensive Against Palestinians," ibid., September 26, 1977, p. 3, col. 2; "Israel Says Cease Fire Is in Effect in Southern Lebanon Border Area," ibid., September 27, 1977, p. 1, col. 1.

32. Moshe Gammer, "Armed Operations," *Middle East Contemporary Survey* 2 (1977–1978): 202 [hereinafter cited *MECS*].

33. "Israel Again Bombs Southern Lebanon; Artillery in Action," *NYT*, November 12, 1977, p. 1., col. 1; "Rockets Landed in Fields," ibid., p. 5, col. 3; "Israel Sends Letter to UN," p. 5, col. 4; Gammer, "Armed Operations," 202.

34. "2 Gunmen in Cyprus Kill Top Cairo Editor and Take off with 17," *NYT*, February 19, 1978, p. 1, cols. 6; "Up to 15 Egyptian Commandos Die Trying to Free Hostages on Jet When Cypriot Soldiers Open Fire," ibid., February 20, 1978, p. 1, col. 6; "Cyprus Wasn't Told of Commandos' Aim," ibid., February 21, 1978, p. 1, col. 5.

35. "20 to 30 Die in Israel in Blaze and Gunfight as Invaders Seize Bus," *NYT*, March 12, 1978, p. 1, col. 6; p. 14, cols. 3–4.

36. "Fatah Admits Raid," *NYT*, March 12, 1978, p. 1, col. 6.

37. "Begin Vows to 'Cut Off Evil Arm' of Group Responsible for Raid," *NYT*, March 14, 1978, p. 1, col. 3.

38. "Major Fighting Ends," *NYT*, March 16, 1978, p. 1, col. 6, p. 16, cols. 1–2; "Israel's Intervention in Lebanon," *MECS* 3 (1978–79): 65.

39. Ezer Weizman, *The Battle for Peace* (New York: Bantam, 1981), pp. 276–77; Yair Evron, *War and Intervention in Lebanon* (Baltimore, Md.: Johns Hopkins University Press, 1987), pp. 76–77.

40. "Israel in Cease-Fire," *NYT*, March 22, 1978, p. 1., col. 2, p. 10, cols. 1–2; "Israel's Intervention in Lebanon," *MECS* 2 (1977–78): 65.

41. See "Chronology of Events (August 1978–August 1979," *MECS* 3 (1978–79): 187.

42. "Chronology of Events (August 1978–August 1979)," *MECS* 3 (1978–79): 190; "40 Reported Killed as Israelis Raid Lebanese Borders," *NYT*, January 20, 1979.

43. "Chronology of Events (August 1978–August 1979)," 186–92.

44. Yaniv, *Dilemmas of Security,* p. 77.

45. "Israeli Ships Shell Lebanon in Reprisal for Guerrilla Raid," *NYT*, April 23, 1979, p. 1, col. 6; p. 4, cols. 3–6.

46. "Chronology of Events (August 1978–August 1979)," 193

47. The new policy was announced by Begin in an address to the Likud members of the Knesset on April 24, 1979. "Begin Vows Tough Reprisals," *NYT*, April 25, 1979, p. 1, col. 1.

48. "Begin Offers Talks with the Lebanese," *NYT*, May 8, 1979, p. 3, cols. 1–2.

49. "Chronology of Events (August 1978–August 1979)," 195; "Civilians Flee Southern Lebanon as Guerrillas and Rightists Fight," *NYT*, May 31, 1979.

50. "Chronology of Events (August 1978–August 1979)," 196.

51. Ibid.

52. Ibid., pp. 196–97.

53. Ibid., p. 197.

54. Ibid.

55. Ibid., p. 198; "US Condemns Raids by Israeli Planes on Lebanese Coast," *NYT*, July 24, 1979, p. 1, cols. 4; p. 9, cols. 1–2.

56. "Chronology of Events (August 1978–August 1979)," 198; "Israel Reports Its Troops Strike Deep in Lebanon," *NYT*, July 25, 1979, p. 3, col. 4.

57. "Chronology of Events (August 1978–August 1979)," 198.

58. Ibid., 199–200.

59. Moshe Gammer, "Areas of Armed Conflict: South Lebanon; Palestine Liberation Organization Operations," *MECS* 3 (1979–80): 142–49.

60. "Israelis Retake Kibbutz Nursery, Kill 5 Terrorists, Free Hostages," *NYT*, April 8, 1980, p. 1, cols. 1–2; p. 3, cols. 1–3.

61. Gammer, "Areas of Armed Conflict: South Lebanon; Palestine Liberation Organization Operations," 149.

62. Ibid., Table 8: "Israeli Operations Against Fida'i Bases in Lebanon (April–August 1980)," p. 162.

63. Gammer, "Armed Operations," *MECS* 5 (1980–81): 214–15.

64. Ibid., 214.

65. Ibid., p. 214.

66. Ibid., p. 214–17.

67. Ibid.

68. Ibid., 217; Israel Hits Northern Lebanon as Syrians Fight Christians," the *Washington Post* [hereinafter *WP*], June 4, 1981, A17, cols. 1–3.

69. Itamar Rabinovitch, "The Lebanese Crisis," *MECS* 5 (1980–81): 167–68.

70. Ibid.

71. Ibid.

72. Ibid., p. 169.

73. Gammer, "Armed Operations," 217–18.

74. Ibid.

75. "US Dismayed at Raid, Delays Decisions on F16s," *WP*, July 18, 1981, A1, col. 5; A14, cols. 1–4; "Reagan Halts F16s for Israel; Haig Cites New Violence," ibid., July 21, 1981, A1, cols. 6; A9, cols. 3–6.

76. Gammer, "Armed Operations," 218.

77. "Israel and PLO Agree to Cease-Fire," *WP*, July 25, 1981, A1, cols. 1–5; A19, cols. 1–3.

78. See Alexander M. Haig, *Caveat: Realism, Reagan and Foreign Policy* (New York: Macmillan, 1984), p. 332.

79. "Recent Arms Acquisitions by the PLO in Lebanon," *Information Briefing* 330/2.8.81/3.06.06 (3.10.06) (Jerusalem: Israel Information Center, 1981), pp. 1–2.

80. See Haig's account, *Caveat*, pp. 330–33; Yaniv, *Dilemmas of Security*, pp. 107–08;

Zeev Schiff and Ehud Ya'ari, *Israel's Lebanon War;* edited and translated by Ina Friedman (New York: Simon & Schuster, 1984), pp. 65–71.

81. Ibid., p. 91.

82. Ibid.

83. Ibid., pp. 97–100.

84. Evron, *War and Intervention in Lebanon,* p. 124.

85. The phases are suggested by Rashid Khalidi, *Under Siege: P.L.O. Decisionmaking During the 1982 War* (New York: Columbia·University Press, 1986), pp. 47–48. Khalidi places the beginning of the war on June 4, when Israeli carried out preventive/attrition attacks. Most commentators consider June 6 the first day of the war.

    My account of the 1982 Lebanon war is based primarily on Moshe Gammer, "The War in Lebanon: The Course of Hostilities," *MECS* 6 (1982): 128–57; Schiff and Ya'ari, *Israel's Lebanon War;* Richard A. Gabriel, *Operation Peace for Galilee* (New York: Hill & Wang, 1984); Trevor N. Dupuy and Paul Martell, *Flawed Victory: The Arab-Israeli Conflict and the 1982 War in Lebanon* (Fairfax, Va.: HERO Books, 1986); Avner Yaniv, *Dilemmas of Security;* and R. Khalidi, *Under Siege.*

86. Gammer, "The War in Lebanon: The Course of Hostilities," *MECS* 6 (1982): 137; Gabriel, *Operation Peace for Galilee,* pp. 84–85; Dupuy and Martell, *Flawed Victory,* pp. 98–104.

87. Gabriel, *Operation Peace for Galilee,* p. 85; Dupuy and Martell, *Flawed Victory,* p. 109.

88. Gammer, "The War in Lebanon: The Course of Hostilities," 137; Gabriel, *Operation Peace for Galilee,* pp. 84–86; Dupuy and Martell, *Flawed Victory,* pp. 105–06.

89. Gammer, "The War in Lebanon: The Course of Hostilities," 137; Gabriel, *Operation Peace for Galilee,* pp. 84–92; Dupuy and Martell, *Flawed Victory,* pp. 102–03, pp. 108–09.

90. Gammer, "The War in Lebanon: The Course of Hostilities," 137; Gabriel, *Operation Peace for Galilee,* pp. 87–90; Dupuy and Martell, *Flawed Victory,* p. 101.

91. Gabriel, *Operation Peace for Galilee,* pp. 91–92; Dupuy and Martell, *Flawed Victory,* p. 109.

92. Gabriel, *Operation Peace for Galilee,* pp. 91; Dupuy and Martell, *Flawed Victory,* pp. 112–13.

93. Gabriel, *Operation Peace for Galilee,* p. 92.

94. Gammer, "The War in Lebanon: The Course of Hostilities," *MECS* 6 (1982): 139; Gabriel; Dupuy and Martell, *Flawed Victory,* p. 112.

95. Gabriel, *Operation Peace for Galilee,* pp. 94–95; Dupuy and Martell, *Flawed Victory,* p. 116.

96. Gabriel, *Operation Peace for Galilee,* p. 95; Dupuy and Martell, *Flawed Victory,* p. 130.

97. Gabriel, *Operation Peace for Galilee,* pp. 95–96.

98. Ibid., pp. 96–97.

99. Ibid., p. 97.

100. Schiff and Ya'ari, *Israel's Lebanon War,* pp. 156–66.

101. Gammer, "The War in Lebanon," 139–41; Schiff and Ya'ari, *Israel's Lebanon War,* pp. 166–68; Gabriel, *Operation Peace for Galilee,* pp. 97–100; Dupuy and Martell, *Flawed Victory,* pp. 119–21.

102. Gammer, "The War in Lebanon," 139; Schiff and Ya'ari, *Israel's Lebanon War,* pp. 171–80; Gabriel, *Operation Peace for Galilee,* p. 100; Dupuy and Martell, *Flawed Victory,* pp. 121–22.

103. Gammer, "The War in Lebanon," 141–42; Gabriel, *Operation Peace for Galilee,* pp. 100–102; Dupuy and Martell, *Flawed Victory,* p. 132.

104. Gabriel, *Operation Peace for Galilee,* pp. 102–04.

105. Ibid., p. 104.

106. Ibid., p. 105; Dupuy and Martell, *Flawed Victory,* p. 133.

107. Gammer, "The War in Lebanon," 141; Gabriel, *Operation Peace for Galilee,* p. 105; Dupuy and Martell, *Flawed Victory,* p. 133.

108. Gabriel, *Operation Peace for Galilee,* p. 105.

109. Ibid., p. 107; Dupuy and Martell, *Flawed Victory,* p. 134.

110. Gabriel, *Operation Peace for Galilee,* pp. 107–08; Dupuy and Martell, *Flawed Victory,* p. 134.

111. Schiff and Ya'ari, *Israel's Lebanon War,* pp. 181–94.

112. Gammer, "The War in Lebanon," 142; Dupuy and Martell, *Flawed Victory,* p. 138.

113. Gammer, "The War in Lebanon," 142; Gabriel, *Operation Peace for Galilee,* pp. 108–12; Dupuy and Martell, *Flawed Victory,* p. 138.

114. Haig, *Caveat,* p. 346.

115. Gammer, "The War in Lebanon," 143; Dupuy and Martell, *Flawed Victory,* p. 155.

116. Gabriel, *Operation Peace for Galilee,* p. 139.

117. Ibid., p. 141.

118. Ibid., Dupuy and Martell, *Flawed Victory,* p. 155.

119. "Israeli Units Permit Restoration of Water, Power in West Beirut," *WP,* July 8, 1982, A17, cols. 5–6; A21, cols. 1–2; Gabriel, *Operation Peace for Galilee,* p. 143.

120. Gabriel, *Operation Peace for Galilee,* pp. 142–44; Dupuy and Martell, *Flawed Victory,* p. 156.

121. Gabriel, *Operation Peace for Galilee,* pp. 144–46.

122. Gammer, "The War in Lebanon," 145; Gabriel, *Operation Peace for Galilee,* p. 146; Dupuy and Martell, *Flawed Victory,* p. 157.

123. Gabriel, *Operation Peace for Galilee,* p. 146.

124. Gammer, "The War in Lebanon," 145; Gabriel, *Operation Peace for Galilee,* pp. 146–47.

125. Gabriel, *Operation Peace for Galilee,* p. 147; Dupuy and Martell, *Flawed Victory,* p. 157.

126. Gabriel, *Operation Peace for Galilee,* p. 146.

127. Gammer, "The War in Lebanon," 146; Gabriel, *Operation Peace for Galilee,* pp. 150–51; Dupuy and Martell, *Flawed Victory,* p. 159.

128. Gammer, "The War in Lebanon," 146; Gabriel, *Operation Peace for Galilee*, pp. 151–54; Dupuy and Martell, *Flawed Victory*, p. 160.

129. Dupuy and Martell, *Flawed Victory*, p. 160.

130. "Begin Rejects US Pressure," *WP*, August 5, 1982, A1, cols. 2–3; A29, cols. 3–4; "US Urges Pullback: Israel Rejects UN Observers," ibid., August 6, 1982, A1, cols. 1–3; A21, cols. 1–3.

131. Gammer, "The War in Lebanon," 147–48; Gabriel, *Operation Peace for Galilee*, p. 155.

132. Gammer, "The War in Lebanon," 148; Gabriel, *Operation Peace for Galilee*, pp. 155.

133. Gammer, "The War in Lebanon," 148; Gabriel, *Operation Peace for Galilee*, pp. 155–56.

134. Gabriel, *Operation Peace for Galilee*, pp. 156–57; Dupuy and Martell, *Flawed Victory*, p. 161.

135. Schiff and Ya'ari, *Israel's Lebanon War*, pp. 223, 225; Gabriel, *Operation Peace for Galilee*, pp. 157–58; Dupuy and Martell, *Flawed Victory*, p. 162.

136. Schiff and Ya'ari, *Israel's Lebanon War*, pp. 225–27; Gammer, "The War in Lebanon," 148; Evron, *War and Intervention in Lebanon*, p. 149.

137. Gammer, "The War in Lebanon," 148.

138. See the discussion of the Sabra and Shatilla massacres in Chapter 7.

139. See Table 3: "The Evacuation of the Palestine Liberation Organization and Syrian Units From Beirut," in Gammer, "The War in Lebanon," 154.

140. "Moves Seen Against Arafat Within PLO," *WP*, May 16, 1983, A1, col. 1; A15, cols. 1–4; "Rebellion in Fatah Causes Arafat to Take Security Precautions," ibid., May 30, 1983, A20, col. 1; Adam M. Garfinckle, "Sources of the Al-Fatah Mutiny," *Orbis* 27 (1983): 603–40.

141. "Arafat Backers, PLO Rebels Clash in East Lebanon," *WP*, June 5, 1983, A1, col. 5; A22, cols. 1–4; A23, cols. 1–4; "PLO Rebels Seize Major Arafat Base," ibid., June 22, 1983, A1, col. 1.

142. "Syria Abruptly Ousts Arafat as PLO Rebellion Mounts," *WP*, June 25, 1983, A1, col. 4–6; A22, cols. 1–2.

143. "Arafat Forces Trapped in North Lebanon by Syrians," *WP*, September 26, 1983, A1, col. 2–5; A8, cols. 1–2; "PLO Chief, Guerrillas Quit Tripoli," ibid., December 21, 1983, A1, col. 1; A22, col. 6.

144. "3 Israelis Killed in Ambush by Guerrillas in Lebanon," *WP*, June 11, 1983, A17, cols. 2–3.

145. "Israel Sets Pullback in Lebanon," *WP*, July 21, 1983, A1, col. 1; A19, cols. 1–3.

146. "Bomb in Tyre Kills 39; Israeli Planes Retaliate, Strike PLO Near Beirut," *WP*, November 5, 1983, A1, col. 1; A20, cols. 1–2; "Lebanon's New Burst of Terror," *Newsweek*, November 14, 1983, pp. 60–61; Moshe Gershovich, "Armed Operations," *MECS* 8 (1983–84): 98–101; ibid., "Chronology of Events," p. 110.

147. "Israeli Warplanes Bomb 2 Camps of Moslem Radicals," *WP*, November 17, 1983, A1, col. 6; A28, col. 1.

148. "French Jets Strike Shiite Position in Eastern Lebanon," *WP*, November 18, 1983, A1, col. 6; A22, col. 1.

149. "Israelis Bomb Lebanese Sites, Lose One Plane," *WP*, November 21, 1983, A1, col. 6, A20, cols. 1–3.

150. "Israel Vows to Continue Raids in Lebanon," *WP*, December 22, 1983, A1, cols. 1–4.

151. See Gershovich, "Chronology of Events," *MECS* 8 (1983–84): 111–13.

152. Ibid.

153. Ibid., p. 113.

154. Avram Schweitzer, "Israel," *MECS* 9 (1984–85): 487–90.

155. Ibid.

156. Joshua Teitelbaum, "Armed Operations," *MECS* 9 (1984–85): 86–87.

157. See "Chronology of Events (October 1984–December 1985)," *MECS* 9 (1984–85): 95–104.

158. Ibid., pp. 97–100.

159. Force 17 is the "semiautonomous Praetorian Guard of Chairman Yasir Arafat." Most of its members operate under diplomatic cover. Neil C. Livingstone and David Halevy, *Inside the PLO* (New York: Morrow, 1990), pp. 72–73.

160. Ibid., "The Larnaca Attack and the Israeli Response," pp. 90–91.

161. Ibid., "The Achille Lauro Affair," pp. 91–93.

162. "Italian Jury Gives Cruise Ship Killer 30-Year Sentence," *NYT*, July 11, 1986, A1, col. 4; A6, cols. 1–4.

163. Ibid., A6, cols. 1–4.

164. "Arafat Condemns Raids on Civilians," *NYT*, November 8, 1985, p. 3, cols. 1–3.

165. "The Attacks at the Airports of Rome and Vienna," ibid., pp. 93–94.

166. Uzi Rabi and Joshua Teitelbaum, "Armed Operations," *MECS* 10 (1986), p. 74.

167. Ibid.

168. Uzi Rabi and Joshua Teitelbaum, "Armed Operations," 74–6.

169. "Bomb found at London Airport," *WP*, April 18, 1986, A25, cols. 1–6; Rabi and Teitelbaum, "Armed Operations," *MECS* 10 (1986), p. 78.

170. "Blast at El Al Counter Injures 13 in Madrid," *WP*, June 27, 1986, A21, cols. 1–2; "Palestinian, Spaniard Held in El Al Bombing," ibid., June 28, 1986, A17, cols. 1–2.

171. "Israelis Speculate on Recent Attacks," *WP*, September 8, 1986, A23, cols. 4–5; Rabi and Teitelbaum, "Armed Operations," 79–80.

172. "Israeli Warplanes Hit 2 Lebanese Villages," *WP*, January 5, 1987, A19, cols. 4–6; A21, cols. 1–5; "Bomb Kills 4 Pro-Israeli Militiamen," ibid., A17, cols. 3–4.

173. Hirsh Goodman, "Analysis: Can the SLA Hold On?," *Jerusalem Post* Int. Ed., January 17, 1987, p. 2, cols. 1–2; "Israel Has Doubled Its Forces in South Lebanon," ibid., February 21, 1987.

174. "Pro-Israel SLA Bolstered," *Jerusalem Post* Int.Ed., February 28, 1987, p. 1, cols. 1–2.

175. "Israel Says It Halted Ship Carrying PLO Guerrillas," *WP*, February 8, 1987, A27, cols. 4–6; "Israel Navy Seizes 50 Fatah Men," *JPI*, February 14, 1987, p. 1, cols. 1–3.

176. See, for example, "Food Runs Out at Besieged Beirut Camp," *WP*, February 8, 1987, A27, cols. 4–6; "Battle Halts Beirut Camp Relief Efforts," ibid., February 14, 1987, A25, col. 1, A38, cols. 1–4.

177. "Amal, Palestinians Agree to Truce in Camps War," *WP*, April 6, 1987, A16, cols. 5–6; "Palestinians, Shiites Reach Accord," ibid., September 13, 1987, A30, cols. 5–6.

178. "Syrians Enter Beirut Camp; Refugees Describe Horrors," *WP*, April 4, 1987, A1, cols. 4–5; A17, cols. 1–3; "Syrians Deploy Southward in Lebanon," ibid., April 15, 1987, A27, cols. 1–3, "Israel Watching Damascus Moves: Syria Halts Troops at 'Red Line,' " *JPI*, April 25, 1987, p. 1, cols. 4–5; David Rudge, "Syria Move is Threat to PLO," ibid., April 25, 1987, p. 3, cols. 1–5.

179. "3 Guerrillas Killed in S. Lebanon Clash with Israeli Troops," *WP*, March 29, 1987, A21, cols. 3.

180. "Israeli Helicopters Raid Suspected Guerrilla Bases," *WP*, April 10, 1987, A19, col. 1.

181. "Israeli Air Raid Kills 3 in Southern Lebanon," *WP*, April 12, 1987, A28, col. 1.

182. "PLO Squad Is Crushed Inside Israel," *WP*, April 20, 1987, A1, col. 4; A20, cols. 1–5.

183. "Rabin Warns Israel May Strike in Lebanon," WP, April 22, 1987, A24, cols. 1–2.

184. "PLO Blamed for Attacks in North," *JPI*, May 2, 1987, p. 1, col. 1; p. 4, cols. 4–5.

185. "Israeli Jets Bomb PLO in South Lebanese Camps," *WP*, May 2, 1987, A24, cols. 4–6; "Israeli Raid Kills 10 at Refugee Site," ibid., May 7, 1987, A43, cols. 1–2; "Israeli Warplanes Strike Palestinians," ibid., May 9, 1987, A16, cols. 1–2; "Jets Bomb PLO Bases," *JPI*, May 16, 1987, p. 1, col. 2; p. 2, cols. 3–5; "Israel Bombs in Lebanon," *WP*, May 19, 1987, A26, cols. 4–5.

186. "Lebanon Annuls PLO Agreement," *WP*, May 22, 1987, A29, cols. 5–6; A35, col. 6.

187. See David Rudge, "Background: Terror Guns Point South Again," *JPI*, May 28, 1987, p. 1, cols. 1–3; p. 2, cols. 3–5.

188. "Lebanese Shiites Hit Pro-Israeli Militia," *WP*, December 22, 1987, A18, cols. 4–6.

189. "A New Pattern of Terror: Fatah and Fundamentalists," *JPI*, September 5, 1987, p. 6, cols. 4–5.

190. "Israeli Raid Kills 40 in Lebanon," *WP*, September 6, 1987, A25, col. 6; A30, col. 6.

191. Ibid., "Questionable Bombing," *JPI*, September 19, 1987, p. 23, col. 3.

192. "Militias Clash in Sidon," *WP*, November 17, 1987, A24, col. 3.

193. "Palestinian Guerrillas Kill Six Israeli Soldiers," *WP*, November 26, 1987, A1, cols. 1–4; A56, cols. 1–2; "Israel Cites Army Blunders in Raid on Base," ibid., November 27, 1987, A1, cols. 1–3; A47, cols. 1–3; "Israelis Disciplined After Raid," ibid., December 3, 1987, A43, col. 1; A48, cols. 1–2; "IDF Probes Lapses That Cost Six Lives," *JPI*, December 5, 1987, p. 1, cols. 4–5; 2, col. 1; "Heads Roll in Wake of Hang-Glider Raid," ibid., December 12, 1987, p. 1, cols. 4–5; p. 2, cols. 1–2.

194. David Rudge, "North Faces 'Uneasy Summer,' " *JPI*, April 30, 1988, p. 4, cols. 1–3.

195. "P.L.O. Accuses Israel in Killing of Senior Military Figure in Tunisia," *NYT*, April 17, 1988, p. 1, cols. 4–5; p. 16, cols. 4–6; "High Backing Seen for Assassination," *WP*,

April 21, 1988, A1, col. 2; A31, cols. 1–6; "Abud Jihad: A Strong Right Arm to Arafat Who Lived by the Sword," *NYT,* April 17, 1988, p. 16, cols. 4–6.
See Livingstone and Halevy, *Inside the PLO,* pp. 31–58.

196. See Richard Deacon, *The Israeli Secret Service* (London: Hamilton, 1977); Steward Stevens, *The Spymasters of Israel* (New York: Macmillan, 1980); George Jonas, *Vengeance* (New York: Simon & Schuster, 1984).

197. Uzi Rabi and Joshua Teitelbaum, "Armed Operations," 124–26; "Israeli Army Raids S. Lebanon," *WP,* May 3, 1988, A1, col. 1; A23, cols. 2–3; "Lebanese Edgy After Sweep by Israelis," ibid., A26, cols. 5–6; "Israeli Troops Hunt Guerrillas in S. Lebanon," ibid., May 4, 1988, A1, col. 1; A26, cols. 1–4; "Israel Kills 40 Shiites, Pulls Back," ibid., May 5, 1988, A1, col. 6; A27, cols. 1–4; "Israeli Troops Battle Shiite Forces and Destroy Village in Lebanon," *NYT,* May 5, 1988, A1, cols. 2–3; A16, cols. 4–6; "Israeli Raid Sends Villagers Fleeing from Once-Scenic Lebanese Resort," *WP,* May 5, 1988, A16, cols. 1–6; "Some Israelis Question Incursion into Lebanon," ibid., May 6, 1988, A23, cols. 1–3; A29, cols. 1–2; "Blow against terror, but North Still Wary," *JPI,* p. 1, cols. 1–5; p. 2, cols. 4–5.

198. Rabi and Teitelbaum, "Armed Operations," 124–26.

199. For examples of 1988 IDF air raids, see "Israeli Warplanes, Gunships Attack Positions in Lebanon," *WP,* January 3, 1988, A24, cols. 5–6; "Air Strikes on Terror Targets," *JPI,* January 9, 1988, p. 2, col. 5; "Israel Hits Guerrilla Sites in Lebanon," *WP,* March 25, 1988, A28, cols. 1–3; "Rival Shiite Militiamen Adhere to Beirut Truce," ibid., May 13, 1988; A30, cols. 5–6; "Israeli Raid in Lebanon," ibid., November 23, 1988, A15, col. 1.

200. "Bomb Kills 7 Israelis in Lebanon," *WP,* October 20, 1988, A1, col. 6; A34, col. 1; "Israeli Leaders Vow Vengeance for Killing of Seven Soldiers," ibid., October 11, 1988, A29, cols. 1–2; "Israeli Jets Raid Lebanon, Kill 15," ibid., October 22, 1988, A1, cols. 2–4; A19, cols. 1–3; "Israeli Hit New Targets in Lebanon," ibid., October 25, 1988, A21, cols. 1–4; "Raids by Israel, Allied Militia Kill 19 in Southern Lebanon," ibid., October 27, 1988, A56, cols. 1–4.

201. Rabi and Teitelbaum, "Armed Operations," 126–27.

202. "Israeli Copters Pound Amal Base," *Washington Times,* December 30, 1988, A7, cols. 4–6.

203. "Arafat's Rivals Behind Terror," *JPI,* March 25, 1989, p. 1, cols. 4–5; p. 2, cols. 1–3.

204. "Arafat Faction of PLO Linked to Terrorism, Israelis Charge," *WP,* February 2, 1989, A30, cols. 4–6.

205. "Israeli Raid Hits School In Lebanon," *WP,* March 1, 1989, A17, cols. 1–4; A19, cols. 5–6.

206. "Israelis Kill 4 Guerrillas In Lebanon," *WP,* March 3, 1989, A34, col. 1; "Palestinian-Israeli Clashes Pose Threat in Lebanon," ibid., March 10, 1989, A27, cols. 3–6.

207. "Israelis Kill 3 Guerrillas in S. Lebanon," *WP,* March 14, 1989, A21, cols. 1–2; "3 Arabs, 1 Israeli Soldier Die in Separate Clashes, ibid., March 19, 1989, A31, cols. 4–5.

This view is supported by Eyal Sisser in his draft of "Armed Operations," *MECS* 13 (1989): 14–15, furnished to the author by Asher Susser.

208. "Israelis, Arafat Forces Avoid Clashes," *WP*, March 28, 1989, A20, cols. 4–6.

209. "Israelis Say 3 Infiltrators, Soldier Killed," *WP*, June 5, 1989, A13, col. 1.

210. "Israel warns Syrians against 'extreme move,' " Jerusalem *Post*, June 10, 1989, p. 1, cols. 3–4, p. 2, cols. 1–2.

211. "Israeli Planes Strike in Lebanon," *WP*, June 15, 1989, A30, col. 1.

212. "Arafat's Fatah using terror, despite vow," *JPI*, July 22, 1989, p. 2, cols. 1–2.

213. "Israelis Seize Imam In Lebanon," *WP*, July 29, 1989, A1, col. 6, A13, cols. 1–2; "Israel Snatches a Sheik," *Newsweek*, August 7, 1989, p. 36, cols. 2–4.

214. "Man in Beirut Videotape Probably Was Higgins, FBI Experts Say," *WP*, August 8, 1989, A12, cols. 1–6.

215. "American Attacked In Israel," *WP*, August 9, 1989, A14, cols. 1–4.

216. "Suicide Car Bomb in Lebanon Hurts Israeli, Lebanese Troops," *WP*, August 10, 1989, A28, cols. 4–6.

217. "Israeli Warplanes Bomb Shiite Target in Lebanon," *WP*, A18, cols. 5–6.

218. "Israeli Troops Wounded," *WP*, September 14, 1989, A35, col. 1; "Another terrorist attack from Jordan," *JPI*, September 23, 1989, p. 1, col. 3; p. 2, cols. 1–2.
The increase in terrorist activities originating in Jordan was attributed to individual initiatives and to some loss of control by the Jordanian government which was viewed as doing its best to prevent terrorist operations against Israel. Eyal Zisser, "Armed Operations," *MECS* 12 (1989) [forthcoming]; draft supplied to the author.

219. "Israelis Rocket Base," *WP*, September 15, 1989, A24, cols. 3–4.

220. "Terrorism threat in S. Lebanon," *JPI*, September 23, 1989, p. 2, cols. 3–4.

221. "Terrorist killed in clash," *JPI*, October 21, 1989, p. 3, cols. 3–4.

222. "Israeli Report Says Arafat Group Ordered 12 Attacks on Civilians," *WP*, October 26, 1989, A36, cols. 1–2.

223. "Suicide attack on navy patrol boat," *JPI*, November 11, 1989, p. 3, cols. 1–2.

224. "Terrorists wiped out on Egyptian border," *JPI*, December 16, 1989, p. 5, cols. 1–2.

225. "Israel Conducts 2 Attacks in Lebanon," *NYT*, December 26, 1989, p. 3, cols. 1–3; "Lebanon Criticizes Israeli Raids," *WP*, December 28, 1989, A31, col. 5; Lebanon to Lodge Complaint At UN Against Israeli Raids," *NYT*, December 28, 1989, p. 7, col. 6.

226. "Israel Seems Ready to Linger in S. Lebanon," *WP*, October 20, 1989, A33, cols. 1–3; A35, cols. 1–5.

227. Prime Minister's Bureau: Advisor for Countering Terrorism, *P.L.O. Terror—A Year since its Renunciation (Dec. 15, 1988—Dec. 15, 1989)* (Special Report Dec. 1989).

228. United States Department of State, *PLO Commitments Compliance Act: Report on Nine Attempted Incursions* (Washington, D.C. March 19, 1990).

229. State Department, *PLO Commitments Compliance Act*, p. 3.

230. Embassy of Israel, Washington, D.C., *The State Department Report on the PLO*, March 21, 1990.

231. State Department, *PLO Commitments Compliance Act*, p. 3.

232. Ministry of Foreign Affairs, *The PLO: Has it Complied with its Commitments?* (Jerusalem, May 1990).

233. "Beach Attack by Arab Speedboats Foiled by Israel," *NYT,* May 31, 1990, A1, cols. 2–4; "Israeli Forces Block Attack By Two Palestinian Boats," *WP,* May 31, 1990, A1, cols. 1–2; A32, cols. 1–4.

234. "Alleged Raider Says Civilians In Tel Aviv Were His Targets," *WP,* June 7, 1990. A30. cols. 1–2.

235. "Beach Attack by Arab Speedboats Foiled by Israel," *NYT,* May 31, 1990, A1, cols. 2–4; A16, cols. 1–3; "Israeli Forces Block Attack By Two Palestinian Boats," *WP,* May 31, 1990, A1, cols. 1–2; A32, cols. 1–4.

236. "Arafat Denies P.L.O. Tie to Raid But His Mild Stand Troubles U.S.," *NYT,* June 1, 1990, A1, cols. 4–5, A13, col. 1; "PLO Refuses To Condemn Israel Raid," *WP,* June 8, 1990, A27, cols. 1.

237. "P.L.O. Is Said to Start Inquiry Into Raid on Israel," New York *Times* (International), June 14, 1990, A5, cols. 1–5; "President Suspends PLO Talks," *WP,* June 21, 1990, A1, col. 6; A32, cols. 1–2.

238. On July 15, 1990, at a meeting in Tunis of Arab countries, Arafat rejected as "out of the question" the U.S. demand that he discipline Abul Abbas. "Arafat Rebuffs U.S. On Disciplining Rebel," *WP,* July 16, 1990, A15, cols. 1–2 Abul Abbas refused to resign from the PLO's Executive Committee, as suggested by Egyptian Foreign Minister Esmat Abdel-Meguid. "Disagreement in PLO," Ibid., July 17, 1990, A13, col. 2.

Part II

The International Law of War in Israel's War with the PLO

3

The Contemporary
International Law of War

Most civilizations have developed some kind of law to regulate relations
between different members of their political systems—tribes, city-states,
kingdoms, empires. The modern international system developed after the
Thirty Years War and is generally referred to as the Westphalian system,
referring to the Treaty of Westphalia of 1648 ending that war. The Westphalian international system has been characterized by a multiplicity of sovereign states, lacking any superior power to establish and enforce international
law and order. Accordingly, modern international law has been developed
in a primitive, decentralized international legal system. In this system law
is developed, interpreted, applied and enforced by the states and other
subjects of the law. The law that emerges is seldom universally accepted
but considered in force if it is generally observed by most of the states most
of the time. This law, properly understood, is not the "black letter" law of
international conventions that superficially resembles the legislative statutes
of domestic law. Rather, international law consists of patterns of behavior
and, in the felicitous word of Myres McDougal, "expectations" as to
legally permissible behavior.[1] Underlying international law are fundamental
principles such as the right of self-defense and the principle of humanity
which are derived from natural law or some form of higher law. In the
words of the preamble to 1907 Hague Convention IV Respecting the Laws
and Customs of War, these are "the principles of the law of nations, as they
result from the usages established among civilized peoples, from the laws
of humanity, and from the dictates of the public conscience."

The Emergence of the Contemporary
International Legal Order

In the international legal order (world public order, in McDougal's
terminology) as it developed from 1648 to 1919, the patterns of behavior
and expectations regarding legally permissible behavior that were consid-

ered most important were those reflecting the practice of the most powerful states, as well as the states most relevant to a particular subject. Thus, British practice obviously was decisive in the development of the law of the sea, Britain being a powerful maritime power. The Netherlands was not a powerful state but it was an important maritime state, so Dutch practice was important. Because of the political, economic and military superiority of the European states and the United States, modern international law was Western international law; non-Western states were obliged to accept this law as they entered the international legal system. This was so much the case that non-Western states often retained Western international lawyers to represent them at international conferences.

This understanding of international law was challenged by the communist regime that took power in Russia in 1917. Marxist doctrine held that law is a superstructure reflecting the values and dynamics of a social substructure. Law in feudal, bourgeois or socialist societies simply reflected the power realities and values of those societies. Western international law naturally reflected the power realities and values of the Western bourgeois states. A socialist state should not be bound by law reflecting Western bourgeois values, and, anyway, power realities were destined to change as the bourgeois powers and their international system succumbed to the contradictions that would destroy them.

On the other hand, the Soviet Union of the interwar period, the sole bastion of Marxist-Leninism, existed precariously and required intercourse with the rest of the world. Doctrine had to be compromised and ingenious explanations had to be invented to explain the international law of coexistence. The Soviets proved adept at using international law as a political-psychological instrument. When on the defensive, the Soviets relied heavily on the most conservative interpretations of international law and defended them with the exhaustive tenacity of the Bolsheviks.[2]

However, the Soviet challenge to Western international law did not significantly alter that law. Western dominance continued through the Second World War. The first real challenge to the international legal order came in the postwar period from Latin American and other states dissatisfied with the law of the sea. Claims of sovereignty over continental shelves and maritime areas extending out to two hundred miles challenged traditional concepts of freedom of the seas and of modest three-mile limits for territorial waters. The inconclusive 1958 Geneva Conference on the Law of the Sea marks the end of the dominance of the great powers over the law of the sea.

Meanwhile, an even greater challenge to Western dominance of international law was building up. The emergence of scores of new nations in the

Third World in the 1950s fundamentally altered the structure and processes of the international legal system. In the United Nations and other international organizations and in international conferences, the commitment to the principle of sovereign equality, to one-state-one-vote, meant that the non-Western, Third World nations had overwhelming numerical superiority. If law was to be based on majority rule, the new nations were the majority and would henceforth make the law. Moreover, these nations could and often did reject existing legal prescriptions, e.g., regarding nationalization and expropriation of private property owned by foreigners, on the grounds that they did not share the values of the "colonial" powers and that they had not participated in the law-making processes in the colonial era. Legal systems are generally based on an assumed status quo. The new nations and others rejected the status quo assumed by the older Western nations and demanded a new international order, particularly a New International Economic Order.[3]

The changed character of contemporary international law was dramatically illustrated in the long process that produced the 1982 Montego Bay United Nations Convention on the Law of the Sea.[4] The Third World majority insisted on establishing an International Seabed Authority whose structure and powers were unacceptable to the United States and other Western maritime powers interested in exploiting mineral nodules from the deep seabed. The United States refused to sign the convention and many powerful maritime powers have failed to ratify it. The Third World majority got the convention it wanted but it did not obtain the adherence of the United States and other states that are both powerful and highly relevant to maritime practice.[5]

To be sure, most of the provisions of the 1982 convention are generally accepted. Indeed, the United States's position is that they are customary international law. Moreover, there is a very substantial body of international law that is widely accepted and applied notwithstanding the doctrinal and practical differences that separate different parts of the international political/legal system. But the Third World challenge to Western international law has produced a situation wherein some attempts to create international legal norms may be misleading. If a putative legal prescription is merely the expression of a numerical majority of states and is not accepted by some of the most powerful and relevant states, it may not be indicative of the patterns of practice and expectations of the international legal system.

For example, if the vast majority of states adhere to a convention on space law to which the United States and the Soviet Union are not parties, expectations of space practice would be more realistically grounded in U.S. and Soviet practice than in the prescriptions of the space convention.

Beyond the complications inherent in efforts to develop effective international law for a divided and conflictual international system there is a perennial characteristic of international law, namely, the difficulty of maintaining legal restraints on issues of high politics. Obviously, it is much easier to develop law regulating comparatively low-level international relations where there is near-universal common agreement. When a state's perceived vital interests are at stake, as is the case when it is engaged in an international or civil war, it may be disinclined to subordinate those interests in order to comply with international law. Nevertheless, there exists a substantial body of international law governing armed conflict and it will be summarized in this chapter. Moreover, there are fundamental principles, such as the right of self-defense and the principle of legitimate military necessity, which both authorize and limit a state's recourse to armed force.

The Sources of International Law

First, however, the sources of international law must be reviewed. They are authoritatively laid down in Article 38 of the Statute of the International Court of Justice as follows:

    a. international conventions, whether general or particular, establishing rules expressly recognized by the contesting states;
    b. international custom, as evidence of general practice accepted as law;
    c. the general principles of law recognized by civilized nations;
    d. subject to the provisions of Article 59, judicial decisions and the teachings of the most highly qualified publicists of the various nations, as subsidiary means for the determination of rules of law.

There is an implied order of priority in this rendition of the sources of international law. Presumably, international conventions, particularly those intended to have universal application and adhered to by the great majority of states, provide the most important prescriptions of international law. They most resemble domestic legislation. They are the most convenient source of international law to cite and they appear to be the most clear-cut evidence of international practice and expectations.

On the other hand, international conventions may not always be persuasive evidence of international law. In the final analysis, international law must reflect the practice and expectations of states. If a convention does this, it is a very useful source of law. If, however, there are gaps between the black letter law of a convention and the practice and expectations of states, some provisions of the convention may not be a realistic reflection of the law actually in force. This is not to say that breaches of conventional international law readily render it null and void, any more than national legislation is vitiated by its violations. The issue is a matter of balancing the need for order and stability through international conventional law and the need to recognize the changing patterns on international behavior and expectations. This issue will arise frequently in the discussion of the international law of war.

Custom as a source of international law also has its strengths and weaknesses. On the one hand, custom is the essence of international law, since it reflects patterns of behavior and expectations in international interaction. These patterns of behavior and expectations may prove that states habitually recognize and abide by the customary legal prescriptions. Conventional law is more clear and easier to demonstrate, but custom, if it can be proven, is the heart of international law. The problem is to prove custom.

To begin with, there is the problem, alluded to earlier, of balancing qualitative versus quantitative evidence of custom. By qualitative, I mean evidence that the most powerful states and/or those most relevant to a subject accept a rule of customary international law. By quantitative, I mean evidence that many states, irrespective of power and relevance, accept that rule. As indicated, in the present international system there may be a tension between the positions of the most powerful and relevant on a subject and the majority of members of the international political/legal system. If the 1982 Montego Bay Convention receives the requisite number of ratifications, the regime for the deep seabed of that convention clearly becomes conventional international law. However, if the United States and other states that have the capacity and interest to develop the deep seabed on unilateral or multilateral bases continue to ignore the convention's deep seabed regime, the convention is not sustained by customary international law.

A further difficulty with customary international law is temporal. There are at least two temporal problems. First, there is the question of how long it takes before a rule of customary international law is clearly established. In the classic decision on the subject by the United States Supreme Court, the *Paquete Habana* case, court judged in 1900 that a rule of customary international law exempting fishing smacks from capture in time of war had been developing since the fifteenth century, and was clearly established. The rule had been so clearly established and generally observed for so long that the Court had no difficulty in accepting it as binding.[6] But suppose the case had come up in 1800; would the custom have been so clearly established?

International lawyers distinguish between law in the making, *lex ferenda,* and established law, *lex lata*. Obviously, it usually takes some time before a sufficient sample of state behavior and expectations is established to warrant the contention that a rule of customary international law has been created. Moreover, the decision to accept or reject a rule of customary law *de lege ferenda* and declare that it is now *de lege lata* is a judgment call on which reasonable people can differ.

It is often claimed that customary international law is an unsatisfactory source of international law precisely because it takes a long and undetermined amount of time to be recognized and accepted, whereas conventions provide the kind of immediate legal guidance found in domestic legislation. This may be true in some cases, but customary international law has sometimes been established very rapidly in the contemporary period. Agreement to the minimum claim of President Harry S. Truman to exclusive jurisdiction and control over the continental shelf was already clear before it was confirmed by the 1958 Continental Shelf Convention.[7] Acceptance of two hundred-mile exclusive fishing zones, initially so resisted in the late 1940s and the 1950s, was completed in the 1970s well before it was confirmed in the 1982 Montego Bay Convention.[8]

However, there is a second temporal aspect of customary international law that may limit its utility, namely, its vulnerability to being overtaken by events. This is well illustrated in the *Paquete Habana* case. In 1900 it was still possible to hold that a rule of customary international law protected Cuban fishing smacks from being captured as prizes of war during the Spanish-American War. By 1918, after the first of our twentieth-century "total wars," no one could be confident that any kind of vessel would be immune from capture. By 1945 it would be clear that a suspect vessel of any kind would probably be strafed and shot out of the water.

In summary, custom is the ultimate source of international law but it is difficult to determine whose practice and expectations (in McDougal's terms, whose "authoritative decisions") make custom and when a rule of customary international law is created and when it is terminated. The task is often increased by the paucity of hard evidence of state practice. In general, only the most advanced and affluent states make available archives relevant to international law, particularly on issues of vital interests. Nevertheless, the international law practitioner or scholar must endeavor to gather evidence of practice and to report it, attempting to distinguish in the process his or her preferred version of what the law should be from the evidence of what the law actually is.

Finally, among the three main sources of international law there are general principles. Three kinds of general principles can be distinguished:

(1) principles of comparative law, e.g., the principle of prescription, that the passage of time may alter the legal status of a controversy; the principle of estoppel, that a party, having taken a particular position, may not change its position to the detriment of another party;

(2) principles of international law, e.g., the principle of freedom of the seas, the principle of sovereign equality and nonintervention, the principle of self-determination;

(3) principles of natural law, e.g., the inherent right of self-defense, basic human rights irrespective of the extent to which they are effectively protected by conventional or customary international law.

Clearly, these three kinds of principles of law overlap, e.g., the right of self-defense is recognized for individuals in comparative law and for both individuals and states in international law and natural law. However, the relative importance accorded to these three kinds of general principles determines an individual's understanding of international law. If only the comparative law general principles are understood as sources to international law, a person will have a rather narrow, technical understanding of it. If broad play is given to the highly political general principles of international law, such as self-determination or nonintervention, the approach will be much broader and potentially controversial. If natural law principles are invoked as "higher law" there are possibilities both for enriching the positive law, as with the condemnation of crimes against humanity at Nuremberg, and for endangering it, as may be the case with appeals for just or holy wars in the name of justice.

Cognizant both of the positive and negative aspects of appeals to natural law, I write from the natural law tradition which, whatever its weaknesses and dangers, gave birth to international law. I reverse the order of relative importance of the three main sources of international law. I place general principles of all three kinds—comparative law, international law and natural law—first. I place customary international law, the actual behavior and expectations of states, second. Conventional international law is third, valuable to the extent that it accords with customary practice and expectations and conforms to general principles, including those of natural law.

As to the subsidiary sources of international law, judicial decisions, both of national and international tribunals, may be of great assistance provided one is always aware that they are not binding in international law generally as are national court decisions within their jurisdictions. Even the decisions of international tribunals are not generally binding, being confined to the particular parties and cases in question. Nevertheless, judicial decisions can provide evidence of the law and legal arguments that are useful even if the decisions themselves are not precedental, not in the domestic law sense *stare decisis*.

Finally, the writings of international law publicists are invaluable to the extent that they furnish evidence of the law and legal arguments in a reliable and convenient form. They may also be valuable for their creative suggestions for improvement of the law—so long as these are clearly distinguished from their description and analysis of the law as it is.

With these observations on the character of contemporary international law generally as background, the international law of war may be discussed.[9]

International War-decision Law:
The *Jus ad Bellum*

In international law, as in just war doctrine which contributed greatly to its development, the law of war is divided into two main parts: the war-decision law concerning the legal permissibility of recourse to armed force, still referred to frequently by the classic title *jus ad bellum*, and the war-conduct law, still called the *jus in bello*.

Before proceeding to a summary and analysis of these two bodies of law, a word should be said about my retention of the old term "the law of war." The generally used term today is "the law of armed conflict." This term is employed in the war-conduct conventions sponsored by the International Committee of the Red Cross and it has been adapted to some extent by the American military, notably in the Air Force's Pamphlet 110-31, *International Law—The Conduct of Armed Conflict and Air Operations* (hereinafter cited as AFP 110-31).[10] To me, "conflict" is a broad term that sounds somewhat vaguer than "war." I prefer the harsher term "war" and the traditional term "law of war."

The most fundamental principle of war-decision law is the principle of legitimate self-defense. It is a principle of natural law and of the international law of war. International law recognizes the natural law character of the right of self-defense in Article 51 of the United Nations Charter, wherein the right is referred to in English as an "inherent" right, in French as "le droit naturel de défense légitime" and similarly ("imprescriptible") in the Russian version.[11]

Article 51 provides:

> Nothing in the present Charter shall impair the inherent right of individual or collective self-defense if an armed attack occurs against a Member of the United Nations, until the Security Council has taken the measures

necessary to maintain international peace and security. Measures taken by Members in the exercise of this right of self-defense shall be immediately reported to the Security Council and shall not in any way affect the authority and responsibility of the Security Council under the present Charter to take at any time such action as it deems necessary in order to maintain or restore international peace and security.

A second general principle of international war-decision law is that the first use of armed force is prohibited. This principle is not necessarily a principle of natural law although modern just war doctrine tends to support it, as will be seen. This principle has been developed since the end of the First World War as evidenced by the League of Nations Covenant, the Kellog-Briand and other pacts purporting to outlaw war as an instrument of foreign policy, in the articulation and application of the concept of Crimes Against Peace at the Nuremberg and Tokyo War Crimes Trials of Major War Criminals,[12] and in other war crimes trials, and most importantly in Article 2 (4) of the United Nations Charter, which provides:

All members shall refrain in their international relations from the threat or use of force against the territorial integrity or political independence of any state, or in any other manner inconsistent with the Purposes of the United Nations.

Under the UN war-decision regime there are only two legal bases for recourse to armed force: UN enforcement action ordered by the Security Council under Article 42 and individual or collective self-defense as provided in Article 51. Leading publicists have argued that there is a third legal basis for recourse to armed force, namely, in humanitarian intervention to protect human rights. This view has not been widely accepted and, as observed below, we lack a good example of such humanitarian intervention.[13]

Since Article 2 (4) is often held out to lay down an absolute prohibition of any recourse to force except Security Council enforcement action or immediate self-defense "if an armed attack occurs," in the language of Article 51, it is important to understand the assumptions that underlay the UN war-decision regime and their relation to the actual pattern of international practice since 1945. Modern war-decision law has been based on two principal assumptions from the time of the League of Nations Covenant to the present. The first is that improved institutions for peaceful settlement of disputes—conciliation, good offices, mediation, arbitration, adjudication—would largely remove the need for states to have recourse to war as an instrument of foreign policy. War would be exceptional, indeed, aberrational. Supporting this assumption was the belief that modern war, especially total war, e.g., the first and second World Wars, is so destructive that any reasonable person can see that it is not a rational instrument of policy.

The second assumption underlying modern war-decision law is that it would be possible to establish a system of collective security that would deter and, if necessary, suppress any threat to the peace. A global international organization—first the League of Nations, then the United Nations—would have a virtual monopoly of force, similar to that existing in most states. When an aggressor threatened the peace, the overwhelming majority of nations would contribute to an international force that would defeat the state that had broken the rule prohibiting use of force except in legitimate self-defense.

Neither of these two assumptions proved to be realistic. In the League of Nations period, states such as Japan, Germany and Italy were not content to settle disputes or pursue national goals through peaceful means. In the United Nations era it has been amply demonstrated that there are scores of conflicts which do not lend themselves to peaceful resolution, conflicts rooted in profound ideological, religious, racial and other differences which lead to wars notwithstanding the general recognition of the dreadful price of modern war in all of its forms.

In the League of Nations period, collective security failed because the principal powers possessed of the means to deter and suppress threats to the peace failed to do so in time. In the United Nations era the Security Council, theoretically a source of effective enforcement action, failed to function because of the superpower rift as well as the ability of other permanent members of the council to block action with their vetoes, e.g., Britain and France in the 1956 Suez crisis.

As this is written, a Security Council enforcement action, appears to have been mandated by Resolution 665 authorizing the use of force in the blockade of Iraq following that state's aggression in Kuwait. United Nations forces were interdicting supplies to and exports from Iraq under S.C. Res. 661. S.C. Res. 665:

> *Calls upon* those Member States co-operating with the Government of Kuwait which are deploying maritime forces to the area to use such measures commensurate to the specific circumstances as may be necessary under the authority of the Security Council to halt all inward and outward maritime shipping in order to inspect and verify their cargoes and destina-

tions and to ensure strict implementation of the provisions related to such shipping laid down in Resolution 661 (1990).*

The United States and other maritime states blockading Iraq employed a variety of methods, including firing warning shots, to stop, inspect and divert Iraqi vessels or other vessels bound to or from Iraq. As of November 1990 no armed resistance had been offered to these coercive acts.

On November 29, 1990 the Security Council passed Resolution 678 authorizing the use of force, if necessary, to implement its resolutions concerning Iraq's conquest of Kuwait and related actions. Security Council Resolution 678 in its operative parts:

1. DEMANDS that Iraq comply fully with Resolution 660 (1990) and all subsequent relevant resolutions and decides while maintaining all its decisions, to allow Iraq one final opportunity, as a pause of good will, to do so;
2. AUTHORIZES member states cooperating with the Government of Kuwait, unless Iraq on or before Jan. 15, 1991, fully implements, as set forth in paragraph 1 above, the foregoing resolutions, to use all necessary means to uphold and implement the Security Council Resolutions 660 and all subsequent relevant Resolutions and to restore international peace and security in the area.
3. REQUESTS all states to provide appropriate support for the actions undertaken in pursuance of paragraph 2 of this resolution.†

Even though an enforcement action against Iraq was carried out by the United States and other members of the UN coalition against Iraq, the status of UN war-decision law may not be fundamentally or permanently changed. The UN reaction to Iraq's 1990 aggression may turn out to be a unique case. One can think of other possible conflicts, e.g., between India and Pakistan, where Security Council permanent members and other members might support different belligerents. Their vetoes and other votes might block Security Council action. In any event, it is very difficult to imagine a case where the Security Council members would support Israel to the extent that they have supported Kuwait and Saudi Arabia. Subject, then, to the possibility that Security Council mandated enforcement action against Iraq proves to be precedental in UN practice, I must hold to the view that individual and collective self-defense remain virtually the sole practical

---

* S/RES 665 (1990), 25 August 1990
† S/Res. 678 (1990), 29 November 1990

legally permissible forms of recourse to armed force in most conflict situations.

There have been debates over the interpretation of the right of individual and collective self-defense, some of which are not relevant to this study. The most important of these debates concerns an issue that is relevant to this study, namely, the debate over anticipatory or preemptive self-defense. Strict constructionists limit self-defense to reactions to antecedent attacks. A more liberal view, which I hold, supports the legal permissibility of preemptive attacks in cases where there is a clear and present danger of attack, as in the case of Israel's preemptive first strike against Egypt in the 1967 June War.[14]

The argument for a right of anticipatory or preemptive self-defense is that in some cases the prospects for effective defense turn on the ability to strike first. A state facing imminent aggression may reasonably argue that to wait until an aggressor actually attacks is to reduce greatly, possibly fatally, the prospects for effective self-defense. Obviously, evidence of the aggressor's capabilities and intentions must be very strong and each case must be judged with the understanding that the presumption against the first use of armed force must be overcome.

In addition to the war-decision law governing measures of individual self-defense, there is a considerable body of law that arises out of the legal option of collective self-defense. This is the law relating to armed intervention. Nonintervention is a general principle of international law. The principle purports to prohibit political, psychological, economic and military intervention. The principle of nonintervention is reiterated in countless international conventions, particularly those of regional organizations such as the Organization of American States and the Organization of African Unity and in UN General Assembly resolutions. It is a perennial part of the pronouncements of Third World conferences.[15] The fact that interventions of all kinds are numerous, to the point that it is difficult to reconcile international practice with the principle of nonintervention and its conventional formulations, does not seem to impress those who hold it out as an absolute.

However, there have been, in practice, exceptions to the broad principle of intervention. To limit them to cases of armed intervention they are:

(1) intervention by treaty right, e.g., the right and duty of the United States to intervene in Panama to protect the canal;
(2) intervention by invitation of an incumbent government, usually justified as counterintervention against the antecedent intervention of another power, e.g., U.S. counterintervention against North Vietnam in the Vietnam War;

(3) intervention to protect and evacuate nationals and others endangered in a civil war, e.g., the Stanleyville rescue mission in the Congo civil war;

(4) humanitarian intervention to protect a people from their own tyrannical government, a category that has no examples that are not tainted by the selfish interests of the intervening states, e.g., India in the Bangladesh War, Vietnam in the occupation of Kampuchea.

While these possible bases for armed intervention are highly relevant to many contemporary conflicts, they are not relevant to Israel's war with the PLO. The international war-decision law relevant to this war is the law of self-defense. Israel's claims to self-defense measures against the PLO and others in counterterror operations and in the 1982 Lebanon War will be examined in Chapters 4 and 5.

International War-conduct Law:
The *Jus in Bello*

International war-conduct law is based on three general principles: military necessity, humanity and chivalry. They may be defined as follows:

Military necessity consists in all measures immediately indispensable and proportionate to a legitimate military end, provided that they are not prohibited by the law of war or the natural law, when taken on the decision of a responsible commander, subject to review.[16]

Humanity is the principle, implicit in legitimate military necessity, that military action should not cause unnecessary or disproportionate damage or suffering and that it should not violate the principle of discrimination or noncombatant immunity from direct intentional attack.[17]

Chivalry is the principle that enjoins honorable behavior, even toward enemies, and prohibits treacherous behavior such as violations of truces.[18]

While it is important to keep alive some commitment to respect for the principle of chivalry, the principles of military necessity and humanity are the key sources of normative guidance in the law of war. It should be observed that, in their insistence that only what is truly necessary and proportionate be done, they are closely related to the military principle of economy of force.[19] In modern just war [doctrine, war-conduct law,] *jus in bello,* emphasizes the principles of proportion and discrimination or noncombatant immunity as the principal restraints on belligerent conduct. Since the international war-conduct law has not been able to develop many effective rules governing weapons and means of war, as distinguished from humanitarian aspects of war such as protection of prisoners of war and

civilians, both legal and moral evaluations of the means of warfare emphasize the issues of proportion and discrimination governed by the principles
of military necessity and humanity.

In my analyses of war conduct, I combine the principles of proportion
and discrimination in a comprehensive principle of legitimate military
necessity which, in addition to requiring that means be proportionate to a
legitimate military objective and discriminate with respect to noncombatants and civilian targets, requires that belligerent actions be consonant with
the laws of war and the dictates of natural law, and that they be taken on
order of a responsible commander and subject to review. The review will
usually be conducted within a belligerent's own military and political
hierarchy. Depending on the fortunes of war, it may be conducted by an
enemy in war crimes proceedings. Finally, the review of world opinion and
of other governments has become an important consideration in an era of
global communications.[20]

Customary war-conduct law, some of it dating from ancient times,
developed over the centuries. In the nineteenth century humanitarian trends
encouraged the codification of this customary war-conduct law. A very
important contribution to the codification movement was made in the United
States in 1863 when the Lieber Code, General Orders 100, was promulgated
to guide the conduct of the Union Armies. Francis Lieber was a German
emigré, a professor of law who was familiar with customary war-conduct
law as it had evolved in Europe. He drafted General Orders 100 at the
request of President Lincoln. The code not only provided authoritative
formulations of customary law and general principles for framers of later
international conventions, it encouraged the issuance of manuals on the law
of war in national military establishments.[21] Lieber's code was to be followed by a series of U.S. Army manuals on *The Law of Land Warfare* (FM
27-10), as well as manuals issued by the Navy and Air Force.[22] Many other
nations have produced field manuals and training materials to guide their
armed forces.[23] While such manuals and materials may not always reflect
the actual practice of the armed forces they at least provide evidence of
legal guidelines that belligerents attempt to follow.

The Hague Conferences of 1899 and 1907 produced conventions on land
warfare. The latter, 1907 Hague Convention IV, is still in force and is
an important source of war-conduct law.[24] Two Geneva Conventions on
Prisoners of War, 1906 and 1929, were supplanted by the 1949 Geneva
Prisoner of War Convention.[25] Altogether there are four 1949 Geneva
Conventions presently in force, the other three concerning the wounded
and sick, the wounded and sick at sea, and civilians. The last, also known
as the Fourth Geneva Convention, is particularly relevant to Israel's occupa-

tion of the West Bank in Gaza, as well as to the partial occupation of Lebanon, 1982–85, to be discussed in Chapters 7 and 8, respectively.[26]

Use of chemical and biological warfare is prohibited except in response to its use by enemies by the 1925 Geneva Gas Protocol.[27] The 1972 Geneva Convention prohibits the development, production and stockpiling of bacteriological (biological) and toxic weapons.[28] Gas warfare, rampant in World War I, was not employed by any belligerent in World War II except by the Japanese against China. Although the 1925 Geneva Gas Protocol is really only a no-first-use agreement which could collapse at the first use of gas by a belligerent, abstention from use of gas warfare in World War II, the Korean War and other wars provided substantial evidence that the prohibition of the 1925 Geneva Gas Protocol was confirmed by customary international law.[29] It was regrettable, therefore, that the United States employed nonlethal riot control gas and defoliants in the Vietnam War. While these means could be defended as less destructive than other, permissible means, their introduction opened a Pandora's box of legal justifications that had previously been closed.[30] More recently, use of gas warfare by Iraq against Iran and against Iraqi Kurds and, allegedly, by the Soviets in Afghanistan has raised the spectre of a new destructive dimension to warfare in which chemical means would be combined with long-range missile capabilities to conduct countervalue warfare.[31]

The use of napalm and other means that may cause superfluous suffering is limited by the 1980 Weapons Geneva Convention.[32]

Two protocols additional to the 1949 Geneva Conventions were signed by many states, including the United States, in 1977. Protocol I applies to international conflict.[33] Protocol II applies to noninternational conflicts.[34] After review, the United States refused to ratify the 1977 Geneva protocols, in large measure because it was concluded that Protocol I was too permissive in its treatment of irregular forces and terrorists. The 1977 Geneva protocols have not yet received enough ratifications to go into force. They may provide evidence of war-conduct law, some *de lege ferenda,* some *de lege lata,* but they do not have the force of the 1907 Hague and 1949 Geneva conventions.

These are the principal sources of conventional law relevant to Israel's war with the PLO. Their relation to customary international law as evidence by the practice and expectations of contemporary belligerents varies. This issue will be pursued in succeeding chapters. One general observation may be made from the outset, however. With the exception of 1977 Geneva Protocol II, these conventions were drafted largely to deal with problems of conventional war between states. Even when their framers envisaged hostilities with irregular forces, they had in mind partisan bands fighting as auxiliaries to conventional forces, as in Russia in World War II, or as resistance forces fighting for the liberation of their country from enemy occupation, as in France. In the latter case partisan operations were conducted in the expectation that conventional forces of their own state, e.g., the Free French forces and their allies, would return to recover their country. It seems very unlikely that the framers of these conventions envisaged anything like Israel's long war with the PLO, a national liberation movement that has never had a state with a sovereign government and whose principal mode of fighting is terrorism.

The problems of applying conventional war-conduct law to Israel's war with the PLO will become evident. One that is inherent in the conflict is that a major incentive for observance of the law of war is largely missing, namely, the prospect of reciprocity for proper conduct. Commanders and lawyers attempting to persuade troops that they should observe the law of war usually emphasize hopes for reciprocity: if you observe the law, the enemy is more likely to. In a war that mainly takes the form of terrorism versus counterterrorism, there is little basis for reciprocity in observance of the law. On the contrary, in the wake of an indiscriminate terrorist attack, the troops may be disposed to indiscriminate retaliation. Firm discipline and professional training are required to curb the natural instinct to strike back more or less in kind.

Traditionally, war-conduct reprisals, retaliation with normally illegal means, have been held out as a sanction for the law of war.[35] The efficacy of war-conduct reprisals is questionable and most of the obvious forms of *jus in bello* reprisal, e.g., against prisoners of war or civilians when one's own prisoners of war or civilians have suffered from illegal behavior, are prohibited by the 1949 Geneva Prisoner of War Convention, Article 13, and the 1949 Geneva Civilians Convention, Article 33.

In the end, conformity to the standards of international war-conduct law is primarily based on a nation's value system and sense of honor. Moreover, there is good reason to believe that use of illegal means may not be to a belligerent's advantage and may, indeed, be disadvantageous. Concrete illustration of these issues will be forthcoming.

Relation of International War-decision and War-conduct Law

In the practice of the United States and other Western states, there is an insistence on the separate character of the war-decision law (*jus ad bellum*) and the war-conduct law (*jus in bello*). At Nuremberg, François de Menthon, the French prosecutor, attempted to combine war-decision and war-conduct law. De Menthon argued that since Hitler's wars were crimes against peace, every action contributing to their conduct was a crime. This argument was rejected without comment by the Nuremberg International Military Tribunal.[36] It was later rejected explicitly by an American Nuremberg military tribunal.[37] Unfortunately, the argument appealed to communist governments and was advanced both in the Korean and Vietnam wars to justify the claim that all American and allied prisoners of war were *per se* war criminals.[38]

With this in mind, the United States and other Western states have repeatedly insisted that the status of a belligerent as putative aggressor or victim of aggression engaged in legitimate self-defense must not affect the obligation of all belligerents to obey the laws of war and to benefit from them.[39]

In a pluralistic and conflictual world, this is a logical and fair approach to the laws of war. It is appropriate to the international law of war. However, modern just war doctrine, with its focus on the central concept of just cause, necessarily integrates its war-decision and war-conduct law, always relating judgments of conduct to the ultimate just cause and the other just war conditions such as right intention.

There is, then, a fundamental difference between the international law of war and modern just war doctrine. In the international law of war, judgments about the legal permissibility of recourse to armed force and the conduct of hostilities are supposed to be kept strictly separated. As will be seen in Chapter 10, in the moral order of just war doctrine judgments about the moral permissibility of recourse to force and the conduct of hostilities are intertwined in a complex series of moral analyses.

Notes

1. Myres S. McDougal, "The Identification and Appraisal of Diverse Systems of Public Order," in *Studies in World Public Order,* Myres S. McDougal and Associates, eds. (New Haven, Conn.: Yale University Press, 1960), pp. 13–14.

2. On Soviet theory and practice regarding international law see Kazimierz Grzbowski, *Soviet Public International Law-Doctrines and Diplomatic Practice* (Leyden: Sijthoff, 1970); G. I. Tunkin, *Theory of International Law,* William E. Butler, trans. (Cambridge, Mass.: Harvard University Press, 1974).

3. See Stephen Krasner, *Structural Conflict* (Berkeley: University of California Press, 1985).

4. UN Doc. A/Conf.62/122 (1982); *International Legal Materials* 21 (1982): 1245–1354.

5. See Bernard Oxman, David D. Caron and Charles L. O. Buderi, *Law of the Sea: U.S. Policy Dilemmas* (San Francisco: ICS Press, 1983).

6. *The Paquete Habana, The Lola,* 175 U.S. 677 (1900).

7. See 1958 Geneva Convention on the Continental Shelf, 49 U.N.T.S. 311; T.I.A.S. No. 5578.

8. The United States, the leading opponent of the claims to extensive fishing zones, claimed a two hundred-mile exclusive fishing zone under the 1976 Magnuson Fishery Conservation and Management Act, and an Exclusive Economic Zone of two hundred miles in a March 10, 1983, proclamation by President Reagan. *International Legal Materials* 22 (1983): 461.

9. On the characteristics of the contemporary international legal order and international law, see Wolfgang Friedmann, *The Changing Structure of International Law* (New York: Columbia University Press, 1964).

10. U.S. Department of the Air Force, *International Law—The Conduct of Armed Conflict and Air Operations, 19 November 1976,* AFP 110-31 (Washington, D.C.: Department of the Air Force, 1976).

11. See J. L. Brierly, *The Law of Nations,* ed. Sir Humphrey Waldock (6th ed.; Oxford: Oxford University Press, 1963), pp. 418–19.

12. Article 16 of the League of Nations Covenant provided that if "any Member of the League resort to war in disregard of its covenants under Articles 12, 13 or 15 [to rely on peaceful means of settling disputes], it shall ipso facto be deemed to have committed an act of war against all other Members of the League, which hereby undertake immediately to subject it to . . . [diplomatic and economic sanctions, supplemented by military sanctions recommended by the League Council]."

    The Kellog-Briand Pact of August 27, 1929, and other treaties for the renunciation of recourse to armed force are cited by the Nuremberg International Military Tribunal in its judgment. See Office of United States Chief of Counsel for Prosecution of Axis Criminality, *Nazi Conspiracy and Aggression—Opinion and Judgment* (Washington, D.C.: GPO, 1947), pp. 46–54.

13. For arguments favoring humanitarian intervention with armed coercion, see, for example, Myres S. McDougal and W. Michael Reisman, "Rhodesia and the United Nations: The Lawfulness of International Concern," *American Journal of International Law* 62 (1968): 1-19; Richard B. Lillich, "Forcible Help by States to Protect Human Rights," *Iowa Law Review* 53 (1967): 325–51; idem, "Humanitarian Intervention: A Reply to Ian Brownlie and a Plea for Constructive Alternatives," in *Law and Civil War in the Modern World,* ed. John Norton Moore (Baltimore: Johns Hopkins University Press, 1974), pp. 229–51; idem, "Intervention to Protect Human Rights," *McGill Law Journal* 15 (1969): 205–19.

14. William V. O'Brien, "International Law and the Outbreak of War in the Middle East," *Orbis* 11 (1967): 692–723. Yoram Dinstein terms the Israeli action in the 1967 June war "interceptive self-defense." See his *War, Aggression and Self-Defence* (Cambridge: Grotius, 1988), pp. 180–81.

15. See, for example, Articles 15–17 of the 1949 Charter of the Organization of American States, T.I.A.S. No. 2361; UN GA Res. 2131 (XX) of December 21, 1965, in *American Journal of International Law* 60 (1966): 662.

16. See AFP 110–31, 1-5-6; FM 27-10 War Department, *Rules of Land Warfare* (Washington, D.C.: GP, 1940), p. 1 (hereinafter cited as FM 27-10 (1940). I survey and analyze most of the definitions of military necessity in William V. O'Brien, "The Meaning of 'Military

Necessity' in International Law," *World Polity* 1 (1957): 109–76; see also idem, "Legitimate Military Necessity in Nuclear War," ibid. 2 (1960): 35–120.

17. AFP 110–31, 1-6; FM 27-10 (1940), p. 2.

18. Ibid.

19. AFP 110-31, 1-6.

20. O'Brien, "The Meaning of 'Military Necessity' in International Law" and "Legitimate Military Necessity in Nuclear War."

21. Instructions for the Government of Armies of the United States in the Field, General Orders 100, are reproduced as Appendix ii in Naval War College, *International Law Discussions, 1903: The United States Naval War Code of 1900* (Washington: GPO, 1904), pp. 115–39.

22. See the Army's *The Law of Landwarfare*, FM 27-10 (Washington, D.C.: Department of the Army, July 1956); AFP 110–31 (1976); Department of the Navy, *The Commander's Handbook for the Law of Naval Operations* (Washington, D.C.: Naval Warfare Pub. 9, 1987).

23. For example: in Britain, the War Office, *The Law of War on Land, Being Part III of the Manual of Military Law* (London: Her Majesty's Stationery Office, 1958); in Norway, Utgitt Av Det Kgl. Utenriksdepartement, *Overenskomster Vedrorende Krigens Rett Som Norgw Star Tilsluttet* (Oslo: Grondahl & Sons Boktrykkeri, 1969); in Sweden, Carl-Ivar Skarstedt, ed., *Krigets Lagar: Folkrattsliga Konventioner Gallande under krig, neutralitet och ockupation* (Stockholm, 1979) and Torgil Wulff, *Handbook i folkratt: under krig, neutralitet och ockupation* (Stockholm, 1980).

24. Hague Convention II Respecting the Laws and Customs of War on Land, July 29, 1899, Malloy's Treaties, II: 2043–2057; Hague Convention IV Respecting the Laws and Customs of War on Land, October 18, 1907, 36 Stat. 2277, Treaty Series no. 539.

25. Geneva Red Cross Convention, June 11, 1906; Geneva Convention Relating to the Treatment of Prisoners of War, July 27, 1929, U.S. Treaty, IV: 5224, LNTS 2734; Geneva Convention Relative to the Treatment of Prisoners of War, 12 August 1949, 6 UST 3316; T.I.A.S. 3364; 75 UNTS 135.

26. Geneva Convention for the Amelioration of the Condition of the Wounded and Sick in the Field, 12 August 1949, 6 UST 3114, T.I.A.S. 3362, 75 UNTS 31; Geneva Convention for the Amelioration of the Condition of the Wounded and Sick and Shipwrecked Members of Armed Forces at Sea, 6 UST 3217, T.I.A.S. 3363, 75 UNTS 85; Geneva Convention Relative to the Protection of Civilian Persons in Time of War, 6 UST 3516, T.I.A.S. 3365, 75 UNTS 135.

27. Geneva Protocol for the Prohibition of the Use in War of Asphyxiating, Poisonous, or Other Gases, and of Bacteriological Methods of Warfare, 17 June 1925, 26 UST 571; T.I.A.S. 8061; 94 LNTS 66.

28. Geneva Convention on the Development, Production, and Stockpiling of Bacteriological (Biological) and Toxin Weapons and on Their Destruction, April 10, 1972, 26 UST 57; T.I.A.S. 8062.

29. William V. O'Brien, "Biological/Chemical Warfare and the International Law of War," *Georgetown Law Journal* 51 (1962): 1–63.

30. I discuss the status of chemical warfare and the use of nonlethal chemical means by the U.S. in Vietnam in William V. O'Brien, *The Conduct of Just and Limited War* (New

York: Praeger, 1981), pp. 59–60, 105–10. See Guenter Lewey, *America in Vietnam* (New York: Oxford University Press, 1978), pp. 248–66.

31. See "Iraq Acknowledges Its Use of Gas But Says Iran Introduced It in War," *New York Times,* July 2, 1988, p. 3, cols. 3–5; "Chemical War: Threat in Third World," ibid., August 5, 1988, p. 8, cols. 1–3.

    On alleged Soviet use of chemical warfare in Afghanistan, see Elisa D. Harris, "Sverdlovsk and Yellow Rain: 2 Cases of Soviet Noncompliance?" *International Security* 11 (1987): 41–95.

32. Geneva Convention on Prohibitions or Restrictions on the Use of Certain Conventional Weapons Which May Be Deemed to Be Excessively Injurious or to Have Indiscriminate Effects, October 10, 1980, *International Legal Materials* 19 (1980): 1523–36.

33. Geneva Protocol Additional to the Geneva Conventions of 12 August 1949 and Relating to the Protection of Victims of International Armed Conflicts (Protocol I), December 12, 1977, UN Doc. A/32/144 (1977), *International Legal Materials* 16 (1977): 1391–1441.

34. Geneva Protocol Additional to the Geneva Conventions of 12 August 1949 and Relating to the Protection of Victims of Non-International Armed Conflicts (Protocol II), December 12, 1977, UN Doc. A/32/144 (1977), *International Legal Materials* 16 (1977); 1442–49.

35. The U.S. Army's FM 27-10 (1956) states: "Reprisals are acts of retaliation in the form of conduct which would otherwise be unlawful, resorted to by one belligerent against enemy personnel or property for acts of warfare committed by the other belligerent in violation of the law of war, for the purpose of enforcing future compliance with the recognized rules of civilized warfare. For example, the employment by a belligerent of a weapon the use of which is normally precluded by the law of war would constitute a lawful reprisal for intentional mistreatment of prisoners of war held by the enemy."

    FM 27-10 (1956) states that reprisals should only be employed after other remedies have been exhausted, that they not be taken against protected civilians and prisoners of war, that they should only be taken under the direct order of a responsible commander and that, "the acts resorted to by way of reprisal need not conform to those complained of by the injured party, but should not be excessive or exceed the degree of violence committed by the enemy." No. 487, *Reprisals,* p. 177.

    See Karl Kalshoven, *Belligerent Reprisals* (Leyden: A. W. Sijthoff, 1981).

36. Nuremberg International Military Tribunal, *Trial of Major Criminals,* V (Proceedings, 9 January–21 January 1946): 387–88, 417.

    See Paul de la Pradelle, "Le procès des grands criminels de guerre et le développment du droit international," from the *Nouvelle revue de droit international privé* (Paris: Editions Internationales, 1947), 15–17.

37. Nuremberg Military Tribunals, *Trials of War Criminals* (15 vols; Washington, D.C.: GPO, 1949–51), XI ("The Hostage Case"), "Opinion and Judgment," 1246–47.

38. See Howard S. Levie, "Maltreatment of Prisoners of War in Vietnam," in *The Vietnam War in International Law,* ed. Richard A. Falk (4 vols.; Princeton, N.J.: Princeton University Press, 1969–76), 2: 363–66; 380–96.

39. Dinstein, *War, Aggression and Self-Defence,* pp. 145–51.

4

War-decision Law:
Reprisals or Self-defense?

In this chapter I will summarize the arguments over the legal permissibility of Israeli counterterror measures as they have been debated in the United Nations Security Council. The arguments made and the decisions taken in these debates have provided the greater part of the evidence of the state of international war-decision law in the UN era on counterterror reprisals and/ or self-defense as it has been interpreted by governments and publicists. Part of the reason for the emphasis on Security Council practice may be respect for its authority. I suspect, however, that such respect is largely limited to international lawyers and to internationalists who believe in the United Nations as a matter of faith despite its disappointing record.

A better reason for paying attention to the practice of the Security Council is that it may reflect the positions of a great variety of states, presumably expressed authoritatively. Of course, the degree of respect accorded Security Council practice also varies with the extent to which it accords with one's own political sympathies.

On the other hand, there are many reasons for discounting Security Council practice, ranging from a low opinion of its real authority to disagreement with its political/ideological implications. However, there is a further reason for not accepting this Security Council practice as authoritative: rejection of the Security Council's interpretations of law and of its decisions on the grounds that they are based on faulty legal rationales and are unreasonable. In an advanced legal order such as the United States, the law is routinely criticized and sometimes opposed on such grounds. In the primitive international legal order, legal prescriptions and decisions laid down by bodies that largely lack the power of sanctions should be persuasive on their own merits in order to elicit respect.

This chapter is a revised version of "Reprisals, Deterrence and Self-Defense in Counterterror Operations," *Virginia Journal of International Law* (1990): 421–78.

In this chapter I will summarize UN Security Council practice concerning Israeli and other counterterror measures and outline Israel's arguments that have been rejected by the council. I will then submit my reasons for refusing to accept the Security Council's prescriptions and decisions relating to Israeli counterterror operations. I will conclude with my own interpretation of the right of self-defense as it applies to Israeli counterterror measures against the PLO.

The reader may ask why it is necessary to devote the bulk of a long chapter to Security Council practice regarding Israeli counterterror measures when this practice is then to be discounted as bad and unfair law. There are several reasons for undertaking an extensive review of the Security Council debates and decisions on this subject. In the first place, very few people, including international lawyers, have seriously considered the legal issues involved. Given the prospects for continuing recourse to terrorist activities emanating from sanctuary states, it is important to clarify the issues involved in counterterror operations. This is an issue which is important in the Israeli case because of the ever-present threat of escalation and/or broadening of Israel's war with the PLO. Beyond that, the status of counterterror measures in international war-decision law needs clarification because such measures may well be considered necessary by other states—as in the case of the U.S. attack on Libyan bases in 1986.

Second, few have understood that the Israeli counterterror measures are taken in the context of a protracted war of national liberation, not simply in response to a few scattered terrorist incidents. In order to judge the merits of Israeli actions, it is necessary to inquire into their context in terms of patterns of hostilities in Israel's war with the PLO. Third, it is worthwhile to confront the fact that the Security Council has consistently refused to condemn PLO terrorism explicitly. Indeed, while most states condemn terrorism in general, many are understanding of the PLO's recourse to terror because of their sympathy with its national liberation goals and some of the communist and Third World states openly endorse a kind of "just terrorism" by the PLO.

Finally, it is important to review Israel's treatment by the Security Council in order to make the point that the PLO's terrorist attacks have obliged Israel to react with measures that have brought general condemnation, thereby greatly weakening Israel's political and moral position. After reading the account of the Security Council's arguments and decisions, Israel's counterarguments, relevant recent U.S. practice, and my own analysis of counterterror war-decision law, the reader may judge the issues.

The Qibya Precedent

An Israeli woman and two of her children were killed on October 12, 1953, when *fedayeen* infiltrators threw a hand-grenade into a house in an Israeli village. Defense Minister Pinhas Lavon, IDF Chief of Staff Mordechai Makleff and Chief of Operations (and Chief of Staff designate) Moshe Dayan reacted to the news of the terrorist attack with an immediate decision to retaliate. Prime Minister Ben-Gurion, on a leave of absence, was present when the decision was made but did not participate in the discussion and decision.

A special organization, Unit 101, commanded by Major Ariel "Arik" Sharon, had been formed earlier in the year to carry out counterterror retaliatory raids. Sharon led Unit 101 in a raid against the West Bank village of Qibya on the night of October 14–15, 1953. The plan was to destroy a number of houses in Qibya, a known base and refuge for *fedayeen* infiltrators.

Most of the villagers fled and slight resistance by the Jordanian Army was easily overcome. However, a number of villagers, mainly women and the elderly, hid in the houses which were not thoroughly searched. As a result, many were killed when the houses were destroyed, a total of forty-two civilian deaths in the operation. Jordanian reinforcements escalated the fighting before the Israelis withdrew.[1]

The Qibya raid was widely denounced. An embarrassed Ben-Gurion attempted to avoid official Israeli responsibility, claiming the raid was carried out by outraged "inhabitants of border settlements."[2] The means employed in the raid were indiscriminate, not because there was an intention to kill non combatants but because there was a failure to take reasonable measures to assure that they would not be killed. The Qibya raid is an operation Israelis would as soon forget. Yet it remains a critical starting point for the legal debate over what are generally called Israeli reprisals.

The issue in this debate is not only—or should not be—whether the Qibya raid or any other Israeli counterterror action was conducted in a manner violative of the law of war. That is a separate issue. The first issue is a war-decision law issue, namely, whether reprisals are legally permissible under UN war-decision law. The conduct of the reprisal raid is a separate and important issue.

Jordan complained about the Qibya raid to the UN Security Council. In the Security Council debate emphasis was placed on the claim that Israel had not only violated Article 2 (4) prohibiting recourse to armed force generally but had violated the 1949 truce agreement with Jordan.[3] Abba Eban argued for Israel that the terrorist attack of October 12, 1953, was only the most recent of many. He argued that the Israeli action constituted legitimate self-defense against an "accumulation" of *fedayeen* infiltrations and terrorist attacks.[4] The Security Council rejected Eban's argument and condemned the Qibya raid.[5]

The Security Council's resolution condemning Israel for the Qibya raid set a precedent for Security Council practice in cases of Israeli counterterror actions.[6] It also was precedental for other cases of Israeli retaliation, e.g., against Syrian forces shelling Israeli fishing boats in the Sea of Galilee or Israeli farms near the border.[7] In 1972 the English publicist Derek Bowett, one of the most authoritative writers on contemporary war-decision law, published a monographic article in the *American Journal of International Law* summarizing and analyzing the Security Council's practice with regard to reprisals.[8] He based his article on the record of twenty-three cases, twenty of them Israeli, the others British and Portuguese.

Bowett on the
Self-defense/Reprisal Distinction

Bowett's treatment of the subject deserves restatement. He began by acknowledging a great gap between the consensus that reprisals were illegal and international practice and expectations. Granting the danger of an international legal "credibility gap,"[9] Bowett undertook to restate and clarify contemporary war-decision law. He distinguished two forms of "self-help": self-defense and reprisals. These two forms, Bowett explained, have in common three "preconditions":

(1) The target state of self-help measures must have committed an antecedent international delinquency against the state employing self-help measures;

(2) the claimant state must have reasonably exhausted all peaceful means of redress and protection;

(3) the "use of force must be limited to the necessities of the case and proportionate to the wrong done by the target state of self-help measures."[10]

However, Bowett explained, these two forms of self-help differ in "their aim or purpose." "Self-defense," he stated, "is permissible for the purpose of protecting the security of the state and the essential rights—in particular the rights of territorial integrity and political independence—upon which that security depends." Bowett then maintained: "In contrast, reprisals are punitive in character: they compel the delinquent state to abide by the law in the future. But coming after the event and when the harm has already been inflicted, reprisals cannot be characterized as a means of protection."[11]

Having stated what he considered to be the correct legal distinction between self-defense and reprisals, Bowett, always objective and candid, acknowledged that it was difficult to discern a state's motive or purpose, distinguishing a motive of protection from one of retribution. Moreover, Bowett observed, "the dividing line between protection and retribution becomes more and more obscure as one moves away from the particular incident and examines the whole context in which the two or more acts of violence have occurred."[12] Indeed, "within the whole context . . . an act of reprisal may be regarded as being at the same time both a form of punishment and the best form of protection for the future, since it may act as a deterrent against future acts of violence by the other party."[13]

In the passage just quoted, Bowett put his finger on the central issue in the debate over Israeli reprisals. The reprisal/self-defense distinction as explained by Bowett and as applied in numerous Security Council debates and decisions rests on the proposition that self-defense measures must be limited to passive defense, i.e., resistance to an attack in progress. This distinction denies the possibility of self-defense measures designed to deter future attacks which may be anticipated, based on a pattern of accumulated past attacks and good intelligence.

Deterrence is always integral to self-defense. If a deterrent posture is sufficiently credible, threatening unacceptable damage to an aggressor, self-defense measures will be unnecessary. However, counterterror deterrence cannot prevent terrorist attacks in the way that nuclear and/or conventional deterrence can prevent nuclear or conventional aggression. Because of the difficulty of deterring terrorist organizations and individual terrorists from attempting terrorist operations, counterterror deterrence requires the capability and will to attack the sources of terrorism to deter its continuation. This deterrence is not based solely on the threat of unacceptable damage but the *demonstration* of unacceptable damage. As discussed in Chapter 1, the Israeli counterterror deterrence/defense strategy has been to attack the terrorists in the states that give them sanctuary in order to deter those states as well as the population around terrorist bases from supporting or acquiescing in terrorist operations.[14]

If self-defense is limited to on-the-spot resistance to terrorist attacks, a state targeted by terrorists is at a grave disadvantage. Its right of self-defense is not effective. It would have virtually no deterrent dimension as far as the terrorists were concerned and none at all as regards the states and local populations which support terrorist operations.

This practical dilemma, acknowledged by Bowett, was not reflected in

Security Council practice with respect to Israeli reprisals. Bowett's 1972 article, covering Security Council debates and decisions from 1953 through 1970, summarized the Council's practice as follows:

(1) The Security Council condemned reprisals as illegal, not a justified form of self-defense.
(2) Reprisals were characterized as "punitive" and, therefore, legally impermissible.
(3) The Security Council, having condemned reprisals generically, frequently emphasized additional rationales for condemning them, e.g., disproportionate character, lack of sufficient provocation, and the fact that they were premeditated.
(4) The Security Council refused to look at the whole context of an action, rejecting the claim of a right of self-defense against on-going threats against the background of an accumulation of attacks.
(5) Security Council practice was sometimes mitigated by an avoidance of a condemnation of Israel on pragmatic grounds that it would serve no useful purpose.[15]

Bowett, considering this Security Council practice unrealistic, suggested that this pattern of stern condemnation of Israeli reprisals might be altered to produce "a partial acceptance of 'reasonable' reprisals."[16] He suggested the possibility of developing UN "fact-finding machinery" to assist a "community review" of controversial reprisal actions.[17] This suggestion was not heeded by the Security Council. Indeed, in studying Security Council practice concerning Israeli reprisals since 1972, I have never found a mention of Bowett's article. It appears that the Security Council members believed that they could obtain all the facts they required through the Secretary General and the UN organizations at his disposal, e.g., UNTSO, UNIFIL. In any event, while there often is a need for more facts about particular cases of Israeli reprisals, the fundamental issue at stake has been whether reprisals, if they are by some standard "reasonable," can legitimately be assimilated into the right of self-defense.

Security Council Practice on Reprisals, 1971–1989

I will pick up the account of Security Council practice regarding Israeli counterterror operations from the point where Bowett's summary and analysis ends. The discussion will show that Israel employed a variety of counterterror operations, broadly justified as legitimate self-defense against an on-going terrorist threat, not as "reprisals"—even though the Israelis themselves sometimes referred to them as "reprisals."

Between 1972, when Bowett's article appeared, and the July 1976 Entebbe rescue mission, the Security Council held eight major debates on Israel's counterterror operations. Generally speaking, the debates revolved around three types of Israeli operations. The first type were rather standard IDF incursions into Lebanon which came after Israeli warnings to the Beirut government to keep its territory from being used as a base for armed attacks against Israel.[18] The Security Council's response, as in Res. 313 of February 28, 1972, was to demand that Israel "desist and refrain" from any operations against Lebanon and withdraw any Israeli forces forthwith.[19]

The second type of operations debated in the Security Council concerned the Israeli reactions to spectacular and bloody Palestinian terrorist actions. The list of terrorist actions here include: the Lod Airport attack of May 12, 1972 (twenty-five dead and forty-two wounded); the murder of eleven Israeli Olympic athletes in September 1972; the attack on Kiryat Shemona of April 1974 in which eighteen were massacred, including five women and eight children, some of whom were thrown from the upper windows of an apartment building; the May 1974 attack on Maalot in which twenty Israeli high school students were killed during an attempted rescue mission; and the June 1974 raid on an apartment house in Nahariya in which three civilians were killed.[20]

As a rule, the Security Council condemned Israel's use of force unless a resolution was vetoed by the U.S. (as happened when the U.S. vetoed a condemnation of Israel's reaction to the Munich massacre). Frequently, the Security Council would deplore "all acts of violence" without mentioning the PLO but would specifically condemn Israel by name.[21] In fact, the Security Council turned back American attempts to include indirect condemnations of PLO terrorism, as when it tried to have the words "as at Kiryat Shemona" included after a condemnation of "all acts of violence."[22] Finally, despite its repeated demand that Israel cease any actions against Lebanon, the Security Council never responded to Israel's demand that Lebanon be reminded of its obligation to prevent armed attacks from its territory.[23]

The third type of Israeli operations debated in the Security Council were the instances of Israeli "preventive" raids. These occurred twice, the first after the Israelis mounted a covert raid in Beirut in April 10, 1973, in which they killed a number of PLO leaders and destroyed or damaged several headquarters of PLO organizations.[24] The second was another attack in Lebanon, this one being a large air raid on December 2, 1975. While the air raids followed recent PLO attacks, it appears that they had a strong political purpose as well as the usual military one of preventive/attrition. They came in the wake of a series of diplomatic reversals for Israel, including the UN's pending decision to seat the PLO as an observer and the November 1975 "Zionism is Racism" resolution.[25] The 1975 air raids caused considerable collateral damage, e.g., an estimated 75 killed, 120 wounded.[26] They were almost universally condemned and were criticized in the Israeli media.[27]

In both of these cases, a majority of Security Council members voted to condemn Israel. Resolution 332, approved after the 1973 raid, condemned Israel by name while "deeply deploring" "all recent acts of violence resulting in the loss of life of innocent civilians. It can be deduced from the record that this language referred to the PLO's activities, but the organization was not mentioned and there was no command for it to "cease forthwith" its terrorist operations or for Arab states to prevent or punish them.[28] The December 1975 air raids produced no Security Council resolution because the United States vetoed a draft resolution rather than permit it to condemn Israel and threaten sanctions.[29]

After Israel's Entebbe rescue mission (which was not a reprisal in the strict sense, but did spark a debate on whether Israel's right of self-defense included the defense of Israeli nationals held hostage),[30] the next significant debate came during the Litani operation of March 1978. This operation, essentially a full-scale invasion which greatly exceeded previous Israeli incursions into Lebanon, had been sparked by the "Country Club" raid.[31] Because of the size of the Israeli operation, the Security Council's reaction was qualitatively different: it endorsed the formation of the UNIFIL to police the IDF withdrawal and serve as a buffer in south Lebanon. But the principle of the Security Council's action did not change: Resolution 425 of March 19, 1978, demanded that Israel "cease its military actions against Lebanese territorial integrity and withdraw forthwith."[32]

The debates during the Israeli-PLO "mini-war" of July 1981 were brief, perhaps out of respect for the delicate American diplomacy being conducted by Philip Habib.[33] The Security Council did pass Resolution 490 calling for an immediate cease-fire and reaffirming its commitment to Lebanese sovereignty. The next Security Council debate on Israeli counterterror measures took place in a single session following the October 1, 1985, air raid on the PLO's headquarters in the suburbs of Tunis. Security Council Resolution 573 of October 4, 1985, condemned the Israeli attack, demanded that Israel "refrain from perpetrating such acts of aggression or from threatening to do so," urged member states to "dissuade Israel from resorting to such acts," and supported Tunisia's right to reparations.[34]

The United States had been opposing resolutions on Israeli-PLO hostilities that were not "balanced." In this case the U.S. abstained on a resolution that made no reference to PLO terrorism. This was understood to be in deference to the U.S. desire to maintain friendly relations with Tunisia, which had been cooperative in facilitating the relocation of major PLO elements after their evacuation from Beirut in August 1982.[35] The U.S. abstention, making possible passage of S.C. Res. 573, was in contrast with original indications that President Reagan accepted the raid as justified. At the time, his spokesman, Larry Speakes, stated: "As a matter of policy, retaliation against terrorist attacks is a legitimate response and an expression of self-defense."[36]

While abstaining, the U.S. representative, Vernon Walters, urged that those employing terrorist violence should be condemned. In an important statement about the right of self-defense against terrorist attack, Walters said:

> We speak of a pattern of violence, but we must be clear. It is terrorism that is the cause of this pattern, not responses to terrorist attacks. . . . [we] recognize and strongly support the principle that a State subjected to continuing terrorist attacks may respond with appropriate use of force to defend itself against further attacks. This is an aspect of the inherent right of self-defense recognized in the United Nations Charter. We support this principle regardless of attacker, and regardless of victim.[37]

Israel did not participate in the debate over the assassination of Khalil El Wazir/Abu Jihad. An American abstention made it possible for the Security Council to pass Resolution 611 of April 25, 1988, condemning Israel. While condemning assassination and supporting Tunisia's sovereignty and territorial integrity, the U.S. abstained because the resolution "disproportionately places all blame for this latest round in the rising spiral of violence in the Middle East on one event only while failing to mention other actions that preceded it. It also includes language which is suggestive of Chapter VII sanctions."[38]

Security Council Debates on
Israeli Counterterror Reprisals, 1970–1989

The treatment of Israeli reprisals and/or self-defense measures in the Security Council from 1970 to 1989 rested on the basis of the council's practice from 1953 to 1970, as reported and analyzed by Bowett. In summarizing Security Council practice from 1970 to 1989, I repeat the arguments and determinations of law, as well as ancillary political judgments, that prevailed in the earlier practice and supplement them with arguments and themes, some more political than legal, that recur in the council's debates. In consistently rejecting Israel's claim that its counterterror measures against the PLO and its supporters constituted acts of legitimate self-defense, the Security Council members repeatedly made arguments, decisions and judgments that fell into three rough categories: (1) condemnation of Israeli acts as reprisals not justified as self-defense measures; (2) reiteration of the position that Israel's only legitimate remedy to its security problem was to engage in peaceful negotiations leading to Palestinian self-determination and that her counterterror measures endangered prospects for such negotiations; (3) justification or toleration of PLO terror viewed as a natural consequence of Israel's treatment of the Palestinians, somewhat mitigated by a tendency to "deplore" violence of all kinds.

In rejecting Israel's self-defense claims, the Security Council tended to make four broad arguments. The first argument accused Israel of violating UN procedure and the Security Council's previous resolutions. For example, in the debate on S.C. Res. 313 of February 28, 1972, Kosciusko-Morizet (France) complained: "Since the attack carried out against the Beirut airport, the Council has adopted no less than five resolutions denouncing Israeli interventions in Lebanon."[39] (This point was made in every debate on Israeli reprisals).* Security Council members also complained that Israel consistently failed to report its recourse to force to the Security Council as required by Article 51 or to seek peaceful remedies.[40]

Second, the Security Council asserted that Israel's actions were reprisals, not acts of self-defense, and that reprisals were legally impermissible. For example, in the debate over Israel's post-Munich attacks, Ortiz de Rozas (Argentina) reiterated Argentina's "views regarding what we consider reprisals, excesses in the exercise of self-defense. . . . While we condemn acts of terrorism, we also condemn acts of reprisal, since they flout the Charter and they are contrary to the purposes on which this very organization rests."[41]

As part of the argument, the Security Council consistently held that each Israeli action must be judged in isolation. The Israeli claim that counterterror actions should be evaluated in the context of an accumulation of past and potential future attacks was always rejected. In particular cases, it was judged that there was no "immediate" and "indispensable" necessity for the

---

* In substantiating these summary generalizations, I quote and cite in notes only typical examples, reflecting the broad spectrum of states making some points and the more particularistic perspectives, e.g., regional, political-ideological, of states making other points.

Israeli action. This approach invoked the criteria for use of force of Daniel Webster in the *Caroline* case, which concerned destruction by British and Canadian forces of a ship carrying insurgents attempting to invade Canada from New York State in 1837.[42]

Some Israeli actions were condemned not only for not being "immediately necessary," but because they were "preventative" rather than "punitive." Thus, in the debate over Israel's December 2, 1975 air raids, de Guiringuad (France) asserted:

> Contrary to previous situations, these bombings are not reprisals against terrorist actions waged in the territory of Israel. As avowed by the Israeli authorities themselves, these are operations of a preventive nature.
>
> At any rate, neither reprisals, nor, above all, prevention are concepts which are accepted in international relations.[43]

Moreover, Israeli warnings to Lebanon and Syria, demanding that they meet their international responsibility to prevent armed attacks from emanating from their territory or face the consequences, were condemned as threats in violation of Article 2 (4) and evidence that subsequent Israeli attacks were "premeditated."[44]

The third broad argument from the Security Council contended that, notwithstanding their prima facie illegality, Israeli reprisals were ineffective and counterproductive.[45] In the debate on S.C. Res. 332 of April 21, 1973, Sen (India) claimed that "the Israeli policy, if followed, will lead to intolerable lawlessness and absurdities," e.g., the Arabs would be justified in carrying out indiscriminate raids in states that supported Israel."[46]

Finally, in some cases, Israeli actions, already condemned as reprisals which are illegal per se, were also judged disproportionate and indiscriminate. For example, in the debate on S.C. Res. 316 of June 26, 1972, de Guiringuad (France) observed, "If they were reprisals, they were in any case condemnable; if this was the exercise of self-defense, the Israeli reaction was obviously out of proportion."[47]

In the debate on the post-Munich raids Malik (USSR) complained: "These barbarous bombings have resulted in the death of many peaceful inhabitants and considerable material damage."[48] The issues of proportion and discrimination were particularly emphasized in the debate over Israel's December 2, 1975, air raids by, e.g., Abel Meguid (Egypt);[49] Saito (Japan);[50] Oyono (Cameroon);[51] de Guiringaud (France);[52] Huang (China);[53] Zahawis (Iraq);[54] and Chale (Tanzania).[55]

A second broad set of arguments and decisions emphasized that peaceful negotiations leading to Palestinian self-determination were Israel's only legitimate remedy and that her counterterror actions prejudiced peace negotiations.[56]

A third set of arguments tolerated, condoned or, in some cases, justified the PLO's terror attacks on Israel. Israel's alleged wrongs—occupation of the West Bank and Gaza, alleged oppression of the Palestinians, attacks on the PLO, etc.,—in the view of the Arab states, many other Third World states and the communist states, fully warranted the PLO's war of national liberation and, by implication, its terrorist strategies and tactics.

In the debate on S.C. Res. 313 of February 28, 1972, Malik (USSR) made a frequently repeated claim:

> The struggle of the courageous Arab patriots to liberate their lands from the Israeli racist usurpers is as just, justifiable and legitimate as the struggle of the heroic African freedom fighters to liberate their Territories and the peoples of Angola, Mozambique, Southern Rhodesia, and Guinea (Bissau) from the white racist and fascist oppressors who have usurped their native lands.[57]

Abdulla (Sudan) stated in the debate on S.C. Res. 316 of June 26, 1972: "We think that this [the Palestinians'] is a true liberation movement, and that the words 'acts of violence' that might have been used in some of the discussion do not apply."[58] Rahal (Algeria) pressed this point in the debate on S.C. Res. of April 23, 1973: "There is Palestinian terrorism, just as yesterday there was Algerian terrorism, in which we glory, and which it occurred to no one to describe at that time as Arab terrorism."[59]

In the debate on the Israeli Litani operation, Harriman (Nigeria), who was chairman of the Ad Hoc Committee on the Drafting of an International Convention Against the Taking of Hostages, disputed Herzog's (Israel) use of the word *terrorist,* declaring:

> Here I wish to reiterate that my Government does not believe that any liberation movement should damage its prestige by taking hostages, and that the noble fights for liberation should be based on very high values. I believe that the PLO at no stage in its war for liberation has abused privilege; at no stage has it terrorized; it is at war.[60]

Alternatively, India and some Western states took the view that, while they deplored terrorist violence, they could understand how the Palestinians could be driven to employ it by Israeli injustice and oppression.

In the debate on S.C. Res. 316 of June 26, 1972, Sen (India) blamed Israel for the failure of peace negotiations and stated:

In these circumstances, how can we deny to the Arabs, particularly the Palestinian Arabs, their right to reclaim their own territories? What is the extent to which any Arab Government can restrain its people when they are so blatantly denied what is justly theirs? This is not to say, of course, that Israel does not have the fullest right to self-defense in its own territory as defined and recognized by the United Nations. But that right surely cannot be exercised by such theories as pre-emptive or preventive strikes or by a desire to teach the Lebanese such a lesson that they will no longer care or dare.[61]

In the same debate de Guiringaud (France) observed:

Of course, it is up to the Lebanese Government to control as best it can the activities of the *fedayeen* based on its territory, but we all know perfectly well that this is a *de facto* situation which is the direct result of the occupation by Israel of territories conquered by force and due to the lack of settlement of the conflict.[62]

A recurring argument was that there should be different standards for judging the use of force by a state, member of the United Nations, and a revolutionary movement; the former to be held to stricter standards.

Sen (India) stated in the debate on Israel's post-Munich raids:

Lastly, we must draw a distinction between the acts of terrorism by private groups and the acts of military vendetta by organized governments. Surely we have the right to expect a better standard of behavior from governments than from fanatics, however devoted they may be to their cause.[63]

This argument was made frequently by France.[64]

Arab, other Third World and communist states charged that Israel was an aggressive, expansionist state bent on further conquest.[65]

Arab, other Third World and communist states charged Israel with "state terrorism," a term covering all forms of Israeli counterterror measures, including standard military counterforce attacks.[66]

All states condemned terrorism in general, and some Western states condemned PLO terror, but there was no specific condemnation of PLO terror in any of the council resolutions.[67] A trend developed to "deplore" violence from any quarter, thereby implicitly deploring PLO terror.[68]

Some states counseled the PLO that its use of terror was counterproductive. Sen (India), in the debate over Israel's post-Munich raids, condemned PLO terrorism, stating:

It is equally clear that we condemn those activities and we do not see how the Arab cause, however just, can be served, far less furthered, by such methods.[69]

In the debate on S.C. Res. 332 of April 21, 1973, de Guiringaud (France), referring to the PLO's terrorist acts in Khartoum and Cyprus, stated:

We as much as any deplore and condemn all acts of violence, particularly taking of hostages, which nothing can justify. . . . I do not think the Palestinian cause gained anything from such an infringement of the most elementary human rights.[70]

Israel's Self-defense Arguments

Throughout all of the Security Council debates on its counterterror measures, from 1953 to the present, Israel has argued that these measures are justified by the right of self-defense. Since official Israeli statements sometimes characterize these measures as reprisals, it is clear that Israel rejects the distinction between permissible self-defense and impermissible reprisals consistently made by the Security Council when dealing with Israeli counterterror measures.

Israel's claims to the right to attack the PLO in sanctuary states have been based on two arguments. First, Israel claims that a state, such as Jordan, Syria or Lebanon, that fails to meet its international responsibility to prevent, repress and punish armed forces organizing and launching attacks on another state from its territory, is liable to self-defense measures by the target state. A fortiori, a state that supports armed forces by permitting them to establish bases and training facilities, by supplying them with weapons, materiel and technical advisors, by making agreements providing for cooperation with their conduct of operations, is rightly subject to attack by the target state.

The Israeli argument was expressed by Tekoah in the debate on the S.C. Res. 316 of June 26, 1972:

The question, however, is not only responsibility for the massacre which occurred at Lod a few weeks ago, for that slaughter of innocent civilians was, after all, a mere culmination of a continuous pattern of attacks against the lives of innocent civilians—men, women and children—which have been carried on for years now from Lebanese territory.[71]

As the Lebanese body politic collapsed into chaos, the Israeli argument emphasized the patent inability of the government in Beirut to control South Lebanon. In the debate on the Litani Operation, Herzog asserted:

> The prevailing situation in Southern Lebanon has been for several years . . . one in which the Government of Lebanon has lost control and, I dare say, sovereignty over a significant part of its own territory.
>
> In the light of this situation, in the light of the unmistakable increase in PLO presence and weaponry in the area, in the light of the build-up which we have observed in the past few months, in the light of the PLO's declared intention to repeat atrocities like the one carried out in Israel last Saturday, the Government of Israel was left with no alternative. It acted in accordance with its legitimate national right of self-defense, the inherent right to defend its territory and population *and to ensure that no more barbaric attacks will be launched against it in the future* [emphasis added].
>
> Finally, the aim of the Israeli Defense Force's operation was not revenge or retaliation. . . . It was and is to clear the PLO once and for all from the areas bordering on Israel, which it used mercilessly for repeated aggression against my country.[72]

Second, Israel has claimed that its recourse to self-defense measures has been necessary because of the complete failure of the Security Council even to acknowledge, much less condemn or take action to prevent, Arab terrorist attacks against Israel.

Tekoah expressed this frequently reiterated Israeli complaint in the debate on S.C. Res. 316 of June 26, 1972:

> If one examines Security Council resolutions it appears as if Jewish blood and Jewish grief are of no concern to the Council. It is only when Israel as a last resort strikes back in self-defense to repel and avert attacks and protect the lives of its citizens that the Council seems to awaken to action.[73]

Israel has argued that its counterterror self-defense measures should be judged in the context of on-going hostilities, not as a series of discrete incidents evaluated out of context. From Eban's 1953 argument to the present, Israel has justified its counterterror measures as necessary and proportionate in view of the context of accumulated attacks and the clear prospect of a continued pattern of such attacks. This was the Israeli position from 1953 until the PLO began its attacks in 1965. To that point the context was one of *fedayeen* attacks primarily sponsored and controlled by one of the Arab states. The Israeli position became even more cogent once the

PLO was organized and began its war of national liberation against Israel. From that point to the present, Israel has been at war with the PLO because the PLO is at war with Israel. The hostilities in the war are discontinuous and usually conducted at a low level. Nevertheless, it is a war. Israel has argued that its self-defense measures, emphasizing their deterrent effects, should be judged as proportionate to the requirements of this on-going war.

Bowett observes:

> Indeed, on many occasions Israeli spokesmen have gone further than even the "accumulation of events" thesis and, starting from the premise that Israel is engaged in a struggle for survival, have argued that Israel's entire policy is based on self-defense. . . . One finds this theme repeated by Mr. Tekoah, speaking in the Security Council debate on the Es-Salt raid of March, 1969:
>
> ". . . *Israel has been in a state of self-defence since 1948. It will so remain until the Arab governments agree to end the war waged against Israel and conclude peace"* [emphasis added].[74]

For many years the United States has concurred with the other members of the Security Council in rejecting these Israeli arguments. When the United States has vetoed or abstained from voting on Security Council resolutions rejecting the Israeli claims and condemning the Israeli actions, it has been on the grounds that the resolution failed to condemn Arab as well as Israeli violence. However, in recent times the United States has taken actions and justified them with legal arguments very much like those so long advanced in vain by Israel. In one case, the attack on Libyan bases linked with terrorism, the United States invoked the right of self-defense against a continuing terrorist threat. In the other case, retaliatory actions against Iran in the Persian Gulf while the U.S. Navy was protecting neutral shipping, there was no issue of counterterrorism, but there was one, widely ignored, of maintaining the distinction between self-defense and reprisals. These two cases must now be examined.

U.S. Recourse to Armed Force: Libya and the Persian Gulf

Following several years of naval and air confrontations between the United States and Libya in the Gulf of Sidra, and a surge of terrorist activities, many traced to Libya, dictator Moammar Gadhafy threatened further terrorist attacks on the United States in early 1985.[75] The threat materialized when terrorists bombed La Belle Discotheque in West Berlin, killing two American servicemen and a Turkish civilian and wounding 229 persons, including 78 Americans. The United States had evidence linking Gadhafy to this attack and others pending. U.S. Air Force and Navy aircraft thereupon attacked Libyan bases linked to terror operations on April 15, 1986.[76]

A number of Third World and communist states, including many not then members of the Security Council, condemned the American raid as an act of aggression, not justified by self-defense. Following the strict interpretation of UN war-decision law long applied against Israel, these states argued that there was no antecedent "armed attack" by Libya.[77] Moreover, they claimed that the U.S. charges of Libyan involvement in terrorism was unsubstantiated.[78] Great emphasis was placed on the allegedly indiscriminate nature of the raid, to the point that Libya claimed that no military targets had been hit.[79]

The United States position in the Libyan debate was virtually identical with the well-established Israeli position of counterterror self-defense. The United States claimed that the raid was an act of self-defense intended to disrupt and deter a pattern of terrorist threats and aggressions against American nationals and interests. Efforts to deal with Gadhafi's terrorist activities by nonmilitary means had been unsuccessful. Gadhafy's long record of terrorist threats and activities and compelling evidence of future terrorist actions warranted the U.S. attack on the sources of terrorism.[80]

The United Kingdom supported the American position. Earlier in the year Prime Minister Margaret Thatcher, alarmed at U.S. threats of action against Gadhafy, had stated that retaliatory or preemptive strikes against another country to punish or prevent terrorism was "against international law" and a policy that could lead to "a much greater chaos."[81] Now the position of Mrs. Thatcher's government was that such measures were permissible if they were proportionate—and the U.S. measures were proportionate.[82]

A resolution condemning the United States was defeated. Negative votes were cast by Australia, Denmark, France, the United Kingdom and the United States, while Venezuela abstained.[83] Later, the General Assembly condemned the U.S. Libyan raid.[84]

In the Security Council debate over the U.S. Libyan raid, we have the first explicit claim by a state other than Israel to a right of counterterror self-defense that extends beyond immediate defense of territory to a broad deterrence/defense posture that includes protection of nationals and interests from future terrorist attack. This right is only explicitly upheld by the United States and the United Kingdom. It is implicitly condoned to some degree by the Western states that voted against the resolution condemning the United States. All other members of the Security Council in 1986 and the great majority of other states that participated in the debate held to the strict view that self-defense is limited to immediate defense against an "armed attack" and terrorist attacks do not constitute an "armed attack."

However, this narrow view of UN war-decision law did not prevail when the U.S. Navy used armed force in the Persian Gulf in 1987–88. At that time efforts were being made by UN Secretary General Perez de Cuellar and various states to end the Iran-Iraq war. An important element in these efforts was the attempt to pressure Iran, apparently the party more reluctant to accept a cease-fire, by restricting its capability for attacking neutral shipping, ultimately destined for Iraq, in the Persian Gulf . Starting in July 1987, the United States began conducting escort operations of U.S.-flagged Kuwait tankers in the Gulf. By the end of April 1988 the U.S. extended its escort services to any ship requesting them, provided it was not carrying war materials.

These escort operations led to a number of armed clashes with Iran. For example, when the Iranians began attacking shipping with small arms fire from gunboats operated by the Revolutionary Guards, U.S. helicopters intercepted and sank three of the gunboats as they were attacking the helicopters' floating base anchored in international waters off Kuwait.[85] The Iranians then fired Silkworm surface-to-surface missiles from mobile launchers on the captured Fao Peninsula at ships anchored in Kuwait waters, damaging two ships and the sea island terminal. The United States made a "measured response" in an attack that destroyed an Iranian oil platform on October 19, 1987.[86] Thereafter, there were no Iranian attacks until April 1988.

When renewed Iranian mining of the Persian Gulf in April 1988 resulted in damage to a U.S. ship on April 14, 1988, the United States retaliated on April 18, 1988, with attacks on Iranian oil platforms and in a day-long series of hostilities clashed with Iranian speedboats and aircraft. An Iranian frigate and four gunboats were sunk and another gunboat frigate severely damaged by U.S. naval gunfire, antiship missiles and bombs.[87]

There was no Security Council debate on these hostilities. In some cases the U.S. forces clearly acted in self-defense. In other cases, as in the retaliatory strikes of October 19, 1987, and April 18, 1988, U.S. attacks were not "immediate" responses to an attack in progress. They could easily be characterized as "preventive" deterrent measures and, as readily, as "punitive."

Although the U.S. involvement was motivated by a desire to end the Iran-Iraq war and to protect neutral shipping, U.S. operations were not enforcement actions under Chapter VII of the UN Charter. However desirable in terms of helping terminate a dangerous war and protecting neutral shipping, they constituted an intervention on one side of a war, the side of the original aggressor.

The United States was not condemned for violating UN war-decision law in the Persian Gulf. Actions that would have been condemned by the Security Council, applying its customary narrow interpretation of the right of self-defense—e.g., reprisals, not immediately necessary against an attack in progress, punitive as well as preventive—were not questioned, much less condemned.

Israeli Counterterror Reprisals/Self-defense: A Dissenting Opinion

UN Security Council practice regarding counterterror reprisals, almost entirely concerned with Israeli actions, is abundantly clear. The overwhelming majority of states hold to the narrow view of self-defense that denies that right to the kind of counterterror strategies pursued by Israel. This majority includes communist and Third World states hostile to Israel but it also includes Western and other states that are either friendly to Israel or neutral. It is true that many of these states may be influenced by political and economic considerations that may oblige them to vote against Israel but international law, like any law, can seldom be removed from political and economic influences.

This Security Council practice purports to be based on the conventional law of the UN Charter as well as on the general principles of law respecting recourse to armed force. The opinions of publicists, a secondary source of international law, have overwhelmingly maintained the armed reprisals are legally impermissible since they are not recognized as a form of legitimate self-defense.[88] To be sure, there have been efforts by publicists such as Bowett, Falk, Lillich and others to develop some concept of reasonable reprisals, but it must be conceded that they are very much in the minority.[89]

A publicist should not misrepresent the state of international law on a particular subject because he or she disagrees with it. I concede that there is substantial evidence that war-decision law on counterterror reprisals, as applied in consistent Security Council condemnation of Israel's recourse to them, is indeed the law in force. Having said that, I contend that this law is unrealistic, based on a faulty model of the international political and legal system and unpersuasive legal arguments, and manifestly unfair.

The Security Council practice with regard to Israeli reprisals has been *unrealistic* because it denies the element of deterrence in self-defense. The Israeli experience has been that passive defense measures are necessarily inadequate to protect a nation from persistent terrorist attacks emanating from sanctuary states. Counterterror strategy and tactics may legitimately require the option of attacking terrorism at its sources, even if that involves attacking them in a sanctuary state.

The Security Council's denial of the right of deterrence is particularly unrealistic in view of the fact that Israel has been in a continuing war with the PLO. This war is less continuous in terms of hostilities and usually conducted at a low-intensity level than conventional wars, but it is a continuing war. Deterrence and defense, therefore, take on long-range magnitudes. This is reflected in the constant Israeli references to the longer and larger contexts of particular actions, to the "accumulation" of terrorist actions, to "patterns" of such actions. It is unrealistic to expect a state, particularly one with Israel's security problems, to reconcile itself to renunciation of the deterrent and preventive/attrition elements in its counterterror strategy.

The Security Council's practice has, moreover, been based on a *faulty model of the international political and legal system and unpersuasive legal arguments*. The systemic model reflected in the Security Council's handling of "reprisals" is a pristine 1945 UN Charter model. It assumes the existence of collective security and effective machinery for the resolution of profound differences such as those in the Arab-Israeli conflict. Recourse to force or the threat of force is strictly limited by Article 2 (4), the enforcement provisions of Chapter VII, and Article 51. Self-help measures of armed coercion are strictly limited to "immediate" defense against an "armed attack." The value of avoidance of recourse to force is paramount. Concern for justice, however defined, is subordinated to the general prohibition of force except as UN enforcement or self-defense narrowly defined.[90]

The reality of the political and legal system is one in which there is virtually no collective security, enforcement action by the Security Council having proved to be improbable. Machinery for peaceful settlement of disputes has been variable but notoriously insufficient to deal with dilemmas such as those of the Arab-Israeli conflict. That being the case, there is ample warrant for broad interpretations of Article 51. Moreover, given the fact that much of contemporary conflict takes the form of subversive intervention, exported revolution, indirect aggression and transnational revolutionary warfare emphasizing terrorism, strict interpretations of the right of self-defense against "immediate armed attacks," limited to reaction, are not compelling. On the other hand, the communist and Third World majorities value justice for their favorite national liberation movements over the value of avoiding armed conflict, and Western states have sometimes done the same, as, for example, in the Reagan Doctrine.[91]

Nevertheless, Security Council practice has assumed a situation in the Middle East where peace exists, and the presumption is always against any recourse to force—except, for many, by national liberation movements such as the PLO. Whenever Israel uses armed force against the PLO, since 1970 usually in Lebanon, the action is viewed as an aberrational breach of the peace. This "peace," of course, is one in which Egypt, alone of the Arab states, recognizes and has diplomatic relations with Israel and Iraq has not even agreed to an armistice ending the 1949 war. It is also a "peace" during which the Arab states support and encourage the PLO's war of national liberation and provide it sanctuaries, bases and support. It is a "peace" in which most of the Security Council members at any given time do not have diplomatic relations with Israel and are openly hostile. The contrast, then, between the Security Council's model of the international political and legal system and the real world, particularly as regards Israel's position in the Middle East, is stark.

From this faulty view of the systematic setting, the Security Council makes *legal arguments that are generally unpersuasive*. Indeed, the council record is conspicuous for the scarcity of serious legal arguments. No delegate remotely approached the level of Bowett's analysis of reprisals and self-defense, or, indeed, even cited Bowett's 1972 monographic article. Other publicists are seldom cited, except by the Israelis.

After the precedental 1953 Res. 101 on Qibya, the Security Council soon settled down to a pattern of rejecting the Israeli arguments out of hand, and what little legal argument there was took the form of reiteration of the Qibya precedent and the reprisal/self-defense distinction with little elaboration. Reprisals were legally impermissible because the Security Council had already said that they were, *res judicata*. As the years went by, participants in Security Council debate simply ticked off the number of resolutions condemning Israeli reprisals.

At the least, there should have been some serious reassessment of the council's view of Israeli reprisals once it became clear that Israel was at war with the PLO, an organization pledged to destroy Israel through a war of national liberation. There was no such reassessment. Once the blanket rejection of reprisals had been reiterated, the standard view, explained by Bowett, that reprisals were not permissible as self-defense measures because they were "punitive" was repeated. There was no acknowledgment of the point made by Bowett that it might be difficult to distinguish "punitive" measures from deterrence/defense measures, that deterrence is integral to effective self-defense. For Israel, "punishment" is believed to be functional to the requirements of counterterror deterrence/defense.

Likewise, the Security Council condemns "preventative" counterterror as not "immediately necessary," often citing Secretary of State Daniel Webster's dictum in the *Caroline* case that self-defense measures "should be confined to cases in which the 'necessity' of that self-defense is instant, overwhelming, and leaving no choice of means, and no moment for deliberation."[92] However, given the duration and magnitude of Israel's war with the PLO from 1964 to the present, the interpretation of "necessity" is very different from that in a single unique incident along the U.S.-Canadian border in 1837.

As Bowett has noted, Security Council practice has sometimes been internally inconsistent, e.g., condemning reprisals as disproportionate and/ or indiscriminate when they had already been ruled legally impermissible per se. The issue of proportionality of Israeli counterterror measures warrants separate treatment in which each case should be examined in its total context. Suffice it to say that the referent of proportionality for the Israelis is rarely some specific terrorist act or acts but rather the overall pattern of past and projected acts, the "accumulation" of acts to which the Israelis have been referring ever since Eban's 1953 argument in the *Qibya* case.

One could concede to Israel the right of self-defense measures to deter and defend against terrorism, including the right to attack terrorist positions in sanctuary states, and still condemn specific major counterterror campaigns, individual operations or particular acts within them. This would be in line with Bowett's and Falk's suggestion that a concept of "reasonable reprisals" might be developed. However, this has not occurred in Security Council debates and decisions. Even the United States has routinely condemned Israeli counterterror operations, albeit insisting that equal condemnations of PLO violence be made.

The upshot is that the version of self-defense applied by to Israel by the Security Council is one of purely passive defense within Israel's territory. The only exception to this practice has been in the case of the U.S. Libyan raid, in which the United States, supported by the United Kingdom, argued essentially the Israeli position that effective counterterror self-defense may require preventive/attrition attacks on the sources of terrorism in another state. The great majority in the Security Council and the other states participating in the debate, as well as the great majority in the General Assembly, rejected the American version of the Israeli counterterror self-defense argument. Nevertheless, I find the legal assumptions and reasoning underlying this majority view to be unpersuasive.

Finally, the Security Council's practice has been *unfair*. A double standard has been explicitly developed, not only by communist and Third World states but by states such as France, in which states members of the United

Nations are to be held to the strict UN war-decision law while national liberation movements are, in effect, excused from any restrictions. A kind of holy war warrant has been extended to the PLO, and many communist and Third World states insist that what the PLO has been doing is not "terrorism" but prosecution of a just war of national liberation. In typical holy war fashion, the war-decision, *jus ad bellum,* judgments about the war of national liberation have swallowed up any concern for the war-conduct, *jus in bello,* issues. While condemning terrorism in general, the communist and Third World countries, in effect, have sanctioned a kind of "just terrorism" by the PLO—and any other national liberation movement that has their approval.

According to this view, Israel's remedy for PLO terrorism is to grant the Palestinians self-determination. Pending that, Israel is expected to endure deserved terrorist attacks to which it may only respond with passive defense measures.

Recognition of the lack both of realism and fairness in UN war-decision law on reprisals, as applied to Israel, is found in the evolution of U.S. practice from 1972 on. From the veto of the resolution condemning Israel's 1972 post-Munich attacks to the veto of resolutions lacking "balance" during the 1982 Lebanon War (to be discussed in the next chapter), the United States has insisted that condemnations of Israeli recourse to force be balanced by explicit condemnations of PLO terrorism. The U.S. abstention in the vote on Security Council Res. 573 of October 4, 1985, condemning Israel's Tunis raid, was a special case and at variance with the initial judgments of President Reagan. Ultimately, the United States adopted the classic Israeli claim of counterterror self-defense in justifying its April 15, 1986, attacks on Libya. While the American arguments of April 1986 were rejected by a majority of the Security Council and General Assembly, no one questioned U.S. reprisals in the Persian Gulf in 1987–88.

The U.S. reprisals in the Persian Gulf fit much more clearly into the classic concept of exceptional use of force in reply to an illegal act of aggression than do the Israel counterterror measures. Whereas Israel has been at war with the PLO since 1964, the United States was not at war with Iran in 1987–88. If the UN war-decision law as applied to Israel by the Security Council had been applied to the U.S. retaliatory measures in the Persian Gulf, the United States would have been limited to "immediate" defense against Iranian attacks. However, since the purpose of U.S. activities in the gulf was approved by the UN, acts of armed coercion that were not "immediately necessary" in the sense of the constantly invoked *Caroline* precedent were readily accepted. They were apparently "reasonable reprisals," notwithstanding the Security Council's long-standing position that reprisals are not part of legitimate self-defense and are generically impermissible.

The majority view, as evidenced in Security Council practice and the opinions of publicists on counterterror reprisals, is clear, but it is unrealistic in its demands on the victim of prolonged terrorist warfare. It is based on faulty legal assumptions and reasoning. Finally, it is unfair since it severely restricts the counterterror deterrence/defense possibilities of the state targeted by terrorists while according a virtually unlimited warrant to national liberation movements approved by the majority to wage terrorist warfare.

However, in contrast to the willingness of the great majority of states to condemn Israeli counterterror reprisals, there is a striking unwillingness on the part of the same states to apply sanctions against Israel. To be sure, they apply the sanction of nonrecognition and nonintercourse, and some of them, e.g., oil-producing Arab states, have in the past punished states that were supportive of Israel. But opposition to Israeli counterterror measures, large and small, has otherwise been limited to diplomatic pronouncements and UN resolutions. In the periods of intensive Israeli-PLO hostilities, e.g. in Lebanon, 1972–75, in the 1978 Litani Operation, in the 1982 Lebanon War, the Arab states did not intervene with armed force to protect the PLO, and other states did not seriously press for sanctions against Israel. Indeed, it is rare for sanctions to be mentioned in draft resolutions condemning Israeli actions, a somewhat vague suggestion of sanctions in the December 1975 draft resolution that was vetoed by the United States being an exception.[93] How, then, to judge the state of international law regarding reprisals in general and counterterror reprisals in particular?[94]

Clearly, this law has not been enforced. It does not affect the practice and expectations of states that are highly relevant to the problem of terrorist attacks emanating from foreign sanctuaries. There are many indications that terrorism may become the principal form of aggression in the international system. States whose encounters with terrorism have hitherto been minor and sporadic may confront protracted terrorist campaigns, as has Israel. The terrorism of the future, experts predict, may take much more deadly forms, including the possible use of chemical, bacteriological or even nuclear weapons. Is there any doubt that a state facing such threats is going to strike at their source if at all possible? Prudence, reflecting political and military realities, will no doubt limit the cases of counterterror operations comparable to those of the Israelis, but when the necessity is sufficient, they may be mounted.

What would be the shape of a war-decision law recognizing reasonable reprisals as an integral part of the right of legitimate self-defense? A realistic and fair war-decision law governing counterterror attacks on terrorist bases and activities in sanctuary states that have failed to prevent, suppress and punish terrorist operations would have recognized that such measures are a form of legitimate self-defense. This right of self-defense should extend to the protection of a state's nationals abroad, e.g., against aerial hijacking, hostage taking and other terrorist attacks.

Despite Security Council practice and the opinions of the majority of publicists, the reprisal/self-defense distinction and the judgment that reprisals are legally impermissible should be abandoned. The distinction between actions taken in self-defense and actions taken to punish antecedent armed "delicts" (delinquencies) as a self-help sanction of the law is unrealistic given the lack of Security Council enforcement of the UN war-decision law regime and the competing holy war/just revolution doctrines and practices flourishing in the present international system.[95]

Even if the Security Council and international legal doctrine conceded that, in the absence of effective collective security, some form of reasonable reprisal should be recognized, it would be difficult if not impossible to obtain a consensus on which uses of force were "delictual" and which were "sanctions" for the UN war-decision regime. A more sensible approach would be to assimilate what have been called armed reprisals into the right of legitimate self-defense, an approach suggested by Dinstein's term "defensive reprisal." Dinstein observes:

> A juxtaposition of defensive armed reprisals and on-the-spot reaction discloses points of resemblance as well as divergence. In both instances, the use of counterforce is limited to measures short of war. But when activating defensive armed reprisals, the responding state strikes at a time and a place different from those of the original armed attack.[96]

Contrary to Security Council practice and the opinions of most publicists, the right of self-defense should be interpreted as taking two forms. As Dinstein suggests, they should be: (1) "on-the-spot reaction" and (2) "defensive reprisals" at "a time and a place different from those of the original armed attack." Both forms of self-defense may be needed and in counterterror operations "defensive reprisals" are indispensable. Whether such self-defense measures are "short of war," such as the U.S. actions in the Persian Gulf, or part of a "war" depends on the nature and duration of the conflict.

The concept of reprisals as isolated and/or intermittent acts of retaliation against antecedent delinquencies, acts which are not "immediately necessary," envisages very occasional breaches of the peace and is quite irrelevant to a continuing pattern of hostilities over a protracted period, as in Israel's war with the PLO or even the operation of Gadhafi's terrorist network. Interestingly, these and other considerations lead Barsotti in a monographic chapter on reprisals to exclude Israeli reprisals from evidence of state practice. Barsotti concludes that reprisals are legally impermissible, a position based in considerable part on the judgment that there have been very few "reprisals" by his definition—which bypasses Israeli practice.[97]

Warnings to sanctuary states should not be treated as "threats to the peace," and it should be presumed that most counterterror measures will be "premeditated," given continuing terrorist threats. It should also be accepted that the best defense against terrorism, assuming competent passive defense, may be deterrence based on preventive/attrition operations. However, counterterror deterrence and defense measures must not be unlimited. Requirements for "reasonable," legally permissible measures of legitimate self-defense against terrorism should be as follows:

(1) The purpose of the counterterror measures should be to deter and render more difficult further terrorist attacks.

(2) Counterterror measures should be proportionate to the purposes of counterterror deterrence and defense, viewed in the total context of hostilities as well as the broader political-military strategic context.

(3) Discrimination in counterterror measures should be maximized by target selection, rules of engagement governing operations and the exercise of command responsibility to ensure that means are discriminatory in practice.

(4) Counterterror measures must not be influenced by demands for vengeance, but should conform strictly to the functional necessities of their purpose.

In the present international political and legal system, the basis for implementing war-decision as well as war-conduct law must be the self-imposed constraints growing out of a state's basic values. Neither international organizations such as the United Nations nor "world opinion" can be trusted to be objective and fair, given the double standards and variety of "just war," "holy war" or "just revolution" claims currently flourishing. However, a state's basic values should include limitation of recourse to armed force by the principles of proportion and discrimination. These principles should not be violated in reaction to the excesses of terrorism. Moreover, even a state engaged in a bitter war with terrorist enemies must adhere to the end of just and lasting peace as a goal of the conflict. Measures that unnecessarily prejudice this goal should not be taken.

Application of these perennial principles to counterterror warfare is necessarily difficult and controversial, but this is usually true of legal and moral dilemmas. Reconciling the necessities of counterterror deterrence and defense with the prerequisites for peace with justice remains a challenge, not only for Israel but for any state that becomes the target of one of the varieties of "just" or "holy" wars that may grow out of the sources of conflict and violence so abundantly visible in the contemporary world.

Notes

1. Howard M. Sachar, *A History of Israel* (2 vols.; New York: Knopf, 1976; Oxford University Press, 1987) 1: 444; Michael Bar-Zohar, *Ben-Gurion* (New York: Delacorte, 1978), pp. 203–04; Uzi Benziman, *Sharon: An Israeli Caesar,* trans. Louis Rousso (New York: Adama Books, 1985), pp. 51–54; Gideon Rafael, *Destination Peace* (New York: Stein & Day, 1981), pp. 32–34; Dan Kurzman, *Ben-Gurion* (New York: Simon & Schuster, 1983), pp. 359–61.

2. Sachar, *History of Israel,* 1: 444.

3. See the agenda adopted by the Security Council, 8 U.N. SCOR (627th mtg.), p. 7; Major General Bennike (chief of staff of the United Nations Truce Organization), ibid. (630th mtg.), pp. 2–18; Eban (Israel), ibid. (632d mtg.), pp. 5–7; Haikal (Hashemite Kingdom of Jordan), ibid. (638th mtg.), pp. 1–19.

4. Eban (Israel), ibid. (637th mtg.), pp. 1–42, esp. pp. 15–20. see Derek Bowett, "Reprisals Involving Recourse to Armed Force," *American Journal of International Law* 66 (1972): 5–6 (hereinafter cited as Bowett, "Reprisals").

5. S.C. Res. 101 of November 24, 1953, *Resolutions and Decisions of the Security Council, 1953* (hereinafter, *UNSC R&D, [year]*), pp. 4–5.

6. The Israeli accumulation of events argument for self-defense was made by Israel and rejected by the Security Council in February and September 1955, the Sharafi and Qalqila incidents of September and October 1956, the Suez invasion of October 1956, and the Samu incident of November 1966. See Bowett, "Reprisals," pp. 5–6.

7. Lake Tiberias, December 1955; Lake Tiberias, March 1962; Bowett, p. 6.

8. Ibid., pp. 1–36.

9. Ibid., pp. 1–2.

10. Ibid., p. 3.

11. Ibid.

12. Ibid.

13. Ibid.

14. See Chap. 1 above.

15. Bowett, "Reprisals," pp. 4–21.

16. Ibid., p. 21.

17. Ibid., pp. 29–30.

18. See Chap. 2 above.

19. *UNSC R&D, 1972,* p. 13.

20. See Chap. 2 above.

21. See S.C. Res. 316 of June 22, 1972, *UNSC R&D, 1972,* p. 14; and 347 of April 24, 1974, *UNSC R&D, 1974,* pp. 3–4.

22. Scali (U.S.), 29 U.N. SCOR (1969th mtg.), pp. 18–20, 21.

23. *UNSC R&D, 1974,* pp. 3–4. On some occasions, the Security Council took no action after Israel formally complained; see 29 U.N. SCOR, Supplement for April–June, 1974, S/11326, p. 161.

24. Tekoah (Israel), 28 U.N. SCOR (1705th mtg.), pp. 23–26; "Raid by Israelis at Beirut Kills 2 Fatah Leaders," *New York Times* [hereinafter *NYT*], April 10, 1973, p. 1, col. 8; ibid. col. 7; p. 7, col. 1; "Premier Quits in Lebanon; Raid Reprisal, Israel Says," ibid., April 11, 1973, p. 1, col. 3.

25. The Zionist is Racism resolution is GA Res. 3379 (XXX) of November 10, 1975. For other pro-PLO and anti-Israeli resolutions passed in this period see Sachar, *History of Israel,* I, 826–827; Harris Okun Schoenberg, *A Mandate for Terror: The United Nations and the PLO* (New York: Shapolsky, 1989), pp. 281–282.

26. "Israeli Jets Hit Palestinian Sites in Lebanon Raids," *NYT,* December 3, 1975, p. 1, col. 7. For descriptions of the Israeli raids and estimates of casualties, see Ghorra (Lebanon), 30 U.N. SCOR (1859th mtg.), p. 46; Abel Meguid (Egypt), ibid., p. 56; Allaf (Syria), ibid., p. 66; Aql (PLO), p. 76.

27. "A Debate Flares in Israel Over Air Raids in Lebanon," *NYT,* December 5, 1975, p. 3, col. 1.

28. *UNSC R&D, 1973,* p. 8–9. Sudan claimed that S.C. Res. 332 did not condemn any recent acts of violence by the PLO. Abdulla (Sudan), 28 U.N. SCOR (1711th mtg.), pp. 7–11. Apparently China, Guinea and the Soviet Union objected to the implications of the resolution, since they abstained. Kenya voted for the resolution precisely because it condemned all violence. Odero-Jowi (Kenya), ibid., p. 17.

29. See Moynihan (U.S.A.), 30 U.N. SCOR (1860th mtg.), pp. 3–5; ibid. (1862d mtg.), pp. 27–32; the votes on the U.S. amendments, ibid., pp. 61–62; the vote on the draft resolution vetoed by the U.S., ibid., p. 63.

30. See, for instance, Scranton (U.S.A.), 31 U.N. SCOR (1941st mtg.), p. 115.

31. See Chap. 2 above.

32. *UNSC R&D, 1978,* p. 5.

33. On Habib's mission, see Steven Speigel, *The Other Arab-Israeli Conflict* (Chicago: University of Chicago Press, 1985), pp. 412–13.

34. *UNSC R&D, 1985,* p. 23.

35. "Reagan Tries to Mend Fences with Tunisia after the Israeli Raid," *NYT,* October 6, 1985, A22, cols. 1–2.

36. "U.S. Supports Attack, Jordan and Egypt Vow to Press for Peace," *NYT,* October 23, 1985, A1, cols. 4–5; A9, col. 1.

37. Walters (U.S.A.), 40 U.N. SCOR (2615th mtg.), pp. 111–12.

38. Okun (U.S.A.), 43 U.N. SCOR (2810th mtg.), pp. 26–30.

39. 27 U.N. SCOR (1643d mtg.), p. 12. See, for example, references to Israel's failure to comply with Security Council resolutions during the debate on Israel's December 2, 1975,

air raids by Ghorra (Lebanon), 30 U.N. SCOR (1859th mtg.), pp. 42–43, 48–50; Abel Meguid (Egypt), ibid., pp. 59–60; Malik (U.S.S.R.), ibid. (1860th mtg.), pp. 8–12; Jackson (Guyana), ibid. (1861st mtg.), p. 6; Oyobo (Cameroon), ibid., p. 11.

40. India especially emphasized this point. See Sen (India), 28 U.N. SCOR (1709th mtg.), p. 18.

41. De Rozas (Argentina), 27 U.N. SCOR (1662d mtg.), p. 12.

42. See, e.g., de Rozas (Argentina), 27 U.N. SCOR (1644th mtg.), p. 3. On the *Caroline* case, see John Bassett Moore, *A Digest of International Law* (8 vols.; Washington, D.C.: GPO, 1906) 2: 412. See my comments on the *Caroline* case, p.   above.

43. De Guiringaud (France), 30 U.N. SCOR (1861st mtg.), p. 16. See Louet (France) in the debate on S.C. Res. 490, 36 U.N. SCOR (2093d mtg.), pp. 13–15. Similar views were expressed by Nuseibeh (Jordan), ibid. (2092d mtg.), pp. 28–30; Chebaane (Tunisia), ibid. (2093d mtg.), p. 12; Parsons (U.K.), ibid., pp. 16–20; Elarby (Egypt), ibid., pp. 23–27.

44. See, e.g., Kabbani (Lebanon), in the debate on S.C. Res. 313 of February 28, 1972, 27 U.N. SCOR (1643d mtg.), pp. 1–3. In the debate of S.C. Res. 347 of April 24, 1974, see, e.g., Naffah (Lebanon), 29 U.N. SCOR (1766th mtg.), pp. 6, 8; Malik (USSR), ibid. (1767th mtg.), pp. 4–5; Anwar Sani (Indonesia), ibid., pp. 17–18.

45. See, e.g., de la Gorce (France), 27 U.N. SCOR (1662d mtg.), p. 9.

46. Sen (India), 28 U.N. SCOR (1709th mtg.), pp. 14–15.

47. De Guiringaud (France), 27 U.N. SCOR (1650th mtg.), p. 2.

48. Malik (USSR), 27 U.N. SCOR (1662d mtg.), p. 9.

49. Abel Meguid (Egypt), 30 U.N. SCOR (1862d mtg.), p. 87.

50. Saito (Japan), ibid. (1860th mtg.), pp. 17–18.

51. Oyono (Cameroon), ibid. (1861st mtg.), p. 12.

52. De Guiringaud (France), ibid., p. 17.

53. Huang (China), ibid. p. 21.

54. Zahawis (Iraq), ibid. (1862d mtg.), pp. 13–15.

55. Chale (Tanzania), ibid., p. 22.

56. See, e.g., in the debate on S.C. Res. 313 of February 28, 1972, Malik (USSR), 27 U.N. SCOR (1643d mtg.), p. 6; Kosciusko-Morizet (France), ibid., pp. 11–12; Vinci (Italy), ibid. p. 14; Longerstaey (Belgium), ibid., p. 15; Sen (India), ibid. (1644th mtg.), p. 11; in the debate on S.C. Res. 332 of April 21, 1973, Sir Colin Crowe (U.K.), 28 U.N. SCOR (1708th mtg.), pp. 8–10; Odero-Jowi (Kenya), ibid. (1709th mtg.), p. 11; de Guiringaud (France), pp. 28–30; in the debate over the December 2, 1975 Israeli air raids, Rydbeck (Sweden), 30 U.N. SCOR (1861st mtg.), p. 13; Chale (Tanzania), ibid. (1862d mtg.), p. 22.

57. Malik (USSR), 27 U.N. SCOR (1643d mtg.), p. 7. Huang (China) spoke in similar vein, ibid. (1644th mtg.), p. 14. In the debate on S.C. Res. 316 of June 26, 1972, the justice of the Palestinian cause was stressed by Huang (China), ibid. (1648th mtg.), pp. 12, 18; Bishara, ibid. (1649th mtg.), p. 4; Sharaf (Jordan), ibid., p. 6; Diop (Guinea), ibid., p. 17; Mojsov (Yugoslavia), ibid., pp. 19–20; Malik (USSR) (1650th mtg.), p. 7.

58. Abdulla (Sudan), 27 U.N. SCOR (1650th mtg.), p. 5.

59. Rahal (Algeria), 28 U.N. SCOR (1706th mtg.), p. 7.

60. Harriman (Nigeria), in the debate on the Litani Operation, 33 U.N. SCOR (2072d mtg.), p. 7.

61. Sen (India), 27 U.N. SCOR (1649th mtg.), p. 14.

62. De Guiringaud (France), ibid. (1650th mtg.), p. 2.

63. Sen (India), 27 U.N. SCOR (1662d mtg.) p. 4. See Komatina (Yugoslavia), ibid., p. 2.

64. See, for example, de Guiringaud (France) in the debate on S.C. Res. 347 of April 24, 1974, 29 U.N. SCOR (1767th mtg.), pp. 29–30; in the debate on Israel's December 1975 air raids, 30 U.N. SCOR (1861st mtg.), p. 16.

65. Charges that Israel was an aggressive, expansionist state were made, e.g., in the debate of S.C. Res. 316 of June 26, 1972 , by Malik (USSR), 27 U.N. SCOR (1648th mtg.), pp. 9–10; Abdulla (Sudan), ibid., p. 11; Huang (China), ibid., p. 12; Diop (Guinea), ibid. (1649th mtg.), p. 16. This charges were routine in most debates on Israeli recourse to force.

66. For charges of Israeli "state terrorism," see e.g., in the debate on S.C. Res. 316 of June 26, 1972, Malik (USSR), 27 U.N. SCOR (1650th mtg.), p. 7; in the debate over S.C. Res. 332 of April 21, 1973, Abdulla (Sudan), 28 U.N. SCOR (1706th mtg.), pp. 68–71; Anwar Sani (Indonesia), ibid. (1708th mtg.), p. 11; in the debate on S.C. Res. 347 of April 24, 1974.; in the debate over Israel's December 2, 1975, air raids, Abel Meguid (Egypt), 30 U.N. SCOR (1859th mtg.), pp. 56–57.

67. Examples of condemnation of PLO terror by Western states are found in the remarks of such delegates as Jamieson (U.K.) in the debate of S.C. Res. 313 of February 28, 1972, 27 U.N. SCOR (1643d mtg.), p. 13; Bush (U.S.), in the debate on S.C. Res. 316 of June 26, 1972, ibid. (1649th mtg.), p. 13.

68. See, e.g., in the debate on S.C. Res. 313 of February 28, 1972, Vinci (Italy), 27 U.N. SCOR (1643d mtg.), p. 14; Bush (U.S.), ibid. (1644th mtg.), p. 12; in the debate on S.C. Res. 316 of June 26, 1972, Bush (U.S.), ibid. (1649th mtg.), pp. 13–14; Von Ussel (Belgium), ibid., p. 15; Nakagawa (Japan), ibid., p. 15.

69. Sen (India), 27 U.N. SCOR (1662d mtg.), p. 3.

70. De Guiringaud (France), 28 U.N. SCOR (1709th mtg.), p. 26. See also de Guiringaud (France), 29 U.N. SCOR (1767th mtg.), p. 28.

71. 27 U.N. SCOR (1648th mtg.), p. 14.

72. Herzog (Israel), 33 U.N. SCOR (2072st mtg.), pp. 6–7. Herzog supported the claim to self-defense against armed bands operating from another state with quotations from D. W. Bowett, *Self-Defense in International Law* (1958), pp. 185–86; Fawcett, "Intervention in International Law: A Study of Some Recent Cases," Academie de droit international, 2 *Recueil des cours* (1961): 347–421: 363; Green Haywood Hackworth, *Digest of International Law* 2 (1941): 296–7, the last citation concerning the U.S. incursion into Mexico, 1916–17.

73. 27 U.N. SCOR (1649th mtg.), p. 25.

74. 24 U.N. SCOR (1468th mtg.), p. 6. Bowett, "Reprisals," p. 6.

75. For a comprehensive and authoritative account of the events leading to the April 15, 1985, raid on Libya, see W. Hays Parks, "Crossing the Line," *U.S. Naval Institute Proceedings* 112 (1986): 40–46 (hereinafter cited as Parks, *Crossing the Line*).

76. Ibid., pp. 45–51.

77. Demevi (Ghana) made the most systematic statement on the proposition that no "armed attack" had occurred. 41 U.N. SCOR (2677th mtg.), p. 32. See, e.g., Dubinin (USSR), ibid. (2675th mtg.), pp. 6–7; Al-Ansi (Oman), representing the UN Arab group, ibid. pp. 23–25; Kunadi (India), citing Prime Minister Rajiv Gandhi's statement on behalf of "the entire Non-Aligned Movement then meeting in New Delhi," ibid., pp. 47–52; Li Loye (China), ibid., p. 53; Djoudio (Algeria), denying self-defense, "which cannot be invoked in the absence of an act of aggression, and in this case there was no such act by Libya," ibid. (2676th mtg.).

78. See, e.g., Al-Ansi (Oman), ibid. (2675th mtg.), pp. 25–25; Dumevi (Ghana), ibid. (2680th mtg.), pp. 32–33.

79. See, e.g., Al-Ansi (Oman), ibid. (2675th mtg.), p. 23; Velazco San Jose (Cuba), ibid., pp. 37–38; Hucke (German Democratic Republic); ibid. (2676th mtg.), pp. 24–25; Azzarouk (Libya), ibid. (2674th mtg.), pp. 11–12.

80. Walters (U.S.), ibid. (2674th mtg.), pp. 13–18.

81. "Thatcher: Reprisal Strikes Illegal," *Washington Post* [hereinafter *WP*], January 11, 1986, A1, col. 1.

82. Sir John Thompson (U.K.), 41 U.N. SCOR (2679th mtg.), pp. 13–27.

83. Ibid. (2682d mtg.), p. 43.

84. Resolution 41/38 in *Resolutions and Decisions Adopted by the General Assembly, 16 September–19 December 1986*, Supplement 53, pp. 34–35; "UN Vote Adopts Resolution Rebuking US on Libya Raid," *NYT*, November 21, 1986, p. 13, col. 6; "Raid on Libya Condemned by U.N. General Assembly," *WP*, November 21, 1986, A30, cols. 5–6.

85. "US Says Copters, Answering Shots, Sank 3 Iran Boats," *NYT*, October 9, 1987, p. 1, cols. 5–6.

86. "US Destroyers Shell Iranian Military Platform in Gulf," *WP*, October 20, 1987, A1, cols. 1–5.

87. "U.S. Retaliates, Hits Iran Oil Platforms in Gulf, *WP*, April 18, 1988, A1, cols. 1–5; A22, cols. 3–5; "U.S. Sinks or Cripples 6 Iranian Ships in Gulf Battles; No American Losses Reported, but Helicopter Missing," ibid., April 19, 1988, A1, cols. 5–6; A22, cols. 1–2.

88. Barsotti's recent work on reprisals, "Armed Reprisals" in A. Cassese, ed., *The Current Legal Regulation of the Use of Force* (Dordrecht: Nijhoff, 1986), pp. 79–110, preserves the distinction between reprisals and self-defense but diminishes its impact by excluding Israeli "reprisals" from the evidence of state practice because there is no consensus as to whether they can be considered responses to antecedent delinquencies. Barsotti cites an impressive list of publicists who make the distinction and hold that "reprisals" are legally impermissible, a list that includes publicists cited in support of this position by Bowett in his 1972 article. See Barsotti, "Armed Reprisals," p. 102, n.1.

89. Among publicists arguing for some kind of right of reprisal are Bowett, "Reprisals," pp. 21, 32; Richard Falk, "The Beirut Raid and the International Law of Reprisal," *American Journal of International Law* 63 (1969): 415–43; Richard B. Lillich, "Forcible Self-Help Under International Law," U.S. Naval War College, *International Law Studies* 62 (1980), 129–138; *Readings in International Law from the Naval War College Review, 1947–1977*, R. B. Lillich and J. N. Moore, eds., vol. II, *The Use of Force, Human Rights and*

General International Legal Issues, pp. 130–38; 131–33; Julius Stone, *Aggression and World Order* (1958), pp. 94–98; Barry Levenfeld, "Israeli Counter-Fedayeen Tactics in Lebanon: Self-Defense and Reprisals under Modern International Law," *Columbia Journal of Transnational Law* 21 (1982) 35: I have argued against the reprisal/self-defense distinction in William V. O'Brien, *The Conduct of Just and Limited War* (New York: Praeger, 1981), pp. 24–27.

90. See J. L. Brierly, *The Law of Nations* (6th ed.; New York: Oxford University Press, 1963), Sir Humphrey Waldock, ed., pp. 414–15.

91. See Thomas M. Franck, "Who Killed Article 2 (4)? or Changing Norms Governing the Use of Force by States," *American Journal of International Law* 64 (1970): 809–20.

92. On the *Caroline* case, see Moore, *A Digest of International Law* 2:412, cited in n.59 above.

93. See above, p. 106.

94. My skepticism about unsanctioned war-decision laws is similar to the positions of Prof. Michael Reiseman and his Yale colleagues, evidenced in W. Michael Reisman and Andrew R. Willard, eds., *International Incidents: The Law That Counts in World Politics* (Princeton, N.J.: Princeton University Press, 1988). This approach is described and applied in Chapter V.

95. Robert W. Tucker argues persuasively that the reprisal/self-defense distinction does not hold up under rigorous analysis and is not reflective of state practice. "Reprisals and Self-Defense: The Customary Law," *American Journal of International Law* 66 (1972): 586–95.

96. Yoram Dinstein, *War, Aggression and Self-Defense* (Cambridge: Grotius, 1988), p. 203.

97. Barsotti, "Armed Reprisals," pp. 87–90.

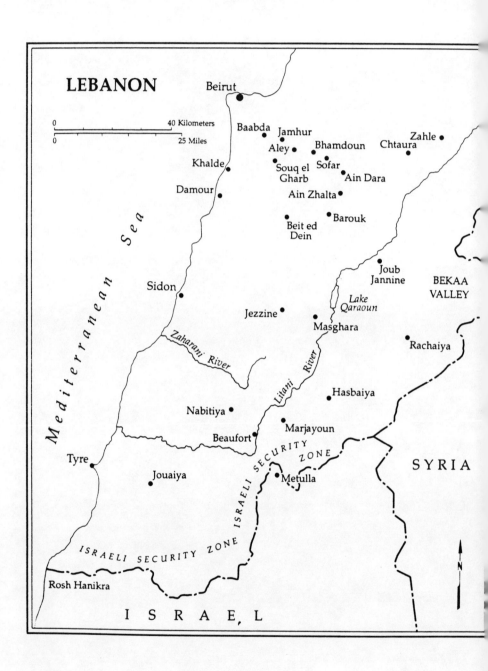

LEBANON

Beirut

0 — 40 Kilometers
0 — 25 Miles

Baabda Jamhur
Aley Bhamdoun Chtaura Zahle
Khalde Sofar
Souq el Ain Dara
Gharb
Damour Ain Zhalta
Barouk
Beit ed
Dein

Mediterranean Sea

Joub
Jannine **BEKAA VALLEY**

Sidon *Lake Qaraoun*

Jezzine Masghara

Rachaiya

Zaharani River

Litani River

Hasbaiya

Nabitiya

Marjayoun

Beaufort

ISRAELI SECURITY ZONE **SYRIA**

Tyre

Jouaiya Metulla

ISRAELI SECURITY ZONE

N

Rosh Hanikra

I S R A E L

5

The 1982 Lebanon War and War-decision Law.

The 1982 Lebanon War was, from Israeli perspectives, a major escalation of a war that the PLO initiated at a very low level of intensity in early 1965. For years Israel had responded to PLO attacks, mostly of a terrorist nature, with low-intensity counterterror measures. Sometimes these involved incursions into Lebanon, and in recent years they had centered on support of the SLA in the Security Zone. The 1978 Litani Operation had lasted three months and involved the occupation of considerable Lebanese territory, but it had merely pushed the PLO back for a time. The 1982 invasion of Lebanon, in contrast, was conceived as a knock-out blow to the PLO.

As described in the previous chapter, the Security Council, world opinion and the majority of international-law publicists had consistently denied Israel the right to make counterterror attacks against the PLO in Lebanon or any other sanctuary state. The right of reprisal for a continuing pattern of terrorist attacks was not recognized. Now Israel contemplated going beyond occasional reprisals as an expression of self-defense and launching, in effect, a campaign justified as anticipatory, preemptive, self-defense. This campaign would not be justified as preempting the kind of conventional threat faced at the start of the 1967 June War. There the clear and present danger was conventional aggression which might have destroyed Israel. The clear and present danger in 1982 was of a different character and magnitude. In 1982 the threat came from a much more dangerous PLO, possessed of conventional capabilities that could make northern Israel population centers uninhabitable. Under the umbrella of this conventional countervalue capability, the PLO would be able to continue terrorist operations undeterred by the prospect of effective Israeli countermeasures. The PLO threat that Israel had failed to remove in July 1981 was still there and, so Israeli strategic thinking went, it would have to be removed sometime. June 1982 was the time.

The major Israeli invasion of Lebanon could have occurred much earlier

133

than June 1982. When Ariel Sharon became defense minister in August 1981, he promptly directed that plans be made for a campaign in Lebanon that would destroy the PLO as a military force. Sharon also planned to drive the Syrians out of Lebanon and make possible the installation of a Christian Lebanese government that would make peace with Israel. If feasible, these objectives were obviously very desirable for Israel. However, Israel could not launch this campaign until it had plausible evidence that the PLO had broken the Habib cease-fire of July 24, 1981.

The Precarious Habib Cease-fire

Not surprisingly, there were different interpretations of the cease-fire. It was based on a July 24, 1981, statement by Ambassador Philip Habib: "I have today reported to President Reagan that as of 13:30 hours local time, July 24, 1981, all hostile military action between Lebanese and Israeli territory, in either direction, will cease."[1]

There was no text of the cease-fire agreement that Habib had negotiated with the Lebanese and Saudi governments acting as intermediaries for the PLO. Israel interpreted the agreement as barring any PLO military or terrorist activity anywhere, including against the Haddad militia in Lebanon or against Israelis or Israeli interests around the world. The PLO and the United States interpreted the agreement as being limited to hostilities between Israel and the PLO across the Lebanese border.

The agreement was vulnerable to claims of violation because of these different interpretations. Moreover, it was vulnerable because of the nature of the PLO's federation of resistance groups. Arafat did not control many of them and he had trouble controlling elements in his own Fatah organization, who soon became restless and eager to renew terrorist operations. It was an open question, therefore, just how many and how serious breaches of the cease-fire would be considered sufficient to warrant the claim that it was void and that hostilities could be resumed.

Sharon and other Israeli officials and military officers increasingly shared their planning for a major campaign in Lebanon with U.S. officials. Habib was appalled when briefed on this subject by Sharon in December 1981.[2] Secretary of State Alexander Haig, however, was more sympathetic. In January 1982, while in Jerusalem and Cairo supporting Egyptian-Israeli negotiations, Haig was told by Begin that the PLO threat would have to be dealt with. Haig answered that permissible Israeli military action would have to be in response to "an internationally recognized provocation," to which Israel might make a "proportionate response." Subsequent correspondence between Begin and Haig concerning interpretation of Haig's formula was inconclusive.[3]

In this context, General Yehoshua Saguy, director of Israeli military intelligence, came to Washington on February 3, 1982. Saguy told Haig that Israel had lost 17 dead and 288 wounded in ten PLO violations of the cease-fire and that further violations would trigger large-scale Israeli attacks on the PLO. Haig instructed Ambassador Sam Lewis to inform Begin that an attack such as that described by Saguy would seriously affect U.S.-Israeli relations. Begin agreed to defer the action if the United States would assure relief through diplomacy from PLO attacks. PLO restraint seemed to result from U.S. initiatives with Saudi Prince Fahd and Jordan's King Hussein.[4]

Meanwhile, another issue provided Israel with an incentive to attack the PLO. Israeli efforts to develop non-PLO Palestinian local government and political alternatives in the occupied territories had failed conspicuously by the end of 1981. From March to May 1982 there were civil disturbances in the West Bank. Israeli leaders linked the PLO to these problems and believed that a crushing defeat of the PLO would have a sobering effect on the Palestinians in the territories.[5]

Israel made no effort to conceal its plans for a major campaign against the PLO in Lebanon. The plan was discussed in the *New York Times* and outlined by John Chancellor on the NBC Nightly News on April 8, 1981.[6] All that was needed was evidence that the PLO had broken the cease-fire with "an internationally recognized provocation."

Israel detected a number of "provocations" in April 1982. Yacov Barsimantov, an Israeli diplomat, was killed by terrorists in Paris on April 4, 1982. An Israeli soldier was killed by a mine in the Security Zone. The PLO denied responsibility, but Israel officials warned that such terrorist acts were violations of the cease-fire and that Israel would strike at terrorist organizations "without mercy," wherever they sought refuge. On April 10 Arafat warned the PLO to be ready for an Israeli attack. Lebanon's President Elias Sarkis pleaded with the United States to prevent renewal of hostilities.[7]

The IAF attacked PLO targets on April 21 and May 9.[8] On May 13, Prime Minister Menachem Begin declared that the accumulation of PLO terrorist activities rendered the cease-fire null and void. The PLO responded to the Israeli air raids with some shelling of northern Israel but, in Haig's words, in "such an obviously ineffective way as to give no excuse for an Israeli escalation."[9]

Meanwhile, Israel completed evacuation of Sinai as scheduled, destroying Jewish settlements in the process despite emotional domestic resistance.

Peace with Egypt seemed secured. Israel could now concentrate on the PLO in Lebanon.

Sharon visited Washington late in May and outlined his plans for a Lebanon campaign to Haig and his staff. Haig reiterated the need for a major provocation and a proportionate response, but Sharon insisted on Israel's right to defend itself in its own way.[10]

The *casus belli* was supplied by an assassination attempt in London which seriously wounded Israeli ambassador to Great Britain Sholom Argov. When Begin's Cabinet met on June 4, 1982, evidence was reported indicating that the London attack was the work of the renegade Abu Nidal terrorist group. Begin and IDF Chief of Staff Rafael Eitan brushed this explanation aside, contending that "they're all PLO." The Argov attack was considered the last straw, the last provocation.[11]

On June 4, 1982, the IAF bombed the empty Beirut sports stadium, exploding a PLO ammunition dump, and carried out other air attacks against the PLO. The PLO now reacted as in July 1981 with artillery attacks on twenty Israeli towns, resulting in the wounding of three civilians.[12]

The Israeli Cabinet authorized Operation Peace for Galilee on June 5, 1982. Begin informed the United States that this operation was to be limited to a drive forty kilometers (twenty-four miles) into Lebanon in order to rid southern Lebanon of PLO forces and bases "so that all our civilians in the region of Galilee will be set free of permanent threat to their lives."[13] However, the Israeli forces soon passed the forty-kilometer limit, engaged the Syrians and besieged Beirut.

Israel's Claim of Self-defense

In the Security Council debate on Israel's attack, Yehuda Blum, the Israeli representative, once more advanced the argument of self-defense in response to an accumulation of terrorist attacks. He stated:

> This recent attempt on the life of Ambassador Argov is only the climax of a long campaign of terror that has been waged against my country and against my people in Israel and throughout the world. . . . This Council may ignore the fact that since July of last year there have been approximately 150 acts of terrorism instigated by the PLO, originating in Lebanon, against Israelis and Jews in Israel and elsewhere: in Athens, Vienna, Paris and London.[14]

Blum said that the PLO often "denies responsibility for its activities" but that, whatever the "aliases" used by terrorist groups, "they all serve the same purpose."[15]

Israel's justification for the Lebanon campaign was that it was an act of self-defense against a long-standing terrorist war waged from PLO headquarters and bases in Lebanon. The July 24, 1981, cease-fire which had interrupted that war had, in Israel's view, been broken by the PLO, thereby warranting resumption of hostilities. This position, of course, was based on the Israeli interpretation of the 1981 cease-fire. While there had been only a few terrorist attacks from Lebanon into Israel, there had been "approximately 150 acts of terrorism" if one counted international terrorism and attacks against the Haddad militia in the Security Zone.

The Security Council Debate: War-decision Law Issues

Once again, the Israeli self-defense argument was rejected by the Security Council. States as different as Great Britain and Ireland, on the one hand, and the Soviet Union, on the other, considered that it was Israel that had broken the cease-fire.[16] A number of states contended that the Argov incident only provided a pretext for Israel to carry out a long-premeditated invasion.[17] The PLO and its supporters argued that it was not responsible for the London terrorist attack.[18] Several states—e.g., the U.K., France, Guyana, and Spain—condemned the London terrorist attack but asserted that it did not justify Israel's massive reaction.[19] Western European states decried Israel's operations that brushed aside UNIFIL.[20] The Western states and Egypt reiterated the position that force was not the answer to the problem; only a solution based on Palestinian self-determination would bring security and peace.[21]

In addition to claiming the right of self-defense in a continuing war, Blum made a number of points in rebuttal during the debate. The Security Council had never condemned Arab terrorist attacks against Israel.[22] The Security Council had never discussed the situation in Lebanon; the PLO state-within-a-state from which terrorist attacks were launched; the Syrian military occupation of large parts of the country; the resulting collapse of the Lebanese government. Indeed, Blum claimed that it was Israel that most wanted restoration of Lebanese sovereignty and territorial integrity.[23]

Blum argued that, since Lebanon could not or would not meet its responsibilities to prevent armed attacks from being prepared and launched from its territory, Israel had no alternative to self-help in the form of self-defense. Recourse to self-defense measures was, moreover, necessitated by the fact that the Security Council had never afforded Israel any relief despite its many complaints of PLO terrorist activities originating in Lebanon.[24]

From the outset the Security Council debate also concerned issues of Israel's conduct of the war. These will be discussed in the next chapter.

The Security Council quickly passed Resolutions 508 (June 5) and 509 (June 6), calling for cessation of hostilities and then for an Israeli withdrawal.[25] The PLO was applauded for immediately accepting these resolutions, while Israel was condemned for ignoring them.[26]

However, a further resolution was vetoed by the United States. Ambassador Jeanne Kirkpatrick stated that Resolutions 508 and 509 "contained balancing language that took account of the fact that the conflict in Lebanon and across the Lebanese-Israeli border is complex in its origin and that its resolution will require compliance in deed as well as in word with the resolutions of the Security Council. Unfortunately, the resolution before us is not sufficiently balanced to accomplish the objective of ending the cycle of violence and establishing the conditions for a just and lasting peace in Lebanon."[27]

On June 26, 1982, the United States vetoed a resolution introduced by France that undertook to resolve not only the current conflict but to initiate a process leading to a Palestinian state.[28] Ambassador Charles Lichenstein stated that, while the United States supported many elements in the resolution, it failed "to call for the essential requisite for the restoration of the authority of the Government of Lebanon, that is, the elimination from Beirut and elsewhere of the presence of armed Palestinian elements who neither submit to nor respect the sovereign authority of the Lebanese Government."[29] The U.S. favored a cease-fire and withdrawal of both Israeli and PLO forces "from the areas of Beirut," monitored at Lebanon's request by UN observers.[30]

A series of exchanges between Ireland's Dorr and Israel's Blum raised but hardly resolved the issue of the proportionality of Israel's invasion of Lebanon to the injuries it had suffered and could expect to suffer. On June 8, Dorr doubted that Israeli losses to terrorism in Israel and elsewhere "over recent years" approximated the "deaths and injuries caused by the recent major Israeli air attacks on Beirut."[31] Blum violently rejected this "bizarre" and "silly" "bookkeeping" approach in this and another exchange with Dorr.[32] Unfortunately, Blum tended to respond with dramatic challenges to put a price on the life of any one victim of terrorism. That naturally led Dorr to affirm his respect for any human life.

The real point of this debate was never adequately developed. The issue should have been the proportionality of the overall Israeli counterterror policy, culminating at this point in the war in Lebanon, with the referent being the overall injury and threat to Israel posed by the PLO, not simply the number of casualties on each side. The impact of terrorism goes far beyond the actual number of casualties it causes. Terrorism may have an enormous psychological impact on a target society, forcing it to exist in a perpetual state of emergency. This is its genius as a means of coercion.[33]

Israel's 1982 Lebanon War:
Aggression or Self-defense?

The legal permissibility of Israel's 1982 Lebanon war may be judged, in the first instance, by evaluating the claim of self-defense. Second, Israel's legal claim may be judged in the light of the reaction of the states of the international legal system, which presumably reflected their understanding of and expectations about state practice. Practice and expectations may be deduced from the official pronouncements of states and from their behavior. It is not uncommon for pronouncements and behavior to signal different patterns of behavior and expectations. As argued in Chapter 3, even pronouncements that take the form of treaty commitments may not be conclusive evidence of state practice and expectations. Thus, statements and votes in the UN Security Council or General Assembly or in other forums, as well as official statements and diplomatic correspondence, may or may not be evidence of legal norms actually being observed. "Paper law" must be confirmed by behavior.

If international law consisted mainly of treaties and authoritative pronouncements from states, Israel's 1982 Lebanon War could easily be branded as illegal aggression, as it has been in the Security Council, the General Assembly, in countless pronouncements by the governments of the world, by self-appointed war crimes commissions and international-law publicists.[34] However, if international law is evidenced by the practice, i.e., behavior and expectations of states, the case is more complicated. Since this is my understanding of international law, I must examine the war-decision issues of the 1982 Lebanon war in terms of the actual practice and expectations of states. First, I will make my own evaluation of Israel's claim to exercise the right of self-defense in the 1982 Lebanon War.

Evaluating Israel's self-defense claim is complicated because key Israeli decision-makers had different understandings of Sharon's strategic objectives and, accordingly, of the true magnitude of the claim. Key Israeli decision-makers had at least three different rationales for the necessity of the invasion and, consequently, three possible referents for the calculus of proportionality. These rationales were:

(1) The PLO's terrorist attacks since the Habib cease-fire were intolerable and Israel must act to prevent continuation of such attacks.

(2) The perpetuation and strengthening of the PLO's conventional countervalue capabilities to attack northern Israel were intolerable and
required action to drive the PLO out of range of northern Israel.

(3) The very existence of the PLO, its state-within-a-state in chaotic
Lebanon and its base for terrorist operations in Beirut, were intolerable. The PLO must be destroyed as a political and military/terrorist
force in Lebanon.

Critics of Israel's 1982 self-defense claims always emphasize the fact
that there were only a few terrorist attacks against Israel itself during the
Habib cease-fire period. However, the PLO's war with Israel has always
been waged on a worldwide basis. In the first place, Israeli diplomats have
been attacked as far away as Bangkok, and attacks on Israeli diplomats
triggered the 1982 war. Second, Israel identifies with Jews everywhere and
the PLO has made non-Israeli Jews and synagogues targets around the world.
Even if terrorist attacks from Lebanon into Israel virtually stopped during
the Habib cease-fire, 150 terrorist attacks against Israelis or non-Israeli
Jews around the world could not be ignored. There was a necessity to
respond to these attacks. It remains, presently, to discuss the means that
might be proportionate to that end.

The necessity to remove the conventional countervalue PLO threat to
Israel was critical. It seems not to have been understood by very many
outside of Israel. This threat challenged the whole Israeli counterterror
deterrence/defense strategy. It transformed the PLO's weapons of choice
from the level of grenades and submachine guns to artillery and rocket
launchers that could fire into northern Israel from distances up to seventeen
miles. This new capability had been demonstrated in July 1981, and although casualties and damage had been comparatively light, the random
violence of the PLO's bombardments had rendered many of northern Israel's
population centers uninhabitable.

This was a threat of major proportions, but its implications were even
more intolerable. By linking its bombardments of Israeli population centers
to Israeli counterterror preventive/attrition raids, the PLO was able to put
the Israelis in a profound practical and moral quandary. The decision to
strike at terrorist bases in Lebanon in order to deter and prevent more
terrorist attacks became simultaneously a decision to bring down PLO artillery and rocket fire on Israeli cities, towns and settlements. Should Israel
forgo its traditional preventive/attrition attacks on the PLO and limit itself
to passive defense measures in order to spare northern Israeli population
centers, or should it continue its counterterror attacks at the expense of
those population centers? The necessity implied by this quandary was that
of permanently driving the PLO out of range of northern Israel.

Beyond this view of necessity, there was the fundamental Israeli percep-
tion of the PLO as a permanent threat to be removed only by defeating it
definitively and depriving it of any base in a country bordering Israel. From
this perspective, the traditional counterterror preventive/attrition raids had
contained the PLO's terrorism, but the prospect was for an indefinite continuation of this terrorist-counterterrorist war. Moreover, the Litani Operation
had demonstrated that merely pushing the PLO back and then withdrawing
was only a short-term solution.

To be sure, it could be argued that the Palestinian liberation movement
could not be definitively defeated. However, Israel could certainly deprive
the PLO of its substantial bases in its state-within-a-state in Lebanon and its
headquarters in Beirut. Israel could defeat and scatter the PLO's armed
forces numbering upwards of 15,000 men and capture its sizeable caches
of weapons, munitions, vehicles and materiel. Moreover, by intervening
in Lebanon and assuring the installation of a friendly Christian government,
Israel could be assured of a safe border with Lebanon.

In addition to these three ascending views of necessity, Israel also perceived the necessity of defeating and discrediting the PLO so that the
Palestinians in the occupied territories would not look to it for leadership.

With these referents of necessity in mind, it is possible to make general
statements about the proportionality of Israel's actions in the 1982 Lebanon
War. If the PLO abstained from its countervalue attacks on northern Israel,
the Israelis could have responded to the pattern of terrorism experienced
during the cease-fire with a resumption of occasional preventive/attrition
attacks on PLO targets in Lebanon. If it appeared that the terrorist attacks
suffered were mainly executed by hardline anti-Arafat elements, Israeli
attacks could concentrate on groups like the PFLP-GC and leave the Fatah
bases alone.

If, as was likely, Arafat would not be able to hold back on artillery and
rocket attacks on Israeli population centers in response to Israeli attacks on
any PLO elements, the necessity would be for resolving the quandary created
by the PLO's conventional countervalue capabilities. A proportionate response would be to escalate counterforce attacks on the PLO's conventional
forces, as the Israelis had been doing in July 1981, and hope that the
northern Israeli population centers could endure the PLO's artillery and
rocket attacks long enough for the Israelis to suppress their sources. But
this might not be realistic, given the experience of July 1981, when the
military thought they were close to winning but the civilians were unwilling
to suffer any longer.

Another proportionate response would be a variation on the Litani Operation, and this seems to have been what was agreed to by Begin's Cabinet.

At this point two issues need to be distinguished. One is the proportionality of Sharon's solution to the dilemma. The other is the way in which he misled Begin and the cabinet as he tried his solution.

There is considerable strategic logic in the Sharon position that another Litani would not suffice and that only a comprehensive campaign that destroyed the PLO would solve Israel's problem. But this is not the concept that Sharon presented to Begin and the Cabinet. He obtained approval for another Litani Operation, intending all along to pursue the goal of a definitive defeat of the PLO. In the process he badly divided the Israeli government, military and people. While he seemed to have been comparatively successful as of August 1982, his ambitious goals were ultimately not achieved. However, with respect at least to the part of Sharon's grand design that envisaged the complete defeat of the PLO, Israel's claim of a self-defense rationale for the 1982 war is plausible for the second version of necessity, namely, removing the PLO's conventional countervalue forces from range of northern Israel, not merely temporarily (as in the Litani Operation) but permanently.

Obviously, if the third version of necessity—the need to remove the PLO as a serious enemy with a base in a country bordering Israel—is accepted, the Israeli invasion could be proportionate.

How were the Israeli claims of necessity and proportionality judged by the members of the international political/legal system? The question has been studied by D. Brian Hufford and Robert Malley in a book of case studies of international "incidents" edited by Professor W. Michael Reisman and Andrew W. Willard.[35] Reisman defines an international incident

> as an overt conflict between two or more actors in the international system.
> It must be perceived as such by other key actors and resolved in some
> nonjudicial fashion. Finally, and of critical importance, its resolution
> must provide some indication of what elites in a variety of effective
> processes consider to be acceptable behavior. Though the incident is
> "resolved" in a factual if not authoritative sense, without the judicial
> imprimatur that routinely indicates law in domestic settings, the incident
> may often be a more reliable indicator of international law than are codes
> or case law.[36]

In a case study of the 1982 Lebanon War, Hufford and Malley present a summary and analysis of reactions to the Israeli self-defense claims. They divide states into those that do not even acknowledge that Israel has self-defense rights vis-à-vis the PLO—e.g., the Soviet Union and other communist states, the Arab and other Third World states—and those that acknowledge Israeli self-defense rights in principle but usually question their invocation in individual cases—e.g. the United States and other Western states and Japan.[37] Their survey is brief but it suffices because the main point is that there was no serious effort to sanction Security Council and individual nations' condemnations of Israel's invasion.

Although Security Council enforcement action with armed force under Article 42 was impossible, any interested state might have justified military intervention as collective self-defense of the PLO and the Syrian forces. The legal situation was, of course, confused, Normally, the collective self-defense would be of Lebanon, but it was not altogether clear that "Lebanon" wanted to be defended against the Israelis as much as it wanted to be free of the PLO and the Syrians. Indeed, there was no clearly defined "Lebanon" or generally accepted Lebanese government. In any event, it was unnecessary to explore such complicated theories of collective self-defense because none of the states denying Israeli legitimacy and self-defense rights volunteered to come to the aid of the PLO and the Syrians.

Perhaps armed intervention was too much to ask. In that case there would still be nonmilitary political and economic sanctions. The Arab states had demonstrated that they could use the oil and other economic "weapons" to punish states that supported or tolerated Israel and its policies. They did not have the practical capability of reviving the oil weapon with the potency it had formerly had, but there was no serious effort to use it or any other economic weapon. Admittedly, they had probably already used up whatever political leverage they possessed relevant to the Arab-Israeli conflict.

That left the United States and other Western states that might have applied political and economic sanctions. The United States, of course, stands apart and alone as Israel's friend, ally and source of indispensable financial and military assistance. The United States's position regarding this war is unclear and controversial. As long as Haig was secretary of state, there was good reason to contend that the United States had given— and continued to give—Israel a "green light." Indeed, as one of my more insightful students observed when we discussed this in class, "The United States gave Israel a green light because it did not give Israel a red light."

When Haig was replaced by George Shultz, it was thought that U.S. policy would be less sympathetic to Israel. In the event, sharply increased U.S. criticism of Israel probably was more the result of Israel's escalation of the fighting in late July 1982 and its coverage by the media. While the United States condemned Israeli military tactics, the Habib mission apparently never altered the firm commitment to evacuating the PLO from Beirut. The American commitment to the Multi-National Force (MNF), originally an American idea, assumed the defeat and evacuation of the PLO to be desirable. Clearly, any UN sanctions against Israel would have been blocked by an American veto.

The other Western states and Japan, as well as some Third World states, maintain good relations with Israel and recognize its need and right to self-defense, but are far less tolerant of Israeli security policies than is the United States. These states regularly condemn Israeli counterterror strategies and reiterate their conviction that Israeli security will only be assured when Palestinian self-determination is achieved. These states could have imposed collective or unilateral political and economic sanctions on Israel to back up their condemnations in the Security Council and official pronouncements. They did not do so.

What did occur, as Hufford and Malley point out, was an evolution of disapproval from grave to more grave. The states that recognized Israel and its security problems disapproved of the invasion when it was characterized as a limited incursion up to 40 kilometers. However, they mitigated their disapproval by accepting the limited incursion as unfortunate but not necessarily disproportionate. When the Israelis besieged Beirut, the disapproval of these states became more severe. When the attacks on the PLO in Beirut became more violent from July 21 on, their disapproval became even more severe. In effect, by their behavior the states disapproving of Israel's invasion tacitly conceded that it was initially proportionate to the necessities of its stated purpose, "Peace For Galilee," but more strongly condemned it as disproportionate when its obvious as well as stated purpose became the definitive defeat of the PLO and its expulsion from Beirut. Still, no serious political or economic pressures were applied by the Western states and Japan.

As Hufford and Malley bring out, these states tacitly accepted the Israeli goal of forcing the PLO armed forces to evacuate Beirut. Indeed, France and Italy contributed troops to the MNF that was to intervene simultaneously with the PLO's evacuation. The upshot was that no one came to the aid of the PLO and Syrians, and no one seriously opposed the Habib plan to evacuate the PLO from Beirut. The Soviets only opposed the MNF for reasons having nothing to do with support of the PLO.

Hufford and Malley conclude:

> The necessity of the Israeli invasion was to some extent legitimated, first by an absence of concrete measures to stop the invasion, then by the implicit acceptance of its rationale. Indeed, by espousing the view that the PLO and Syria were "occupying" forces, certain elites confirmed the necessity of some kind of action. In effect, Israel's presence was perceived as no more illegitimate than that of the other two parties, while possibly creating the opportunity to remove all foreign intervention. But although

the need for the invasion was, at least implicitly, recognized, a limit on the extent of the invasion was activated through application of the norm of proportionality.[38]

If the 1982 Lebanon War "incident" indeed provides an important example of self-defense and the interpretation of "necessity" and "proportion," it leaves a major question unanswered: how to reconcile the accepted end and the condemned means? As Hufford and Malley say, the main Israeli end, expulsion of the PLO from Beirut and most of Lebanon, was accepted—however reluctantly—but the Israeli means were condemned as disproportionate. Yet it is very unlikely that "proportionate" means as widely interpreted by interested states, for example, a limited 40-kilometer Litani-type incursion, would have produced the end that was ultimately accepted.

For those for whom international law is deduced from the resolutions of organizations like the Security Council and the official pronouncements of states, Israel's 1982 Lebanon war was not a permissible exercise of the right of self-defense.[39] For those, including myself, for whom international law is deduced from fundamental principles such as the right of self-defense and state practice as evidenced by patterns of state behavior and expectations, the 1882 Lebanon War was a war that was condemned by resolutions and pronouncements unsupported by sanctions and, therefore, a war that was reluctantly tolerated and whose principal end was accepted.[40] If Hufford and Malley are correct in their judgment that relevant international elites judged Israel's self-defense means to be disproportionate, I would have to reiterate the point that the principal end was accepted, and it could hardly have been achieved without the means employed. There is warrant for finding the means proportionate; justified as legitimate self-defense.

By "means" I understand the overall purpose and scope of the war, not all of the strategies and tactics employed therein. These will be discussed in Chapter 7. Israel's self-defense "means," in the sense of international war-decision law, *jus ad bellum,* have been discussed here from the perspectives of international law. Emphasis has been placed on the practice of states, both in the form of resolutions and pronouncements and of patterns of state practice in terms of behavior and expectations. In Chapter X, I will analyze the war-decision-law issues of reprisals and self-defense from the somewhat different perspectives of just war doctrine.

Notes

1. "Israel and PLO Agree to Cease-Fire," *Washington Post* [hereinafter, *WP*], July 25, 1981, A1, cols. 1–5; A19, cols. 1–3.

2. Ze'ev Schiff and Ehud Ya'ari, *Israel's Lebanon War,* edited and translated by Ina Friedman (New York: Simon & Schuster, 1984), p. 66.

3. Alexander M. Haig, *Caveat* (New York: Macmillan, 1984), pp. 326–27.

4. Ibid., pp. 332–33; Schiff and Ya'ari, *Israel's Lebanon War,* pp. 67–68.

5. Ibid., pp. 43, 71, 233–34, 304. On unrest in the West Bank and Gaza in early 1982, see Chap. 8 below.

6. Haig, *Caveat,* p. 333; Schiff and Ya'ari, *Israel's Lebanon War,* p. 69.

7. Haig, *Caveat,* p. 333.

8. Schiff and Ya'ari, *Israel's Lebanon War,* p. 91.

9. Haig, *Caveat,* p. 333; Schiff and Ya'ari, *Israel's Lebanon War,* p. 91.

10. Haig, *Caveat,* p. 333.

11. Schiff and Ya'ari, *Israel's Lebanon War,* p. 98.

12. Schiff and Ya'ari, *Israel's Lebanon War,* p. 102; Haig, *Caveat,* p. 336.

13. Haig, *Caveat,* p. 333.

14. Blum (Israel), 37 U.N. SCOR (2374th mtg.), p. 27.

15. Ibid.

16. Sir Anthony Parsons (U.K), 37 U.N. SCOR (2374th mtg.), p. 11; Dorr (Ireland), ibid; Orleandrov (Soviet Union), ibid. p. 22.

17. See, e.g., Zaki (Egypt), ibid. (2375th mtg.), pp. 63–65; Pinies (Spain), ibid. (2377th mtg.), p. 4; Ling Qing (China), ibid. (2376th mtg.), p. 22; Nowak (Poland), ibid., p. 31.

18. Abdel Rahman (PLO), ibid. (2374th mtg.), pp. 18–20; Maksoud (League of Arab States), ibid., p. 32.

19. Sir Anthony Parsons (U.K.), ibid. (2374th mtg.), p. 11; Barr de Nauteuil (France), ibid., pp. 34–35; Karran (Guyana), ibid. (2375th mtg.), p. 47; Pinies (Spain), ibid. (2377th mtg.), p. 4.

20. Dorr (Ireland), ibid. (2379th mtg.), p. 6; Scheltema (Netherlands), ibid., pp. 34–35; Thunborg (Sweden), ibid., p. 62.

21. Sir Anthony Parsons (U.K.), ibid. (2379th mtg.), p. 18, citing the EEC's June 13, 1980, Venice Declaration; Thunborg (Sweden), ibid., pp. 63–65; Barre de Nanteuil (France), ibid. (2381st mtg.), p. 7; Meguid (Egypt), ibid. (2384th mtg.), pp. 13–22.

22. Blum (Israel), ibid. (2374th mtg.), p. 27; ibid. (2375th mtg.), pp. 16–17, 33; ibid. (2376th mtg.), p. 11.

23. Blum (Israel), ibid. (2374th mtg.), pp. 28–30; ibid. (2375th mtg.), pp. 21–22, 23–25; ibid. (2376th mtg.), pp. 8–11.

24. Blum (Israel), ibid. (2374th mtg.), pp. 28–30; ibid. (2375th mtg.), pp. 27–30; ibid. (2375th mtg.), pp. 8, 9–10, 12–15, 17; ibid. (2376th mtg.), pp. 11–12.

25. *Resolutions and Decisions of the Security Council 1982* pp. 5–6 (hereinafter cited *UNSC R&D* [year]).

26. See, e.g., Pinies (Spain), 37 U.N. SCOR (2377th mtg.), p. 3; Dorr (Ireland), ibid., p. 11.

27. Mrs. Kirkpatrick (U.S.), ibid. (2377th mtg.), pp. 8–10. See Haig's account of the internal debates within the Reagan Administration over the U.S. vote in *Caveat,* pp. 338–39.

28. 37 U.N. SCOR (2381st mtg.), pp. 8–10.

29. Lichenstein (U.S.), ibid. (2381st mtg.), p. 11.

30. Ibid.

31. Dorr (Ireland), ibid. (2377th mtg.), p. 12; argument repeated, ibid. (2379th mtg.), pp. 7, 82.

32. Blum (Israel), ibid. (2377th mtg.), p. 311; ibid. (2379th mtg.), pp. 58–60, 61.

33. For a searching analysis of the issue of proportionality in the 1982 Lebanon War, see D. Brian Hufford and Robert Malley, "The War in Lebanon: The Waxing and Waning of International Norms," in W. Michael Reisman and Andrew R. Willard, *International Incidents: The Law That Counts in World Politics* (Princeton, N.J.: Princeton University Press, 1988), pp. 144–80.

34. See, e.g., Sean McBride, ed., *Israel in Lebanon: Report of the International Commission to Enquire into Reported Violations of International Laws by Israel During Its Invasion of the Lebanon,* Sean McBride, Chair (London: Ithaca, 1983) [hereinafter, *McBride Report*]; W. Thomas Mallison and Sally V. Mallison, *The Palestine Problem in International Law and World Order* (Essex: Longman, 1986), pp. 291–323.

35. Reisman and Willard, *International Incidents.*

36. W. Michael Reisman, "International Incidents: Introduction to a New Genre of International Law," in Reisman and Willard, *International Incidents,* pp. 15–16.

37. Hufford and Malley, "The War in Lebanon," pp. 164–76.

38. Ibid., p. 180.

39. See *McBride Report,* pp. 1–26; Mallison and Mallison, *The Palestine Problem in International Law and World Order,* pp. 277–323.

40. Dinstein characterizes the 1982 Israeli "incursion" into Lebanon as "extraterritorial law enforcement," "designed to destroy a vast complex of Palestinian bases from which multiple attacks across the international frontier had originated," necessitated by the inability of the Lebanese government to put an end to the "Palestinian military presence." Yoram Dinstein, *War, Aggression and Self-Defence* (Cambridge: Grotius, 1988), p. 226. Dinstein considers "extra-territorial law enforcement (his term) a form of self-defense. Ibid., pp. 225–26.

6

War-conduct Law in
Israeli Counterterror Action

As discussed in Chapters 1 and 2, Israeli counterterror operations include, in addition to passive defense measures, offensive initiatives that almost always occur in a neighboring Arab country or on the sea. To the best of my knowledge, none of these operations has been intentionally countervalue in character, i.e., aimed at almost wholly civilian targets. Consequently, most of the issues of war-conduct law in counterterror operations will be discussed in the context of attacks on targets in which PLO *fedayeen* and civilians were intermingled to a great extent.

The normative evaluation of Israel's counterterror strategies and tactics rests primarily on the two basic principles of military necessity and humanity in which the principles of proportion and discrimination are foremost. In this chapter I will not discuss other principles and prescriptions of the law of war—e.g., regarding treatment of prisoners or of civilians—since they will be treated extensively in discussing the conduct of the 1982 Lebanon War and the occupation of the West Bank and Gaza.

In my normative evaluation of Israel's conduct of counterterror operations, I will employ my concept of *legitimate military necessity* as a comprehensive tool of analysis. Legitimate military necessity requires that the means of war be proportionate to a military objective, discriminate, and limited by the laws of war, subject to the control of a responsible commander and subject to review. This concept includes both the principles of military necessity and humanity as they are generally understood, as well as the prescriptions of the law of war.

Review of actions claimed to be justified by military necessity should be conducted with a belligerent's chain of command by responsible commanders. If actions or patterns of action are sufficiently important, they should be reviewed by responsible political authorities since the military instrument must always be consonant with political policies and subject to civilian control. The military necessity of an action or policy will also be judged by public opinion in the belligerent state, and by public opinion around the world. Theoretically, claims of military necessity are subject to review in international war crimes proceedings, and there are some excellent analyses of such claims in the war crimes trial decisions that followed World War II. However, the political-military circumstances necessary for the conduct of anything like fair international war crimes proceedings have not existed since World War II.[1] On the other hand, alleged violations of the principle of legitimate military necessity have been reviewed in national court martial proceedings, e.g. by the U.S. in Vietnam.[2] Finally, claims of legitimate military necessity are reviewed by the UN Security Council and General Assembly, as well as by regional organizations and private organizations such as Amnesty International.

It is difficult in practice to separate issues of necessity and proportionality from issues of discrimination. By employing the comprehensive principle of legitimate military necessity, this difficulty may be overcome. Moreover, since my own understanding of the principle of discrimination is that collateral damage resulting from belligerent actions must be proportionate to the legitimate military necessity of the action, proportionality and discrimination are inseparable whenever the target is of mixed military/civilian character.

Israel has carried out thousands of counterterror attacks on the PLO. It would take a large contingent of military historians, international lawyers and moralists to evaluate these attacks in terms of their compliance with the standards of legitimate military necessity. I will take a sample of Israeli counterterror operations and evaluate them by the standards of legitimate military necessity. Most of this sample will be taken from cases that were debated in the UN Security Council. This will, of course, mean that there will be some particularly controversial cases in the sample. Moreover, it is already clear from the previous chapter that the Security Council has been extremely critical, not only of Israel's recourse to armed force but of the conduct of its counterterror operations. I will not review every case discussed in the Security Council, only some of those in which particular emphasis was placed on Israel's conduct of operations as distinguished from objections to the fact that Israel had had recourse to armed force.

However, there are good reasons to make use of the cases debated in the Security Council. First, the proceedings of these debates usually provide factual details not easily assembled from other sources. To be sure, alleged facts are themselves controversial and competing versions must be acknowledged. But if this convenient source is utilized with care and balanced, when possible, by other sources, it makes the presentation of case studies more feasible.

Second, although Israel has usually lost its debates in the Security Council, it has had the opportunity to give its own justifications for the actions in question. Independent observers can decide what version of the facts seems most plausible and whether the Israeli justifications or the arguments of those who reject them are more persuasive.

Third, as I have demonstrated in the preceding chapter, I reserve the right to differ with the Security Council in general or its members in particular. I do not consider the war-conduct issues of Israel's counterterror operations to have been definitively and finally decided in the Security Council. I will judge the actions in question and the arguments about their legal permissibility on their merits as I see them. From the evaluations in terms of legitimate military necessity of these cases I will offer some general conclusions about the legal permissibility in general of Israel's conduct of its counterterror war with the PLO.

The starting point in the evaluation of belligerent actions under the principle of legitimate military necessity is the plausibility of the necessity claimed and the proportionality of the means to the military goal. The military end referent to which the means must be proportionate must be made clear from the outset. Much as in the debate over the legal permissibility of counterterror reprisals as self-defense, the proportionality of Israeli counterterror operations to be discussed here have to be seen as part of a pattern of continuing terrorist challenge and counterterror response. Contrary to the general attitude taken in the Security Council, proportionality of Israeli counterterror measures should not be judged simply by comparing the damage done by the most recent terrorist attack with the damage done by a subsequent Israeli counterterror attack. Rather, the proportionality of the Israeli action should be judged in the context of the pattern of recent hostilities.

Delineating this context is, admittedly, an undertaking that can be subjective and controversial, but it must be attempted. The context of recent hostilities represents the middle ground between the Security Council's limitation of the context to the most recent incident and Israel's propensity to look at every action as part of a long war and calculate proportionality in terms of the total context of that long war.

In any war a belligerent's record will be a mixture of actions that conform to or deviate from the standards of legitimate military necessity. An analysis of the legal permissibility of a belligerent's actions must look for a general pattern of conformity to or deviation from those standards. In terms of recent American experience, it makes a difference whether incidents such as the My Lai massacre were, as Secretary of the Army Stanley Resor claimed, aberrational, or whether they were commonplace.

Karameh
March 21, 1968

As discussed in Chapter 2, the battle of Israeli forces with Fatah and other elements of the PLO on March 21, 1968, at Karameh village and refugee camp and the accompanying clashes in a wide area of the East Bank of the Jordan was important to the rising prestige of the PLO. The crushing defeat and loss of the West Bank in the 1967 June War left Jordan bitter and committed to continuing the war with Israel by other than conventional means. This means was increased support of PLO *fedayeen* terror against the Israelis in the West Bank and in Israel. Jordan's policies toward the PLO changed from permissive to overtly supportive.

Arafat's Fatah headquarters was largely moved from Damascus to Jordan. Fatah's main operational headquarters was in Karameh. This was confirmed by the Israeli troops when they attacked and occupied the town.[3] Few inhabitants remained in Karameh.[4] Fatah troops wore camouflage uniforms and were in organized units. To be sure, King Hussein's regime was aware of the dangers of the growing strength and prestige of the PLO, dangers that were finally confronted in September 1970. But at the time of the Karameh battle, the trend was in the direction of substantial Jordanian support for the PLO, principally the Fatah element which was emerging as the leader under Arafat.

The Jordanian forces supplied the PLO units with intelligence. They covered PLO *fedayeen* with artillery and mortar fire when they were launching and withdrawing from terrorist operations. Moreover, by March 1968 the Jordanian forces were increasingly active in independent harassing attacks on both Israeli military and civilian targets, mainly in the form of firing across the Jordan River, for instance, at a jeep on patrol or a tractor in a field.

The extent of the level of terrorist attacks against Israel, now overtly supported by Jordan, is reflected in Israel's complaints to the Security Council prior to the Karameh operation.[5] The Security Council's agenda for the debate on the Karameh raid included Israel's complaint about PLO terrorist attacks and Jordanian complicity in them as well as Jordan's complaint over the Karameh Operation.[6] Israel's Tekoah presented the council, during the debate, updated enumerations of current terrorist attacks and instances of the Jordanian military firing on Israeli military and civilian targets.[7]

The immediate terrorist incident that preceded the Karameh operation was the explosion of a mine under a bus full of schoolchildren on March 18, 1968. The accompanying doctor and another man were killed, and twenty-eight children were injured.[8] The context of this incident was described to the Knesset by Prime Minister Eshkol:

> Lately, the terror organizations have established open bases near the cease-fire line which serve them as training bases from which they cross the border to carry out murder, mining and sabotage acts. From 15 February until last night these gangs carried out thirty-seven acts of sabotage, in which six civilians and soldiers were killed, and forty-four civilians and soldiers wounded.[9]

The fighting at Karameh has been briefly described in Chapter 2.[10] In judging the conformity of the Israeli forces to the principles of legitimate military necessity, it is instructive to compare the Karameh Operation with earlier raids aimed at breaking up local centers of terrorist activity and deterring its recurrence. The Israelis had justified earlier raids in terms of the necessity of breaking up centers of terrorist activity and deterring its recurrence in a particular locality. Israel justified the Karameh Operation on the basis of a much larger goal, namely, destruction of the principal PLO base in Jordan, source of a wide range of terrorist activity all along the Jordan Valley.

It was the intention of the IDF to surround Karameh and kill or capture the bulk of the *fedayeen*. Dayan states that ground mist prevented the timely landing of the troops in helicopters so that many of the *fedayeen,* including Arafat, escaped.[11] As discussed in Chapter 2, the battle was costly in terms of casualties on both sides and damage to Karameh. Was the Israeli operation necessary, proportionate and discriminate?

With the Fatah/PLO terrorist war being waged vigorously, there certainly was a military/security necessity to hit at the source of terrorist activity. In terms of war-conduct law, the means were proportionate to the objective of destroying the major Fatah base. The problem was that the operation did not succeed in achieving its objective completely, and it provided an opportunity for the *fedayeen* to demonstrate their fighting qualities as distinguished from their terrorist accomplishments.

Finally, the issue of discrimination in this case is very different from cases where the PLO forces and civilians were closely intermingled. In the latter there was the difficulty, typical in counterterror/counterguerrilla operations, of collateral damage in a mixed military/civilian target. The Israelis claimed, with persuasive supporting evidence, that Karameh's normal population had largely been displaced by the time of the battle. Visiting journalists had found Karameh to be a bustling military/terrorist base, not an essentially civilian place, in which there was a *fedayeen* presence.[12] It appears that while other Israeli raids hit civilian areas within which there were legitimate military/security targets, Karameh was primarily a major military target which included some remaining noncombatants and civilian targets.

Although the operation conformed to the requirements of the principle of legitimate necessity, Karameh was a disappointing victory for Israel and a defeat from which the PLO in general and Fatah in particular gained prestige and confidence. It was condemned by the Security Council in Resolution 248 of March 24, 1968, which also deplored "all violent incidents in violation of the cease-fire" ending the 1967 June War.[13] Nevertheless, the Karameh battle was followed by intensified Jordanian fire assaults across the Jordan River and continued terrorist activity from Jordan. Jordanian and Israeli complaints made to the Security Council on March 29, 1968, produced no council action except a statement by the council president that the council was "deeply concerned at the deteriorating situation."[14]

Es Salt
August 4, 1968

The period between the March 21, 1968, Karameh Operation and a major Israeli air raid on Fatah's base at the town of Es Salt, roughly midway between Amman and the Allenby Bridge over the Jordan, was one of continued intensive *fedayeen* terrorist attacks in the West Bank and Israel accompanied by Jordanian fire assaults across the river. Israel responded with an increased use of air attacks on Fatah bases. On June 4, 1968, the IAF hit *fedayeen* bases at Irbid. While a Jordanian complaint to the Security Council about a raid on Irbid raid was still pending, the IAF carried out a major preventive/attrition air raid on Fatah bases at Es-Salt on August 4, 1968.

Jordan's Ambassador El-Farra reported Israeli armor attacks in the area adjacent to the Prince Abdullah Bridge and Suamah concurrently with the Es-Salt air raid and claimed that these attacks resulted in the deaths of five persons, including two women and one child and injuries to twenty civilians.[15] El-Farra put the casualties at Es-Salt at "thirty-four Jordanians" killed and "eighty-two Jordanians" wounded.[16]

Renewing charges made in March and April, El-Ferra claimed that Israel was deliberately attacking Jordanian agriculture, notably citrus and banana crops, and had used napalm to destroy banana trees.[17] He also charged the Israelis with deliberately attacking civilians and Red Crescent vehicles.[18]

Israel brought counterclaims and complaints to the Security Council, contending that Jordan had continuously violated the injunction of Security

Council Resolution 248 of March 24, 1968, by continuing to support terrorist attacks (a number of which were described) on Israel and by its own repeated fire attacks across the Jordan River.[19] Israel's Tekoah stated that "the Salt area has become known as the center of terrorist operations."[20] Accordingly, Tekoah reported:

> Yesterday at 1300 hours local time Israeli aircraft took action against the terror bases from which these attacks against Israel emanate. The action was directed against two terrorist bases in the Salt area, including the central headquarters of the El-Fatah organization, stores of ammunition and sabotage equipment, training facilities and barracks. These were the only targets. The town of Salt and the Jordanian army camps in its vicinity remained outside the scope of the action.[21]

Tekoah supported his statement, inter alia, with an account of the raid by an Arab journalist for the *Christian Science Monitor:*

> For nearly four hours on 4 August Israeli jets bombed, strafed, rocketed two large advance training areas of Arab *fedayeen [guerrillas]* south and west of the town of Salt, eighteen miles northwest of Amman.[22]

Basing his calculations on reports of funerals for the victims of the Salt raid, Tekoah accounted for the thirty-four deaths by enumerating twenty-eight Palestinian *fedayeen,* an Iraqi officer, a Jordanian officer and four Jordanian soldiers. None of the dead were Jordanian civilians as claimed by El-Ferra.[23]

The Security Council voted unanimously for Resolution 256 of August 16, 1968, which condemned the Salt raid.[24] The raid was described by U.S. representative George Ball as "excessive and repressive."[25]

I consider the Salt raid to be, indeed, "repressive." It was intended to "repress" the continuing pattern of *fedayeen* terrorist attacks from Jordan and the supporting actions of Jordan. It appears to have been a straightforward counterforce attack which avoided civilian targets. Collateral damage does not appear to have been disproportionate to the legitimate military objective. The raid was conducted in conformity with the principle of legitimate military necessity and was not "excessive" to the requirements of deterrence and defense against a major, continuing terrorist threat.

**Post-Munich Massacre Attacks
September 7–17, 1972**

Israel held Syria, Lebanon and Egypt responsible as "accomplices" in the September 5, 1972, Munich massacre of eleven Israeli Olympic athletes since those countries actively supported Fatah or permitted it and other PLO elements to operate freely in their territories. Two days after the Munich massacre the Israelis began attacking PLO targets in Lebanon and Syria. Two IDF company-strength armor incursions, supported by helicopters, were launched into Lebanon on September 7, 1972. Israel claimed that these operations had begun within Israel in reaction to *fedayeen* infiltration attempts and continued a mile into Lebanese territory.[26]

The IAF carried out simultaneous strikes on 10 PLO bases deep in Lebanon and Syria on September 8. This was the biggest IAF operation since the 1967 June war. An Israeli-Syrian air battle over the Golan on September 9 resulted in the downing of three Syrian aircraft, as there were artillery exchanges between the Israelis, the Lebanese and the Syrians.[27] On September 10 Israeli Chief-of-Staff Elazar stated that the Israeli attacks in Lebanon and Syria were a response not only to the Munich massacre but also to the rising wave of terrorist attacks from Lebanon and Syria. Elazar said that every effort was made to avoid civilian casualties and damage, but pointed out that the terrorist bases were located near civilians.[28]

Syrian forces retaliated for the IAF raids with bazooka fire against the Hussania area of the Golan Heights occupied by Israel.[29] An IDF armored task force crossed the Lebanese border on September 16, 1972, and conducted a search-and-destroy operation against PLO bases in the Ainata area. The purpose of the September 16 operation was to root out terrorists and to persuade Lebanese villagers in the area not to cooperate with them.[30]

The task force penetrated twelve miles into Lebanon, sweeping through more than a dozen villages in three columns. The Israelis destroyed about 130 houses from which PLO fire had been received, at least forty PLO *fedayeen* were killed and twenty PLO *fedayeen* and Lebanese soldiers captured. The IDF stressed that the attack was against the PLO forces, estimated at three to four thousand, not the Lebanese Army.[31] In a radio address, Israeli Chief of Intelligence Chaim Herzog said that it was up to the Lebanese government and people whether Israel would conduct more deep raids into their country.[32] The Israeli force withdrew from Lebanon on September 17, 1972, having encountered heavy resistance that delayed the return of some elements.[33]

On September 20, 1972, Arab sources reported that the PLO, under pressure from the Lebanese Army, had accepted new restrictions on its operations in Lebanon. Arab League General Secretary M. Riad mediated a new understanding between Lebanon and the PLO, the details of which were not disclosed.[34] However, Israel remained skeptical as to Lebanon's ability and willingness to restrain the PLO.[35] Starting October 15, 1972, the IAF hit PLO targets in Lebanon and Syria. Israel stated that these air raids and those that followed were not retaliatory, but the first move in implementing a new policy of initiating action against the PLO in a protracted war against terrorism.[36]

It would appear that, while outrage at the Munich massacre sparked this new phase in Israel's response to PLO terror, the basic strategic requirements of counterterror deterrence/defense called for a change in emphasis from retaliation to preventive/attrition strategies and tactics. Thus the military necessity for these operations was not primarily one of avenging Munich but of seizing the initiative in a continuing war with terrorists operating from the sanctuaries of Lebanon and Syria. The proportionality of the Israeli attacks should be measured in reference to this necessity, not to the Munich massacre. The serious nature of the PLO's position in south Lebanon may be judged from the heavy fighting during the Israeli incursion of September 14–17, 1972.

The proportionality of the Israeli operations of this period must also be judged in relation to the objective of deterring the Lebanese government and the local populations in areas of PLO operations from supporting or tolerating the preparation and initiation of terrorist attacks on Israel. In this regard, the hurried consultations and secret agreements between the Lebanese government and the PLO are significant. The Lebanese government was finding Israeli incursions and air attacks to be "unacceptable damage." Yet, as I remarked in Chapter 2, even at this time, when there was still a more or less effective government in Lebanon, it was not possible for it long to rein in the PLO's terrorist operations against Israel.

Israeli Operations Following
Kiryat Shemona

Reference has been made in Chapters 2 and 4 to the April 11, 1974, terrorist attack at Kiryat Shemona. The brutal killing of eight children, four women and six male civilians by the terrorists naturally aroused demands for effective retaliation. It was in this context that Defense Minister Dayan issued one of the statements of Israeli policy which appears to call for countervalue attacks on locales from which PLO *fedayeen* operate, these attacks being intended to inflict unacceptable damage on the sanctuary states and populations. Such statements were regularly condemned by the Security Council as "threats" of legally impermissible action.[37]

Dayan warned that if Lebanon did not control the PLO, Israel would continue its preventive/attrition raids until all of southern Lebanon was a desert.[38] Restating basic Israeli counterterror deterrence/defense doctrine while commenting on an IDF incursion into Lebanon on the night of April 12–13, Dayan stated:

> It was not revenge. There can be no revenge for what took place in Kiryat Shemona. We did not try to match that disaster, not by the scale nor by the methods. . . .
> Our objectives this time were political, not military. . . . We are trying to explain that we are not the police of Lebanon. Each government is responsible for what is taking place inside its territory. We have no doubt that the Government of Lebanon knows that the three murderers who killed the Israelis in Kiryat Shemona came from the headquarters of the Jibril group in Beirut. . . . The Government of Lebanon knows where to find him and his group of murderers and it is their job to do it.
> We made all the villagers aware that . . . it is their business to go to their government and tell them that they have to take care no terrorists cross the border into Israel. That was the message.[39]

The IDF raids of the night of April 12–13 were directed against several Lebanese villages from which the PLO *fedayeen* had launched their attack against Kiryat Shemona. Houses believed to have had a PLO connection were dynamited, ten of them in Ett Taibe, the village nearest Kiryat Shemona.[40]

This case has two elements: preventive/attrition and deterrence. As preventive attrition the IDF operation attacked the sources of local terrorist attacks. If the Israelis had good intelligence, which is probable, they destroyed houses that had been used by the *fedayeen* in preparing and launching the Kiryat Shemona and other terrorist attacks. By destroying these houses and by sweeping the area, the IDF demonstrated to the local population and to the Lebanese government that Dayan's warning should be taken seriously. The Israelis demonstrated that there would be a price for support and/or acquiescence in PLO terrorist activities.

The Israeli operation was proportionate both to the need to obstruct future PLO terrorist attacks from these villages as well as to the requirement to deter the local populace and the Lebanese government from supporting and/or condoning such attacks. The Israeli operation was discriminate, destroying buildings used by the *fedayeen* for terrorist operations. Of course, there is no way for an outsider to evaluate the accuracy of Israeli intelligence in this or any of the cases of counterterror operations. I assume that it was good and that the houses destroyed could fairly be considered military targets. Civilian casualties appear to have been minimal.

"Preventive" Air Raids
December 2, 1975

As discussed in Chapter 4, IAF air raids of December 5, 1975, on PLO bases located in refugee camps did not appear to be primarily based on specific military/security necessities but were carried out to make a political point. They came in the wake of a series of UN actions designed to support the PLO and to enhance its position in UN debates.[41] The relation of the raids to military/security necessity was very broad. The IDF Spokesman stated "that Israeli planes bombed suspected guerrilla bases in Lebanon as a warning to the Palestinians not to be encouraged by United Nations developments into staging further attacks on Israel."[42]

In contrast to the Israeli actions discussed above, then, the context of the December 2, 1975, raids was not so much one of a substantial accumulation of terrorist activities but, rather, one of diplomatic victories for the PLO. Moreover, the targets attacked reflected, in part, the fact that the raids were designed more to make a political point than to accomplish a military/ security mission demanded by the state of hostilities. One of the target areas hit was near the northern Lebanese border. Although it was part of the PLO network of bases and a plausible military target, it was not closely related to hostilities on the southern border, as, for example, Karameh or Es Salt had been when the war was being waged across the Jordanian-Israeli border.

However, the other main target area was at Nabitiya, a well-known PLO stronghold in southern Lebanon. There was a much clearer military necessity to attack the PLO at Nabitiya. The upshot is that the December 1, 1975, raids appear to be more difficult to justify, in the first place, because their context was more one of PLO political victories than of PLO terrorist attacks and because at least one of the two main target areas was remote from the Israeli border.

In the second place, the December 2, 1975, raids were hard to justify because they caused great civilian damage.

Noting that casualty figures were incomplete because bodies were still in the rubble, Ambassador Ghorra (Lebanon) stated that "a large number of both the Lebanese and Palestinian victims were women and children."[43] The *New York Times* quoted an estimate of the casualties in the raids at 75 killed and 120 wounded.[44]

Was this disproportionate collateral damage, and if so, who was at fault? The PLO's practice of colocating its military/terrorist bases with refugee camps has contributed greatly to civilian casualties and damage throughout the war with Israel. Nevertheless, Israel has an obligation to minimize civilian casualties and damage when it attacks PLO forces in refugee camps and local population centers. In this case it is hard to tell just what damage was done to the PLO and to compare it with the civilian damage.

If we accept the claim of Lebanon that a large part of the damage was to civilians, including women and children, the Israeli raids were rightly condemned as disproportionate to any persuasive military purpose and indiscriminate. All participants in the Security Council debate considered the raids particularly disproportionate and indiscriminate. This included the United States, even though it vetoed a resolution condemning Israel and threatening sanctions because of the failure to condemn PLO terrorism.[45] The raids were criticized in Israel.[46]

My concurrence, in this instance, with the views of Security Council members and the domestic Israeli and foreign critics of the December 2, 1975, raids does not mean that I would confine Israeli counterterror measures to reprisals for recent terrorist attacks. In a continuing war, Israel has the right to hit the PLO with preventive/attrition attacks at times and places of its own choosing. However, those attacks should not be justified simply on the broad claim that any blow that weakens the PLO is permitted. There must be some more concrete military necessity for the Israeli action. In the case of the December 2, 1975 raids, there actually was a plausible rationale for attacking Nabitiya in southern Lebanon in the area from which most PLO terrorist operations were launched. Perhaps the Nabitiya raid should be considered separately from the raid in the north. But even the Nabitiya raid was not linked to a major accumulation of terrorist initiatives at that time—not surprisingly, since the PLO was occupied with the Lebanese civil war.

In my view, the requirement to demonstrate a clear military necessity for an operation is increased when the military target is intermingled with civilian targets. If the PLO can be caught in the open, e.g., in a convoy or maneuvering in open country, its forces are fair game at any time. However, when PLO forces are in bases colocated with civilian centers, a higher military necessity to engage them should be required.

The Litani Operation
March 14–June 13, 1978

The 1978 Litani Operation has been described briefly in Chapter 2. The original purpose of the operation was to create a six mile security zone in Lebanese territory adjacent to the border. Although the operation was triggered by the "Country Club" terrorist attack of March 11, 1978, its purpose was to carry out major preventive/attrition actions that would have long-term effects rather than retaliation. An important constraint in the conduct of the Litani Operation was the Israeli policy of minimizing IDF casualties. This required a conservative tactical approach with emphasis on using overwhelming firepower to suppress enemy strong points. The operation was successful to a degree. Many *fedayeen* were killed, their arsenals, stores and bases destroyed, and the bulk of their forces driven back behind the Litani River.[47] UNIFIL moved into the area, forming a substantial but not impenetrable obstacle to *fedayeen* seeking access to the border. However, as noted in Chapter 2, the Litani operation left the PLO intact as a military/terrorist threat, and the 1982 Lebanon War was in great measure the result of a determination to go beyond Litani's partial successes.

There was a military necessity for the Litani Operation. The context of the operation was a continuing state of hostilities in southern Lebanon which the Lebanese government could not begin to control or even influence. It was a context in which Colonel Saad Haddad's Christian militia continued to fight a desperate battle for survival against the PLO. It was a context in which the south Lebanese Shiites were caught in the middle, bitterly resenting the PLO and the fighting and destruction it had brought to their area. In these circumstances the Israelis decided that instead of a series of limited attacks they would make one large, comprehensive effort to clear the area from which the *fedayeen* had been attacking Israel and the Christian militia.

The strategies and tactics employed were, unfortunately, not always proportionate and discriminate as they should have been, even when the PLO's tactic of mingling with the civilian population is taken into consideration. The IDF's rules of engagement called for minimizing civilian casualties.[48] However, Defense Minister Ezer Weizman was to observe later that "there was too much firing into civilian population centers—even though these were precisely the places where the terrorists were sheltered; in one case, three of our paratroopers were killed while a white flag was hoisted in front of them."[49]

Journalists reported "a path of destruction" in the areas of the fighting. H. D. S. Greenway of the *Washington Post* sums up both the extent of civilian damage and the tactical dilemma of fighting the PLO in population centers:

> The scope and sweep of the damage here makes a mockery of Israeli claims to have staged surgical strikes against Palestinian bases and camps. But, then, such military surgery was never possible, as the Palestinians were deeply entrenched and living among the civilian population.[50]

Michael Walzer, basing his opinion on American press reports, observed that it was

> clear that air power and artillery also were used in ways that turned civilians into targets, killing innocent people and driving thousands from their homes. One hundred thousand refugees, perhaps more: another "success" that no one should want to celebrate. In some areas the Israelis fought well indeed: entering villages to seek out PLO fighters and accepting risks in order to do that, rather than bombarding villages from great distance like the Americans in Vietnam. But mostly they used their fire power, the reflex of a modern army, in what can only be called indiscriminate fashion.[51]

One aspect of the fighting in the Litani Operation that should be kept in mind was that many of the population centers in the area had lost a good part, sometimes most, of their normal civilian populations. Weizman describes al-Him, a village at the end of "the Arafat trail," inhabited solely by PLO *fedayeen*, its inhabitants having fled and their homes looted by the Christian militia.[52]

The conduct of the Litani Operation apparently did not always meet the standards of legitimate military necessity. On the positive side, the major fighting was concentrated in the area from which the PLO waged its terrorist war against Israel and its conventional war against the Christian militia. The Israeli attacks were counterforce in nature and there were efforts to minimize collateral damage, despite the PLO's continued practice of mingling with civilians.

However, the policy of minimizing civilian damage was not always implemented in practice. As remarked several times, modern conventional firepower combined with a policy of minimizing one's military casualties by expending bullets instead of men will lead to excessive collateral damage. The collateral damage caused by the Israelis in the Litani Operation appears to have resembled that caused by the American forces in Vietnam.

Israeli-PLO Hostilities
July 10–14, 1981

The July 1981 Israeli-PLO hostilities followed a series of events described in Chapter 2: the Syrian Missile Crisis, the return of the Sinai to Egypt, the attack on the Iraqi nuclear reactor, and Begin's victory in the June elections. Apparently, Begin thought it was now time to resume preventive/attrition attacks on the PLO and that they were more necessary than ever because of the PLO's conventional build-up.[53] Begin had been asked by Sadat at a June 4, 1981, summit meeting not to resume attacks on the PLO in Lebanon, and although Begin declined to agree, the Israelis had not attacked the PLO since. Meanwhile, the United States had also asked that Israeli not resume attacks while Philip Habib was pursuing his mission to resolve the Syrian missiles in Lebanon issue. However, on July 10, 1981, on the same day that Habib returned to the Middle East, the IAF bombed and strafed PLO "antiaircraft gun emplacements north of the Zaharani River and a convoy of vehicles mounted with Katyusha rocket launchers moving south of the river."[54] Within hours, the PLO rocketed Kiryat Shemona, injuring thirteen people.[55]

The IAF shot down a Syrian MIG that intervened while it was conducting a raid on July 14 on PLO ammunition depots and training bases on the Mediterranean coast south of Damour and near Nabatiya. The PLO reported six *fedayeen* and Lebanese villagers were killed and thirty-five wounded in the raids.[56] On July 15 the PLO responded with heavy rocket attacks on Nahariya and Kiryat Shmona, killing three and wounding thirteen.[57]

The IAF attacked a regional headquarters of the PFLP near Damour, an Arab Liberation Front headquarters south of Sidon, and "training and terrorist departure" bases south of Tyre on July 16, 1981. The IAF also destroyed three bridges used by the PLO over the Zaharani River. Although the raids were termed "preventive" by the Israelis, Deputy Defense Minister Mordechai Zippori, attending a funeral for two victims of the Nahariya rocket attack, warned that the dead Israelis would be "avenged." The preventive rationale for the air raids was expressed by Zippori:

> We knew they were trying to prepare themselves to hit us [with long-range artillery and rockets] and we are trying to prevent that. And I think we prevented many, many operations that would have been carried out if we didn't strike them. But it seems that the lesson wasn't enough and we shall have to deal with them in the future.[58]

Israeli chief of staff Lt. Gen. Raphael Eitan explained that the IAF was now shifting away from direct military objectives and hitting the PLO's infrastructure. He said:

> In the past, we attacked only direct military objectives and not the infrastructure. Now, these attacks will make it ever more difficult to assemble a military force. This is not a final solution. Their ability is being cut down. If this continues, we shall have to think of other ways of attacking them.[59]

In one of the most controversial actions in Israel's long war with the PLO, the IAF attacked Fatah and DFLP headquarters in Beirut in a heavy half-hour air raid on July 17, 1981. These headquarters were located in an area heavily populated by Palestinians, many the families of the *fedayeen*. When one of the bombs skipped off its target, it hit an apartment house that was totally destroyed, killing most of the occupants.[60]

The Lebanese government put the casualties from the raid at 300 dead and 800 wounded.[61] Concurrently with the Beirut raid, the IAF attacked bridges and the coastal highway, which was also hit by Israeli naval fire. These attacks cut off southern Lebanon and causing a severe gasoline shortage, since the main refineries were south of Sidon.[62]

Prime Minister Begin made the decision to make the Beirut attack following the massive katyusha attack on Nahariya. He had promised during the recent elections that he would put an end to rocket and artillery attacks on northern Israel, and there had been increasing indications of popular discontent because of the continuation of the PLO bombardments. Begin declared that Israel had hitherto avoided hitting civilian population centers and directed its attacks only a "military targets of the terrorists." He stated:

> Now, too, we will not intentionally direct our fire against the civilian population. We shall, however, continue to attack terrorist bases and headquarters, even if they are purposefully located in the vicinity of or within civilian concentrations. Responsibility shall fall on those who seek immunity for themselves by knowingly endangering civilians.[63]

The shift to attacks on the PLO's headquarters and infrastructure was justified by Israeli officials and IDF officers as a response to the PLO's new conventional capabilities. The preventive/attrition strategies and tactics developed since 1979 had, by 1981, succeeded in reducing greatly the PLO's infiltrations and terrorist activities, but now the threat of harassing countervalue rocket and artillery attacks was rendering civilian life in northern Israel dangerous.[64]

The U.S. government, which had been about to lift the suspension of deliveries of F16 jet fighter bombers to Israel, the suspension having been imposed in protest against the Israeli attack on the Iraqi nuclear reactor, now decided to continue to hold back the aircraft because of the Beirut bombing.[65]

Major fighting lasted for almost a week after the Beirut air raid. While Israeli commandos, naval forces and aircraft struck PLO bases and infrastructure, the PLO attacked Israeli civilian centers in the north with artillery and rockets. For the first time in Israel recent history, the Israeli civilian population broke and fled.[66] Kiryat Shemona and other towns and settlements in northern Israel became virtual ghost towns.[67] Finally, Israel and the PLO agreed to a cease-fire, announced by Habib, on July 24, 1981.[68]

To evaluate the Israeli conduct of the July 1981 hostilities it is necessary, first, to understand their purpose, since they were initiated by Israel. The purpose of the Israeli attacks on the PLO in Lebanon was to break up the PLO's growing conventional forces. This was to be done in three principal ways:

(1) by attacks on conventional formations and their bases, their arsenals, vehicle pools, and general infrastructure;
(2) by attacks on bridges and roads used by the PLO in moving its forces into position to attack Israel and the Christian militia;
(3) by attacks on the headquarters, general and regional, of Fatah and other PLO elements.

All of these means would be considered reasonable in an ordinary conventional war. In this case, of course, there is a severe problem of meeting the requirements of the principle of legitimate military necessity, since the Israeli actions take place in a country that is not at war with Israel and whose population is drawn into almost every aspect of the hostilities by the tactics of the PLO.

Once again, the principle of legitimate military necessity demands the balancing of the belligerent's right to do what is militarily necessary and his duty to maximize the protection to civilians enjoined by the principle of humanity. This balancing becomes increasingly difficult as one proceeds through the three principal types of actions taken by the Israelis. In attacks on PLO military/terrorist formations and bases priority should be given to military necessity over humanity, although serious efforts to limit collateral damage should be made. However, it seems to me that in destroying bridges and roads which are used by the whole population of the unhappy country in which the hostilities are taking place, considerations of humanity should be given more weight. Finally, when PLO headquarters are attacked, usually in a heavily populated area, respect for the principle of discrimination should have priority over claims of military necessity.

These general observations do not produce obvious judgments in most cases. Each case must be evaluated on its own merits. In my view, the general pattern of Israeli attacks in the first category—namely, on PLO formations and bases—conformed to the requirements of proportion and discrimination demanded by the principle of legitimate military necessity. The targets were important military targets the destruction of which was essential to the purpose of the campaign, i.e., the blunting of the PLO's conventional capabilities. Collateral damage appears to have been proportionate to the important military accomplishments of the Israeli attacks.

With respect to the second category of Israeli attacks there is more doubt. It certainly was a military necessity for Israel to interdict the lines of communication and supply connecting the PLO forces in Beirut and other parts of the country from the *fedayeen* forces being attacked in south Lebanon. However, very considerable damage to Lebanon's road systems and bridges was caused. Petroleum supplies, concentrated in the south, were cut off, causing a gas shortage that affected transportation and communication for the Lebanese. Of course, from the Israeli point of view, these interdiction attacks were more than justified by the need to diminish the PLO's ability to continue its countervalue attacks on northern Israeli population centers.

Ultimately, the permissibility of the Israeli interdiction attacks turns on acceptance of the necessity of restricting the movement of a major conventional military force that was openly using the roads and bridges of Lebanon to get into position to attack Israeli population centers. There is a difference between Lebanon tolerating PLO bases from which *fedayeen* go on terrorist missions with submachine guns and grenades and Lebanon tolerating the passage of convoys of military vehicles mounting rocket launchers or antiaircraft guns proceeding openly over Lebanese roads and bridges. If a government and people permit the latter, destruction of some of their roads and bridges and a gas shortage may not be a disproportionate price to pay.

The July 17, 1981, air raid on Fatah and DFLP headquarters in Beirut was justified by the Israelis on the grounds that the place where terrorist strategies and tactics were conceived and ordered was a legitimate military target. Begin placed responsibility for foreseeable collateral damage on the PLO leaders who located their headquarters in heavily populated areas. I would agree that these headquarters were a legitimate military target that might be attacked if sufficient efforts were made to limit collateral damage. The definition of "sufficient efforts" in practice is difficult. The Israelis claim that the main collateral damage, in the destroyed apartment house, resulted from a bomb "skipping" after it hit its proper target. However, as the United States armed forces have learned in a number of wars and operations such as the attack on Libyan terror bases in 1986, accidents of this kind may be expected.

Whatever the intention of the Israelis, the July 17, 1981, Beirut raid caused civilian damage disproportionate from any known military advantage achieved. The raid was condemned unanimously in the Security Council in S.C. Res. 490 of July 21, 1981.[69] It did not meet the demands of the principle of legitimate military necessity. In their attacks on regional PLO headquarters outside of the Beirut area, it appears that the Israelis did use proportionate and discriminate means despite the problem of colocation of PLO and civilian targets.

Overall, if one excludes the July 17 Beirut raid, the Israeli conduct of hostilities in July 1981 met the standards of legitimate military necessity. While some of the attacks may have pressed the priority of military necessity over humanity to an unacceptable point, the general pattern was of actions that were proportionate to serious military objectives and were reasonably discriminate. This record, it must be observed, is remarkable, given the utterly indiscriminate rocket and artillery attacks by the PLO on population centers in northern Israel.

Air Raid on PLO Headquarters, Tunis

Following the murder of three Israelis in Cyprus by members of the PLO unit "Force 17," and a rise in terrorist activity, the IAF attacked PLO headquarters, which included "Force 17," in Borj Cedria, a suburb of Tunis, on October 1, 1985. Tunisian casualty estimates were of seventy-three killed, including twelve Tunisians, eight of whom were policemen, and hundreds injured. The raid destroyed much of the headquarters and Arafat's personal quarters.[70] As discussed in the preceding chapter, the U.S. abstained from an otherwise unanimous vote for S.C. Res. 573 of October 4, 1985, condemning the raid.[71] The initial reaction of President Reagan had been that the raid was a justifiable self-defense measure.[72]

Defense Minister Rabin claimed that there had been a dramatic increase in PLO terrorism and asserted: "We decided the time was right to deliver a blow to the headquarters of those who make the decisions, plan and carry out terrorist activities."[73] In the Security Council debate, Israel's Netanyahu argued that a state such as Tunisia which permitted its territory to be used as a terrorist base must take the consequences. He claimed that the raid was proportionate to the damage suffered by Israel from terrorists and to the future damage to be prevented.[74]

The context of the Tunis raid was, indeed, one of rising terrorist activity. Shortly after the raid the Achille Lauro maritime hijacking occurred, followed by the massacre of travelers near El Al ticket counters in the Rome and Vienna airports on December 27, 1985. It can be assumed that Israeli intelligence correctly estimated the threat of escalating terrorism. By hitting the main PLO headquarters Israel could cripple the terrorist campaign. PLO headquarters resemble military more than civilian governmental headquarters, although both military and civilian functions are performed at them. Arafat and many of the top PLO leaders have been linked specifically to the conception, planning and implementation of terrorist operations. There is a military necessity for attacking such headquarters. Indeed, there is much to be said for attacking the top of the PLO's chain of command rather than carrying out numerous attacks at lower levels.

The question remains, as in the July 17, 1981, Beirut raid, whether an attack for which there is an important military need can be carried out with reasonable discrimination. In this case, as distinguished from that of Beirut, it seems to me that the PLO headquarters was more removed from a major population center. True, the suburb of Borj Cedria was a civilian target. But it contained a major military target. As a general proposition, it would seem that those who resided in the immediate vicinity of the PLO's headquarters should have known that they were in a dangerous area. It should be noted that most of the fatalities caused by the raid were Palestinians and that the Tunisians killed were mostly policemen.

In this case, as in virtually all others, we confront the problem of judging the effectiveness of deterrent actions as well as of preventive/attrition measures. We grapple with the problem of guessing at what might have occurred had the measures not been taken. Had Israel not bombed PLO headquarters on October 1, 1981, what would have been the pattern of PLO terrorist activity? Certainly it would have been greater. No organization could function as efficiently after such an attack on its headquarters. It can be assumed that the military/security advantage gained by the raid was substantial and that the means were proportionate. They were also comparatively discriminate. Perhaps through successful efforts to limit collateral damage and perhaps in part through luck, compared to the experience on July 17, 1981, the raid on a populated area did not cause the massive damage of the Beirut raid. I conclude that the military objective was legitimate and the means proportionate and discriminate.

Assassination of
Khalil El Wazir/Abu Jihad

The assassination of Khalil El Wazir/Abu Jihad on April 16, 1988, has been described in Chapter 2. Despite Israeli refusal to take responsibility, the evidence is strong that this was an Israeli operation. Was it justified under the principle of legitimate military necessity?

The issue is complicated by the intermingling of political and military character in a person such as Khalil El Wazir/Abu Jihad. A purely political figure—e.g., a treasury minister or the equivalent—is not a military target.

A defense minister might be a military target. A chief executive who, like the President of the United States, is commander-in-chief of the armed forces, might be considered a military target. However, the general practice of belligerents and conventional wisdom has tended to raise a blanket moral presumption against assassination without too much attention to these distinctions. Moreover, in the case of the United States, there is an executive order prohibiting assassination as a means for U.S. policy.[75]

Whatever Khalil El Wazir/Abu Jihad's political functions, he was known by the Israelis as the man responsible for the 1978 Country Club raid and a number of recent terrorist actions, as well as the chief PLO coordinator with the leaders of the *intifada*.[76] In terms of military utility it would make as much sense to kill Abu Jihad, to use his *nom de guerre,* as it would to kill a drug lord in Colombia. Does the principle of humanity provide some overriding normative reason not to do so? That reason could not be supplied by the principle of discrimination because Abu Jihad was a military/terrorist commander organizing and dispatching terrorist operations.

It is my belief that the rationale for the presumption against assassination is more prudential than principled. Both political and military leaders and commanders may feel instinctively that assassination may open a Pandora's box that all leaders and commanders—as well as their wives and families—would regret. An open season on political leaders and military commanders would be profoundly destabilizing. We have the experience of Mafia and other gangster vendettas to instruct us.

In my view, the assassination of Abu Jihad was not violative of the international law of war. He was, by any standard, a combatant in a war fought largely outside the normal belligerent arenas and he died in his home rather than on a battlefield, just as most of the victims of his operations died in noncombat environments. Whether it was prudent to assassinate Abu Jihad, given the possibility of retaliation in kind, is something that the Israelis should have thought about seriously and should think about in the future should they be inclined to take out another PLO terrorist leader.

Israel's Conduct of Counterterror Operations

The foregoing survey of Israeli counterterror operations has included cases wherein disproportionate and indiscriminate means were used. However, in the majority of the cases studied I have concluded that the Israeli actions were reasonably proportionate and discriminate. This general conclusion is, of course, at variance with the consensus in the Security Council debates on these cases. There are, I believe, several reasons for the difference between this consensus and my own view. First, the Security Council members condemned *any* Israeli recourse to force except in passive defense within Israeli territory, and they tended to condemn any particular Israeli action as disproportionate and indiscriminate. Second and very important, the usual referent for proportionality in Security Council debates has been the terrorist act or acts immediately preceding the Israeli measures. I have rejected this approach and taken the recent context of the Israeli action, including the accumulation of terrorist acts and the prospects for their continuation, as the referent for proportionality. Third, the Security Council members routinely condemn any action that causes any civilian damage as indiscriminate. I balance the proportionality between the military necessity of the Israeli action and the collateral damage. Fourth, I acknowledge the requirements of deterrence as well as those of weakening the enemy's capabilities for further attacks. I consider prevention a legitimate referent for proportionality.

Even with this different approach, I find that a number of Israeli counterterror measures have been either clearly disproportionate and indiscriminate or have been borderline. However, my finding in this sample of a number of cases ranging from single actions to prolonged campaigns is that there is a general pattern of compliance with the principle of legitimate military necessity. This judgment reflects a recognition that the task of locating and fighting the PLO is made very difficult by that organization's tactic of intermingling its forces and bases with the civilian population. Were Israel to adopt a more restrictive approach to hostilities with the PLO, sacrificing further the requirements of military necessity for the goals of humanity, it would not be able to engage its forces at all except when they were intercepted in Israel.

Notes

1. United Nations War Crimes Commission, *Law Reports of Trials of War Criminals* (15 vols.; London: United Nations War Crimes Commission/His Majesty's Stationery Office, 1947–49).

2. See Guenter Lewy, *America in Vietnam* (New York: Oxford University Press, 1978), 10, pp. 343–73.

3. Tekoah (Israel), 23 U.N. SCOR (1404th mtg.), pp. 6–7.

4. Tekoah (Israel), ibid. (1404th mtg.), p. 7.

5. Tekoah (Israel), ibid. (1401st mtg.), p. 5.

6. Ibid., p. 1.

7. Tekoah (Israel), ibid., pp. 5–6; ibid. (1407th mtg.), pp. 19–20.

8. Statement of Prime Minister Eshkol, quoted by Tekoah (Israel), ibid. (1401st mtg.), p. 6.

9. Prime Minister Eshkol's statement of March 21, 1968, to the Knesset, quoted by Tekoah (Israel), ibid. (1401st mtg.), p. 6.

10. See Chapter 2 above.

11. Moshe Dayan, *Moshe Dayan: Story of My Life* (New York: William Morrow, 1976) p. 415.

12. See Tekoah's quotation of a *New York Times* account of the return of the *fedayeen* to Karameh: "Karameh camp was swarming today with men carrying Soviet-made machine guns and grenades and voicing pride over the fight they put up yesterday." Tekoah (Israel), 23 U.N. SCOR (1406th mtg.), p. 1.

13. *UNSC R&D, 1968*, pp. 1–2.

14. See 23 U.N. SCOR (1409th–1412th mtgs.).

15. El-Farra (Jordan), ibid. (1434th mtg.), p. 3.

16. Ibid.

17. Ibid., p. 4; ibid. (1434th mtg.), pp. 8–9.

18. Ibid., pp. 3–5.

19. Tekoah (Israel), ibid. (1434th mtg.), pp. 5–9.

20. Tekoah (Israel), ibid., p. 8.

21. Tekoah (Israel), ibid.

22. Quoted by Tekoah (Israel), ibid. (1437th mtg.), p. 10.

23. Tekoah (Israel), ibid.

24. *USNC R&D, 1968*, p. 10.

25. Ball (U.S.), 23 U.N. SCOR (1440th mtg.), p. 2.

26. "Lebanon Is Raided by Israeli Patrol," *New York Times* [hereinafter, *NYT*], September 8, 1972, p. 1, col. 1; p. 12, cols. 1–2.

27. "3 Syrian Planes Downed in Clash with Israelis," *NYT*, September 10, 1972, p. 1, col. 8; p. 16, cols. 1–4.

28. "Top Israeli General Calls Raids Only 'Part of Continuous War,' " *NYT*, September 11, 1972, p. 12, col. 2–3.

29. "Syrians Casual on Israeli Threat," *NYT*, September 14, 1972, p. 12, cols. 2–3.

30. "Israeli Raid into Lebanon Sets off Heavy Fighting, Tanks and Planes Clash," *NYT*, September 17, 1972, p. 1, col. 8; p. 28, cols. 4–6.

31. "Israelis Report That Armored Force Is Holding Ground within Lebanon," *NYT*, September 17, 1972, p. 28, cols. 3–5.

32. Ibid.

33. "An Israeli Briefing on Raid: 'No Looting—I Repeat, No Looting," *NYT*, September 18, 1972, p. 4, cols. 4–8.

34. "Commandos Said to Yield to Beirut," *NYT*, September 21, 1972, p. 17, col. 1; "Lebanese Premier Says the Guerrillas Accept Restrictions," ibid., p. 6, col. 1.

35. See statement of General Aharon Yariv, military intelligence director, "Israeli Military

Aide Says That Lebanon Is 'Not Ready' to Stop Guerrilla Operations in South," *NYT*, September 28, 1972, p. 13, cols. 1–7.

36. "Israel's Planes Strike 5 Targets in Lebanon, Syria," *NYT*, October 16, 1972, p. 1, col.; p. 16; col. 1; "Syrians Hit Twice by Israeli Planes," ibid., October 31, 1972, p. 1, col. 4; p. 10, cols. 4–6.

37. See Chapter 4 above.

38. This warning was cited by Naffah (Lebanon), 29 U.N. SCOR (1766th mtg.), p. 6. See "Dayan Says Raids Against Lebanon Will Be Continued," *NYT*, April 14, 1974, p. 1, col. 8; p. 3, cols. 3–6.

39. Quoted in 29 U.N. SCOR (1766th mtg.), p. 22; "Dayan Says Raids Against Lebanon Will Be Continued."

40. "Israelis Attack Border Villages in Lebanon," *NYT*, April 12, 1974, p. 1, col. 4; p. 3, col. 8.

41. See Chapter 5 above.

42. Quoted by Abdel Meguid (Egypt), 30 U.N. SCOR (1859th mtg.), p. 57.

43. Ibid., p. 46.

44. "Israeli Jets Hit Palestinian Sites in Lebanon Raids," *NYT*, December 3, 1975, p. 1, col. 7.

45. See Moynihan (U.S.), 30 U.N. SCOR (1860th mtg.), pp. 3–5; ibid. (1862d mtg.), pp. 27–32; vote on draft resolution, ibid., p. 63.

46. "A Debate Flares in Israel over Air Raids in Lebanon," *NYT*, December 5, 1975, p. 3, col. 1.

47. Ezer Weizman, *The Battle for Peace* (New York: Bantam, 1981), pp. 276–79.

48. Ibid., p. 272.

49. Ibid., p. 279.

50. "Israel Leaves a Path of Destruction," *Washington Post* [hereinafter, *WP*], March 25, 1978, A1, cols. 4–6; A8, cols. 1–4.

51. "Israel in Lebanon," *New Republic*, April 8, 1978, pp. 17–18.

52. Weizman, *The Battle for Peace*, p. 275.

53. "Israeli Fear of Guerrilla Buildup Triggered Beirut Strike," *WP*, July 25, 1981, A18, cols. 1–6.

54. "Israeli Planes Strike Palestinian Targets in Lebanon," *WP*, July 11, 1981, A17, cols. 1–3.

55. Ibid.

56. "Israelis, in Lebanon Raid, Down Syrian MIG," *WP*, July 15, 1981, A18, cols. 1–4.

57. "Rocket Barrage Kills 3 in Northern Israel," *WP*, July 16, 1981, A20, cols. 1–4.

58. "Israel Bombs PLO Sites, Bridges in Lebanon After Rocket Attacks," *WP*, July 17, 1981, A19, cols. 1–6.

59. Ibid.

60. "Israeli Jets Bomb Beirut; Palestinian Toll Is Heavy," *WP*, July 18, 1981, A1, cols. 4–6; "Begin's Blitz on Beirut," *Newsweek*, July 27, 1981, p. 38.

61. "Begin's Blitz on Beirut."

62. "Israeli Jets Bomb Beirut; Palestine Toll Is Heavy."

63. "Begin Widens Targeting to PLO Sites in Cities," *WP,* July 18, 1981, A1, col. 4; A14, cols. 1–4.

64. Ibid.

65. "U.S. Dismayed by Raid, Delays Decision on F16s," *WP,* July 18, 1981, A1, col. 5, A14, cols. 1–4.

66. Avner Yaniv, *Dilemmas of Security* (New York: Oxford University Press, 1987), pp. 88–89.

67. "Artillery Roars as U.S. Seeks Israeli-Palestinian Truce," *WP,* July 19, 1981, A19, cols. 1–6; "Israel, PLO Trade New Assaults," ibid., July 20, 1981, A1, col. 6; A20, cols. 3–4; "Israeli Ground Units Hit Sites in Lebanon," ibid., July 21, 1981, A1, col. 5; A9, cols. 1–2; "Israel Rejects U.S. Appeals for Cease-Fire with Lebanon," ibid., July 22, 1981, A1, col. 5; A25, cols. 1–2; "Living under Gun Frays Nerves of Those Left in Israeli Border Town," ibid., A23, cols. 3–5; A26, col. 1; "Shelling Heavy across Border," ibid., July 23, 1981, A1, col. 4; A16, cols. 1–2; "Weinberger's Critical Remark Called 'Astonishing' by Begin," ibid., July 24, 1981, cols. 1–2; A17, cols. 1–5.

68. "Israel and PLO Agree to Cease-Fire," *WP,* July 25, 1981, A1, cols. 1–4; A19, cols. 1–3.

69. *UNSC R&D, 1981,* p. 5.

70. "Israeli Planes Attack PLO in Tunis, Killing at Least 30; Raid 'Legitimate,' U.S. Says," *NYT,* October 1, 1985, A1, col. 6; A8, cols. 4–6.

71. *UNSC R&D, 1985,* p. 23.

72. "U.S. Supports Attack, Jordan and Egypt Vow to Press for Peace," *NYT,* October 2, 1985, A1, cols. 4–5; A9, col. 1. See Chapter 4, pp. 106–7, and notes 35–37.

73. "Israel Calls Bombing a Warning to Terrorists," *NYT,* October 1, 1985, A8, cols. 1–3.

74. Netanyahu (Israel), 40 U.N. SCOR (2615th mtg.), pp. 86–87.

75. Executive Order 12333 (December 4, 1981), "U.S. Intelligence Activities," *Weekly Compilation of Presidential Documents* 17 (1981), Part 1, "Conduct of Intelligence Activities," no. 2.11, p. 1346.

76. "Abu Jihad: A Strong Right Arm to Arafat Who Lived by the Sword," *NYT,* April 17, 1988, p. 16, cols. 4–6.

7

War-conduct Law in the
1982 Lebanon War

As in the preceding chapter, Israel's record of war conduct in the 1982 Lebanon War will be evaluated in terms of the principle of legitimate military necessity that requires acts of war to be proportionate to a legitimate military objective, discriminate and in conformity with the principles and prescriptions of the law of war, subject to review. Whereas the evaluation of Israel's conduct of counterterror operations was confined to the issues of proportionality and discrimination, in this chapter it will be necessary to consider, in addition to proportionality and discrimination, issues of particular weapons and means of war, and treatment of prisoners of war and civilians.

The 1982 Lebanon War lasted for almost three months and involved hostilities on a longer and more protracted scale than any other part of Israel's war with the PLO. It was followed by an Israeli occupation of large parts of Lebanon that lasted almost three years. As was the case with the evaluation of the more than twenty-five years of Israeli counterterror actions against the PLO, it is necessary to select typical—as well as controversial—samples of Israeli belligerent practice in order to make some general judgments about Israel's compliance with war-conduct law. I will draw these samples from the different phases of the war excepting those involving hostilities between Israel and the Syrians. I do not believe that there are any distinctive war-conduct issues in those hostilities and there is much to be discussed with regard to the Israeli-PLO hostilities.

For an evaluation of Israel's conduct of the 1982 Lebanon War in terms of the requirements of the principle of legitimate military necessity, I will assess selected cases of combat to determine whether the Israeli actions were proportionate and discriminate. These cases will be drawn from the different phases of the war and include:

(1) assaults on PLO forces in towns or villages;
(2) assaults on fortified PLO refugee camps;

173

(3) the siege of Beirut, including:
  (a) artillery and naval bombardments;
  (b) air raids;
  (c) ground attacks.

In addition to the evaluation of the extent to which the principles of proportion and discrimination were observed in selected Israeli combat actions, I will discuss issues relating to particular weapons or means of warfare, namely:

(1) cluster bombs;
(2) phosphorous;
(3) siege tactics, e.g., denial of electricity, water, food, medical supplies, fuel for medical facilities.

Next I will discuss the treatment of PLO *fedayeen* captured by the Israelis: their status, conditions of incarceration, access to the International Committee of the Red Cross (ICRC).

Finally, I will discuss the treatment of civilians, Lebanese and Palestinian, during the hostilities of 1982. This discussion will include the legal and practical status of the Israeli occupation authorities, military government functions, responsibility of Israel for the activities of Major Haddad's Christian militia, and Israeli responsibility for the Sabra and Shatilla massacres.

Proportion and Discrimination

In the initial days of the 1982 Israeli invasion of Lebanon, the Israeli forces were only engaging the PLO. The hostilities east of the coastal road were not conducted in heavily populated areas. The PLO forces were quickly overcome and there were no particular issues of lack of proportionality and discrimination in the conduct of Israeli operations. These issues are, however, raised in the case of Israeli attacks on fortified Palestinian refugee camps, notably those near Tyre and Sidon. They are also raised in the assault on Sidon itself. Once Beirut was placed under siege, it was inevitable that the issues of proportion and discrimination would become acute. I will examine the conduct of Israeli operations in these difficult battles.

Palestinian Fortified Refugee Camps and the Battle for Sidon

The battles for Palestinian fortified refugee camps are well described by Ze'ev Schiff and Ehud Ya'ari, two of Israel's most distinguished military correspondents, one of whom witnessed the battle for the Ein Hilweh camp as a war correspondent.[1] They observe that well after the Israeli forces had moved beyond Tyre, PLO forces held out in camps—in Rashidya for four days and in Burj Shemali for three and a half. The fortified refugee camps presented a problem in many ways. First, they resembled old towns, with narrow streets and alleys. Second, they were heavily fortified with seventy-four bunkers in Rashidiye and eighty in Burj Shemali. Bunkers and shelters were connected with extensive tunnel systems. Substantial stocks of weapons and munitions, as well as supplies, were stored in the camps.

Above all, the camps presented a problem because they were densely populated by civilians, including many children. The Israelis were committed to minimizing their own casualties but they were also pledged to limit casualties among noncombatants.[2] Faced with determined, sometimes fanatical, resistance by PLO forces, the Israelis could have stood off and leveled the camps and killed everyone in them with their superior firepower. This option was not taken. Instead, the Israelis tried to isolate and subdue portions of the defense, bit by bit, until the whole camp was taken. There was, of course, no way that any fighting at all could be conducted in the camps without major civilian damage. Israel took the time to minimize it.

I will mention only a few camps located near Tyre and Sidon. However, the Israeli tactics in attacking other camps, of which there were many, were similar to those employed in these cases.[3]

As the Israeli forces prepared to attack Tyre and the nearby fortified refugee camps, they warned the civilians in the town and in the camps of the impending attacks and offered them safe passage to the rear of the Israeli lines or to the beach. Before the assault on Tyre the noncombatants were advised by leaflets and loudspeaker announcements that they had two hours to evacuate. Dupuy and Martell, respected American military historians and analysts, observe that these warnings deprived the Israelis of the element of surprise but were motivated by a desire to minimize civilian casualties and to avoid antagonizing the Lebanese people. Dupuy and Martell note that the same warnings were given before the attacks on Sidon and Nabatiya.[4]

Of the battle for the Rashidiye camp Gabriel, another American military historian and analyst, says:

> Fighting was moderately heavy, and the Israeli capture of the camp was more difficult because of their concern for Israeli and civilian casualties. Israeli units had strict instructions not to use satchel charges or even hand grenades when entering buildings. This concern for civilian casualties marked almost all IDF operations throughout the war, especially in the

areas of Tyre and Sidon, where it reduced the speed with which the Israelis were able to overcome enemy opposition.[5]

The slow reduction of the Rashidiya and Berj Shemali camps near Tyre tied up important Israeli assets, but it did not otherwise hamper the advance which had already proceeded north. However, the battle for the Ein Hilweh camp, just east of Sidon, was important to the continuation of the advance. There is little room to by-pass Sidon to the east because of the mountains. The main attack north had to go through Sidon with the Ein Hilweh camp on the attackers' right flank.

On June 7 a battalion of the Golani Brigade attacked Ein Hilweh from the south. The Israelis found that each advance was followed with a return of the PLO defenders to its rear through which succeeding Israeli forces had to fight. Heavy shelling failed to solve the problem and the Israelis withdrew for the night. They resumed the attack on the morning of June 8. This time artillery fire was reinforced with tactical air strikes at PLO positions in the camp as well as in Sidon.

The Israelis then attempted to clear the camp of civilians by dropping leaflets urging them to evacuate. This apparently had little effect. Meanwhile, attempts to break through the main road north through Sidon had also been unsuccessful, despite what Schiff and Ya'ari describe as "generous air support."[6] At this point Colonel Eli Geva's brigade was authorized to try to by-pass Sidon by a difficult road through the mountains to the east, and by the 9th this unit was able to link up with Yaron's force that had made an amphibious landing at the estuary of the Awali River above Sidon on June 6 and had been waiting since for the arrival of link-up forces from the south. However, this precarious route through Druze country was not deemed adequate. The main coastal highway had to be cleared. Sidon and the Ein Hilweh camp had to be taken.

The assault on Sidon, down the main street and one parallel to it, on June 9, was supported by what Schiff and Ya'ri describe as "a merciless artillery bombardment that created a rolling screen of fire" and tactical air strikes against PLO strong points.[7] By afternoon the way through Sidon was open, leaving the Ein Hilweh camp and the Sidon casbah occupied by the PLO forces. It should be mentioned at this point, however, that although the defenders of the camp were PLO troops, the commander was a mullah, Haj Ibrahim, who had taken command when the regular PLO commander, Haj Ismail, had fled. An Islamic fundamentalist, Haj Ibrahim inspired the defenders to desperate resistance.[8]

Recalling that the casbah had been held by the PLO against the Syrians in 1976, the Israelis decided that it would have to be taken by using overwhelming firepower that would destroy much of it. This tactic was successful in three days, with no Israeli casualties.[9]

As the battle for the Ein Hilweh camp continued on June 10, the Israelis captured two mosques north of the camp that had been the source of heavy fire. They were then confronted with a major problem. The next objective that had to be taken because it was a major strong point was the camp hospital. Inside were the medical personnel, the wounded and sick and many civilians seeking refuge there. The Israeli commander tried on five different occasions to effect the evacuation of the hospital, using PLO members and local citizens to explain that the battle for the area was over and that further resistance was suicidal. Mullah Haj Ibrahim rejected all of these overtures.[10]

The Israelis resumed the block-by-block reduction of the camp, capturing the main bunker on June 12. Mopping up continued until June 14, the mullah having met an uncertain fate, when the last defenders in a mosque were killed.[11] Gabriel asserts that "the Israelis took the Ein Hilwe camp with very small loss of civilian life" and that "the number of Israeli casualties . . . was considerably higher than it would have been had the IDF brought its firepower to bear."[12]

The principle of legitimate military necessity requires that a belligerent action be truly necessary for the achievement of a legitimate military end, that it be proportionate to that end, that it be discriminate and that it be otherwise permissible under the laws of war. As a general proposition, it can be said that the military necessity for the Israeli actions against the fortified refugee camps and Sidon was clear, consonant with normal military practice.

Given the missions of the troops involved in the actions just described, there can be no question that, from a military point of view, the Rachidiya fortified refugee camp could not be left alone, deep in the rear of one of the Israelis' main line of advance. The case of military necessity with respect to capturing Sidon, including the casbah, and the Ein Hilweh camp is even more clear. They stood as a bottleneck in the main line of advance and had to be cleared.

If there was a military necessity in each of these cases, were the means employed proportionate and discriminate? The referent for proportionality in each of these cases is the military objective of either protecting the rear of an advance and/or making possible the continuation of the advance. By the standards of modern conventional war, these means were proportionate. However, the Israeli actions obviously caused many civilian casualties and very great civilian damage. Does that mean they were excessively indiscriminate?

I would argue that the Israeli actions were not indiscriminate for two reasons. First, the Israelis had a preconceived policy of limiting civilian casualties and damage in such situations and they attempted to implement it. Specifically, the Israelis attempted repeatedly to separate the civilians from the PLO defenders and to remove them from the combat zone. In so doing they sacrificed the element of surprise. Second, the Israelis turned to use of heavy artillery bombardments and air strikes after first trying to take the objectives with infantry assaults. Third, even when the Israelis brought heavy firepower to bear, they aimed it at clear tactical objectives, moving from strong point to strong point rather than simply leveling the area as they could have. This was done at the expense of considerable delay in getting the troops involved on to their missions in the north. Fourth, the PLO commanders not only deliberately intermingled their troops with civilians, they prevented civilians from accepting offers to evacuate.

Throughout the war there was a continuing battle of civilian casualty estimates. Shortly after the battles for Tyre and Sidon the Lebanese police claimed that 9,583 persons had been killed and 16,608 wounded in the first eleven days of fighting. The Lebanese Red Crescent estimated that 2,000 civilians had been killed in Sidon and was the source of a claim that there were over 10,000 civilian casualties overall.[13] It was some time before the word got around that the head of the Lebanese Red Crescent was Yasir Arafat's brother. The Lebanese Red Crescent also was the source of an estimate of 600,000 displaced persons for whom United Nations relief supplies and assistance were requested. The ICRC estimated 300,000 displaced persons, while the Israeli government estimate was 20,000, mostly Palestinians.[14] Following a denunciation of the ICRC's role in the war by Israeli Health Minister Eleazar Shustak, the ICRC denied responsibility for the figures of 10,000 dead and 600,000 displaced, stating that the only figure it had given so far was for 47 dead and 247 wounded in Tyre.[15]

On June 22, 1982, the Israeli government estimated the overall civilian casualties in the battles for Tyre and Sidon as 460 dead and 450 wounded. An Israeli Foreign Ministry background paper stated that "local sources, such as Lebanese physicians and hospital staff, estimate the dead in the major southern Lebanese towns as follows: Sidon—400, Tyre—50, Nabatiyah—10." The Israelis pointed out that many of the refugees then on the move were returning to southern Lebanese areas from which the PLO had been expelled.[16]

I conclude that Israeli intentions, rules of engagement, conduct of hostilities and the casualty figures are persuasive evidence that the IDF's and IAF's conduct of operations up to the siege of Beirut was consonant with the principle of military necessity in that it was proportionate to legitimate military objective and discriminate and observant of the laws of war.

The Siege of Beirut

The issue of military necessity in the siege of Beirut was more complex than that in the battle for Sidon or the fortified refugee camps. There were, of course, greatly differing opinions as to what the Israeli forces should do once they reached Beirut. However, hardly anyone aspired to capture Beirut. Indeed, many responsible Israelis opposed attacking it in any way. The reason the IDF was encircling Beirut was to force the evacuation of the PLO, not only of its fighting forces but of its headquarters. The dilemma was to find means of coercion and/or persuasion that would effect this purpose.

The Israelis were in a "fight and negotiate" situation. They needed enough military coercion to support a diplomacy, carried on by American envoy Philip Habib, that would achieve the purpose of forcing the PLO's evacuation from Beirut. The military necessity, then, was not a straightforward necessity to destroy the enemy forces or to gain territory, but to provide an effective, appropriate form of coercion in support of Habib's diplomatic negotiations.

The two principal figures in this "fight and negotiate" process, Habib and Sharon, were about as ill-matched as possible. Habib was a dove who deplored the use of armed force and who had bitterly opposed Israeli use of armed force in the past and in the present war. Sharon was a super-hawk who believed that the solution to any security problem was to demolish the enemy. Moreover, Habib was an American, undertaking to negotiate on behalf of Israel. Sharon was an Israeli, often suspicious of his own country-men when it came to security policies and particularly suspicious of an American dove.

The "fight" and "negotiate" elements in such situations need to be coordinated and mutually supporting. Too much or too little of the wrong kind of either element can negate the other. Thus the proportionality of a measure of the "fight element" should be judged in terms of the referent of success in the diplomatic quest. This kind of situation accentuates the limited war principle, espoused by Clausewitz and many other strategists, that the military instrument must always be subordinate to and in the service of the political instrument of policy.

In the war against terrorism, the Israelis had sought to threaten and deliver unacceptable damage on the PLO and those that supported its war against Israel. In this phase of that war, the Israelis sought to inflict unacceptable damage on the PLO holding out in Beirut. This necessarily meant, also, unacceptable damage on the city that the PLO had declared to be its Stalingrad. No military necessity justified unlimited damage either to the PLO or Beirut. The necessity was for enough damage to persuade the PLO to get out.

From June 14 to 25 the Israeli forces encircling Beirut subjected the PLO to artillery bombardments and air attacks. The PLO responded with artillery, rocket and mortar fire. There were also constant exchanges of small arms fire. On June 25 Habib protested strongly to Washington that Israeli attacks on the PLO and the consequent PLO return fire made negotiations impossible. The Lebanese government was near collapse and without it there was no intermediary with the PLO. Secretary of State Haig persuaded the Israelis to cut back on air and artillery attacks, but fighting still continued within a mile and half of the presidential palace. At U.S. insistence a cease-fire was arranged, permitting Lebanese negotiators to move in safety. Israel discontinued its air attacks altogether and did not resume them until July 21.[17]

In the ensuing period there were many breaches of the cease-fire, but the level of hostile interaction was limited. At this time the Israelis conducted intensive psychological warfare operations with leaflets, loudspeakers and radio announcements, and mock bombing runs, warning the inhabitants of Beirut that they should leave the city to escape the fighting. Water and electricity were cut off on July 5,[18] but restored at President Reagan's insistence on July 7.[19] Artillery, rocket and gunboat attacks on PLO positions continued, leading to intense duels on July 9 in which the PLO employed 130 mm. guns and katyusha rockets. After Israeli probes around the airport met with strong PLO resistance on July 11, a cease-fire went into effect and held until July 21.[20] During this time delivery of food supplies to West Beirut was blocked, only an occasional delivery by the Red Cross being permitted.[21]

At this point it is important to recognize that Israel's objective of forcing the PLO to evacuate Beirut had been accepted by the United States and was the goal of Habib's diplomacy. In instructions sent to Habib on June 28, the U.S. sought the following:

(1) a cease-fire in place;
(2) evacuation of all PLO leaders and troops, carrying only their personal weapons;
(3) adjustment of Israeli lines after an agreement was reached and implementation was in progress;

(4) assumption of control by the Lebanese Army, with factional forces surrendering their arms to the Army;

(5) eventual withdrawal of all foreign forces—Israeli, Syrian, PLO—from Lebanon.[22]

These objectives were announced by President Reagan in a news conference on June 30, 1982. In his statement Reagan conceded that Israel had not promised not to enter Beirut.[23]

To reiterate, then, the main objective of the siege of Beirut was to force the evacuation of the PLO, following which the other objectives would be pursued. As of the lull in the fighting between June 27 and July 21, what were the prospects for achieving the main objective of the campaign?

There are varying accounts of the progress of Habib's diplomacy. Rashid Khalidi states that Arafat delivered a signed note to Lebanese Premier Shafiq el-Wazzan on July 2 in which he agreed to evacuation, confirming earlier oral assurances to this effect.[24] (It had been reported on June 28 that the PLO had "reached a formal agreement 'in principle' with the Lebanese government to leave Lebanon with most of their guerrillas and sent the accord through U.S. diplomatic channels to Israel for a response.")[25] However, there were a number of obstacles to an evacuation agreement. One was to find countries that would accept the departing PLO forces; Arab states were not forthcoming at first.

Another was the inadequate Lebanese Army, which, it became clear, could not handle the responsibilities suggested for it. Accordingly, some kind of multinational force would be necessary and it took time to obtain agreement on the character, mandate and timing of arrival of the multinational force. These problems were important because both sides insisted on security guarantees, the Israelis that the PLO would pull out entirely and the PLO that the Palestinians left behind would be protected from the Israelis and hostile Lebanese elements. Finally, throughout the negotiations the PLO attempted to exact some concessions for leaving, such as, recognition by the United States, permission to retain a purely political presence in Beirut.

It is important to understand these issues in order to judge the proportionality of the military measure taken by Israel, beginning July 22. Two broad versions of the situation were plausible. One was that Arafat had already accepted evacuation in principle and was simply trying to salvage the best terms possible, including the perfectly reasonable provision for the protection of the Palestinian civilians to be left in the areas occupied by the Israelis. The other was that Arafat had not truly accepted the inevitability of evacuation and was stalling.

If the first version was essentially accurate, little if any further military coercion was needed. What was needed was continuation of the diplomatic process to work out the details necessary to effect the evacuation and, in time, to pursue the other objectives. If the second version of the situation was valid, the "negotiate" element needed some more "fight" element in order to push Arafat over the threshold of full acceptance of the inevitability of evacuation.

Sharon, as might be expected, believed the second version of the situation. Moreover, the PLO contributed mightily to his conviction that the PLO had not given up hope of surviving its predicament. At this time the PLO elements in Syrian-controlled areas of the Bekaa Valley infiltrated the Israeli lines and carried out small guerrilla attacks. PLO forces also managed to get close enough to the Israeli border to launch katyusha rocket attacks on towns in northern Galilee, thus mocking Begin's claim that this campaign would free Galilee of the threat of such attacks.[26]

The Israelis responded to these new PLO attacks with what they termed "disproportionate force."[27] Israeli air attacks, explicitly linked to the July 21 PLO attacks on Israel, were resumed against PLO positions in Beirut on July 22. Concurrently, the IAF hit PLO and Syrian positions in the Syrian-controlled area. Israel was back to the policy of attempting to deter terrorist attacks by preventive/attrition strikes at their source.

Israeli air attacks against the PLO entrenched in Beirut continued from July 22 through 30 when a cease-fire that lasted until the 31st began. Dupuy and Martell describe the targets in these attacks as "ammunition dumps, troop concentrations, and command headquarters."[28] The air raids were preceded and followed by artillery, tank, heavy machine gun and light arms fire. Collateral damage was heavy.

Israeli armor was massed at the Beirut crossing points on the Green Line separating East from West Beirut on August 2. The PLO was entrenched in the southern part of West Beirut. The Israelis crossed the Green Line on August 4 but soon bogged down, taking heavy casualties in city fighting. Despite protests by President Reagan, who claimed that the Israelis had promised not to enter West Beirut and that the Habib negotiations were being endangered at a critical point, the Israelis maintained their positions.[29] There was little fighting on August 5. On August 6 it was announced that negotiations had been completed for the PLO's evacuation. There was no significant ground action but "two Israeli aircraft demolished two apartment buildings housing PLO arms caches; unfortunately, a number of civilians were killed in the attack."[30]

Rashid Khalidi states that the escalating Israeli military pressures and the collapse of hopes for help through Arab diplomacy "meant that the PLO had little alternative but to accept the hated Habib plan."[31] Khalidi places the PLO's decision to leave in the last three days of July. He says, "By the end of July, however, the PLO had already presented Habib and the Lebanese government with a working paper including a timetable for withdrawal. This is the first concrete indication that it had accepted the approach that had been pushed by Philip Habib since mid-June."[32]

After a lull, the IAF attacked the PLO in Beirut and behind the Syrian lines inland on August 9. On August 10 the Israeli government accepted the Habib plan in principle while Israeli air, naval and artillery forces attacked the PLO camps south of Beirut.[33] On August 11, as negotiations continued, the Israelis continued air, sea and artillery attacks, resumed on August 9, on PLO positions and moved an armored unit north of Beirut to block any attempt to reinforce the PLO from Tripoli, where 10,000 PLO and Syrian troops were stationed. The air strikes and bombardment were concentrated against the "southern Palestinian-inhabited suburbs and refugee camps."[34] Schiff and Ya'ri state: "These blows were conceived as the 'softening-up' stage prior to a ground assault as well as a way of forcing Arafat to climb down a few notches in his terms for an evacuation accord—though Sharon still thought it preferable to take the city."[35]

On August 12, 1982, in the most controversial operation of the war, the Israelis unleashed a massive aerial bombardment against the PLO in Beirut that lasted from 6:00 a.m. to 5:30 p.m. Most of the 128 dead and 400 wounded were civilians.[36] Although the targets were PLO positions, the collateral damage was very great. President Reagan protested vehemently in phone calls to Begin. Reagan brushed aside Begin's claim that the attacks of August 12 were in retaliation for numerous PLO breaches of the ceasefire, terming them "totally out of proportion," causing "more needless destruction and bloodshed," and "unfathomable and senseless."[37] Begin and his Cabinet were shocked and rescinded Sharon's authority to direct the war without prior authorization.

The collateral damage inflicted on Beirut by the massive August 12, 1982, air attacks has been the subject of great controversy. The figure of 128 dead and 400 wounded I have given above is that given by Gabriel. He wrote his book with extensive cooperation from the Israeli government and, although he does not indicate his sources for his figures, I assume that they are from the Israeli government. Schiff and Ya'ari say that "unofficial statistics counted 300 people dead in West Beirut."[38] They say that on August 12, when "it was clear that an agreement on the evacuation was finally within reach," Sharon, "contrary to any scrutable logic, ordered the air force to mount its fiercest attack on the city to date." Schiff and Ya'ari describe "Black Thursday" as "a nightmare in which the saturation bombing came on top of a massive artillery barrage that began at dawn and continued throughout the eleven hours of the air raid."[39]

Gabriel, who says that the massive aerial bombardment was "inexplicable," states that "the major targets of this staggering air, artillery, and naval bombardment were the PLO camps and their military positions in West Beirut and all areas south of the Corniche Masraa." He adds that "undoubtedly by accident, even hospitals were hit."[40]

As against the near-universal condemnation of the air attacks and bombardments of August 12, 1981, by President Reagan and the American government, the UN Security Council, most governments around the world, the world media, which was heavily represented in Beirut, and even Begin and the Israeli Cabinet, there is a dissenting opinion from the experienced military historians and former American combat officers Dupuy and Martell. At this point it should be emphasized that their dissenting view is not so much based on an opinion as to the purpose of the raids and bombardments of August 12 as on their eye-witness view and appraisal of their actual volume. Dupuy and Martell state: "While probably the most extensive Israeli bombardment to date, its intensity was highly exaggerated by press, radio and television reports."[41]

Dupuy and Martell were in Lebanon gathering material for their book on the war. They spent five hours observing the air raids and bombardments of Beirut from a number of vantage points. They devote over three pages to a critique of the media reports of the Israeli attacks, pointing out that the numbers of bombs that were said to have been dropped and the damage inflicted were greatly exaggerated. Indeed, they show that it would have been technically next to impossible for the full Israeli Air Force at maximum strength to drop the number of bombs claimed in reports by BBC radio, the *International Herald Tribune,* the Washington *Post* and other newspapers, radio and television networks.[42] Granting that the day-long ordeal was understandably frightening to civilians, Dupuy and Martell conclude that "to any veteran soldier who had been under air or artillery attack in a combat situation, as the authors had been earlier in their lives, this was a relatively modest bombardment."[43]

After August 12 the Israelis relaxed their military pressure and on August 19 they agreed to the Habib plan for the withdrawal of the PLO, starting August 21 on the arrival of a multinational force (MNF). The evacuation was completed on September 1, ahead of schedule. The evacuees were: 8,144 PLO *fedayeen,* 2,651 PLA members, 3,603 Syrian soldiers, and 664 women and children.[44]

The *Middle East Contemporary Survey* gives the following military casualty figures for the 1982 Lebanon War:

PLO: c. 1,000 killed; over 7,000 captured.
Syria: hundreds killed, c. 1,500 wounded; 294 captured.
Israel: 344 killed; 2,108 wounded; 3 PWs with Syrians; 5 missing in action[45] (some captured by the PLO were killed).[46]

The *Middle East Contemporary Survey* cites figures from an *al-Nahar* survey of Lebanese police and hospital records as follows:

17,825 killed; 30,203 wounded.
2,513 civilians and 9,797 combatants (PLO, Syrians, Lebanese) killed outside of the Beirut area.
5,515 killed in the Beirut area—no breakdown between military and civilian casualties.[47]

It will be noticed that the total number of Arab combatants listed by Lebanese sources as killed far exceeds the total estimated by the *Middle East Contemporary Survey*. Probably the same is true of civilian casualties.

Gabriel has made a serious study of the casualties in the 1982 Lebanon War. He points out that neither Lebanon nor Israel has provided estimates of the casualties in the siege of Beirut. By subtracting estimated casualties from hostilities outside of Beirut, he comes to a figure of civilian casualties in Beirut of 10,000–12,000 dead. He adds that at least 80 percent of the wounded were civilians. Indeed, Gabriel considers the PLO's casualties in the Beirut siege not to have been very high, e.g., 1,000. It should be noted that he estimates PLO fatal casualties in the fighting outside Beirut at 1,400, whereas the *Middle East Contemporary Survey* estimate was 1,000 total for the war. Gabriel's estimates were published later, based on extensive inquiries, including with the Israeli government and military. When Gabriel proposed the figure of 10,000–12,000 civilian fatalities in the siege, the consensus of those whom he consulted—a wide range from many perspectives—was that it was too high, that 4,000–5,000 civilian fatalities was more likely accurate.[48]

Since the issue of proportionality turns on the alleged necessity of military operations, it is necessary to evaluate the proportionality of Israeli actions in the light of Israeli objectives and in the context of the fight and negotiate situation of the Beirut siege. Several phases in that siege seem apparent:

(1) June 10–26: the fighting as Beirut was encircled;
(2) June 27–July 22: Israeli abstention from air attacks on Beirut;
(3) July 22–August 6: heavy Israeli air and ground attacks concurrently with intensive diplomatic negotiations;
(4) August 7–8: lull as diplomatic breakthrough is anticipated; Israeli acceptance of Habib plan pending;
(5) August 9–11: Israel accepts Habib plan on August 9 but continues attacks;
(6) August 12: massive Israeli bombardment.

It seems to me that the proportionality of Israeli actions has to be judged in the light of the probability of success of the Habib negotiations to force the evacuation of the PLO from Beirut. Somewhere in the first phase, June 10–26, disproportionate force was employed. The object of belligerent action was not to destroy the enemy but to support the negotiations with coercive force. When the Israeli force and the reaction to it produced conditions in which the diplomats literally could not meet and communicate it was counterproductive to the fight and negotiate enterprise. This was acknowledged, apparently, when Israel, under American prodding, discontinued aerial attacks after June 25.

During this phase, however, it appears that, on balance, the Israeli attacks were discriminate. I find no evidence of direct intentional attacks on civilian targets. As always, there may have been unintentional attacks on civilian targets. The Israelis were in positions from which they could spot targets and observe artillery fire and air strikes. Their attacks seem to have been counterforce in character. The fact that the PLO had deliberately dug in in a city made considerable collateral damage inevitable. The Israelis attempted to mitigate collateral damage by urging the civilians to leave the combat zone.

The next phase of the siege, June 27–July 22, can be broken down into several subphases. It constitutes a single phase in the sense that it was a period of Israeli abstention from air attacks. However, if one breaks down the phases of the siege in terms of the progress of negotiations, there are several possible thresholds. One might be July 3, when Arafat allegedly promised Lebanon's Premier Wazzan that the PLO would leave. However, this left many controversial issues to be worked out. At this point reasonable people could differ in their evaluation of Arafat's intentions. He may have been genuinely reconciled to evacuation and only trying to salvage some concessions, or he may have intended to stall indefinitely.

If one took the more optimistic view, a comparative lull in hostilities, if not a complete cease-fire, was the appropriate military posture. If one doubted Arafat's acceptance of evacuation, there would be a case for more military coercion. Indeed, it could be argued that the abstention from air attacks had deprived the "negotiate" element of sufficient "fight."

Clearly, Sharon was of the latter view. It would be easy to dismiss Sharon's belief that Arafat was stalling, given Sharon's affinity for forceful measures. However, only Arafat and those close to him would know what his intentions were in early July. There were still hopes that the Arab states and/or the French would come up with something to alleviate his predicament.[49]

The resumption of air attacks against the PLO on July 22 coincided with the air raids in the Bekaa Valley responding to PLO provocations in the south. One could argue that the PLO terrorist and guerrilla attacks in south Lebanon and even against Israeli targets were evidence that the PLO was not reconciled to evacuation. However, it seems likely that the Israelis would have resumed air attacks on Beirut in any event, since negotiations did not seem to be moving very well, a good nineteen days after the July 3 Arafat commitment to Wazzan.

I would give the benefit of the doubt to an Israeli belief that the negotiations needed to be supported by more military coercion and accord a presumption of proportionality to the renewed air raids and ground attacks after July 22. However, the estimates of the situation and consequent analyses of Israeli actions become particularly difficult as the war continues into August. At some point at the end of July or beginning of August, it appears, Arafat really did accept the inevitability of evacuation and the fact that some of the concessions he had sought—e.g., U.S. recognition, continued political presence in Beirut—were not going to be granted. He was now down to bargaining on issues having to do with the actual evacuation, e.g., would the multinational force arrive before, during or after the beginning of the evacuation.

As of early August, then, the necessity to support negotiations with military coercion would seem to be less than it had been on July 22. Accordingly, the massing of Israeli armor at the Green Line separating East and West Beirut on August 2 and the advance into West Beirut on August 4 were inappropriate forms of military coercion, given the apparent proximity of an evacuation agreement. After the announcement that the PLO had accepted the Habib plan on August 6 and that Israeli acceptance (which came on the 10th) was pending, there was no sufficient reason for further attacks, but they continued on August 9–11. Additionally, the IDF moved to the north to block reinforcements from Tripoli. It is difficult to justify any further attacks against the PLO in Beirut after August 6—if their purpose was to support negotiations to secure evacuation.

Two other rationales may be suggested for the Israeli attacks after August

6. One would be that Sharon and his generals did not trust the PLO and wanted to make sure that they did not try to stall in some way. This is a plausible rationale, but given the advanced stage of the negotiations not very convincing. Another, quite different, rationale would be that Sharon had not given up the idea of administering a really decisive defeat to the PLO, that he was not satisfied with a negotiated evacuation, that time was running out on his war to crush the PLO and that he wanted to try one last time to defeat it definitively before he had to step back and watch the PLO leave Beirut. I believe that some combination of these two rationales underlay the Israeli attacks following announcement of the PLO's acceptance of the Habib plan on August 6.

Accordingly, I must judge the Israeli attacks after August 6 to have been disproportionate to the principal objective of forcing the PLO to evacuate Beirut because that objective was essentially achieved. It might be possible to justify these attacks as insurance against last-minute changes of heart in the PLO, but this is a borderline justification. Thus, on August 6 a report from Beirut stated: "The latest heavy exchange of fire came amid mounting skepticism here among Israeli military officials and their Christian Phalangist allies that the besieged guerrillas would ever agree to withdraw peacefully from their West Beirut stronghold without a tangible political prize in return."[50] If the real purpose was simply to inflict more damage on the PLO, these attacks were not justified, given the fact that it was practically impossible to inflict damage on the PLO, which had accepted evacuation, without inflicting more damage on Beirut.

It is difficult to judge the extent to which the Israeli air strikes and bombardments after August 6 were discriminate. It appears that the air strikes more frequently hit targets in the northern part of West Beirut, beyond the main concentration of PLO forces. This may have been justified since the PLO also had headquarters and logistical facilities in the heart of Beirut. For example, on August 6 Jonathan Randal reported that "during an intense, 45-minute air assault, an Israeli warplane destroyed a six-story apartment building that housed a Palestinian guerrilla operations room."[51] Estimates of civilian deaths, including many women and children, ranged from 10 to 250. Randall reported: "The air strike hit the heart of besieged West Beirut, about 100 yards from the office of Prime Minister Shafig Wazzan, who was absent, and about 200 yards away from where this correspondent was standing."[52] An operations room is a prime military target. The PLO placed it in the heart of Beirut, close to the prime minister's office. The presumption should be that the collateral damage should be blamed on the PLO, not the Israelis.

It is virtually impossible to distinguish between the Israelis' duty to minimize collateral damage in operations against an enemy entrenched in a major city and the PLO's duty not to endanger the civilians and their property by operating from their midst. That being the case, I would fall back on the issue of the necessity of the Israeli actions. If there was a plausible military necessity for it, as I think there was for the attacks from July 22 through August 6, and there was evidence of Israeli efforts to minimize collateral damage, I would justify the Israeli attacks as being sufficiently discriminate and censure the PLO for using the city of Beirut as a screen. However, if there was not a compelling military necessity for Israeli attacks, as I tend to believe there was not after August 6, I would consider the collateral damage inflicted excessive.

The Israeli air strikes and bombardments of August 12 should be considered separately from those that preceded them. If there is a plausible argument in favor of the attacks from August 6–11 on the grounds of, in effect, nailing down the reluctant PLO's acceptance of the evacuation without stalling, there appears to be no justification on those grounds for the attacks of August 12. Lacking a plausible necessity, these attacks were disproportionate and excessively indiscriminate. I make this judgment cognizant of the fact that media reports and the reactions of President Reagan and other political leaders may have been exaggerated, bearing in mind the evaluation by Dupuy and Martell.[53] Had the attacks of August 12 been carried out pursuant to a legitimate military necessity, I would be inclined to justify them as proportionate and sufficiently discriminate. What condemns them, then, is the fact that they were not a means to the primary end of the campaign, the expulsion of the PLO from Beirut, since that end was sufficiently assured by August 12. If, indeed, the PLO had subsequently stalled or reneged, Israeli military pressure could legitimately have been resumed.

Overall, I believe that military coercion of approximately the kind applied by Israel was essential to the success of Habib's efforts to persuade the PLO to evacuate Beirut. The thresholds between too little, just enough and too much military force are very hard to fix. It is quite possible that more military pressure, e.g., between June 25 and July 22, might have brought an earlier conclusion to the battle. Indeed, despite my doubts about the post–August 6 Israeli attacks, it is possible that they prevented Arafat from changing his mind or stalling. What I do not justify are attacks on the PLO at great cost to Beirut after the main object of the campaign was reasonably assured.

Most of what has been written or reported on television and radio about Israel's conduct of its Lebanon War condemns it as disproportionate and indiscriminate.[54] A private "International Commission" of international lawyers from several countries, chaired by Sean McBride, investigated "reported violations of International Law by Israel during its invasion of the Lebanon," and concluded that Israel was guilty of disproportionate and indiscriminate use of armed force, a charge seconded by the Mallisons.[55] In contrast, Dupuy and Martell conclude:

> As military historians we can think of no war in which greater military advantages were gained in combat in densely populated areas at such a small cost in civilian lives lost and property damaged. And this despite the PLO's deliberate emplacement of weapons in civilian communities, and in and around hospitals, in violation of those provisions of the Geneva Convention regarding obligations to locate weapons and military installations so as to endanger civilians and populated communities least.[56]

Bombardment of and Intrusions in Medical Facilities

Ordinarily, a war-conduct evaluation would devote a separate section to the record with respect to the medical services for the wounded and sick protected by the First Geneva Convention of 1949. However, it appears that whatever medical facilities the PLO had were intermingled with the much greater facilities of the Lebanese civilian sector. Any attacks on or interference with the civilian medical facilities could constitute a double dereliction in that it would violate the principles both of noncombatant and medical personnel immunities.

In books, reports and journalistic accounts of the 1982 Lebanon War there have been charges that there were widespread instances of Israeli bombardments of hospitals and clinics and that there were also many instances where the Israelis interfered with medical personnel and, in some cases, detained them.[57] Israel answered with charges that the PLO deliberately used medical facilities to store munitions and war material and even to serve as combat positions.[58] It is sad but true that in every modern war when heavy firepower and air strikes are employed, hospitals and other medical facilities are hit. It is difficult to imagine that the belligerents deliberately waste their assets on such targets.

If the Israelis were aware of the nature of their targets, attacks on hospitals would constitute grave breaches of 1949 Geneva Conventions I and IV as well as the principle of discrimination. If they were misinformed about the nature of the target—for example, informed that the PLO was using the hospital for combat purposes—there might be some excuse for the attacks. It is conceivable that the Israeli attacks, aimed at military targets, hit hospitals by mistake. In any event, from a political/psychological point of view, attacks on hospitals always bring widespread condemnations highly damaging to a belligerent's reputation.

The broader issue is difficult to address. Were the instances of Israeli bombardment of hospitals and violent interference with medical personnel so numerous as to form a pattern of deliberate violation of the immunities of those places and personnel? Were the instances of bombardment of medical facilities largely due to the PLO's practice of using them for their own purposes? Was bombardment of hospitals mainly an unfortunate but natural by-product of the use of heavy firepower against forces entrenched in population centers? Was the interference with medical personnel justified by the links of these people to the PLO? My presumption is that sound military practice would lead to compliance with the laws of war and that a belligerent such as Israel would not deliberately divert military assets to attacks on hospitals unless there was good reason to believe that the hospitals contained important military targets.

This evaluation is supported by the observations of Colonel W. Hays Parks (USMC Res.), the leading international law of war expert in the U.S. Army's Judge Advocate General's International Affairs Division. Parks made an official visit to Israel in May 1983 for the secretary of defense "to examine the law of war issues involved in the 1982 Israeli incursion into Lebanon, and specifically to investigate Israeli Air Force (IAF) employment of airpower in light of allegations of 'indiscriminate bombing' by the ICRC and supporters of the PLO."[59] Parks "had access to all-source intelligence" and met with American and foreign military experts as well as Israeli officers. Parks states: "Whatever the feelings of the observers toward Israel, and they were mixed, they were unanimous in their confirmation of the IAF's exercise of care for the civilian population in light of the PLO's efforts at using that population as a shield from attack."[60] Parks particularly criticizes the PLO's practice of emplacing "artillery and antiaircraft weapons on top of or immediately adjacent to hospitals, churches and mosques," to foreign embassies, and of taking battle positions in the lower floors of high-rise apartment buildings.[61]

Controversial Means of Warfare

Against the background of these discussions of the overall compliance of Israel with the principle of legitimate military necessity, it is now appropriate to examine other war-conduct issues. These will be: the Israeli use of cluster bombs and of phosphorous incendiary bombs, the status and treatment of captured PLO *fedayeen* and their allies, and the treatment of civilians in areas occupied by the Israeli forces.

Cluster bombs

The use of cluster bombs or cluster bomb units (CBU) by U.S. forces in Vietnam was criticized. Guenter Lewy's discussion of the subject is instructive. Describing the CBUs, he reports:

> Cluster bomb units are a refinement or special type of fragmentation munition developed during the early 1960s and are usually referred to as improved conventional munitions. They involve a container or dispenser which holds a large number of bomblets or submunitions. Dropped from an aircraft or fired as an artillery round, the dispenser opens to release the bomblets which, depending on the fuse employed, will fragment before, during or after impact. The military utility of the CBU lies in the large area covered by the widely dispersing fragments traveling at high velocity. CBU's proved particularly useful in flak suppression over North Vietnam where they could either knock out the antiaircraft weapons or prevent them from firing by forcing their crew underground. Primarily an antipersonnel weapon, CBUs can also be employed against logistical installations and trucks.[62]

Lewy maintained that cluster bombs were not prohibited by war-conduct law, that they were capable of discriminate use and that they did not inflict unnecessary suffering compared to other weapons commonly used. He concluded: "The practice of states has established the legality of fragment-producing weapons such as hand grenades, artillery projectiles, mines and rockets. Therefore, as the law of war stands today, CBUs cannot be considered illegal per se."[63]

The issue raised by use of CBUs in the Lebanon War was the issue of discrimination. Given the colocation of PLO combat positions and civilian areas, the discriminate use of CBUs was obviously difficult. However, the Israeli government claimed that its use of CBUs was discriminate. On June 27, 1981, Maj. Gen. Aharon Yariv briefed correspondents on the subject. Edward Cody reported from Jerusalem:

> Maj. Gen. Aharon Yariv . . . emphasized that the cluster bombs and shells were not used against civilian targets but rather against what he called "organized resistance, mainly the Syrians, armor and infantry." This reference to Syrian soldiers and apparently to their Palestinian guerrilla allies seemed designed to counter press reports from Beirut that the bombs were used against civilians in Palestinian refugee camps, and, on one occasion, against any Armenian hospital in the Bekaa Valley.
>
> "They were not used against civilians. I mean areas where there were concentrations of civilians," he said.[64]

Israeli use of cluster bombs in the 1978 Litani Operation had brought objections from the U.S. government. It was reported that "Israel informed Washington that their use was a mistake." At that time, "the State Department told Congress . . . that a classified agreement between Israel and the United States in April 1978 reaffirmed Israel's acceptance of the conditions on the use of the cluster bombs." According to Edward Cody's story from Jerusalem, "the Israeli government reportedly had pledged that it would use the cluster bombs and shells only against fortified military positions and only if it were attacked by more than one country."[65]

On July 18, 1982, Israeli radio reported that the Israeli government "told the United States it had not violated its agreement on the use of U.S.-supplied cluster bombs because the weapons had been aimed only against military targets."[66] Israel pointed to the PLO's policy of locating its positions in civilian areas.[67] Previously, the State Department had advised Congress in a confidential letter that "a substantial violation" by Israel of the Arms Export Control Act "may have occurred."[68] President Reagan suspended shipment of cluster-type artillery shells to Israel.[69] It was reported on July 28, 1982, that a secret review had concluded that some violations of the U.S.-Israeli agreement on use of cluster bombs had occurred.[70]

Apparently there was a widespread consensus in the U.S. executive branch and in the Congress that Israeli had used cluster bombs improperly.[71] The Mallisons found that the use of cluster bombs in populated areas violated "a number of basic principles of international law." They stated that "the weapon is indiscriminate, it causes injuries which are excessive in relation to any possible military objective that might be accomplished by its use, and it was directed at areas where the main impact was on civilians."[72] The McBride Commission, likewise, found that the use of cluster bombs in areas where there was a high concentration of civilians caused deaths and injuries from the delayed action of some of the unexploded bomblets as well as from initial explosions, was "contrary to the principle of discrimination."[73]

The matter is not so clear. The military necessity for use of cluster bombs should be considered, not rejected out of hand. The PLO was engaged in hostilities with the Israelis from fortified positions in West Beirut. While there was considerable action in the form of small-arms-fire fights along the defense perimeters, it appears that the major forms of combat were artillery and rocket exchanges and, on the Israeli side, air strikes. The air strikes were resisted with anti-aircraft fire. Use of cluster bombs delivered from aircraft or in artillery shells would be an important means of impairing the ability of *fedayeen* to man the artillery pieces, rocket launchers and anti-aircraft guns and missiles.

Whether the cluster bombs caused disproportionate collateral damage would depend on the targets. If the targets were important PLO combat positions, they could be hit with cluster bombs as well as with regular ordinance. Indeed, in many cases it would be preferable to use cluster bombs against PLO gun, rocket and Anti-aircraft positions rather than to use regular ordnance, which would destroy property. If the targets were not so vital and they were close to known concentrations of noncombatants, military necessity should have deferred to humanity.

Overall, the question is whether the Israeli routinely used cluster bombs against target areas that were mainly civilian and only partly military, or whether they used them mainly against military targets at the cost of some civilian casualties. The critics assume the former.

The Israelis claim the latter. The U.S. government appears not to have accepted the Israeli justifications, but this judgment involves not only the question of the permissibility of using cluster bombs but the question of the use of U.S.-supplied cluster bombs—an emotional and politically explosive question. More recently, the State Department decided to remove the limitations on use of U.S.-supplied cluster bombs and to approve resumption of sales of them to Israel. Israel, which had been producing its own cluster bombs by this time, declined the U.S. offer.

I conclude that the issue is not settled by denying the legal permissibility of cluster bombs in any area where military and civilian targets are colocated. As with most issues of legitimate military necessity, the military utility of a means must be balanced against the humanitarian injunctions to limit civilian damage. Unless the means is illegal per se, e.g., lethal chemical means, permissibility should depend on the proportion between military necessity and collateral damage. In the Israeli siege of Beirut, it seems to me, cluster bombs could have been a particularly appropriate means of suppressing artillery, rocket and anti-aircraft fire. I would therefore reject the judgment of the critics that, in effect, any use of cluster bombs against the PLO entrenched in West Beirut was an egregious violation of the principle of discrimination. Whether that principle was violated would depend on the extent to which the Israelis may have used cluster bombs unnecessarily or in areas where the targets were substantially more civilian than military.

Phosphorous Munitions

Phosphorous shells and bombs are used as artillery markers or smoke-screens. While the use of napalm against mixed military-civilian targets was discouraged by the American Rules of Engagement in the Vietnam

War, except when the survival of U.S./South Vietnamese forces was at stake, use of white phosphorous shells was not included in this restriction.[74]

The Mallisons cite press reports of civilian casualties from white phosphorous shells fired by the Israelis into Beirut and join the McBride Commission in condemning their use. While conceding the permissibility of employing phosphorous munitions against enemy positions in open country, the critics condemn their use in heavily populated areas.[75]

In Article 23 (e) of 1907 Hague Convention IV, "it is especially forbidden . . . to employ arms, projectiles, or materials calculated to cause unnecessary suffering." This is a conventional law expression of the so-called St. Petersburg principle, proclaimed in the 1868 St. Petersburg Declaration, prohibiting means of war that caused "superfluous suffering." Unfortunately, neither belligerent practice nor the writings of publicists have produced a broadly accepted basis for evaluating suffering caused by war means. No means has been banned on the grounds that it caused superfluous suffering, unless chemical warfare could be considered to have been.[76]

During the Vietnam War it seemed that napalm might be banned as causing superfluous suffering, but an ICRC Geneva Conference that attempted to do so was confronted with the fact that most belligerents reserve the right to use napalm, which is extremely useful in attacks on fortified positions and tanks. The Geneva Conference did produce the 1980 Geneva Convention on Prohibitions or Restrictions on the Use of Certain Conventional Weapons Which May Be Deemed to Be Excessively Injurious or to Have Indiscriminate Effects.[77] The 1980 Weapons Convention has not yet been ratified by Israel or the United States.

The issue of use of white phosphorous does not concern a means that is legally impermissible per se but rather a question of the use of the means evaluated in the context of combat situations. Most of the combat in the siege of Beirut took the form of artillery and rocket exchanges. Since white phosphorous is a standards means to mark targets in such exchanges its use was not surprising. What is controversial is whether the Israelis used white phosphorous irresponsibly, given the intermingling of PLO positions with civilian targets. If white phosphorous was employed without adequate consideration for its effects on civilians caught in combat areas, the principle of discrimination and the prohibition of means causing superfluous suffering were violated.

As in the case of artillery bombardments and air strikes, evaluation of use of white phosphorous for the purpose of marking targets turns on the task of balancing the military necessity for the action with the duty to avoid civilian casualties, suffering and destruction as much as possible. I doubt that the critics can prove that the incidents of use of white phosphorous of which they complain resulted from acts unjustified by military necessity. The issue comes down to the fundamental dilemmas of fighting a war in a city, whether the question is discrimination in artillery fire or aerial bombardments or the use of a means such as white phosphorous.

Siege Tactics

As mentioned above, Israel cut off water and electricity for West Beirut during its siege of the PLO entrenched there. Israel also largely prevented relief supplies of fuel, food and medical supplies from entering West Beirut. Under American pressures, the Israelis relented and restored water and electricity after a few days. However, the interdiction of fuel, food and medical supplies caused great suffering in the besieged civilian population. These Israeli siege tactics have been condemned by critics.[78] The UN Security Council repeatedly condemned Israel's siege tactics and demanded that UN, Red Cross and other organizations be permitted to bring relief to Beirut.[79]

Traditionally, the law of war permits a force besieging a defended city or town to "starve it out" by denying access to food, water and other necessary supplies. Indeed, it was considered permissible to drive back noncombatants attempting to flee a besieged place, even with lethal fire.[80] Article 17 of 1949 Geneva (Civilians) Convention IV suggests that such tactics be ameliorated by special agreements:

> The Parties to the conflict shall endeavor to conclude local agreements for the removal from besieged or encircled areas, of wounded, sick, infirm and aged persons, children and maternity cases, and for the passage of ministers of all religions, medical personnel and medical equipment on their way to such areas.

Israel did not make any special agreements of this kind with the PLO, since it did not recognize the PLO as a belligerent. It appears that most of the arrangements for relief convoys were made on an ad hoc basis with the ICRC or some other organization. However, the Israelis repeatedly urged the civilians in West Beirut to leave the combat area. This was a departure from the usual practice of besieging forces. Under the customary law of war, a besieging force may deny civilians in a besieged area from leaving, if necessary by deadly force.[81] In this case, most of the civilians were Lebanese whose part of the city had been taken over as a battlefield by the PLO. It would not have been logical or humane to compel them to remain in West Beirut, although there might be military utility in forcing the PLO to deal with the effects of deprivation of the necessities of life to a large civilian population.

It appears that the principal reason for Israeli reluctance to permit relief convoys to enter West Beirut was the belief that the PLO would take them over and that little would go to the civilians suffering under the siege. I consider the general policy of denying relief to West Beirut to be permissible under the law of war. I am less certain that the Israelis did all that they could have done to make local arrangements for relief assistance supervised by the ICRC or other neutral organizations.

Prisoners of War

There are two basic issues regarding PLO prisoners in Israeli custody: the status of these prisoners under the law of war and their treatment while incarcerated.

Prisoner of War Status

The status and treatment of prisoners of war are the subject of Article 1 of 1907 Hague Convention IV and Article 4 of 1949 Geneva Prisoner of War Convention. These subjects are also covered in the 1977 Geneva Protocols I, which has not been ratified by Israel or the United States, and Protocol II, which has been ratified by the United States but not Israel. Article 4 of the 1949 Geneva Prisoner of War Convention provides that the convention applies to:

(1) Members of the armed forces of a Party to the conflict, as well as members of militias or volunteer corps forming part of such armed forces.

(2) Members of other militias and members of other volunteer corps, including those of organized resistance movements, belonging to a Party to the conflict and operating in or outside their own territory, even if this territory is occupied, provided that such militias or volunteer corps, including such organized resistance movements, fulfill the following conditions:

    (a) that of being commanded by a person responsible for his subordinates;

    (b) that of having a fixed distinctive sign recognizable at a distance;

    (c) that of carrying arms openly;

    (d) that of conducting their operations in accordance with the laws and customs of war.

Throughout its long war with the PLO, Israel has denied PLO personnel
prisoner of war status. The PLO's principal form of armed coercion has
been terrorism which is carried out by *fedayeen* who may be subject to a
responsible commander but who often do not have a uniform or distinctive
insignia, often conceal their arms, and who by definition do not conduct
their operations in accordance with the laws and customs of war. The
Israelis consider all PLO troops to be "terrorists," unentitled to PW status.

In the 1982 Lebanon War Israel continued to deny PW status to captured
PLO troops even though they were now engaged in a conventional war and
would appear, prima facie, to meet the four conditions for belligerent status.
Early in the war an IDF source told the *Washington Post*: "They are terrorists.
We don't refer to them as prisoners-of-war."[82] The source said that while
PLO qualifications under some of the conditions for belligerent status were
arguable, the *fedayeen* clearly did not conduct their operations in accordance
with the laws and customs of war. However, an Army Command source
emphasized that Israel would make certain that the treatment of PLO prisoners would be subject to review by the ICRC and would conform to the
standards of the Geneva Conventions. Apparently, this meant conformity
with the standards of the Fourth (Civilians) Convention, not the Third (PW)
Convention.[83]

The Israeli Ministry of Foreign Affairs conducted a briefing on July 18,
1982, and distributed a statement entitled "The Israeli Operation in Lebanon: Legal Aspects." The briefing paper stated:

> From the outset of the operation, Israel declared to the International
> Committee of the Red Cross that it will apply, as appropriate, the four
> Geneva Conventions. Accordingly, both during and since the hostilities,
> Israel has duly applied these conventions.[84]

The Foreign Ministry's statement said that Syrian soldiers would receive
PW status. No mention was made of Lebanese Army regulars or of members
of the various Lebanese militias. No mention was made of members of
Palestinian units such as the Palestine Liberation Army.[85] All PLO personnel
were denied PW status. The briefing paper stated:

> The PLO and its associated terror groups do not fall within any of the
> categories formulated in the Convention regarding persons entitled to the
> status of prisoners-of-war. They are not "regular armed forces" and do
> not constitute an "organized resistance movement belonging to a party to
> the conflict."[86]

In the December 1982 issue of the *IDF Journal* devoted to Operation Peace For Galilee, Lt. Col. Yoel Zinger reiterated and elaborated on the Israeli position:

> PLO personnel who have been captured by the IDF are not members of the armed forces of a State which is Party to the Conflict neither of Lebanon (against whom Israel is not fighting) nor of Syria. Moreover, they do not cumulatively fulfill all of the four above-mentioned conditions [for PW status, cited above].[87]

Colonel Zinger pointed out that PLO *fedayeen* were often dressed in civilian clothes, that their "operations were usually terrorist, and that they violated the laws of war by deliberately locating missile emplacements, missiles and ammunition dumps within populated civilian areas.[88]

Presumably there were two major reasons for Israel's denial of PW status to PLO personnel. One, stated in the official Israeli explanations, was the fact that the PLO's normal operations were overwhelmingly terrorist in character and therefore not in conformity with the laws of war. The other reason was that extension of PW status to PLO personnel could be construed as a recognition of the PLO as a belligerent, entitled to the rights and bound by the duties of an international person for purposes of the law of war. Traditionally, a state or regime engaged in the counterinsurgency operations of a civil war has refused to increase the prestige of the insurgents by recognizing them as a belligerent entitled to at least some of the rights of a belligerent under the law of war. This was the attitude of the Republic of Vietnam vis-à-vis the Viet Cong.

As long as the PLO's main hostile activity was terrorism, it was easy for Israel to deny its *fedayeen* belligerent status. However, when Israel's attack on the PLO forced a conventional defense, it was not accurate to describe the PLO as terrorists; they were soldiers fighting in ways that met the requirements of the 1907 Hague and 1949 Geneva conventions. A PLO *fedayeen* captured on a terrorist mission into Israel can rightly be held as a criminal and tried before an Israeli military or civil tribunal for criminal, terrorist acts. However, a PLO *fedayeen* who has no known record of participation in terrorist operations and who is captured defending a position in Beirut should not be tried for participating in conventional fighting.

The Mallisons make the argument that only a few of the PLO personnel actually carry out terrorist operations and that the characterization of the entire PLO armed forces as "terrorist" is unwarranted.[89] However, it must be assumed that the great majority of PLO personnel are trained for terrorist operations and that, to varying degrees, they support terrorist operations by protecting PLO bases, by participation in transportation and logistical operations necessary for terrorist operations, by intelligence activities and in other ways. As indicated, I would distinguish the status of a PLO *fedayeen* captured on a terrorist mission and a PLO *fedayeen* defending a base, but they are both part of an overall enterprise that employs terrorism as its virtually sole form of armed coercion.

Israel's policy somewhat resembled that of the Republic of Vietnam with respect to Viet Cong detainees.[90] No belligerent status was recognized, but some of the central features of the PW regime were incorporated into the Israeli treatment of captured PLO *fedayeen*. Lt. Col. Zinger stated in December 1982:

> Though the terrorists are not entitled to the status of Prisoner of War, this does not mean that they are without any legal or humanitarian protection. They must likewise be treated humanely in accordance with the humanitarian principles of international law. Israel has therefore announced that she will treat these detainees in accordance with the provisions of the Fourth Geneva Convention in all matters relative to the granting of humane treatment and conditions of internment. . . . A comparison of the conditions of internment of internees accorded to the Fourth Geneva Convention to those of Prisoners of War accorded by the Third Geneva Convention reveals that as far as the humanitarian conditions accorded to internees is concerned there is no practical difference between the treatment accorded to PoWs and that accorded to other internees beyond the political implications entailed in the granting of Prisoner of War status.[91]

Treatment of Captured PLO Fedayeen

Israel had, in the past, permitted ICRC visits to detention camps in which captured PLO *fedayeen* were held. In the 1982 War the ICRC was not permitted prison visits until July 18. The ICRC was dissatisfied with the terms of visitation and interrupted its visits on July 22. Visits were resumed on July 26 when, apparently, the ICRC was satisfied with the terms of visitation.[92] ICRC visits are essential to the proper operation of the prisoner of war regime. Claims by the detaining power that it is meeting the standards of the PW regime need to be validated by ICRC inspections.

Most of the captured PLO *fedayeen* and Lebanese suspected of aiding the PLO were incarcerated in a special PW camp at Ansar, about fifteen kilometers northeast of Tyre. PLO leaders and *fedayeen* suspected of serious terrorist acts were sent to the Israeli prison of Athlit, near Haifa.[93]

Israel's critics charged that conditions in the Ansar and other detention centers did not meet the standards for treatment of prisoners of war and that that torture and mistreatment of detainees was widespread.[94] In the December 1982 edition of the *IDF Journal* Major Dan Laish offers a description of the Ansar Detention Facility, its living conditions, daily life and the future of the detainees. If accurate, the conditions described were certainly up to the standards of humanitarian law. But most importantly, it appears that the ICRC played its critical role at Ansar. Major Laish stated:

> Representatives of the Red Cross visit the detainees daily and personally interview detainees without the presence of an IDF representative. Likewise, Red Cross doctors are available for consultation by all detainees.
>
> The Red Cross maintains a list of all detainees and every detainee is allowed to send a postcard to his family.
>
> The Red Cross also transfers suggestions and requests made by detainees for the improvement of camp facilities to Israeli authorities. The majority of these requests are complied with. Thus, following a request to install laundry facilities such facilities were provided. When a request for nail-clippers was made, the request was approved and the IDF provided and distributed this item throughout the camp.[95]

The Israeli Forces and the
Civilian Population

From the outset of the 1982 war Israel acknowledged that it was bound to comply with the requirements for belligerent occupation of the Fourth 1949 Geneva (Civilians) Convention.[96] These include the protections of the lives and property of civilians, subjects which have been discussed above under the categories of proportion and discrimination. In general, it appears that Israeli military government conformed to the standards of 1949 Geneva Convention (Civilians) IV. Considerable relief assistance was given to the Lebanese in the occupied areas from the beginning of the war in June 1982 until the final Israeli withdrawal in 1985.

War-conduct issues that are most prominent in Israel's occupation of Lebanon concern the conduct of Major Haddad's Christian militia and the Sabra and Shatilla massacres of Palestinians by Christian Phalange forces.

Haddad's Militia

Under the original Sharon plan the Christian Phalange and other elements loyal to Bashir Gemayel would take over control of Lebanon. Haddad's militia was confined to their narrow strip along the border as the Israelis closed on Beirut. However, as the war progressed, the Israelis, apparently disenchanted with the Gemayel forces because of their reluctance to play

202 / Part II

their expected role in rooting out the PLO, permitted Haddad's forces to deploy to the Zahrani River. Despite objections from the Phalange, Haddad's militia was then encouraged by the Israelis to move up to the Awali River and the Phalangists were pushed north of that line.[97] Haddad's Christians apparently shared the general Lebanese propensity for mistreating other factions when they found the opportunity. There were many instances of violence visited upon inhabitants of towns and villages under the occupation of Haddad's forces and much looting.[98]

Haddad's militia was supplied, trained and controlled by Israel. Presumably, its deployment far north of its narrow enclave was carried out in order to save the Israeli forces some of the burden of security and military government tasks. As things developed, not surprisingly, given the endless hatreds and rivalries of Lebanese politics, the wider deployment of the Haddad militia probably generated a lot more security problems for the Israelis than it solved. While they very likely carried out some necessary security tasks, they apparently engaged in a number of activities that not only were not justified by legitimate military necessity but were counterproductive to Israeli goals. Israel must take responsibility for their excesses.

The Sabra and Shatilla Massacres

Bashir Gemayel, Lebanon's President-elect, was killed in a massive explosion in the Phalangists' party headquarters on September 14, 1982. Prime Minister Begin, Defense Minister Sharon and IDF Chief of Staff Lt. Gen. Rafael Eitan met that evening and made the decision to send the IDF into West Beirut. The purpose of this incursion was twofold: to maintain order and to root out remaining PLO and radical leftists militia personnel in the Beirut area. They agreed that the IDF should not enter the Palestinian refugee camps but should leave the task to the Lebanese Army or the Phalangists. Maj. Gen. Amir Drori, commander of the Northern Command, Brig. Gen. Amos Yaron, commander of the 96th Division surrounding Beirut, and senior Phalangist officers met before dawn on September 15. The Phalangists were requested to order a general mobilization of their forces, impose a curfew on all areas under their control and be ready to join the IDF if fighting occurred. About 6 a.m. on September 15 the IDF entered Beirut, initially encountering no opposition. Presently the Israelis came under fire from leftist militia forces and from the Palestinian camps. The Security Council, in Resolution 520 of September 17, 1982, condemned the murder of Bashir Gemayel but also condemned "the recent Israeli incursions into Beirut in violation of the cease-fire agreements and of Security Council resolutions."[99]

At 8 a.m. September 15, Sharon came to Brig. Gen. Yaron's forward command post, a five-story apartment house, two-hundred meters southwest of the Shatilla camp. While the apartment overlooked the Shatilla camp, it was impossible to see what was happening in the narrow streets and alleys in the camp. Joined by Chief of Staff Lt. Gen. General Eitan, Sharon agreed to the Phalange forces entering the camps to weed out PLO and other hostile elements. He subsequently went to Phalangist headquarters, where he assented to the Phalangist initiative. Maj. Gen. Drori met with Phalangist commanders in the evening of September 15 and advised them that they could go into the Palestinian camps the next day. However, he was uneasy about the enterprise and tried unsuccessfully to persuade the Lebanese Army to go in instead of the Phalange forces.

This was the origin of the operation that became the Sabra and Shatilla massacres, September 16–18, 1982.[100] Public pressures in Israel subsequently obliged the Begin government to appoint the Kahan Commission of Inquiry, headed by Yitzhak Kahan, president of the Supreme Court, and including Aharon Barak, justice of the Supreme Court, and Maj. Gen. (Res.) Yona Efrat of the IDF. The Kahan Report was signed on February 7, 1983. It is my main source for the facts relating to Israel's involvement in the massacres.[101]

A Phalange force of 150 men commanded by Eli Hobeika, chief of Phalangist intelligence, entered the camps at 6 p.m. September 16. The unit was chosen because it was especially trained to screen out *fedayeen* hiding among the general population. A Phalangist officer with a radio set was stationed at Yaron's forward command post. A Mossad liaison officer was at Phalangist headquarters. Yaron, who had earlier experience with the Phalangists and was critical of their behavior, cautioned Phalangist commanders that they must not harm noncombatants.

The Phalangists requested illumination from the Israelis, and mortars fired illuminating shells over the camp intermittently through the night of September 16–17. Meanwhile, the Israelis accumulated evidence that civilians, including women and children, were being killed in the camps. This evidence came from:

(1) reports of Phalangist radio conversations;
(2) reports from the Phalangist officer at Brig. Gen. Yaron's forward command post;
(3) IDF personnel who witnessed killing of noncombatants and other actions indicating violent measures against inhabitants of the camps.

It is not necessary to rehearse all of the details of the failures of the IDF to get timely reports of the massacres to the top commanders. Suffice it to say that these commanders seemed to have had misgivings about the Phalangists' actions but lacked hard evidence until much time had elapsed and the slaughter continued.[102] During the night of September 16–17 the Phalangists requested more illumination from the Israelis. Lt. Col. Triber of Divisional Operations Branch refused, at first, stating that the Phalangists had already killed three hundred people and that they shouldn't have illumination to kill more.

On September 17 the Phalangists asked permission to reinforce the unit in the camps. When Maj. Gen. Drori arrived at division headquarters at 11 a.m., he denied permission to reinforce and, having by this time heard of the events of the previous night, ordered the Phalangists to stop operations in the camps. On that day Drori again tried to get the Lebanese Army to go into the camps, but was once again refused.[103]

Chief of staff Eitan, with Drori and Yaron, visited Phalangist headquarters in East Beirut on the afternoon of September 17. The atmosphere was relaxed. The Phalangists were not confronted with charges of misbehavior and they did not bring up the subject of possible misconduct. The meeting proceeded on the assumption that the necessary job of rooting out the PLO and other hostile *fedayeen* from the camps had been successfully done by the Phalangists. The only problem discussed was American pressure for the Phalangists to leave the camps. The Phalangists requested tractors to destroy illegal buildings in the camps. The Israelis sent them one with the IDF markings removed but it was returned unused.[104]

Eitan returned to Tel Aviv, where he called Defense Minister Sharon. He allegedly told Sharon that the Phalangists had "gone too far" in the camps but that they had now been stopped, that reinforcements had been denied and that they would be out of the camps by 5 a.m. September 18.[105] Lt. General Eitan's phone call was the first official notice given Sharon about events in the camp.[106]

The Phalangists did not leave the camps at 5 a.m. September 18. Brig. Gen. Yaron ordered them to leave, which they did at 8 a.m. It appears that Prime Minister Begin learned of the Sabra and Shatilla massacres only in the evening of September 18, which was Rosh Hashana. Begin and his cabinet had been advised on the evening of September 16 that the Phalangists were entering the camps and, despite warnings from Deputy Prime Minister David Levy that Israel would be blamed if the Phalangists committed crimes, no objections were raised to the operation.[107]

Estimates of the casualties suffered in the Sabra and Shatilla massacres vary greatly. Among many difficulties in making the estimates is that of distinguishing those actually killed in combat operations from those who were simply murdered. The Kahan Report concludes:

Taking into account the fact that Red Cross personnel counted no more than 328 bodies, it would appear that the number of victims of the massacre was not as high as a thousand, and certainly not thousands. According to I.D.F intelligence sources, the number of victims of the massacre is between 700 and 800. . . . This may well be the number most closely corresponding with reality. It is impossible to determine precisely when the acts of slaughter were perpetrated; evidently they commenced shortly after the Phalangists entered the camps and went on intermittently until close to their departure.[108]

The Phalangist forces were guilty of war crimes in the Sabra and Shatilla massacres. It is clear that most of the casualties were noncombatants who were not killed inadvertently in course of combat but were deliberately murdered. Since the massacres occurred in an area that was wholly in the control of the Israeli forces, during an operation ordered and supported by the IDF, Israel as a belligerent and the responsible Israeli civilian officials and military commanders bear some responsibility under international law for the crimes committed by the Phalangists.

The Kahan Commission found no evidence that the Israeli government or the military commanders intended anything like the massacres to occur. The intention was to root out suspected PLO and other enemy personnel hanging on in the Beirut area and still firing at the Israelis. Accordingly, the commission denied any "direct responsibility" on the part of the Israeli government and military or individual officials or commanders for the Sabra and Shatilla massacres. However, the Kahan Commission found that Israel and some of its officials and commanders bore an "indirect responsibility" for the massacres.

The commission ascribed indirect responsibility on three principal grounds:

(1) Those who decided on the entry of the Phalangists into the camps should have foreseen—from the information at their disposal and from things which were common knowledge—that there was danger of a massacre, and no steps were taken which might have prevented this danger or at least greatly reduced the possibility that deeds of this type might be done, then those who implemented them are indirectly responsible for what ultimately occurred, even if they did not intend this to happen and merely disregarded the anticipated danger.

(2) A similar indirect responsibility also falls on those who knew of the decision; it was their duty, by virtue of their position and their office, to warn of the danger, and they did not fulfill this duty.

(3) It is also not possible to absolve of such indirect responsibility those persons who, when they received the first reports of what was happen-

ing in the camps, did not rush to prevent the continuation of the Phalangists actions and did not do everything in their power to stop them.[109]

The Kahan Commission did not fault the decision to employ the Phalangists in the task of clearing the camps of hostile *fedayeen*. It imputed indirect responsibility to those who failed to take measures to monitor and control the Phalangists in order to prevent excesses that any reasonably informed person could have foreseen. There was a long history of massacres and assassinations in Lebanese internal warfare, including a massacre of Christians in Damour and elsewhere during the Civil War. The Israeli officials and commanders should have done everything possible to prevent excesses against noncombatants and to terminate the operation immediately when such excesses were reported.[110]

The Kahan Commission found that Prime Minister Begin failed to keep himself informed as to events in the camps, although he had good reason to be concerned about possible Phalangist excesses.[111] The commission concluded with respect to Sharon:

> It is our view that responsibility is to be imputed to the Minister of Defense for having disregarded the danger of acts of vengeance and bloodshed by the Phalangists against the population of the refugee camps, and having failed to take this danger into account when he decided to have the Phalangists enter the camps. In addition, responsibility is to be imputed to the Minister of Defense for not ordering appropriate measures for preventing or reducing the danger of massacre as a condition for the Phalangists' entry into the camps. These blunders constitute the nonfulfillment of a duty with which the Defense Minister was charged.[112]

Sharon was not found responsible for failure to order a halt to the operation when first reports of trouble reached him since he had been told that the operation was to be terminated the next morning.[113] The commission recommended that Sharon resign or be removed by the prime minister from the position of defense minister.[114]

The Kahan Commission found that Lt. General Rafael Eitan: "did not consider the danger of acts of vengeance and bloodshed being perpetrated against the population of the refugee camps in Beirut; he did not order the adoption of the appropriate steps to avoid this danger; and his failure to do so is tantamount to a breach of duty that was incumbent upon the Chief of Staff."[115] The commission further found other instances of Lt. Gen. Eitan's failure to intervene to stop the Phalangists' operation constituted "a breach of duty and dereliction of the duty incumbent upon the Chief of Staff."[116]

Since Lt. Gen. Eitan was soon to retire as chief of staff and another term was not contemplated, no recommendation was made about him.[117]

Maj. Gen. Yehoshua Saguy, director of military intelligence, was found to have failed in his duties to warn effectively about the dangers of the Phalangists' operation and to have "stepped aside" and let matters take their course, since he was known to be opposed to cooperation with the Phalangists.[118] The commission recommended that he be removed from his position.[119]

The commission lamented the failure of the Mossad liaison officer to express forcibly his concerns about the operation but made no recommendation about him.[120]

The Kahan Commission found that Maj. Gen. Amir Drori had "acted properly, wisely and responsibly" up to the time of Lt. Gen. Eitan's visit on the afternoon of September 17.[121] However, the commission found that Maj. Gen. Drori failed to warn the chief of staff effectively during Lt. Gen. Eitan's September 17 visit and that this failure constituted a breach of duty.[122] Since Maj. Gen. Drori had made efforts to terminate the operation, the committee made no recommendation about him.[123]

The Kahan Commission confirmed charges against Brig. Gen. Amos Yaron: failure to evaluate and check reports of killing and other irregular actions, to pass on information to the chief of staff or to warn him when Eitan visited on September 17, or to stop the Phalangists' actions immediately on receiving reports of the massacre.[124]

The commission recommended that Brig. Gen. Yaron "not serve in the capacity of a field commander in the Israel Defense Forces, and that this recommendation not be reconsidered before three years have passed."[125]

The Kahan Commission's disposition of the legal issues of state and personal responsibility was, in my view fully consonant with international law. However, it is true, as the Italian international law scholar Antonio Cassese points out, that the Kahan Commission did not base its reasoning on Israeli military law or the international law of war. Rather, it relied on moral or religious imperatives.[126] Nevertheless, the commission's handling of the inquiry produced results comparable to those that would have come from a law of war proceedings. The state of Israel was responsible for actions taken by an allied force operating within an area controlled by the Israeli forces. The character and degree of that responsibility depended on the extent to which Israeli officials and military commanders could have prevented the crimes perpetrated by the Phalangists, on the extent to which responsible Israelis acted to repress the criminal behavior, and the extent to which those directly and indirectly responsible for the crimes were punished.

It is true, as Cassese argues, that the concept of "indirect responsibility" was taken by the Kahan Commission from moral rather than legal sources.[127] However, the issue is not so much one of "direct" or "indirect responsibility." The standard of state and individual responsibility is not absolute but reasonable. Responsible officials or commanders are expected to take whatever actions a reasonable person would make in the situation. In the case of a military situation, the standard is one of military professionalism. As my mentor Professor Ernst Feilchenfeld used to put it, there is the standard of "the reasonable colonel," akin to that of "the reasonable man" in civil law. The Kahan Commission judged that, by the standards of a reasonable person, knowledgeable about the actors in the Lebanon wars— as all judged by the commission were—each of the principal Israeli civilian officials and military commanders involved in the Sabra/Shatilla operation failed to meet the professional standards of command responsibility.

They failed to foresee and prevent the massacres. They failed to terminate them promptly, either from failure to acquire and pass on information about the events in the camps or from failure to act when sufficient information was available. The judgments of the Kahan Commission demonstrate once again the close relationship between legality, morality and true military utility. Just as My Lai was an American defeat equal to the worst battlefield defeat, so Sabra and Shatilla were Israeli defeats far surpassing any advantage gained by ferreting out PLO and other hostile elements from the camps.

The injury done to Israel's standing in the world by the Sabra and Shatilla massacres was and remains great. That injury is, however, somewhat mitigated by the fact that Israel did constitute the Kahan Commission, which produced a fair set of judgments and recommendations that acknowledged the indirect responsibility of Israel and its top officials and commanders for the massacres. By contrast, the government of Lebanon, led by Phalangists, made only superficial and belated attempts to investigate the massacres and assess responsibility for them.

War-conduct Law in the Lebanon War

Throughout its report the Kahan Commission emphasizes the gap between the IDF's "battle ethic" and that of the Lebanese factions. Most of the principals testifying before the commission also emphasized this point. Admittedly, Israeli troops must not always have lived up to this "battle ethic," but the emphasis upon it in the Kahan inquiry suggests that the "battle ethic" is deeply imbued in the IDF. This, in turn, casts light on the issues of war conduct discussed in this chapter. Given the emphasis in Israeli training on the "purity of arms" (*tohar haneshek*) concept, it can at least be suggested that the Israeli armed forces intend to conduct operations in consonance with the principles and rules of the international law of war.[128]

On the whole, it appears that Israel substantially met its standard of "battle ethics" in the 1982 Lebanon War. Serious efforts were made to minimize civilian casualties and damage in the drive to Beirut. These efforts were rendered very difficult by the PLO's tactic of fighting from civilian areas. In the siege of the PLO in West Beirut, the problem of fighting with proportionate and discriminate means became even more difficult. I have tried to show how the issue of proportionality should be broken down according to the objectives and the circumstances of a "fight and negotiate" situation, as distinguished from a "defeat the enemy's forces" situation. I have also tried to demonstrate the close relation between proportionality and discrimination, since discrimination turns on the proportion between the legitimate military necessity of the action and the extent of the collateral damage.

As indicated, I conclude that Israel's use of force in the siege of the PLO in Beirut was proportionate to the goal of expelling the PLO and that, given the colocation of military and civilian targets, Israeli force was sufficiently discriminate. I do not, however, find that the continued use of force by Israel after August 6, 1982, was proportionate and discriminate, given the high probability that the goal of the campaign had been achieved.

I conclude that objections to Israeli use of cluster bombs and phosphorous shells are not sustained by the contemporary law of war. In my view, the Israeli treatment of captured PLO and allied personnel conforms with the common practice of states or regimes fighting revolutionary forces to which they do not grant belligerent status. That practice, as in U.S. policy in Vietnam, is to deny PW status but accord detainees a standard of protection, including access to the ICRC, that is satisfactory.

Not much has been written about the conduct of Israeli military government and/or civil affairs during the occupation of large parts of Lebanon from June 1982 to May 1985. I have not found any major complaints. I have also not found recognition of the positive measures taken by Israel to help the Lebanese. It appears that there were excesses, notably looting, by the Christian militia of Major Haddad when they moved from their enclave up to the Awali River. Israel must bear responsibility for their depredations. Finally, I can only join the Kahan Commission in condemning the Sabra and Shatilla massacres for which the Phalangists were directly responsible but for which Israel and its top officials and military commanders must also bear responsibility.

In most evaluations of war conduct there is a mixed record of compliance with and deviation from the law of war. There are usually a number of borderline issues. Inevitably, judgments about war conduct tend to be influenced by judgments about the legal permissibility of the war. World opinion and, eventually, a substantial part of Israeli opinion, opposed or sharply questioned the 1982 Israeli invasion of Lebanon. Accordingly, each facet of that invasion was judged critically. Moreover, the fact that, like Vietnam, this was a television war where civilian damage, suffering and grief were shown all over the world, added to the propensity to condemn Israel's conduct of the war.

In this chapter I have attempted to go beyond the instant judgments of the media and the judgments of self-appointed war crimes investigators. I have attempted to demonstrate how considerations of military necessity and humanity must be balanced—and how difficult this is. My conclusion is that, whatever the prudence of Israel's decision to drive the PLO out of southern Lebanon and Beirut and whatever the disappointments of Israelis with the long-term effects of the war, it was fought in reasonable conformity with the laws of war.

Notes

1. Ze'ev Schiff and Ehud Ya'ari, *Israel's Lebanon War* edited and translated by Ina Friedman (New York: Simon & Schuster, 1984), pp. 139–50.

2. Schiff and Ya'ari, *Israel's Lebanon War*, pp. 139–50; Trevor N. Dupuy and Paul Martell, *Flawed Victory: The Arab-Israeli Conflict and the 1982 War in Lebanon* (Fairfax, Va.: Hero Books, 1986), pp. 105–06; Richard A. Gabriel. *Operation Peace for Galilee* (New York: Hill & Wang, 1984), pp. 85, 87.

3. Dupuy and Martell, *Flawed Victory*, pp. 15–16.

4. Ibid., pp. 105–06.

5. Gabriel, *Operation Peace for Galilee*, pp. 86–87.

6. Schiff and Ya'ari, *Israel's Lebanon War*, p. 143.

7. Ibid., p. 144. See Dupuy and Martell, *Flawed Victory*, pp. 130–31.

8. Schiff and Ya'ari, *Israel's Lebanon War*, pp. 144–45. See Dupuy and Martell, *Flawed Victory*, pp. 130–31.

9. Schiff and Ya'ari, *Israel's Lebanon War*, p. 145.

10. Ibid., pp. 145–48; Gabriel, *Operation Peace in Galilee*, p. 95; Dupuy and Martell, *Flawed Victory*, 133.

11. Schiff and Ya'ari, *Israel's Lebanon War*, pp. 144–50; Dupuy and Martell, *Flawed Victory*, pp. 131–32.

12. Gabriel, *Operation Peace for Galilee*, p. 95.

13. "Israel Disputes Civilian Casualty Figures, Calls Them 'Propaganda,' " *Washington*

Post [hereinafter, *WP*], June 23, 1982, A20, cols. 1–6; "Disagreements Flare over Casualty Toll in Lebanon," June 25, 1982, A27, cols. 1–4.

14. "Israel Disputes Civilian Casualties, Calls Them 'Propaganda,' " cols. 1–2.

15. "Disagreements Flare over Casualty Toll in Lebanon."

16. "Israel Disputes Civilian Casualty Figures, Calls Them 'Propaganda.' " Embassy of Israel, Washington, D.C., "Information Background: The Truth about Civilian Casualties and Refugees in Southern Lebanon," (June 22, 1982); Martin Peretz, "Lebanon Witness," *The New Republic*, August 2, 1982, pp. 16–18.

17. Alexander M. Haig, Jr., *Caveat* (New York: Macmillan, 1984), p. 346.

18. "Lebanese government officials said an Israeli officer forced three engineers to remove a key piece of pumping machinery from the waterworks serving West Beirut and part of East Beirut." "Israel Shells PLO on Edge of Beirut, Enforces Blockade," *WP*, July 6, 1982, A1, col. 5; A14, cols. 4–6.

19. "Israeli Units Permit Restoration of Water, Power in West Beirut," *WP*, July 8, 1982, A17, cols. 5–6; A21, cols. 1–21.

20. Gabriel, *Operation Peace in Galilee*, pp. 143–44.

21. "Food for Beirut Still Blocked by Israeli Lines," *WP*, July 17, 1982, A1, col. 6; A11, cols. 1–2.

22. Haig, *Caveat*, p. 348.

23. Ibid.

24. R. Khalidi, *Under Siege*, pp. 115–16, 131; Haig, *Caveat*, p. 349. The *Washington Post* reported that Arafat signed the agreement on the night of July 3. "Arafat Reportedly Signs Agreement to Withdraw," *WP*, July 4, 1982, A1, cols. 4–6; A18, col. 1.

25. "PLO and Lebanese Agree in Principle on Withdrawal," *WP*, June 29, 1982, A1, col. 6; A12, cols. 1–6.

26. Dupuy and Martell, *Flawed Victory*, pp. 157–58; Gabriel, *Operation Peace in Galilee*, p. 146.

27. Gabriel, *Operation Peace for Galilee*, p. 146.

28. Dupuy and Martell, *Flawed Victory*, p. 159.

29. Gabriel, *Operation Peace in Galilee*, p. 154.

30. Ibid., p. 155.

31. R. Khalidi, *Under Siege*, p. 164.

32. Ibid.

33. Gabriel, *Operation Peace for Galilee*, pp. 155–56.

34. Schiff and Ya'ari, *Israel's Lebanon War*, p. 223. Schiff & Ya'ri state that the IAF mounted 36 sorties on each of the next two days.

35. Ibid.

36. Gabriel, *Operation Peace in Galilee*, p. 157.

37. "Reagan Expresses 'Outrage' at Israeli Assault: Fighting Halted as President Phones Begin," *WP*, August 13, 1982, A1, col. 6; A15, col. 1; Schiff and Ya'ari, *Israel's Lebanon War*, pp. 225–26.

38. Schiff and Ya'ari, *Israel's Lebanon War*, p. 225.

39. Ibid.

40. Gabriel, *Operation Peace for Galilee*, p. 157.

41. Dupuy and Martell, *Flawed Victory*, p. 162.

42. Ibid., pp. 167–70.

43. Ibid., pp. 167–69.

44. Moshe Gammer, "The War in Lebanon," *MECS* VI (1982): 148.

45. Gammer, "The War in Lebanon," citing Ya'agov Erez, "Ha Milhama la Shalom" ("The War for Peace"), *Ma'ariv*, 17 September 1982, pp. 30–38, 42, 61–62.

46. Gabriel, *Operation Peace in Galilee*, p. 83; Schiff and Ya'ari, *Israel's Lebanon War*, p. 121.

47. Gammer, "The War in Lebanon," 150, citing *WP*, September 3, 1982.

48. Gabriel, *Operation Peace in Galilee*, pp. 164–65.

49. See Haig, *Caveat*, pp. 346–47; "New Cease-Fire Halts Bombing of Lebanese Capital," *WP*, June 26, 1982, A1, cols. 5–6; A19, cols. 2–5; R. Khalidi, *Under Siege*, pp. 118–29, 135–65.

50. "Israeli Forces Inch Forward in West Beirut," *WP*, August 7, 1982, A17, col. 1; A20, cols. 1–2.

51. "Israel Launches New Attacks as Talks Advance," *WP*, August 7, 1982, A1, cols. 1–5; A22, cols. 1–3.

52. Ibid.

53. See Dupuy and Martell's evaluation of the August 12, 1982, attacks, p. 183 above.

54. See Joshua Muravchik, "Misreporting Lebanon," *Policy Review* (Winter 1893): 11–66.

55. *Israel in Lebanon: Report of the International Commission to Enquire into Reported Violations of International Law by Israel during Its Invasion of the Lebanon*, Sean McBride, chair (London: Ithaca Press, 1983), pp. 188–89 [hereinafter cited as *McBride Report*]; W. Thomas and Sally V. Mallison, *The Palestine Problem in International Law and World Order* (Essex: Longman, 1986), pp. 365–71.

56. Dupuy and Martell, *Flawed Victory*, p. 173.

57. See *McBride Report*, p. 189; Mallison and Mallison, *Palestine Problem in International Law and World Order*, pp. 358–62.

58. Dupuy and Martell, *Flawed Victory*, p. 173.

59. W. Hays Parks, "Air War and the Law of War," *The Air Force Law Review* 32 (1990): 1–226; p. 166, n. 494.

60. Ibid.

61. Ibid., p. 165.

62. Guenter Lewy, *America in Vietnam* (New York: Oxford University Press, 1978), pp. 266–67, citing Michael Krepon, "Weapons Potentially Inhumane: The Case of Cluster Bombs," in Richard A. Falk, ed., *The Vietnam War and International Law* (4 vols.; Princeton, N.J.: Princeton University Press, 1969–76), 4: 266–74.

63. Lewy, *America in Vietnam*, p. 267.

64. Edward Cody, "Israel Confirms Using U.S.-Made Cluster Bombs," *WP*, June 28, 1982, A15, col. 6.

65. Ibid.

66. "Israel Said to Deny Misuse of Bombs," *WP*, July 19, 1982, A1, col. 4; A20, col. 1.

67. Ibid.

68. Ibid.

69. "President Halts Shipment Of 'Cluster' Shells to Israel," *WP*, July 20, 1982, A1, cols. 3–4; A10, cols. 1–3.

70. "Reagan Bans Indefinitely Cluster Shells for Israel," *WP*, July 28, 1982, A16, cols. 5–6.

71. "President Halts Shipment of 'Cluster' Shells to Israel," *WP*, July 20, 1982, A1, cols. 4–5; A10, cols. 1–3.

72. Mallison and Mallison, *The Palestine Problem*, p. 382.

73. *McBride Report*, p. 97.

74. Lewy, *America in Vietnam*, pp. 242–48.

75. Mallison and Mallison, *The Palestine Problem*, pp. 383–87; *McBride Report*, p. 99.

76. On the difficulties of defining "superfluous or unnecessary suffering" and identifying weapons and means causing it, see the excellent discussion, strongly supported by references to the opinion of leading publicists, in Myres. S. McDougal and Florentino P. Feliciano, *Law and Minimum World Public Order* (New Haven, Conn.: Yale University Press, 1961), pp. 614–22; Julius Stone, *Legal Controls of International Conflict* (New York: Rinehart, 1954), pp. 551–52.
   See the U.S. Army's FM 27-10 comments on the prohibition of means causing unnecessary suffering in 1907 Hague Convention IV, Article 23 (e), no. 34, p. 18.

77. *International Legal Materials* 19 (1980): 1523–36.

78. Mallison and Mallison, *The Palestine Problem*, p. 361; *McBride Report*, pp. 154–61.

79. See S.C. Res. 512 of June 19, 1982, *Resolutions and Decisions of the Security Council*, p. 7; S.C. Res. 513 of July 4, 1982, ibid.; S.C. Res. 515 of July 29, 1982, ibid., pp. 7–8; S.C. Res. 516 of August 1, 1982, ibid., p. 8; S.C. Res. 517 of August 4, 1982, ibid.; S.C. Res. 518 of August 12, ibid., p. 9.

80. McDougal and Florentino, *Law and Minimum World Public Order*, pp. 605–08 and authorities cited therein; U.S. Army FM 27-10, *The Law of Land Warfare* (Washington, D.C.: Department of the Army, July 1956), para. 44 (a), p. 20.

81. See the U.S. Army FM 27-10, *The Law of Land Warfare* (Washington, D.C.: Department of the Army, July 1956), para. 44 (a), p. 20.

82. William Claiborne, "Israel Does Not Consider Palestinians POW's," *WP*, June 13, 1982, A25, cols. 1–3; cited in Mallison and Mallison, *Palestine Problem*, p. 344.

83. Ibid.

84. Israel Ministry of Foreign Affairs, Information Division, Briefing no. 342, p. 4, quoted in Mallison and Mallison, *Palestine Problem*, p. 343.

85. Ibid.

86. Ibid., p. 4.

87. Lt. Col. Yoel Zinger, "Peace for Galilee: The Prisoners," *IDF Journal* 1 (December 1982): 37–38.

88. Ibid.

89. Mallison and Mallison, *Palestine Problem*, p. 346.

90. Lewey, *America in Vietnam*, p. 328.

91. Zinger, *Peace in Galilee: The Prisoners*, p. 38.

92. Jonathan C. Randal, "Israeli Prison Camp Causes Concern in Lebanon," *WP*, July 28, 1982, A1, cols. 2–4; A16, cols. 3–5; cited in Mallison and Mallison, *Palestine Problem*, pp. 350–51.

93. Dupuy and Martell, *Flawed Victory*, p. 137.

94. Mallison and Mallison, *The Palestine Problem in International Law and World Order*, pp. 351–54.

95. Major Dan Laish, "Peace for Galilee: Ansar Detention Facility," *IDF Journal* 1 (December 1982): 38–39.

96. See Chap. 8 below.

97. Schiff and Ya'ari, *Israel's Lebanon War*, pp. 238–39.

98. See "Lebanese in Occupied South Say Israelis Give Free Rein to Lawless Militias," *New York Times*, August 18, 1982, p. 6, cols. 1–6, cited in Mallison and Mallison, *Palestine Problem*, p. 364.

99. *UNSC R&D 1982*, p. 10.

100. See Chap. 13, "Anatomy of a Slaughter," in Schiff and Ya'ari, *Israel's Lebanon War*, pp. 250–85, for a highly informed account of the Sabra and Shatilla massacres, including Schiff's efforts to alert responsible IDF officers and civilian officials to the continuing war crimes.

101. The Commission of Inquiry into the Events at the Refugee Camps in Beirut, *Final Report* (authorized translation; Jerusalem: Reprinted from the *Jerusalem Post*, 1983) [hereinafter cited as *Kahan Report*].

102. See the *Kahan Report*, pp. 12–20.

103. Ibid., p. 17.

104. Ibid., p. 18.

105. Ibid., pp. 18–19.

106. Ibid., p. 19.

107. Ibid., p. 21.

108. Ibid.

109. Ibid., p. 26.

110. Ibid., pp. 26–29.

111. Ibid., p. 31. The commission's discussion of Begin is on pp. 30–31.

112. Ibid., p. 33.

113. Ibid.

114. Ibid., p. 49.

115. Ibid., p. 36.

116. Ibid., pp. 36–37.

117. Ibid., p. 49.

118. Ibid., pp. 37–39.

119. Ibid., p. 49.

120. Ibid., pp. 39–40.

121. Ibid., p. 41.

122. Ibid., p. 42.

123. Ibid., p. 48.

124. Ibid., pp. 42–43. See p. 44 for concluding determination.

125. Ibid., p. 49.

126. Antonio Cassese, "Sabra and Shatilla," in idem, *Violence and Law in the Modern Age,* S. J. K. Greensleaves, trans. (Cambridge: Polity, 1988), p. 79.

127. Ibid., p. 80.

128. On the IDF's emphasis of the "Purity of Arms" (*tohar haneshek*) tradition of moral conduct in war, see Martin Peretz, "Lebanon Eyewitness," *The New Republic,* August 2, 1982, pp. 15–23; Gabriel, *Operation Peace for Galilee,* pp. 171–76.

8

Israel and the Law of Belligerent Occupation in the Occupied Territories

At the end of Israel's War of Independence in 1949, Jordan occupied the area that came to be known as the West Bank. Egypt occupied the Gaza Strip. The borders between the new state of Israel and the areas occupied by Jordan and Egypt were set by the fortunes of war. Armistice agreements were eventually concluded between Israel, Egypt, Jordan, Syria and Lebanon. However, no peace treaties were to be signed except that of 1979 between Egypt and Israel.[1]

Between the end of Israel's War of Independence and the 1967 June War, the status of the West Bank and Gaza was unclear. Gaza was administered by Egypt but not annexed to it.[2] Jordan annexed the West Bank but the annexation was only recognized by Great Britain and Pakistan.[3] Jordanian sovereignty over the West Bank was not recognized by most of the states of the world, including the Arab states. In these circumstances, Jordan's position in the West Bank was one of a military occupant rather than a sovereign.

Accordingly, Israel's conquest of the West Bank in the 1967 June War can be viewed from two legal perspectives. If the West Bank is considered to have been sovereign territory of Jordan, Israel would have displaced Jordan's sovereign control temporarily and subjected the West Bank to belligerent occupation based on total control of the area. Israel would remain as belligerent occupant until the conflict was terminated by some kind of peace treaty that would determine the legal status of the territory.

However, if the West Bank is considered to have been merely under Jordan's military occupation, not its sovereign territory, Israel would have been displacing a competitor for physical control of a portion of the former Palestine Mandate. Jordan, having seized the West Bank by force of arms in 1949 without acquiring sovereignty over it, had now lost it by force of arms.

If the second approach is followed, Israel "occupied" the West Bank, but what it occupied was not part of Jordan but a part of Palestine claimed by both

216

Israel and Jordan. To be sure, Jordan could point to the 1948 UN partition plan that did not grant Israel any territory in the West Bank area. However, the Arabs rejected the UN partition plan and, had they accepted it, the West Bank would have gone to a new Palestinian Arab state, not to Jordan.

In any event, King Hussein, in effect, unannexed the West Bank in July 1988, cutting all legal ties with the area, as well as various governmental functions and forms of support. Since then, the only claimant to the West Bank, besides Israel, has been the PLO and/or any indigenous Palestinian group that may challenge the PLO's position as "sole representative" of the Palestinian people.[4] As for Gaza, it seems to be linked with the West Bank, given Egypt's disinclination to reclaim it.

The unusual histories of the West Bank and Gaza make the application of the international law of belligerent occupation difficult. This law was developed for the case of occupation in time of war of the sovereign territory of one belligerent by another. Moreover, this body of law assumed that wars do not last indefinitely and that eventually there will be a peace settlement that will determine the status of the territory under belligerent occupation. Even if one were to concede that the West Bank was a part of Jordan's sovereign territory when the Israelis occupied it in 1967, a state of suspended hostilities but no peace settlement lasting over twenty years is certainly not the kind of situation envisaged in the international law of belligerent occupation. If one does not concede Jordanian sovereignty over the West Bank at any time, we are, again, confronted with a situation not foreseen by the law of belligerent occupation, a military occupation re-sulting from a war (1948–49) which is only suspended by a truce—and which continues for over twenty years.[5]

The situation is further complicated by Israeli ambivalence as regards annexation of the West Bank and Gaza. Outright annexation would mean demographic changes in Israel that would ultimately cause it to cease to be a predominantly Jewish state, unless it expelled the Arabs wholesale or reduced them to a permanently inferior status. In that case Israel might still be a Jewish state but not a democratic state. Accordingly, the majority view in Israel has been that Israel should hold on to the West Bank and Gaza, mainly for security reasons, and limit Palestinian self-determination to some kind of less-than-sovereign autonomy. The pressures unleashed by the *intifada* have put in question the realism of such a solution.[6] Moreover, the *intifada* itself has engendered Israeli security measures that extend the already long list of issues of belligerent occupation law raised by Israel's long occupation of the West Bank and Gaza.

None of these problems seem to discourage claims to Judea and Samaria based on religious and historic grounds. These grounds are, of course, reinforced by practical stakes in the settlements of the settlers and the Israeli government.

Before discussing the legal issues, a brief overview of the phases of Israel's occupation of the West Bank and Gaza, emphasizing security issues, will be presented. I will then offer a review of the sources and basic principles of the international law of belligerent occupation. Following this I will examine the legal issues raised by Israeli emergency security measures, related both to Israel external war with the PLO and to internal security in the occupied territories. The discussion will be organized in categories having to do with:

(1) use of force and settler violence;
(2) collective punishment;
(3) individual punishment;
(4) discipline of security forces.

Since this book is primarily concerned with issues of recourse to armed force, several controversial Israeli measures of great importance will not be discussed: modification of existing governmental systems, acquisition of land, water rights, general restrictions on property rights and restrictions on travel and correspondence, establishment of Jewish settlements in the Occupied Territories, as well as economic coercive measures before and since the *intifada*.[7]

Israel's Occupation of the West Bank and Gaza

The phases of Israel's occupation of the West Bank and Gaza tend to overlap. They reflect a variety of factors, including Israeli occupation policies, external events in the Arab-Israeli conflict, the behavior of Israeli settlers, changes in the political, economic and social composition of the Palestinian Arab communities, and the activities of resistance movements, including the PLO, independent Palestinians and Islamic fundamentalists such as Hamas. Thus, the first phase to be discussed runs from the beginning of the occupation to the 1972 mayoral elections, but within that period there is another phase, already discussed in Chapter I: the PLO's attempt to conduct a guerrilla/terrorist war of national liberation in Israel and the occupied territories, 1967–68.

The Early Years
June 1967–1972

Israel's initial occupation authority was a military government under Minister of Defense Moshe Dayan. While Dayan's opinions about the ultimate disposition of the territories were ambiguous and shifting, his policy as a military governor was to persuade the Arabs that it was in their interest to live peacefully and productively under overall Israeli rule. If they did they could have considerable self-government but never complete self-determination. If they resisted Israeli rule they would be subject to severe repressive measures.[8] Dayan emphasized the prospects for local self-government by minimizing the IDF presence.[9]

As described in Chapter 2, Arafat attempted to conduct a guerrilla/terrorist war of national liberation in Israel and the occupied territories, roughly from September 1967 to the end of 1968. Naturally, Israel's counterinsurgency measures affected the population of the occupied areas, engendering greater Israeli emphasis on security.[10]

The situation in Gaza was markedly different from that in the West Bank. The Egyptians had left weapons behind in Gaza and there were active PLO agents. They soon controlled the refugee camps and used them as bases for terrorism both against the Israelis and against Arabs cooperating with the Israelis. For example, they bombed and grenaded Arab day laborers waiting to go to work in Israel. This situation became acute at the end of 1970 and came to a head on January 4, 1971, when the Israelis responded to a grenade attack that killed two Israelis with a crack-down directed by Ariel Sharon. Some 13,000 Palestinians were uprooted as bulldozers smashed wider avenues in the refugee camps to permit control. Most of them were sent to al-Arish in Sinai.[11]

Throughout 1971 Sharon conducted relentless operations featuring detentions, curfews and interrogations. It is estimated that 742 *fedayeen* were killed or captured. By the end of 1971 the Gaza insurrection was over.[12]

The catastrophe for the PLO of "Black September" 1970 in Jordan and the continuing ordeal of the PLO which was definitively defeated and ejected from Jordan by July 1971, the collapse of resistance in Gaza and the general effectiveness of Dayan's carrot-and-stick policies produced a period of quiet that permitted mayoral elections in April 1972. The elections brought in mayors who, on the whole, favored a resolution for the West Bank with Jordan and/or Israel.[13]

Growing Unrest Followed by Pessimism
1973–1976

In January 1973 a decision was made to form a Palestinian National Front (PNF) to organize resistance in the territories. An April 10, 1973, Israeli commando raid in Beirut to assassinate PLO leaders outraged the Palestinians and caused the advancement of the arrangements for the PNF, which was established and began operations in August 1973.[14] A wave of unrest and disturbances ensued, partly as a result of Israeli actions that increased Palestinian frustration, from some statements by Dayan to the publication of the Labor party's Galili Plan.[15]

Israel was shaken by the 1973 Yom Kippur War. Israeli superiority over the Arabs was now in question. Moreover, the 1974 Rabat Arab summit's recognition of the PLO as the sole representative of the Palestinian people was a blow to Israeli hopes to deal only with non-PLO Palestinians and Jordan in settling the future of the territories.[16]

In this context Shimon Peres, who became defense minister after the Yom Kippur War, launched a major initiative in October 1975 to give autonomy to the West Bank and Gaza. Perceiving that this implied that there would never be an independent sovereign Palestinian state, the West Bank and Gaza Palestinians reacted with a wave of strikes and civil disobedience.[17]

Riots, which began in Nablus in November 1975 with student strikes, soon spread throughout the West Bank. The disturbances reached a climax in March 1976, when Israeli soldiers stormed secondary schools in Nablus and Ramallah and invaded dorms at Bir Zeit University, beating residents.[18] In addition to expressing resistance to Peres's autonomy plans, the Palestinian uprising of this period had multiple causes including: the establishment of a Gush Emunim settlement near Nablus in December 1975, further expropriations near Ramallah the same month, and an Israeli court ruling (later overturned) permitting Jewish prayers on the Temple Mount. Part of the Israeli response included the permanent stationing of the IDF in some of the West Bank's major towns.[19]

In April 1976 pro-PLO candidates ousted the moderates in local elections.[20] More protests followed, keyed to events such as Israel's Independence Day, Syria's intervention against the PLO in the Lebanon Civil War and anti-Palestinian measures in Kuwait and Jordan, and Israel's imposition to impose a value added tax in the territories.[21] Israeli countermeasures, aided by Palestinian mayors anxious to demonstrate that they turn on and off popular protests, contained the protests. Moreover, by the end of 1976 the outcome of the Lebanon Civil War and the general trends in Israeli politics leading to a Likud electoral victory in 1977 produced a general mood of pessimism among the Palestinians in the territories.[22]

The West Bank Is Judea and Samaria

When Menachem Begin's government took office on June 21, 1977 Israel's policy of holding on to the territories while granting the Palestinians some autonomy became even more adamant. The Likud's constituencies and Begin himself spoke of the West Bank as "Judea and Samaria," integral parts of *Eretz Israel,* or "Greater Israel," Israel's rightful domain based on religious/historic grounds. To be sure, Judea and Samaria were mainly populated by Arab Palestinians, but that could be changed over time by a more aggressive Jewish settlements policy. This policy would be implemented by Ariel Sharon, the new agriculture minister, while the new defense minister, Ezer Weizman, directed the military administration of the territories. Weizman stressed assistance to autonomous municipal governments. These policies, together with the impact of Sadat's November 1977 Jerusalem initiative, led to a period of relative calm.[23]

As Sharon's vision of greatly increased Jewish settlements in the territories became better known and as Israel carried out the 1978 Litani Operation, Palestinian resistance revived. Israeli countermeasures escalated. By the end of 1978 the Israelis were again blowing up houses after having refrained from this practice for three years.[24]

By mid-1981 the military administration was assuming an adversary stance vis-à-vis the mayors, seeking to neutralize them, a policy that became more pronounced when Sharon took over as defense minister in August 1981. However, Sharon then attempted the gambit of the hard-liner seeming to adopt a softer line. He inaugurated a period of "liberalization," ended collective punishments and, in November 1981, introduced a "Civil Administration," with Menachem Milson as its head. Milson, professor of Arabic literature at the Hebrew University, had served both as a veteran officer under Sharon and as chief of Arab affairs in the West Bank government.[25] The object of the policy was to uproot PLO influence in the territories and produce a non-PLO political infrastructure.[26] Policies associated with the plan eventually provoked far-flung disturbances from March to May 1982. During these, thirteen civilians were killed in clashes with the IDF.[27]

From the Lebanon War to the Intifada

The West Bank was quiet during the 1982 Lebanon War but there were major disturbances after the Sabra and Shatilla massacre and during former President Carter's tour of the territories six months later.[28] In 1983–84 rock throwing and other forms of resistance to Israeli rule increased. The defeated Arafat seemed to grow in popularity, an ironic development since a major purpose of the 1982 war had been to disabuse the Palestinians of any hope that Arafat might prevail.[29] Arab mayors were appointed to replace IDF officers and more resources were committed for improving the standard of living in the occupied territories but still the security situation deteriorated.

In the territories, for instance, there were some 133 Molotov cocktail attacks by Palestinians in 1984–85; they increased to 167 in 1985–86.[30]

While there were some months of relative calm, especially the spring of 1985, by August 1985 the IDF was following a new "iron fist" hard line to deal with continuing unrest. Deportations and Administrative Detention were re-established. There ensued a substantial decline in hostile activity.[31] In March 1986, IDF troops were obliged to break up extensive disturbances associated with the annual "Land Day" (March 30) protests. The use of force changed the situation drastically, setting off waves of protests. The most serious protests came in December 1986, when two students were shot and killed at Bir Zeit University, provoking six days of intensive unrest. The use of live ammunition almost immediately in confronting protesters drew criticism within Israel. While successfully clamping down on the unrest, the IDF was reported to be making an intensive search for alternative equipment and methods to deal with riots and disturbances.[32]

The Intifada

The Palestinian uprising, *intifada* in Arabic, began spontaneously on December 8, 1987, after an accident in which an Israeli truck collided with vehicles carrying Arab workmen, killing four and injuring seven in Gaza.[33] The culmination of twenty years of Palestinian resentment of and resistance to the Israeli occupation, the *intifada* was not initiated or, at the outset, controlled by the PLO.[34] In a short time it became a well-coordinated, continuing uprising, with local rather than external PLO leadership, the so-called "Unified Leadership."[35] The Israelis were taken by surprise and their initial reactions were *ad hoc* and unsatisfactory.[36]

Beginning with Rabin's January 19, 1988, announcement of the beatings policy described below,[37] Israel's counterinsurgency policies became more coherent. A number of different tactics and means were used, described in part in the latter parts of this chapter. In general, there was little disposition on the part of the Israelis to take a soft, conciliatory line. Israel's posture was that of a government determined to suppress the uprising wherever and whenever appeared. Counterinsurgency operations were extended to isolated rural villages hitherto left alone.[38]

Israel was faced with a continuing, widespread, violent uprising that persisted despite drastic repressive measures.[39] It took the form of mass demonstrations, establishment of roadblocks, especially with burning tires, and attacks on Israeli security forces, as well as civilians, with stones, objects propelled by sling shots and Molotov cocktails. The *intifada* also was manifested through strikes, boycotts, closure of stores in defiance of Israeli orders and various forms of civil disobedience, e.g., nonpayment of taxes, violation of laws regarding licensing.[40]

In the spring of 1988 the press reported that Israel had developed an "Overall Plan" to deal with the unrest in the occupied territories. The aim of the Overall Plan was to reduce significantly the level of violence and to prevent the *intifada's* leadership from severing the links between the civil administration and the population.[41] The Israeli security measures, in effect, reestablished the "Green Line" between the territories and Israel itself which Begin had tried to erase.[42]

By May 1988 the Israeli counterinsurgency measures combined with the onset of the Muslim month of Ramadan to reduce the level and incidence of violence. Prime Minister Shamir claimed that the territories were "stabilizing" and "approaching a return to order," permitting the reopening of schools for a few weeks.[43]

With the close of Ramadan, violence escalated and by midsummer 1988 it was clear that the violence was complemented and in part driven by a new political dynamic. This was clearly influenced by King Hussein's July 31, 1988, announcement that he was cutting Jordan's ties to the West Bank and by Faisal Husseini's proposal that the PLO declare the establishment of the State of Palestine.[44] Shortly thereafter, defense minister Rabin announced that he was outlawing "popular committees" because of their connection to the violence, but also, and more importantly, because they were intended to displace the Israeli administration. Israel also deported some of the committees' more active members.[45]

By September 1988, Rabin was claiming that the IDF was well on the way to putting down the *intifada*.[46] At the end of the year, General Amram Mitzna, Officer Commanding the Central Front (OCC), also maintained that declining incidents and casualties in the last months indicated that the IDF was regaining control.[47] However, the major political events of late 1988 were having effects that negated these optimistic Israeli judgments. With the declaration of the State of Palestine at the Algiers Arab Summit, November 14, 1988, the Arafat's pronouncements in December 1988, leading to U.S. talks with the PLO, the Palestinian resistance escalated. Shortly after General Mitzna talked of regaining control, the number of violent incidents, deaths and injured went up dramatically: December 9, 1988–January 9, 1989, killed 26 and 492, whereas in the previous month they had been 10/281. The number of incidents rose from 1,595 to 2,790.[48]

On January 17, 1989, Rabin announced a series of new measures to deal with the *intifada*. Included were five-year prison sentences for stone-throwing; $1,000 or more fines for parents of violators under age fourteen; house demolitions in cases where stone-throwing caused serious injuries; and the number of soldiers authorized to fire plastic bullets was increased.[49]

Thus far, Israeli counterinsurgency policies had been almost exclusively hard-line. This is understandable because the Palestinians were not demanding reforms that Israel might extend but independence, something that Israel was not prepared to grant. However, in March 1989 an intelligence report was leaked to the press. It stated that the *intifada* could not be ended in the near future, that there was no serious leadership in the territories outside of the PLO, and that the PLO had moved toward moderation.[50] In April 1989 Prime Minister Shamir initiated a political strategy based on offering elections to the Palestinians so that they might have a significant measure of autonomy—without any prospect for independence.[51]

The spring of 1989 also saw the first large-scale use of economic incentives, which eventually became part of a program to issue new ID cards for Gazans.[52]

As part of an attempt to cut costs and to contain the interference of counterinsurgency duties on regular IDF training, the Israelis began to redeploy their forces away from the small Arab villages in 1989. One of the results of this was an increase in attacks reported by Israeli settlers, especially on the West Bank. By the spring of 1989 there was a rise in violence by settlers on vigilante/retaliation missions.[53]

In August 1989, for the second time in the course of the *intifada,* there were reports that the uprising was dying out. As a result of detentions and deportations of the principal *intifada* leaders and aggressive security force tactics featuring surprise raids to root out activists, local gangs had taken over much of the control. There was increased violence but on a less extensive scale.[54]

The threat of escalation by radical elements within the *intifada* materialized in late November 1989, when terrorists armed with assault rifles killed three IDF reservists in a jeep in the Gaza Strip. Brig. Gen. Zvi Poleg, commanding IDF forces in the Gaza Strip, warned that such attacks could change "the rules of the game." However, it appeared that such actions were not favored by the *intifada's* leadership since a shooting war with the IDF would not be wise and the uprising would likely lose some of its support in world opinion.[55]

Attention focused on suppression of the terrorist gangs who had been killing alleged collaborators and engaging in a wide range of acts of intimidation and violence. At the beginning of December special Israeli antiterrorist troops killed four members of 1989 a "Black Panther" assassination squad and carried out a large-scale raid in Nablus in which they rounded up scores of suspects.[56]

Just before the second anniversary of the outbreak of the *intifada,* Defense Minister Rabin conceded that it could continue for years, but also asserted that Israel "can deal with the attrition better than they can."[57] Rabin was confident that a threefold strategy of ongoing military action, legally imposed punishments and economic pressures would contain the *intifada.* He said, "There is no civil disobedience now, only passive acceptance of the strikes."[58]

By mid-1990 the *intifada* appeared to have reached its lowest ebb with only 8 Palestinians killed in June in clashes with the IDF, the lowest number since the *intifada* began and even less in July. Nearly 1,000 persons had died in the *intifada,* at least 920 of them Palestinians, but the trend continued to be towards deaths in intra-Arab violence, at least 230 overall. These deaths resulted from attacks on alleged Israeli collaborators but also from internecine warfare between resistance factions and simple criminal activity.[59]

Violence in the occupied territories flared up again after the riot on the Table Mount on October 8, 1990. Nineteen Palestinians were killed and more than fifty wounded as the Israeli security forces subdued a mob that assaulted a police station on the Temple Mount and stoned Jewish worshipers at the Western Wall on the Jewish feast of Sukkot. An Israeli investigation blamed the Palestinians and their religious leaders for the incident but faulted the police for inadequate preparations for an expected confrontation. A UN Security Council Resolution condemned the Israeli actions and Secretary General Javier Perez de Cuellar tried to send a UN mission to investigate the incident. Israel refused to accept such a mission on a number of grounds but particularly because the October 8 clash occurred in Jerusalem, Israel's capital.

The Temple Mount incident exacerbated what was already a difficult situation in the territories and in Israel itself. Israeli relations with the United States suffered and Israel was once again the object of UN condemnations at a time when the U.S. was marshalling support for action against Iraq.*

The history of the uprising, as of Israel's war with the PLO and the larger

---

* "Israeli Police Kill 19 Palestinians in Temple Mount Confrontation," WP, October 9, 1990, A1, cols. 4–6; A15, cols. 2–6; "Baker Suggests Greater Restraint by Israel," Ibid. A15, cols. 1–2; "Mild Israel Censure Approved by U.N.," Ibid, October 13, 1990, A1, cols. 5–6; A16, cols. 1–4; "U.S. Joins U.N. Vote Denouncing Israel," Ibid, October 25, 1990, A1, cols. 5–6; A34, col. 1; "Israeli Panel Gives Report on Killings," Ibid, October 27, 1990. A1, col. 1; A20, cols. 1–3.

Evidence of violence following the Temple Mount clash may be found in the following reports: "Israeli Troops Wound 35 Palestinians in Gaza," Ibid, October 19, 1990, A28, cols. 2–4; "Arab Worker Kills 3 Jews in Jerusalem," Ibid, October 22, 1990, A1, col. 6; A16, cols. 1–3; "Israel Closes Its Borders To Entry by Palestinians," Ibid, October 24, 1990, A12, cols. 1–2; A15, cols. 1–3, "3 Arabs Die, 2 Jews Hurt in Attacks," Ibid, October 31, 1990, A36, cols. 1–3.

Arab-Israeli conflict, suggests that many factors will operate to create new phases in the *intifada,* leaving the future of the conflict uncertain.

Principles of the International Law of Belligerent Occupation

As remarked above, it is difficult to fit the law of belligerent occupation to the extraordinary character of Israel's occupation of the West Bank and Gaza. It is, accordingly, important to emphasize the broad principles that underly that law before examining specific issues. While the detailed prescriptions and prohibitions of the international law of belligerent occupation are voluminous and often complicated in their application, the basic principles of this body of law are simple.[60] They are the principles of military necessity and humanity.[61] The belligerent occupant is at war. It has the right to secure its military position within the occupied territory in order to continue the war. If the actual hostilities are interrupted, as in the case of truces, the belligerent occupant has the right to maintain its military position so as not to be disadvantaged should hostilities resume. Whether in time of continuing or suspended hostilities, the belligerent occupant has the right to maintain order in its area of control. The occupant also has a right to draw on the resources of the area to support its operations so long as its use of them is reasonably proportionate to its military necessities.[62]

Under the principle of humanity the belligerent occupant has the duty to replace the displaced government and to provide at least minimal governmental protection and services to the population. In so doing the occupant is traditionally prohibited from enacting major changes in the political, legal, economic and social character of the area unless such changes are required by military necessity or by the principle of humanity itself. For example, American occupying forces in Germany during World War II would have the right to eliminate Nazi institutions, laws and personnel both for reasons of military necessity and humanity.

Traditionally, the relationship between the belligerent occupant and the occupied population has been seen as one of a temporary sovereign to temporary subjects. In exchange for the protection and services provided to the population its members were thought to owe a kind of temporary allegiance to the occupying power. There was assumed to be a kind of tacit contractual relationship in which each side would do its part as long as the other side did its.[63]

This relationship obviously has been subject to strains, particularly in modern conflicts that often bring together armed forces and populations of vastly different political, ideological, racial or other characters. If, on the one hand, the occupying power exploits the area disproportionately and violates the principle of humanity, as the Nazis did in World War II, the tacit contract has been broken and the occupied population has a legal and moral right to defend itself and resist the occupation in any way it can. On the other hand, if, despite general compliance with the principles of military necessity and humanity by the occupying power, elements in the population continue the war through guerrilla warfare or other means, the occupied population has broken the contract and can expect a harsh reaction.[64]

Belligerent occupations, then, usually suffer the strains of the tension between the mutual interest of the occupying power and the occupied population in maintaining a stable status quo and the natural tendency of enemies to upset it to the advantage of their own side. Often this tension is exacerbated by tensions between the desire of a good part, often the majority, of the occupied population to maintain tolerable relations with the occupying power and the determination of resistance activists, often a minority, to fight the occupying power. This frequently engenders a spiral of partisan attacks and reprisals by the occupant to the pain and detriment of the majority of the population—as well as to the occupying power. Of course, either side may justify this pain if it is the price of ultimate victory. The dilemma of the law of belligerent occupation is to balance the requirements of desirable stability between the occupant and the occupied with the exigencies of ultimate victory.

The Law of Belligerent Occupation:
The West Bank and Gaza

The principal sources of the law of belligerent occupation are the 1907 Hague Convention IV and the 1949 Fourth Geneva Convention Relative to the Protection of Civilian Persons in Time of War.[65] The 1907 Hague Convention IV, to which Israel is not a party, is generally considered to be part of customary international law.[66] There is a large body of customary international law to be found in the judgments of war crimes tribunals, national as well as international, following World War II.[67] However, evidence of customary law concerning belligerent occupation in international and other conflicts since World War II is very sparse. Indeed, one problem with discussing the law applicable to Israel's occupations has been that it seems to have been virtually the only case to which international opinion and legal commentaries have paid much attention. This has resulted in large measure from the fact that Israel is an open society wherein it is possible to observe and obtain the facts relating to occupation, whereas access to the details of, for example, Vietnamese policies in Cambodia or Soviet policies in Afghanistan has been very difficult.[68]

The applicability of the 1907 Hague and 1949 Geneva Conventions to the Israeli occupation of the West Bank and Gaza has been an issue on which Israel stands against the world. Although not a party to 1907 Hague Convention IV, Israel follows its provisions as customary law. However, Israel contends that the 1949 Fourth Geneva Convention, to which it is a party, does not apply to its occupation of the West Bank and Gaza. Nevertheless, Israel has announced from the outset of the occupation in June 1967 that she would observe the "humanitarian provisions" of the Fourth Geneva Convention.[69]

The other states that have expressed an opinion and/or voted for resolutions on the subject in international fora, the UN Security Council and General Assembly, the International Committee of the Red Cross (ICRC) all maintain that the 1949 Fourth Geneva Convention applies to the Israeli occupation of the West Bank and Gaza.[70]

The Israelis base their position on an interpretation of Article 2 of the 1949 Fourth Geneva Convention. Article 2 provides:

> In addition to the provisions which shall be implemented in peacetime, the present Convention shall apply to all cases of declared war or of any other armed conflict which may arise between two or more of the High Contracting Parties, even if the state of war is not recognized by one of them.
>
> The Convention shall also apply to all cases of partial or total occupation of the territory of a High Contracting Power, even if the said occupation meets with no armed resistance.

Israel contends that the West Bank and Gaza were not part of the "territory" of Jordan and Egypt, respectively, in June 1967. As discussed in the beginning of this chapter, Jordan's claim to sovereignty over the West Bank was controversial and had been opposed by Israel, particularly in 1950 at the time when Jordan purported to annex that territory. Egypt never claimed sovereignty over the Gaza Strip. Therefore, neither the West Bank or Gaza was part of "the territory of a high contracting power" in the sense of Article 2 (2) of the 1949 Fourth Geneva Convention. Meir Shamgar, former chief justice of the Supreme Court of Israel, Military Advocate General (1961–68), Attorney General of Israel (1968–75), contended that to accept the applicability of the 1949 Fourth Geneva Convention would amount to recognizing the sovereignty of Jordan and Egypt over the West Bank and Gaza, respectively. He also raised questions about the interpretation of and relation between the first and second paragraphs of Article 2 of the Fourth Geneva Convention.[71]

Professor Adam Roberts has criticized the Israeli position on a number of grounds. He points out that it is the first paragraph of 1949 Geneva Convention IV. Article 2, quoted above, that should be applied and that this paragraph applies, *inter alia,* to "any other armed conflict," with no requirement that the territory occupied be that of a High Contracting Party.[72] Roberts raises other objections, including inconsistencies in Israeli positions, and the possibilities for Israel to abuse its position of selective application of the "humanitarian" provisions of the Fourth Geneva Convention.[73]

Shamgar summarizes Israel's approach to the occupied territories:

> From the normative point of view the rule of law in the territories found its expression in the adoption of two main principles of action: (1) the prevention of the development of a legal vacuum by the *de facto* observance of customary international law and the humanitarian rules included in the Hague Rules and the Fourth Convention and furthermore: (2) the supplementation of the above-mentioned rules and provisions by the basic principles of natural justice as derived from the system of law existing in Israel, reflecting similar principles developed in Western democracies.[74]

The second principle refers to Israeli laws which improved on the minimal human rights provisions of the laws inherited by the previous occupant, e.g., repeal of provisions for capital punishment.[75]

Unfortunately, analysis of the Israeli position is complicated by the difficulty of defining or identifying "humanitarian" provisions of the 1907 Hague and 1949 Fourth Geneva Conventions. The ICRC has promoted a usage of "humanitarian" which embraces all of the law of war or, as modern usage has it, international conflict. Thus, the ICRC conferences that produced contemporary law of international conflict conventions are dubbed "humanitarian." If this usage prevails, every substantive provision of the law of international conflict is "humanitarian." This usage ignores the traditional distinction between the law governing means and methods of warfare, e.g., Article 23 of the 1907 Hague Convention IV, and the humanitarian law dealing with subjects such as protecting the wounded and sick, prisoners of war and civilian persons.

The practical effect of the Israeli approach is to apply selectively the law of the Hague and Geneva conventions and customary international law. Presumably what Israel applies is considered "humanitarian" and what she rejects is not.

As remarked earlier, Israel stands alone in its interpretation of the law of belligerent occupation and its application to the West Bank and Gaza. Accordingly, it is possible simply to tick off all of the provisions of that law that Israel declines to observe and to condemn her for each and every violation. Additionally, it is possible to find instances where there is evidence that Israel, while acknowledging that certain prescriptions of the law of belligerent occupation were binding, has not always observed them. These violations are added to the record by various committees of lawyers and by publicists.[76]

A different approach will be taken in this study. Beyond the claims to the West Bank and Gaza, the occupation of those territories is a matter of the survival of the state of Israel. Any relinquishment of those territories in whole or in part will have to be accompanied with the most serious provisions for Israel's security—a point generally recognized in peace proposals. Meanwhile, the occupation of these territories is an important component in Israel's war with the PLO and deterrence/defense posture vis-à-vis possible Arab state enemies that might resume hostilities. Accordingly, the issues of belligerent occupation law raised by Israel's long occupation of the territories should not be viewed solely from the standpoint of lawyers interpreting treaties.[77]

Instead, the requirements of the conventional and customary law of belligerent occupation should be interpreted in the light of the military/security situation in the occupied territories. The law should be interpreted in such a way as to acknowledge legitimate military/security necessities and to balance them against the demands of humanity developed in the law of belligerent occupation.

The issues to be discussed will be analyzed in the context of a continuing war between the PLO and its various allies and Israel. It has been over twenty years since the end of hostilities in the 1967 June War and almost that long since the 1970–71 War of Attrition and the 1973 Yom Kippur War, but Israel's low intensity war with the PLO continues, in the context of the threat of renewed war with Arab states, and its military necessities continue to compete with the claims of humanity in the Occupied Territories. This is not to say that military necessity must always prevail, providing a blank check to Israel's security forces. In each case, considerations of military necessity must be carefully evaluated and balanced against countervailing considerations of humanity. Specifically, measures justified under military necessity must be proportionate to a legitimate military/security end and must be discriminate. Moreover, it is believed that there will be cases where considerations of military necessity and humanity are more complementary than competitive. In the analyses that follow, an attempt will be made to identify the values that underlie the various prescriptions of the Hague and Geneva conventions and to balance those values against Israel's military/security necessities.

Israel's Use of Force in the Occupied Territories

Three categories of force employed in emergency security measures in the territories will be considered: beating; special ammunitions that may be lethal; and deadly force. These categories form a ladder of escalation rather than a chronological ordering of Israeli tactics. Actually, an emphasis on beating replaced deadly force that, in the early days of the *intifada,* caused many casualties.

Beating

In the face of intense criticism at home and abroad of the use of deadly force in suppressing *intifada* violence, Defense Minister Yitzhak Rabin announced a new policy of "force, power and blows" on January 19, 1988. This new policy had been introduced two weeks earlier and Rabin's public announcement was designed to explain it to the troops and the country.[78] Rabin's stark rhetoric and the appearance of Palestinians suffering from the beating policy sparked controversy in Israel. In response, one week later, Rabin expressed concern at reports of "indiscriminate beatings" and clarified the orders, saying that there "shouldn't be blows for the sake of blows."[79]

Israel's Attorney General, Yosef Harish, criticized the beating policy in a letter to Rabin that was later released to the press. Harish warned that "[t]he number of complaints [about beatings after arrest, etc.] raises the suspicion that classifying these incidents as exceptions no longer reflects reality."[80] Consequently, the IDF circulated a "Letter to a Soldier" to acquaint soldiers with the legal aspects of the use of force in suppressing the *intifada.*[81] On February 23, 1988, Chief of Staff Dan Shomron issued a "Dispatch" containing instructions clarifying the use of beatings, stating:

> I would like to clarify and emphasize that force is to be used for the purpose of fulfilling our task according to law and the orders of the army, from which there should be no deviation. *Under no circumstances should force be used as a means of punishment.* The use of force is permitted during a violent incident in order to break up a riot, to overcome resistance to legal arrest, and during pursuit after rioters or suspects—all within the confines of the time and place where the incident occurs. Force is not to

be used once the objective has been attained—for example, after a riot has been dispersed or after a person is in the hands of our forces and is not resisting. In every instance the use of force must be reasonable.[82] (emphasis added)

A year later, General Shomron was called to testify in the court-martial of four members of the Givati Brigade who were charged with manslaughter in the beating death of a Palestinian man from the Gaza Strip. The defense called Shomron to demonstrate that there were "grey areas" in his clarifying policy statement of February 23, 1988, i.e., when an incident is "over," when a suspect stops "resisting." The defense showed that there was a wide discrepancy between the Army's official orders and the IDF's actual practices in Gaza.[83]

The U.S. State Department *Country Report on Human Rights Practices in Israel for 1988* estimated that the number of casualties resulting from beatings was at least thirteen dead and an unknown number wounded.[84] Israel defended the beating policy:

(1) as an alternative to deadly force;[85]
(2) as more effective than other methods, such as smoke and teargas grenades and rubber bullets;[86]
(3) as the best available deterrent.[87]

The critics of the beating policy contend that it was not used for self-defense of the soldiers or to control Arabs resisting arrest in the course of a riot or disturbance but to punish. Al-Haq* claimed that most beating incidents took place when the person concerned was already in the hands of the Army and under circumstances where force was not actually needed to control a situation, e.g., after dispersal of a demonstration. Amnesty International contended that there was little evidence of control of beatings within the chain of command; that there had been few prosecutions and little information on disciplinary measures.[88]

However, by 1990 the Israeli High Court of Justice ordered the court-martial of Colonel Yehuda Meir, former military commander of Nablus, accused of ordering his troops to beat and break the bones of twenty bound and gagged Palestinians from the villages of Beit and Hawara near Nablus in January 1988. Judge Advocate General Amnon Strashnow had argued that Meir had been sufficiently punished when he was reprimanded, relieved

---

* Al-Haq is the Ramallah-based Palestinian affiliate of the International Commission of Jurists and a widely cited human rights monitor. The U.S. Department of State considers al-Haq sufficiently authoritative that it frequently cites al-Haq in its human rights reports.

of his command and given the choice of resigning from the IDF or facing court-martial. He had resigned but retained pension rights. This was the first case of the High Court overruling the IDF judge-advocate general and the first in which an officer of Meir's rank was brought to trial. Defense Minister Rabin stated in a communication to a Knesset member that the IDF's legal system applies to members of all ranks and that three major and five captains had been tried for committing offenses connected to IDF operations in the territories. In the Meir case the High Court rejected the argument that the beatings policy was unclear, holding that Meir's order was clearly illegal. Justice Moshe Bejski stated: "These actions outrage every civilized person, and no lack of clarity can cover this up. Certainly, if the order is given by a senior officer, this officer must be aware that the morality of the IDF forbids such behavior."[89]

Beatings not justified by military/security necessity constitute a grave breach of the 1949 Fourth Geneva Convention, Article 147 of which cites "wilfully causing great suffering or serious injury to body or health" as one of the grave breaches. Even if the convention were not deemed applicable, unjustified beatings would certainly be prohibited by the customary law of war and the principles of military necessity and humanity. Any sampling of media reports on the *intifada* confirms that a very substantial number of beatings have, indeed, taken place in circumstances that did not warrant them and that they were carried out as punishment rather than for the purpose of subduing rioters in acts of violence.[90]

The issue is complicated because the beatings may serve several functions. Officially their function is to serve as a means of immediate self-defense for the military and security forces and as a means of coercion to suppress violence and lawlessness and effect the arrest of the rioters. However, it is clear from the statements of Rabin and others that the beatings are also viewed as a deterrent to *intifada* violence and demonstrations. If the self-defense/repression of violence rationale is emphasized, any beatings not related to those functions are violations of the laws of war. If, however, the deterrent rationale is emphasized, the beatings become a kind of threat of "unacceptable damage" that might deter people from participating in *intifada* demonstrations and violence.

If beatings are to serve as a deterrent as well as a self-defense function, however, they should still be limited to the circumstances of immediate hostilities between the IDF and other security forces and the Palestinians. This would have some deterrent effect. Indeed, it is not clear that beating prisoners after they have been arrested and away from the scene of hostilities would have a deterrent effect. On the contrary, it might very well motivate the Palestinians to continue and escalate the resistance.

Of course, official Israeli practice is to bar beating for the purpose of punishment and this has been demonstrated by the cases when soldiers have been court-martialed or otherwise disciplined for unauthorized beatings. The issue, then, becomes that raised by Amnesty International, namely, whether Israel has made sufficient efforts to control beatings by preventing, suppressing and punishing unauthorized beatings. This is part of the larger problem of assessing the overall record of Israel in controlling and disciplining its military/security forces, to be discussed at the end of this chapter. However, on the specific issue of control of the beating policy it appears that the Israeli record is unsatisfactory.

In its January 3, 1990, Response to Amnesty International, the Israeli Justice Ministry stated:

> At the outset of the rioting, large numbers of IDF members were thrust into a position of having to contend with mobs of rock-throwing rioters. The soldiers' training in conventional warfare did not prepare them for this challenge. Short of using their rifles, the soldiers' main tool to protect life and to restore order in the streets were their night-sticks (billy clubs). The IDF command believed that charging rioters with night-sticks, while more dangerous to the soldiers involved, would ultimately inflict fewer fatalities. This was in fact the case as the number of fatalities dropped. In the meantime, other methods of riot control, such as the use of tear-gas and 22-caliber, rubber and plastic bullets, were introduced on a wider scale.[91]

The Israeli response to Amnesty International then recalls General Shomron's February 1988 "Dispatch" limiting beating and calling for the maintenance of "the law, morals and discipline which we have all been imbued." The Response's section "Appropriate Use of Night-Sticks in Subduing Riots" concludes with the statement that educational programs to "instruct soldiers in lawful behavior" have been conducted to supplement the February 1988 "Dispatch" and other directives.

Clearly efforts were taken from the outset to confine beatings to the circumstances outlined in the rules of engagement but the judgment of Amnesty International that these efforts were not sufficient appears to be warranted, subject to persuasive rebuttal by Israel.

Special Ammunitions

Tear Gas. If the *intifada* is treated as a domestic disturbance there is no question about Israel's right to employ nonlethal riot control chemical means. However, the charge of her critics has been that these means have at times been employed in circumstances that rendered them lethal. Reliable figures of alleged deaths and injuries caused by riot control gas released in confined areas or in ways that caused it to be excessively concentrated have been impossible to obtain for a variety of reasons having to do with access to autopsy reports and official Israeli death certificates. Figures for deaths in 1988 from tear gas range from fourteen (al-Haq) to over forty (Amnesty International). There have also been many reports of miscarriages caused by exposure to tear gas; thirty in 1988, according to al-Haq.[92]

Based on numerous reports of misuse, generally regarding firing riot control gas into enclosed spaces and using the gas in high concentrations, Amnesty International has asserted: "Israeli soldiers are employing it also in such a way as to constitute a punitive measure to harass and intimidate Palestinian residents of the occupied territories."[93]

Several legal issues are raised by the charges against Israel. First, if riot control gases are used as punishment and harassment, then their use violates the principles of proportion and discrimination. There is no sufficient military necessity in such cases to warrant violation of the principle of humanity. Second, if the chemical means are deliberately employed in places and circumstances and in forms that may render them lethal, they are transforming the weapon from the nonlethal to the lethal or deadly force category.

This does not, however, seem to be Israeli policy. The Israeli government stated in January 1990:

> Tear gas of the standard type employed by police throughout the world is used to control riots, and Israeli orders bar its use in closed structures; at times, during a riot, some of the tear gas used outside may penetrate buildings—that effect, however, is unintentional.[94]

The U.S. General Accounting Office supported the Israelis in a report in 1990 when it concluded that the tear gas used by Israel would only be lethal in very high concentrations and that there was insufficient evidence of deaths and miscarriages allegedly caused by Israeli use of tear gas. The report noted that, while tear gas is one of the most "humane forms of riot control," there had been some occasional misuse of it by the Israelis. The misuse, however, was not widespread.[95] The Israelis themselves have hotly contested the charges of their critics, asserting, for instance, that Amnesty International has relied on mere reports of deaths involving tear gas with no medical evidence to substantiate them.[96]

Given the importance of tear gas as a means of riot control and the fact that it often must be used in very crowded urban areas, it is inevitable that allegations of misuse of this means will continue. There are indications that the IDF is taking reasonable steps to respond to misuse, such as the jailing of an IDF reserve officer who threw tear gas grenades into a UN clinic in the Gaza Strip.[97]

Plastic Bullets. The IDF had used rubber bullets in riot control operations but in August 1987, before the *intifada* began, the Defense Minister authorized the use of "plastic bullets" in the occupied territories.[98] These bullets differed from the plastic bullets used by the British Army in Northern Ireland. The British "baton round" is 5 inches long and about 1.5 inches in diameter and generally cannot penetrate the body. The Israeli rounds are small, hard, sharp-edged plastic slugs.

When they were introduced in August 1987, the IDF stated that only officers and specially trained NCO's could fire the plastic bullets. The rules of engagement were to require that the bullets be fired at distances of more than seventy meters; they must be aimed below rioters' knees and women and children below the age of sixteen should not be targeted. At night only officers were to fire the ammunition.[99] Israel's January 3, 1990 Response to Amnesty International states: "Every use of plastic bullets is reported to, and investigated by, the command echelon. The orders stipulate that in every situation the officer has to consider the alternative means of riot control such as the use of rubber bullets or tear gas."[100]

However, the plastic bullets could be used in non-life-threatening situations. This rule of engagement provoked debate when it became clear that the plastic bullets could be a deadly type of ammunition. Through July 1990, plastic bullets have killed 147 Palestinians.[101]

Plastic bullets per se are not an illegal weapon comparable to dumdum bullets or other expanding bullets that cause superfluous suffering.[102] Whether their use in general or in particular cases violates the law of war depends upon the pattern of use. If Israeli soldiers comply generally with the rules of engagement announced when plastic bullets were first introduced in 1987, their use would be legally permissible. Although the permission to use them in situations that were not life-threatening is controversial, it is not clearly violative of law of war standards. However, if the original rules of engagement were not adequately enforced or if they were changed to more permissive rules, it could well be the case that the Israeli use of plastic bullets frequently amounted to the use of deadly force and would have to be evaluated as such.

Legal evaluation of the use of plastic bullets is complicated by the official rationale offered by Defense Minister Rabin. As in the case of the beatings policy, Rabin stressed the value of wounding with plastic bullets as a deterrent. Rabin stated:

> Our purpose is to increase the number of [wounded] among those who take part in violent activities but not to kill them. . . . I am not worried by the increased number of people who get wounded, as long as they were wounded as a result of being involved actively, by instigating, organizing and taking part in violent activities.[103]

This rationale decreases the warrant for treating the plastic bullet issue under the category of deadly force since the explicit purpose of Israeli policy is to wound rather than to kill. The problem still remains, of course, that there have been so many deaths from plastic bullets. But, with the official rationale emphasizing wounding, the issue becomes one of the justification of such wounding with these bullets in situations that are not life-threatening for the soldiers shooting the plastic bullets. Chief of Staff Shomron emphasized repeatedly that use of plastic bullets reduces recourse to live ammunition.[104]

A policy of maximizing woundings with plastic bullets as a deterrent rather than an immediate self-defense measure has been criticized by the United States government and by some Israelis. The Association for Civil Rights in Israel claims that the policy is illegal under Israeli law.[105] The United States's position is:

> The policy of using plastic bullets had admittedly been designed to cause an increase in casualties. We believe that measures must be taken to reduce, rather than to increase, casualties among Palestinian demonstrators.[106]

The *Jerusalem Post* stated editorially that "it is hard to imagine on what grounds the government's legal adviser could justify the non-self-defensive use of plastic bullets."[107] Al-Haq has claimed that the Israelis use of plastic bullets has been deliberately indiscriminate, but this has not been proved.[108] The issue of Israeli use of plastic bullets lies at the threshold of the deadly force issues. The plastic bullet is a substitute for live ammunition. In terms of immediate self-defense of troops in life-threatening situations, it could be a reasonable substitute. However, as a deterrent broadly used to maximize woundings, it is a substitute for less extreme measures such as use of rubber bullets, tear gas and beatings.

If plastic bullets are used indiscriminately against persons not engaged in violence, their use is illegal. But if, as seems more likely to be the case, they are used for the purpose of wounding Palestinians engaged in violence in order to deter them, the issue is not discrimination but proportionality of the means to the deterrent end. Is a policy of deliberately maximizing woundings of Palestinians engaged in violence, as explained by Rabin, a proportionate response to *intifada* violence? This question cannot be answered in the abstract. To judge the policy's proportionality it is necessary to examine the violence that it is supposed to deter. This is also the task of an analysis of Israeli use of deadly force so the two subjects—use of plastic bullets to deter by maximizing wounding at the risk of substantial fatalities and use of deadly force—will be discussed together.

Use of Deadly Force: The IDF

While the tactics and weapons discussed to this point have been controversial and important in Israel's response to *intifada* violence, the use of deadly force with regular live ammunition has accounted for most of the deaths suffered by the Palestinians in the *intifada*. According to one survey, in the period between December 1987 and the end of May 1989, of 463 Palestinians killed by the Israelis, 431 had been killed by gunfire.[109]

As with less lethal means, evaluation of Israeli use of deadly force starts with the rules of engagement (ROEs) and proceeds to an assessment of the extent to which they are followed in practice. According to the Israeli ROEs, live fire is permitted only when the lives of soldiers are in danger. Fire must be directed at specific targets. Soldiers are to aim for the legs. Live ammunition may be used against fleeing suspects only when a serious felony is suspected and, even then, firing may be only a last resort, after calling "Halt or I'll shoot" in Arabic and firing a warning shot in the air.[110]

In defining the circumstances when the lives of soldiers may be in danger, the Israelis have distinguished defense against stone throwing from defense against "petrol bombs" or "Molotov cocktails." The IDF has given permission to use deadly force against those throwing "Molotov cocktails," while denying it in cases of stone throwing.[111]

There is disagreement over the Israeli rules of engagement relating to deadly force and the extent to which they are followed. Amnesty International has asserted that the guidelines are so loose that they have "effectively condoned and even encouraged extrajudicial executions of Palestinians."[112] Al-Haq goes so far as to suggest that, besides the written rules, "other informal and unpublicized guidelines exist, which may differ for each army unit."[113]

Israel contends that all of its military/security measures, including use of deadly force, are permissible under Israeli law, the law of previous rulers in Palestine and international law, and that they are necessary to maintain law, order and the public safety. Some Israelis who have studied the rules in American police forces on the use of deadly force believe that the Israeli

ROEs are even more restrictive. They contend that there are actually fewer occasions when deadly fire is authorized by the Israeli rules than in the American rules. For instance, many American police forces permit the use of deadly fire when threatened with "great bodily harm," while the Israeli rules stress that there must be a true mortal danger before deadly force can be used.[114] Moreover, Ambassador Netanyahu told the UN Security Council at the beginning of the *intifada:*

> We are acting—as is our right under international law—to secure order in the face of violent provocations, and we are doing so with the maximum restraint and in full compliance with the laws that have applied and pertain to those areas for nearly half a century.[115]

Israel frequently notes the differences in casualties in the *intifada* and those that result from "Arab-style pacification."[116] In the first Security Council meeting on the *intifada,* Netanyahu stated:

> Maintaining law and order in the face of deliberate incitement is not an easy task. Our soldiers are under strict instructions. Even when surrounded by mobs whipped up to a frenzy and brandishing Molotov cocktails, iron bars and the like, they are to use non-lethal means such as tear gas and rubber bullets. Live ammunition is to be used only as a last resort, when their lives are threatened or when they have already been injured. However tragic the casualties, their numbers would have been much greater in the absence of this procedure and this restraint. They would undoubtedly have reached the levels of casualties in the disturbances in the period of Jordanian rule in Judea and Samaria—I cited the other day just a handful of disturbances, with 50 persons killed in one day; or, for that matter the hundreds who lost their lives in the disturbances in Mecca recently; or the heavy toll of casualties in the riots in India in recent years—in the Golden Temple, to name only one example, when over 400 persons were killed in one disturbance.[117]

As observed above, Israel's critics deny that the rules of engagement on deadly force are observed. The U.S. Department of State asserts: "These guidelines were often not followed. Soldiers frequently used gunfire in situations that did not present mortal danger to troops, causing many avoidable deaths and injuries."[118] Amnesty International claimed that "despite strict guidelines, live ammunition, particularly high velocity bullets . . . have been used excessively."[119]

Moreover, the necessity and proportionality of frequent Israeli recourse to deadly force has been disputed. Al-Haq maintains that "those creating the 'disturbance' are armed with no more than hand-held missiles such as stones or, at most, iron bars or molotov cocktails."[120] The U.S. State Department asserts that "the IDF, caught by surprise and untrained and inexperienced in riot control, responded in a manner which led to a substantial increase in human rights violations."[121] Criticism of Israeli use of deadly force has come from friendly sources. In an interview in the *Jerusalem Post*, Michael Walzer observed:

> Most soldiers I have talked to believe that a well-trained, well-armed army shouldn't have to kill so many people to contain the type of violence encountered in the territories.

Walzer pointed to the experience of South Korea, where the police and army have clashed for months with tens of thousands of rioting, rock-throwing, fire bomb–hurling students without inflicting heavy casualties.[122]

Despite the great differences in the nature and scope of the conflicts, there is a parallel between the charges of excessive use of deadly force by Israel in combating *intifada* violence and the charges of excessive firepower against U.S. forces in Vietnam. Excessive use of firepower is endemic to modern warfare. The weapons are automatic or semi-automatic, their rate of fire, range and velocity are great. The temptation to employ this awesome fire power in threatening situations is great. Controlled use of fire power requires a degree of training and discipline rarely achieved except by elite units. This is not to suggest an excuse for violating the principles of proportion and discrimination but to state a problem that is universal in the law of war.

Given that this problem exists, it is not enough to condemn a state for excessive use of deadly force, either in a civil war or an international war. Evaluation of the use of firepower should attempt to distinguish extremes and borderline categories. Is the excessive use of fire power so universal as to reflect a policy routinely to rely on overkill? Is excess widespread but apparently more a result of inadequate control than of official policy. Excess sporadic and fortuitous? Is it so rare as to be aberrational?

There is no evidence that excessive use of deadly force is official Israeli policy. There is a widespread conviction, shared to varying degrees by disparate observers such as al-Haq, the U.S. State Department and Michael Walzer, that there is excessive use of deadly force resulting from deficiencies in the training and discipline of troops and the failure to develop adequately nonlethal forms of coercion. This is a serious criticism since the Israeli government and Army are responsible for the conduct of their troops. Having said this, however, Netanyahu's point in the Security Council should be remembered. A comparative study of riot control and counterinsurgency in the Middle East might begin with the practices of Jordan and Saudi Arabia to which he referred and conclude with the techniques employed by Assad in Syria, notably the massacre of over 20,000 opponents in Hama—following what Thomas Friedman calls "Hama Rules."[123]

Of course, Israel does not operate under Hama Rules and should not. While the excessive use of deadly force, including the use of plastic bullets, has not been an official Israeli policy, the efforts to curb such use have not been sufficient. This is an overall evaluation. However, it must be qualified in two respects, namely, as concerns reactions to Molotov cocktail attacks and to circumstances where soldiers are caught by large bodies of Palestinians variously armed.

First, a Molotov cocktail is clearly a lethal weapon and there should be no hesitation in shooting to kill when attacked by an enemy throwing one. IDF rules of engagement on this point are clearly justified.

Second, small bodies of troops or individuals caught in narrow streets or alleys or even in open country might very well be in mortal danger when attacked by a larger body of Palestinians armed with stones, iron bars, knives and other weapons. Some soldiers have even been killed by large stones and cinder blocks dropped from roofs. Al-Haq's argument that the limited weapons carried by the rioters can easily be dealt with does not hold up in many tactical situations. So, while the IDF is correct in prohibiting the use of deadly force against stone throwers as a standard operating procedure, it is certainly likely that there have been situations in which "only" stone throwing might be so life-threatening as to warrant defense with deadly force.

It is worthwhile to reiterate a point about the occasions requiring recourse to force by the Israelis during the *intifada*. Discussions of the subject frequently refer to "demonstrations," and the need for more restrained "crowd control" measures, bringing to mind civil rights demonstrations or "disturbances" implying sporadic unruliness (e.g., at soccer matches or rock concerts). But, as Israel's January 3, 1990, Response to Amnesty International rightly observed, the *intifada,* from the outset, has taken the form of riots in which violence with rocks, iron bars and other weapons and Molotov cocktails were employed. Failure to respond forcibly to *intifada* violence would put Israeli lives at risk. In these circumstances the requirements of legitimate military necessity are great.[124]

Deadly Force: Settlers

In addition to use of deadly force by IDF troops, there is a serious problem with its use by settlers. This problem was already attracting attention before the *intifada*. The Karp Report, by Deputy Attorney General Judith Karp, was released under public pressure in February 1984, concluded that processing of complaints against settler violence was unacceptable.[125]

In the course of the *intifada* the IDF has attempted to lay out rules limiting use of deadly force by civilians. For example, General Amram Mitzna, Officer Commanding (OC) Central [Command], stated that: "a civilian should use his gun solely for self-defense, to extricate himself from a life-threatening situation, when there is no alternative to using his weapon. He is not there to solve the problem, punish someone, or take deterrent action."[126]

However, there is little evidence that this guideline has been enforced effectively. According to the 1989 State Department Country Report, while at least eleven Palestinians have been killed by settlers, only one settler has been charged.[127] Granted that the situation has been very threatening for a long time in the West Bank and that considerable overreaction is to be expected, the failure to limit more effectively settler use of deadly force, particularly in cases of reprisal raids that are not justified by immediate self-defense, represents a serious failure of Israel's counterinsurgency effort.

Collective Punishments

Collective punishment is prohibited by Article 50 of the 1907 Hague Convention IV and Article 33 of the 1949 Fourth Geneva Convention. Article 50 of the Hague Convention IV provides:

> No general penalty, pecuniary or otherwise, shall be inflicted upon the population on account of the acts of individuals for which they cannot be regarded as jointly and severally responsible.

Article 33 of the 1949 Fourth Geneva Convention provides:

> No protected person shall be punished for an offense he or she has not personally committed. Collective penalties and likewise all measures of intimidation or of terrorism are prohibited. . . . Reprisals against protected persons and their property are prohibited.

In this section three types of Israeli counterinsurgency policies that appear to take the form of collective punishment will be examined: demolition of houses, curfews, and closure of schools and universities.

Demolition

Demolition of houses from which subversive activity and/or violent resistance emanated was a British practice during the Mandate period. It was employed frequently in counterterror raids into *fedayeen* base areas in neighboring Arab states and in the West Bank and Gaza prior to the 1967 June War. When Israel took over the territories after the war Dayan, soon employed demolition in the face of PLO guerrilla/terror warfare.[128] Through 1977, 1,224 homes had been destroyed under this policy.[129] House demolition was revived in 1985, accompanied by a policy of sealing off whole houses or even individual rooms. From the beginning of the *intifada* through 1989, 224 houses were destroyed or sealed. In combating the *intifada*, the Israelis have usually destroyed whole houses.[130]

House demolitions are conducted with little prior notice and generally only an accusation that someone connected to the dwelling has been engaged in wrongdoing. In rare cases when there was time to appeal for an injunction from the Israeli High Court, the effort has usually been unsuccessful. While some temporary injunctions were issued in the past, there had never been a decision overturning a demolition order through 1989.[131] This may change as a result of the August 1989 High Court decision.[132]

Israel justifies demolition on two principal grounds. First, it is claimed that demolition is required by military necessity in response to the violence of the Palestinians. Second, demolition is justified as a deterrent to support of or acquiescence in unlawful and violent behavior.

The military necessity argument rests on Article 119 of the British Defense Emergency Regulations, which explicitly permits house demolitions, and on Article 53 of the 1949 Fourth Geneva Convention:

> Any destruction by the Occupying Power of real or personal property belonging individually or collectively to private persons, or to the State, or to other public authorities, or to social or cooperative organizations, is prohibited, *except where such destruction is rendered absolutely necessary by military operations.* (Emphasis added)

The Israeli Commission of Jurists cite Jean S. Pictet's authoritative commentary on the Fourth Geneva Convention:

> The occupying forces may therefore undertake the total or partial destruction of certain private or public property in the occupied territory when imperative military requirements so demand. Furthermore, it will be for the Occupying Power to judge the importance of such military requirements.[133]

Using Pictet, Shamgar has defined "imperative military requirements" as being of two kinds, the second being deterrence:

> . . . on the one hand, there is the necessity to destroy the physical base for military action when persons are discovered committing hostile military acts, and, in this respect, a house from which a grenade is thrown is a military base, not different from a bunker in other parts of the world. On the other hand, there is the necessity to create effective military reaction. The measure under discussion is of utmost deterrent importance, especially in a country where capital punishment is not used against terrorists who kill women and children.[134]

An ancillary argument for demolition is that, as an essentially monetary or material punishment, it is preferable to detention of individuals and certainly to executions, which, as Shamgar points out, are prohibited by Israeli law.[135]

Critics of Israel's house demolition policy argue that it:

(1) is not justified by military necessity;[136]
(2) is an illegal collective punishment;[137]
(3) is unjustified as a deterrent since it is used to deter political activity as well as violence.[138]

The military necessity argument for house demolitions should not be accepted or rejected as covering all cases. While there have not been conventional hostilities in these territories since 1967, there has been serious low-intensity conflict at many times, particularly in the 1967–70, 1975–77 and 1987–present periods. Shamgar is right in claiming military necessity in cases of counterguerrilla or counterterror operations. It then becomes a question of the facts of individual cases whether there is a plausible military/security necessity for a particular demolition. Such a necessity should rest upon a clear connection between the house and acts of violence that warrant the extreme measure of house demolition.

If a Palestinian who has been throwing Molotov cocktails is chased back to a house in which materials for more fire bombs are found, demolition would seem to be justified. If another Palestinian, participating in the same "demonstration" is chased back to a house in which political propaganda materials supporting the *intifada* are found, demolition would not seem to be justified. Admittedly, there will often be a thin line between acts of violence and acts planning and inciting violence.

The difficulty of determining in particular cases whether there is sufficient military necessity for house demolition clearly indicates the need for careful review before a decision to destroy a house. It is to be hoped that the Israeli High Court's August 1989 decision will ensure such review.

The claim that demolition is collective punishment must be judged according to individual circumstances. In some cases the owners of houses might be fully involved in illegal resistance activities and subject to punishment. In others they might be unwilling accomplices and punishment would be "collective." Many cases would fall in between.

The issue of determining the relation between a house and the activities emanating from it to actual violence is obviously also important in evaluating the deterrence justification. What is to be deterred is participation in and/or support of subversive and violent resistance to the Israeli regime. But such a drastic punishment should not extend beyond that. Otherwise, all sorts of expressions of support for the *intifada* would be punished by house demolition. The key to defining what is to be deterred is fidelity to the first justification, military necessity. If Israel relies on Article 53 of the 1949 Fourth Geneva Convention, it must recognize that the military necessity proviso there is an exception to the general prohibition of the article and the destruction of property must be "absolutely necessary." One can agree with Shamgar and disagree with Israel's critics about the degree of military necessity involved in counterinsurgency/counterterror operations, but this does not mean that any participation in *intifada* activities produces a justification for house demolition that is "absolutely necessary."

A final thought on justifications advanced for house demolition, that it is preferable to detention and simply a kind of material punishment or fine, is not persuasive. Loss of a home, particularly a permanent home, is a very serious and painful thing. Loss of a home because of the acts of others, as will be the case more often than not, is particularly painful. It is not clear that detention might not be preferable. At least the house would be there when the detainee was released.

Curfews

Israel imposed curfews in the West Bank and Gaza after the 1967 June war. Curfews were occasionally used from the early 1970s on but became a more important instrument of Israeli security policy in 1983. Al-Haq claimed that through 1988 that there had been some 1,600 curfews imposed during the *intifada,* with at least 400 of them being "prolonged," i.e., longer than three days. In January 1989, for instance, there were 87 curfews in force, with 24 being prolonged curfews.[139]

Israel justifies the use of curfews as:

(1) authorized by British law and practice under the Mandate;
(2) not prohibited by the international law of war;
(3) an effective instrument of security and order;
(4) a deterrent.

Curfews for any purpose are permitted for military commanders by Article 124 of the British Defense Emergency Regulations. They are not prohibited by either the Hague or Geneva conventions. Curfews have proved to be an effective method in the investigation of terrorist attacks, affording a means for apprehending suspects as quickly as possible with the minimum of disturbance of the population. A curfew is also a speedy method of restoring order when breaches of the peace occur during demonstrations.[140]

Sensitive to the charge that curfews are collective punishment, Israelis have justified them as a deterrent. One senior IDF officer stated:

> We have to apply environmental pressure, so as to deter stonethrowers from repeating their deeds. It is difficult for us to find the children who throw stones, and even if we do, what can one do to a child? Therefore, I repeat: the creation of environmental pressure is meant to bring an end to the throwing of stones.[141]

Israel's critics contend that curfews imposed in the occupied territories are:

(1) prohibited collective punishment;
(2) often disproportionate punishment;
(3) violative of the belligerent occupant's duty to maintain conditions of normal public life;
(4) a major Israeli coercive instrument rather than an extraordinary, exceptional emergency measure.

The National Lawyers Guild* recognizes that curfews are not illegal per se, but claims that Israel uses them to punish rather than to contain disorders. Therefore, they are prohibited collective punishment.[142] The Guild further claimed that the IDF "often imposes curfews on whole villages in reprisal for a strike or demonstration," arguing that such curfews were disproportionate punishment.[143]

---

* NLG reports are the products of "delegations" of this New York-based organization, which visited the Middle East in 1978 and 1988.

Al-Haq argues that curfews should be limited by the duty of the occupying power to maintain, as far as possible, conditions for normal public life, particularly by ensuring adequate supplies of food and health services, as required by Articles 55–57 of the 1949 Fourth Geneva Convention.[144]

Here, again, we have a matter of balancing the principles of military necessity and humanity. In part this involves a decision as to which should prevail. The violent behavior that leads to imposition of curfews creates the military/security necessity to restore order. Curfews have been proven to be an effective means of achieving this military/security goals. Moreover, they are a more humanitarian means than alternatives involving use of armed force. To be sure, curfews can produce serious suffering, as in cases when people cannot circulate to obtain food or medical care. Nevertheless, restoration of order and prevention of further violence by curfews would seem both a legitimate military/security means and a relatively humane means.

It is true that the belligerent occupant is required to maintain conditions of normal life as far as is possible. Confronted with violent resistance from the population as prolonged and widespread as that experienced in the *intifada,* the occupying power can hardly be expected to maintain "normal" conditions. What Israel's critics seem to demand is *carte blanche* for revolution, what some Israelis call an "*intifada* de luxe," while expecting the military government to maintain "normal" conditions.[145] As observed in discussing the general principles of the law of belligerent occupation, there is a kind of tacit social contract between the occupying power and the occupied population, based on a mutual interest in stability. When either side breaks that implied contract, it may be expected that the other will alter its behavior accordingly.

One would have to know the details of particular curfews to judge whether they were proportionate measures, given past patterns of behavior and intelligence about the future. But curfews are clearly a military/security necessity, and they are clearly a means of coercion and deterrence, preferable to other means available to the occupying power. As such, there is nothing wrong with their being considered as an important instrument of coercion and control rather than as an exceptional emergency measure.

This leaves the issue of collective punishment. There is no question that curfews are in part a punishment. But, as just argued, they are, more importantly, an effective security measure. In my view, the utility of curfews as a military/security means outweighs the objection that they constitute collective punishment, particularly in a low-intensity conflict as widespread and prolonged as the *intifada.*

Closure of Schools and Universities

Article 56 of the 1907 Hague Convention IV requires occupying powers to treat the property of "institutions dedicated to religion, charity and education, the arts and sciences, even when State property," as "private property." Article 50 of the 1949 Fourth Geneva Convention provides:

> The occupying power shall, with the cooperation of the national and local authorities, facilitate the proper working of all institutions devoted to the care and education of children.

Israel has improved the schools in the West Bank and Gaza during its occupation. A number of colleges and universities were established in the territories. None had existed under Jordanian and Egyptian rule.[146] However, in the territories as in many other parts of the world, schools and universities were at times bases for political propaganda and agitation. This resulted in security intrusions and closures; e.g., Bir Zeit University was closed fourteen times between 1979 and 1987.[147]

The schools and universities became the source of much of the activism and violence of the *intifada*. As a result, the Israeli government closed all of the colleges and universities for the academic year 1988–89. Primary and secondary schools in the West Bank were closed for seven months in 1989. In July 1989, the Israelis began a phased reopening of the schools, although schools are occasionally still closed for extended periods.[148] Schools in Gaza were left open for most of 1989.[149]

Israel justified these closures on the grounds that:

(1) the secondary and even the primary schools are "centers of violent protest";[150]

(2) school closures were effective in reducing support for the *intifada*.[151]

Israel's critics condemn the school and university closures as violations of Jordanian and Israeli law, the Hague and Geneva convention provisions cited above, the International Covenant on Economic Social and Cultural Rights, and the Universal Declaration of Human Rights. They charge that:

(1) Israel has failed to maintain the minimal standard for public education required of an occupying power;[152]

(2) there is no military/security necessity for closing elementary schools;[153]

(3) school and university closures are prohibited collective punishment;[154]

(4) school and university closures have had no noticeable effect on the level of protest.[155]

As in the case of the curfew issue, there is a strong element in these criticism of a wish for a kind of no-fault revolution. It appears that a substantial number, if not the majority, of the troops of the *intifada* are young people, including elementary schoolchildren. They are engaged in throwing stones and Molotov cocktails and other forms of violence. Once again, the issue becomes one of balancing military/security necessity with humanitarian considerations. The Israeli contention that the school and university closures have reduced the incidence of violence is plausible. The argument that this is a collective punishment has less force than in the case of curfews, since the punishment is aimed at a category of major actors in the *intifada*'s violence and the parents who encourage or condone their participation in that violence.

There is one obvious solution to the problem of balancing the requirements of military/security necessity with those of humanity. That is to keep schools free of political agitation and the organization of *intifada* violence. If this can be done, the necessity for closing the schools is removed. Whether this would be possible at the college and university level is more doubtful. The *intifada* is a revolution and revolution has its price. In this case, part of the price is loss of education by the Arab youths of the West Bank.

Measures against Individuals

Administrative Detention

Israeli treatment of individuals detained for participation in Palestinian resistance activities has raised a number of legal and moral issues. Administrative detention, as distinguished from ordinary detention of criminals, was employed in the occupied territories from the end of the 1967 war into the 1980s. After the 1978 Camp David accords, the detention process was changed to ensure more effective, automatic review by military judges. Then, with the introduction of the Civil Administration, administrative detention was discontinued for a time. The practice was reintroduced in August 1985 as part of the iron fist policy. Between August 1985 and the beginning of the *intifada*, 316 Palestinians were held under detention orders and 74 of them remained in detention after it began.[156]

Administrative detention procedures were changed on May 17, 1988, and the liberal changes of 1978 were effectively suspended. Regional military commanders (with the rank at least of colonel) could now issue detention orders that were not subject to automatic review.[157] Estimates of the number of Palestinians held under administrative detention range from 3,000–4,000 to 6,000.[158]

Secret evidence, not divulged to the accused or to his counsel, is often used in administrative detention. Rulings based on secret evidence can be appealed to the High Court, which may review the evidence, but there have been no reversals from the Court. However, some detention periods were shortened or cancelled.[159] It should be noted that "inhabitants of the West Bank, seeking review of adverse actions by the military courts . . . [may apply] to the Israel Supreme Court, sitting in its capacity as a High Court of Justice, for writs of mandamus, habeas corpus and certiorari and for writs of prohibition."[160] This is an unprecedented privilege for an occupying power to grant to occupied people. The High Court has heard cases involving a number of the issues discussed in this chapter, including deportation and house demolitions.

Most detentions were for six months, until August, 1989, when they were extended to one year.[161] In about 20 percent of the cases detention orders are renewed. In some cases renewals continued for years without the accused ever being informed of the charges against him, e.g., the physicist Tayseer al-Aruri, detained from April 1974 to January 1978.[162]

Under administrative detention, access can generally be denied for up to eighteen days, and it can be denied indefinitely for security reasons. Israel has sometimes refused to confirm to consular officials that their nationals were under detention.[163]

Israel defends its administrative detention policy on grounds that it is:

(1) permitted by international and municipal law;
(2) necessary to counterinsurgency;
(3) proven to be a useful counterinsurgency instrument.

Israel invokes Article 78 of the 1949 Fourth Geneva Convention, which provides for subjecting people "to assigned residence or to internment" for "imperative reasons of security." Detention is permitted under Article 111 of the British Defense (Emergency) Regulations and subsequent Jordanian and Egyptian law.[164]

Israel's justification of necessity was expressed by the attorney general on January 26, 1988. He stated that administrative detention

> can be issued only for reasons of state or public security. . . . *This measure is resorted to only in those circumstances where normal judicial procedures cannot be followed because of the danger to the lives of witnesses or because secret sources of information cannot be revealed in*

open court. Typically, such orders are issued against leaders or members of terrorist organizations. (Emphasis added)[165]

The claim of the utility of administrative detention to counterinsurgency efforts was expressed by Defense Minister Rabin:

No one measure alone will extinguish the violence . . . [but] administrative detentions have made it easier for us to arrest the inciting organizers in a wide sweep.[166]

Critics of Israel's administrative detention policy argue that it

(1) exceeds the limits of Article 78 of the Fourth Geneva Convention;
(2) is not an effective, necessary counterinsurgency instrument.

Other critics, including the U.S. State Department, argue that Israel's very broad definition of security under the mandate of Article 78 of the 1949 Fourth Geneva Convention is unjustified. Specifically, they object to the detention of "journalists, editors, trade unionists, student activists, community leaders, doctors, lawyers, and human rights monitors."[167] Denying the effectiveness of detention, Israel's critics invoke an argument frequently made in criticism of regular jails, namely, that they become "finishing schools" for crime or, in this case, revolutionary activity. Ironic references are also made to the fact that Rabin and other Israeli leaders were once detainees and that the experience did not seem to deter them.[168]

It is clear, however, that some sort of administrative detention policy is a counterinsurgency necessity for Israel, particularly since the outbreak of the *intifada*. The legal permissibility of detention policies depends on the manner of their administration. Criticism of the administrative detention policies tends to focus on the issues of due process, conditions of detention, torture and deportations.

Due Process

Al-Haq has complained that the appeals process used in administrative detention is perfunctory and futile because of the pervasive invocation of secret evidence by prosecutors.[169] Critics claim that Israel has not lived up to its agreement with the International Committee of the Red Cross to notify the ICRC within twelve days of an arrest and to permit the ICRC to visit within fourteen days.[170] Further, the "incommunicado detentions" permitted under the amended administrative detention rules of March 1988 prevent families from confirming that their relatives have been detained.[171]

It would take a formidable effort and extraordinary cooperation from a government confronted with a widespread and enduring revolution to obtain the facts necessary to judge how justified Israel's administrative detention procedures have been. The need to protect intelligence sources, a military/ security necessity, has been given overwhelming priority over the due process claims of humanity. As a general proposition this is justified. However, the possibilities of abuse are all too clear. No external review of cases is possible. The ICRC or other organizations can monitor conditions of detention, but no outside review of the merits of individual cases is possible if they do turn on secret information.

The problem is, unhappily, demonstrated by the Shin Bet affair. In April 1984, PLO terrorists highjacked a bus near Ashkelon. Following a shoot-out with security forces, there were two terrorist survivors. They were killed by Shin Bet agents after having been photographed by journalists as they were led away from the bus. The IDF claim that they had died of wounds suffered during the shoot-out was obviously contradicted by the photographs. Investigations of alleged IDF and Shin Bet cover-ups were frustrated by misleading testimony by Shin Bet agents.[172] Attorney general Yosef Harish closed the police file on the Shin Bet affair in January 1987, at which time he released a Justice Ministry report stating that " 'the twilight zone of security' should be controlled by the rule of law." Concluding that the killing of the two captured terrorists was not justified by security needs, the report called on "the bodies responsible for the Shin Bet to draw the "administrative and moral conclusions," and on the Shin Bet "to root out deviations from the law' through education."[173]

The reconciliation of military necessity and the humanitarian requirements of due process can take place only within the Israeli government. There should be a serious review of all cases of administrative detention in which the judges had access to secret evidence. No doubt this would require more judges and lawyers, but the cost would be justified by the prospect of reducing the likelihood of abuses in the administrative detention program.

Conditions of Detention

The first issue raised under conditions of detention is that of transfer of detainees from the West Bank and Gaza to prisons in Israel. This has been done in the case of the Ketziot Camp in the Negev, also known as Ansar III. Sixteen detainees appealed such a transfer to the Israeli High Court, which rejected the appeal.[174]

There have been many charges that the detention centers are not suitable for extended habitation, e.g., confinement in tents in Ketziot, in old British stables in Al-Fara'a near Nablus.[175] Bad conditions and overcrowding led to riots in August 1988, in which two detainees killed in controversial circumstances.[176] There have also been charges of widespread arrest and detention of children, those over the age of fourteen being treated as adults.[177]

Israel responds that Israeli and foreign journalists visit the detention camps and report on conditions. A legal adviser is permanently stationed at each camp. Soldiers stationed at Ketziot told reporters that they had the same food and water rations as the inmates.[178]

Torture

Common Article 3 of all of the 1949 Geneva conventions prohibits "at any time and in any place whatsoever . . . violence to life and person, in particular murder of all kinds, mutilation, cruel treatment and torture." Torture is defined as follows in Article 1 of the 1984 Convention against Torture and Other Cruel, Inhuman or Degrading Treatment or Punishment:

> 1. For the purposes of this Convention, the term "torture" means any act by which severe pain or suffering, whether physical or mental, is intentionally inflicted on a person for such purposes as obtaining from him or a third person information or a confession, punishing him for an act he or a third person has committed or is suspected of having committed, or intimidating or coercing him or a third person, or for any reason based on discrimination of any kind, when such pain or suffering is inflicted by or at the instigation of or with the consent or acquiescence of a public official or other person acting in an official capacity. It does not include pain or suffering arising only from, inherent in or incidental to lawful sanctions.
>
> 2. This article is without prejudice to any instrument or national legislation which does or may contain provisions of wider application.[179]

After years of complaints,[180] a special judicial commission to investigate allegations of torture was appointed under ex–High Court President Moshe Landau in 1987. The Landau Commission found that "physical pressure" had been used by the General Security Service (Shin Bet) against suspects. Torture had been employed in particular in interrogation of alleged terrorists whose court convictions required confessions, given the nature of a case where many witnesses were unavailable or afraid to testify. While the commission stressed that torture had not been used to convict innocent persons, it did find that the Shin Bet had systematically perjured itself in denying to the courts that torture had been employed. While not recommending any measures against the Shin Bet, the Landau Commission recommended that prisoners be able to petition for retrials. The Landau report contained a secret annex which undertook to limit and clearly delineate what sort of "pressure" was permissible.[181]

Charges of torture as well as mistreatment come from former detainees and from families of detainees who died in suspicious circumstances while in custody, particularly when they are not permitted to examine the bodies of their relatives to be represented at official autopsies or to exhume bodies.[182]

Torture as a problem in the law of war has always been a frustrating subject. The law is quite clear in its prohibition of torture, but the term was never defined in the law of war and human rights conventions until the 1984 Convention on Torture. The difficulties of definition and application and the notorious gap between the law and belligerent practice, particularly in revolutionary/counterinsurgency wars, have discouraged realistic analysis of the subject.

Torture, while clearly illegal, has occurred in most contemporary revolutionary/counterinsurgency wars such as those of the French in Indochina and Algeria, the Americans in Vietnam and the British in Northern Ireland. This is not to say that this belligerent practice negates the prohibitions of conventional law. However, our experience has been that torture was deemed necessary even by belligerents that considered themselves law-abiding.

If this is the case, the issue is the control and minimization of physical and mental "pressure" on prisoners of war and detainees. To this end, such pressure should only be applied on the decision of responsible commanders. It should never be applied routinely to all prisoners or detainees but only to those where there is a strong *prima facie* case that they have important information necessary for counterinsurgency operations or that they are guilty of major acts of violence and subversion. Constant command oversight should be exercised to ensure that this pressure does not take forms that cause excessive and irreversible physical and mental damage. This oversight must also ensure that the personnel applying the pressure do not exceed the guidelines laid down for them.

Israel should observe some such legal guidelines. Perhaps it does. Further Israeli investigations, such as that of the Landau Commission, are needed in order for informed judgments to be made on this subject. Meanwhile, neither the simplistic position that torture is prohibited by international law and that Israel is guilty of torture nor the Israeli denial that torture is ever practiced in detention camps contributes to the task of limiting torture to the minimum and controlling that which does occur.

Deportations

Article 49 of the 1949 Fourth Geneva Convention provides in part:

> Individual or mass forcible transfers, as well as deportations of protected persons from occupied territory to the territory of the Occupying Power or to that of any other country, occupied or not, are prohibited, regardless of their motive.
>
> Nevertheless, the Occupying Power may undertake total or partial evacuation of a given area if the security of the population or imperative military reasons so demand. Such evacuations may not involve the displacement of protected persons outside the bounds of the occupied territory except when for material reasons it is impossible to avoid such displacement. Persons thus evacuated shall be transferred back to their homes as soon as hostilities in the area in question have ceased.

From 1967 to 1977, some 1,100 Palestinians as well as two Bedouin tribes, were deported from the West Bank and Gaza. Nine Palestinians were deported in 1978, one in 1979, three in 1981 and none in 1983–85. From December 1987 through July 1989, forty-five had been deported.[183] Israel claims that:

(1) Article 64 of the 1949 Fourth Geneva Convention gives the occupying power the right to take steps to maintain order in the occupied territory and to ensure its own security;[184]
(2) deportations are authorized by Article 112 of the British Defence (Emergency) Regulations;
(3) Egypt and Jordan made deportations, notwithstanding a prohibition against them in the Jordanian constitution;
(4) Article 49 of the 1949 Fourth Geneva Convention forbids mass but not individual deportations.[185]

The Israeli High Court held in *Abu Awad v. the Regional Commander of Judea and Samaria*:

> . . . the powers granted to the [occupying] authority due to the emergency situation are given to it for one purpose alone, that is, for ensuring the public order and security. Dr. Pictet also regards this purpose as a legitimate one. It has nothing to do with the deportations for forced labor, torture and extermination that occurred in the Second World War.[186]

Israel argues, further, that deportation is a more humane sanction against dangerous enemies than execution, the death penalty being prohibited by Israeli law.[187]

Once again, Israel is alone in its interpretation of the 1949 Fourth Geneva Convention. It is generally agreed that the prohibition of deportation in Article 49 should be interpreted strictly as prohibiting all deportations, whatever the reasons. The United States has condemned the practice publicly, while protesting it even more vigorously privately.[188] Critics of Israel's deportation policies have argued that exile "is one of the most inhumane forms of punishment."[189] As in the debate on detention, critics point out that deportation by the British of two future Israeli Prime Ministers, Ben-Gurion and Shamir, did not prevent their cause from succeeding.[190]

Despite the near-universal consensus that Article 49 of the 1949 Fourth Geneva Convention prohibits individual, as distinguished from mass, deportations, there is much to be said for the Israeli interpretation of that article. The historical context in which the convention was drafted would certainly imply that the concern was with the kind of mass deportations carried out by the Nazis. Israel's contextual interpretation of Article 49 is more plausible than the literal, textual interpretation of the United States and the other nations. Moreover, this issue has to be seen in the light of the ambiguity of the applicability of the Fourth Convention to the Israeli Occupation of the territories. Given the length of the occupation and the fact that Israel has claims to the territories, the situation is far more akin to that of a state exercising sovereign powers than of a belligerent occupant exercising limited powers in a temporary, precarious occupation. No one doubts the legal permissibility of a state deporting criminals or subversives under its own domestic law, as the United States does, and indeed as Jordan and Egypt did when they controlled the West Bank and Gaza. Admittedly, Israel is not sovereign in the territories, but it is also not the kind of temporary occupying power envisaged in the Hague and Geneva conventions.

In these circumstances, the issue should not turn on technical interpretations of conventional international law. It should be decided on the basis of a balancing of the requirements of military/security necessity and humanity. As with other issues discussed in this chapter, this, finally, should be done on a case-by-case basis. There should be a persuasive showing that a given individual represents such a threat to security in the territories that the requirements of the law, literally interpreted, and of humanity should be overridden. Beyond making such a case, the issue also calls for the exercise of prudence. Given the adamant opposition of the United States and the majority of nations to Israeli deportation of inhabitants of the territories, it should be asked in each case whether the security gains will be proportionate to the negative effects that deportations have on Israel's relations with its principal ally and with the other nations.

Discipline of Security Forces

The laws of war rely on military discipline within a responsible chain of command. The guidelines necessary for compliance with the requirements of the law of war, as well as with those of government policy, are usually provided in the form of military legal codes, manuals, and in Rules of Engagement (ROEs). The chain of command is responsible for the prevention of violations of military law and ROEs through effective training, leadership and oversight. When it appears that military law and the ROEs have been violated, responsible commanders should investigate, suppress continuing violations and punish those that can be verified through recourse to courts-martial proceedings.

In the case of security operations in the West Bank and Gaza, judicial review goes beyond military courts-martial to appeals to the Israeli court system. Moreover, the Israeli judicial system plays a role in shaping Israeli security policy, notably in approving the ROEs for operations in the territories so that they conform to the requirements of international law.[191] Brigadier General Amnon Straschnow, currently the judge advocate general of the IDF, has full authority in deciding which cases involving apparent violations of Israeli military law and the ROEs should go to trial.[192] However, it appears that in some cases General Straschnow could be overruled by the chief of staff.[193]

Israeli military officers have conceded that the IDF was unprepared for the security operations necessitated by the *intifada* and that there were many violations of military law and the rules of engagement. Educational orientation programs were developed, including showing a film depicting counter-*intifada* operations to troops before they deployed for that duty.[194] Official pronouncements, e.g., from Defense Minister Rabin or from the chief of staff, sought to clarify the ROEs. The approach was that violations were not so much the result of disobedience as of confusion about their interpretation by officers as well as enlisted men.[195]

Nevertheless, reports of behavior clearly violative of these legal and policy guidelines, sometimes in visual form on films and in photographs, have been widespread throughout the *intifada*. Israel has claimed that timely investigations of allegations of illegal behavior have been made by the military police. While conceding that the military police may not be truly impartial, the IDF argues that they have the best access to military units and their personnel and can therefore easily obtain information about their activities.[196]

Critics of the operation of Israel's military legal/discipline system complain of

(1) the difficulty of filing complaints;[197]
(2) the small number of cases and of convictions;
(3) the lack of impartiality of investigations by military police;[198]
(4) the leniency of sentences.[199]

The U.S. State Department Report for 1988 concluded:

> Regulations were not vigorously enforced; punishments were usually lenient; and there were many cases of unjustified killing which did not result in disciplinary actions or prosecutions.[200]

As of June 1990, 69 courts-martial have been convened in Israel, with a total of 111 IDF personnel charged. Of these, 23 have been charged with manslaughter or wrongful death (9 involving firearms), 10 for illegal use of firearms, 45 for maltreatment of Palestinians (16 of those for maltreating detainees), 27 for theft, and one for forcing an inhabitant to sign an untrue declaration. In no cases did prison sentences exceed three and a half years in prison (and that was for theft; no wrongful death sentence exceeded one and a half years in prison); most of those convicted were given suspended sentences, and 26 were demoted in their rank.[201]

The practical utility and the legal and moral justification of the military instrument of policy depend upon control of the use of armed coercion to effect its political purpose. In the case of the *intifada*, Israel has been obliged to use the military instrument but it has not been able to control it sufficiently to meet the requirements of political utility or legal permissibility. This is a general judgment which is tempered with realization of the difficulties of the tasks of the IDF and other security forces.

Conclusions

My evaluation of Israel's record as a belligerent occupant in the West Bank and Gaza stands somewhere between the positions of Israel and her critics. I consider that all the violent means of coercion employed by Israel are legally permissible if used in conformity with the principles of proportion and discrimination. Properly used, beatings, tear gas, plastic bullets and deadly force may be justified by military/security necessity.

Deadly force employed by settlers and other civilians in immediate self-defense may be legally permissible. The pervasive problem for Israel has been lack of adequate control over recourse to all of these means. It appears that disproportionate and indiscriminate use has been made of all of them on a scale sufficient to constitute major deviation from the requirements of humanity for which there is no countervailing adequate argument of military/security necessity.

Justifications based on deterrence rationales tend to blur the picture. I would argue that there is enough deterrent force in recourse to all of these means in proportionate and discriminate ways and that their use, allegedly for deterrence, in ways exceeding the requirements of ordinary military/security necessity is unwarranted.

I consider blanket condemnations of all measures deemed collective punishment to be unrealistic and unjustified. The requirement of Article 33 of the Fourth Geneva Convention that punishable acts must have been personally committed is very difficult to apply in a situation of widespread if not general resistance to the occupying power. If a whole village or school erupts in violence, is not the local population, in the sense of Article 50 of 1907 Hague Convention IV, "jointly and severally responsible"?

However, I consider that there is a major legal and prudential presumption against demolition of houses allegedly related to subversive activity and violent resistance. The possibilities of mistakes, the irreversible character of the sanction, and the presumptive effects of the act, generative of lasting hatred and resentment, counsel against this practice. I am unimpressed by the fact that the British employed it.

On the other hand, I find the Israeli use of curfews and school closures generally permissible, viewed in the light of legitimate considerations of military/security necessities. These means are functional to the requirements of military/security necessity and are preferable to more violent means. They are justified, moreover, by the violent resistance of the occupied population, the price of which is a sacrifice of benefits enjoined by humanity.

Israel's detention policies are generally necessary and legally permissible. Admittedly, they involve dilemmas which are probably beyond the competence of an outsider to resolve. The dilemma of reconciling due process with the requirements of protecting intelligence sources seems to be intractable. Only internal Israeli political/legal processes can sort out and balance the considerations involved. This should be done as matter of national integrity for Israel, as many Israelis constantly urge.

I do not consider the issue of transferring detainees from the territories to Israel to be a major one, notwithstanding the provisions of the Fourth

Geneva Convention. The more important issue is that of conditions of detention. Admittedly those conditions are not good but they are subject to scrutiny by the ICRC, by a variety of other humanitarian organizations, by political and legal activists in Israel, by foreign journalists and others. On the whole, conditions of detention appear to meet minimal standards required by international law.

Torture is an issue that has never been satisfactorily resolved in any revolutionary/counterinsurgency war, including those engaged in by France, the United Kingdom and the United States. The debate over torture in this conflict has not been realistic. Critics condemn torture broadly defined; Israel denies that there is any torture. Of course there is torture. The real issue is how to minimize and control that torture. This should be a priority for the Israeli government.

The issue of deportations should not be resolved on the basis of technical legal arguments. On the whole, I agree with the Israeli contention that the deportation provisions of the 1949 Fourth Geneva Convention ought not to be applied to this belligerent occupation and that the kinds of deportation, such as experienced in World War II, envisaged in the convention are not at all like those carried out by Israel. I would argue for a case-by-case approach, balancing putative military/security necessity with humanity. Prudentially, I would want the case for deportation to be overwhelming on security grounds since the price for deportations that Israel must pay in terms of adverse foreign, especially American, reactions is severe.

In this chapter I have differed with Israel's critics and much conventional wisdom on a number of specific issues of the international law of belligerent occupation. However, as an overall assessment of Israel's coercive measures in combating the *intifada,* I conclude that Israel has not been guilty of deliberate, widespread violations of the law of belligerent occupation as it should be realistically applied to this unique occupation. However, the lack of adequate control of Israel's counterinsurgency forces in the occupied territories has produced a general pattern of behavior that falls below Israel's own officially proclaimed standards and does not serve Israel's national interests well.

Notes

1. Israel signed armistices with Egypt on February 24, 1949, with Lebanon on March 23, 1949, with Jordan on April 3, 1949, and with Syria on July 20, 1949. An armistice was never signed with Iraq. See Alan Gerson, *Israel, the West Bank and International Law* (London: Frank Cass, 1978), pp. 62–64.

2. Meir Shamgar, "The Observance of International Law in the Administered Territories," in John N. Moore, *The Arab-Israeli Conflict*, (Princeton: Princeton University Press, 1975), II: 373. Shamgar notes that the question of applying the Geneva Convention to the Egyptian administration was never raised.

3. Even the UK's recognition was qualified when the UK made reservations about the frontier between the territory and Israel and about the status of Jerusalem. The Political Committee of the Arab League voted that the Jordanian annexation violated previous Arab League resolutions and on that basis Egypt, Saudi Arabia, Lebanon and Syria voted to expel Jordan from the Arab League. The Israelis protested the annexation. See Julius Stone, *Israel and Palestine: Assault on the Law of Nations* (Baltimore: Johns Hopkins University Press, 1981), n. 23, p. 191 and n. 19, p. 200.

4. Hussein Dissolves Jordan Parliament's Lower Chamber," *Washington Post* [hereinafter, *WP*], July 31, 1988, A23, cols. 5–6; A25, col. 6; "Jordan to Cut W. Bank Administrative, Legal Ties," ibid., August 1, 1988, A1, cols. 1–4; A20, cols. 1–4.
    See Asher Susser, *In Through the out Door: Jordan's Disengagement and the Middle East Peace Process,* The Washington Institute Policy Papers no. 19 (Washington, D.C.: Washington Institute for Near East Policy, 1990).

5. For a thorough and thoughtful analysis of the relevance of the international law of belligerent occupation to the West Bank and Gaza, see Adam Roberts, "Prolonged Military Occupation: The Israeli Occupied Territories Since 1967," *American Journal of International Law* 84 (1990): 44-103.

6. See Joseph Alpher and Shai Feldman, eds., *The West Bank and Gaza: Israel's Options for Peace: Report of a JCSS Study Group* (Tel Aviv: Jafee Center for Strategic Studies, 1989).

7. See, for instance, Raja Shehadeh, *Occupier's Law: Israel and the West Bank* (Washington, D.C.: Institute for Palestine Studies, 1985), especially chapters 1–2 and the epilogue; Gerson, *Israel, the West Bank and International Law,* pp. 115–203; Alan Dowty, "Emergency Powers in Israel: The Devaluation of Crisis," in Shao-chuan Leng, ed., *Coping with Crises: How Governments Deal with Emergencies* (Lanham, Md: University Press of America, 1990), pp. 1–43. See also Don Peretz, *Intifada: The Palestinian Uprising* (Boulder, Colo.: Westview, 1990) on Israeli policies prior to the *intifada*, pp. 9–15, 20–23, 27–29; on economic coercion during the *intifada*, pp. 71–74.

8. On early resistance, see Ann Mosely Lesch, *Political Perceptions of the Palestinians on the West Bank and the Gaza Strip* (Washington, D.C.: Middle East Institute, 1980), pp. 33–37.

9. Shabtai Teveth, *The Cursed Blessing* (London: Weidenfeld and Nicolson, 1970), Meron Benvenisti, *The West Bank Data Base Project: A Survey of Israel's Policies* (Washington, D.C.: American Enterprise Institute, 1984), pp. 44–45.

10. See Chapter 2 above.

11. Lesch, *Political Perceptions.* pp. 42–43.

12. See Geoffrey Aronson, *Creating Facts* (Washington, D.C.: Institute for Palestine Studies, 1987) pp. 46–47; Sachar, *History of Israel,* 1: 683–84; also Uzi Benziman, *Sharon: An Israeli Caesar* (New York: Adama, 1985), pp. 115–18.

13. Moshe Ma'oz, *Palestinian Leadership on the West Bank: The Changing Role of the Arab Mayors under Jordan and Israel* (London: Frank Cass, 1984), pp. 102–06.

ack

14. Lesch, *Political Perceptions*, pp. 51–53.
15. Ibid., p. 53; Sachar, *History of Israel*, I: 740–41.
16. See Chapter 2 above.
17. Ma'oz, *Palestinian Leadership*, p. 134; Peretz, *Intifada*, p. 15.
18. Lesch, *Political Perceptions*, p. 70.
19. Ibid., pp. 69–70; Elie Rekhess and Dan Avidan, "The West Bank and Gaza Strip," *Middle East Contemporary Survey* [hereinafter, *MECS*] 1 (1976–77): 213.
20. See Ma'oz, *Palestinian Leadership*, pp. 135–39.
21. Ibid., p. 155.
22. Lesch, *Political Perceptions*, p. 86.
23. Ma'oz, *Palestinian Leadership*, pp. 180–81.
24. Elie Rekhess, "The West Bank and the Gaza Strip," *MECS* 3 (1978–79): 335.
25. Sachar, *History of Israel* II: 159.
26. Ma'oz *Palestinian Leadership*, pp. 198–99; also, Benvenisti, *Data Base Project*, pp. 46–47.
27. Meir Litvak and Elie Rekhess, "The West Bank and the Gaza Strip," *MECS* 4 (1979–80): 367.
28. Elie Rekhess and Meir Litvak, "The West Bank and the Gaza Strip," *MECS* 8 (1983–84): 242; Peretz, *Intifada*, p. 19.
29. Elie Rekhess, "The West Bank and the Gaza Strip," *MECS* 9 (1984–85): 234–35; Peretz, *Intifada*, p. 19.
30. Rekhess, "The West Bank and the Gaza Strip," *MECS* 9 (1984–85): 235.
31. Ibid., 238.
32. Elie Rekhess, "The West Bank and the Gaza Strip," *MECS* 10 (1986): 204–05.
33. Zeev Schiff and Ehud Ya'ari, *Intifada*, edited and translated by Ina Friedman (New York: Simon & Schuster, 1989), pp. 17–29; Thomas L. Friedman, *From Beirut to Jerusalem* (New York: Farrar, Straus, Giroux, 1989), p. 371: Peretz, *Intifada*, p. 39. Deborah J. Gerner, *One Land, Two Peoples: The Conflict Over Palestine* (Boulder, Co.: Westview Press, 1991), pp. 96–100.
34. See Schiff and Ya'ari, *Intifada* for the background of the *intifada*, pp. 51–78, and for the PLO's initially slow reaction to it, pp. 45–50.
35. See ibid., pp. 188–219 on the Unified National Command, and pp. 220–39, on Hamas; Peretz, *Intifada*, on the "Unified National Leadership of the Uprising," pp. 87–94.
36. Schiff and Ya'ari, *Intifada*, pp. 29–45; Peretz, *Intifada*, pp. 42–45; Avner Yaniv, "Israel Comes of Age," *Current History* 88 (February 1989): 69–72, 100–102.
37. See p. 231 below.
38. "Death Toll Rises as Army Gets Tougher," *Jerusalem Post* International Edition [hereinafter, *JPI*], April 9, 1988, p. 1, cols. 3–4; p. 2, cols. 1–3.
39. There were violent protests after the assassination of Abu Jihad; see "Israeli Troops Kill 12 Palestinians," *WP*, April 17, 1988, A1, col. 6; A24, cols. 1–2.
40. See Schiff and Ya'ari, *Intifada*, pp. 79–100, and 101–31; Peretz, *Intifada*, pp. 81–118.

41. "Army Pins Hopes on Overall Plan," *JPI*, April 2, 1988, p. 1, cols. 4–9; p. 2, cols. 4–5.

42. "Uprising Forces Israel to Repaint the 'Green Line,' " *WP*, April 2, 1988, A11, cols. 2–4, A12, cols. 1–4.

43. "Palestinians See Uprising Losing Momentum, but Vow to Continue," *WP*, May 13, 1988, A30, cols. 1–5; "After the Palestinian Intifada," *Newsweek*, May 16, 1988, p. 37; "Uprising in Sixth Month," *JPI*, May 21, 1988, p. 1, cols. 3–4.

44. See Susser, *In Through the out Door,* and press reports cited in n. 5. above.

45. "Israel Outlaws Committees Linked to Palestinian Revolt," *WP*, August 19, 1988, A17, cols. 5–6; "Moves to Block State-in-the-Making," *JPI* August 27, 1988, p. 1, cols. 1–2.

46. "Rabin Says Uprising Failing," *JPI*, September 17, 1988, p. 1, cols. 2–5; p. 2, col. 3.

47. "After a Year of Intifada, the IDF Is Regaining Control," *JPI*, December 17, 1988, p. 1, cols. 2–5; p. 2, cols. 1–2.

48. "The Army and the Intifada," *JPI*, February 4, 1989, p. 1, cols. 3–5; p. 2, cols. 4–5.

49. "Troops Fighting Uprising Tell Shamir It Is Impossible Task," *WP*, January 18, 1989, A1, cols. 5–6; A18, cols. 1–4.

50. Peretz, *Intifada,* pp. 79–80, citing "Israeli Intelligence Report Links Peace Hopes to Talks With P.L.O.," *New York Times* [hereinafter, *NYT*], March 21, 1989, A1, cols. 1–2; A7, cols. 1–4.

51. "Shamir Proposes Elections for Spokesmen of Palestinians," *WP*, April 7, 1989, A1, cols. 1–2; A17, cols. 4–6; "Dual Approach on Uprising Reflects Pressures on Israel," ibid., May 19, 1989, A30, cols. 2–5.

52. "Israel Orders Workers Back to Gaza Strip," *WP*, May 17, 1989, A1, cols. 3–5; A26, col. 1; "Israel Plots Paper Chase Against Intifada," ibid., July 30, 1989, A32, cols. 1–3; "Israel Starts ID Checks for Gazans," ibid., August 18, 1989, A13, cols. 1–4.

53. "Anti-intifada Backlash Gaining Momentum," *JPI*, May 20, 1989, p. 1, cols. 3–4; "Israeli Settlers Striking Back with Vigilante Action Groups," *WP*, June 2, 1989, A1, cols. 4–5; A30, cols. 3–6.

54. "The Intifada: After 20 Months, Cracks in the Edifice," *JPI*, August 19, 1989, p. 1, cols. 1–4; p. 4, cols. 1–3; "Intifada Control Is Now in Hands of Local Gangs," ibid., September 9, 1989, p. 1, cols. 4–5; p. 2, col. 5.

55. "Intifada: Are the Rules of the Game Changing?" *JPI*, November 25, 1989, p. 1, cols. 1–2; p. 2, col. 5.

56. "Israelis Raid W. Bank City, Arrest Scores," *WP*, December 3, 1989, A36, col. 1; "Army Crackdown as Anniversary of Intifada Looms," *JPI*, December 9, 1989, p. 1, cols. 4–5; p. 2, col. 5.

57. "Anniversary of a No-Win Intifada," *WP*, December 7, 1989, A53, cols. 2–3; A56, cols. 2–6.

58. "Intifada 'Under Control,' " *JPI*, December 16, 1989, p. 1, cols. 1–2; p. 2, cols. 4–5.

59. "Arab Uprising Grinds on in Low Gear—For Now," *WP*, July 22, 1990, A21, cols. 4–5; A25, cols. 1–3.

60. On the law of belligerent occupation, see: Ernst H. Feilchenfeld, *The International*

Economic Law of Belligerent Occupation (Washington, D.C.: Carnegie Endowment for International Peace, 1942); Doris Appel Graber, *The Development of the Law of Belligerent Occupation, 1863–1914* (New York: Columbia University Press, 1949); L. Oppenheim, *International Law,* H. Lauterpacht, ed. (7th ed.; 2 vols; London: Longmans, Green, 1952), II: 432–56; Julius Stone, *Legal Controls of International Conflict* (New York: Rinehart, 1954), pp. 723–32; Gerhard von Glahn, *The Occupation of Enemy Territory* (Minneapolis: University of Minnesota Press, 1957); Myres S. McDougal and Florentino P. Feliciano, *Law and Minimum World Public Order* (New Haven: Yale University Press, 1962), pp. 732–832.

61. McDougal and Feliciano base their analyses of belligerent occupation on "the familiar complementary principles of military necessity and humanitarianism." Ibid., p. 739.

62. Ibid., pp. 735–36, 739–71, 790–824.

63. See Stone, "The Duty of Obedience to the Belligerent Occupant," *Legal Controls of International Conflict,* pp. 723–26; McDougal and Feliciano, *Law and Minimum World Public Order,* pp. 790–95.

64. See McDougal and Feliciano, *Law and Minimum World Public Order,* pp. 795–96.

65. Hague Convention No. IV Respecting the Laws and Customs of War on Land and Annex Thereto Embodying Regulations Respecting the Laws and Customs of War on Land, 18 October 1907, 36 Stat. 2277, Treaty Series no. 539; Geneva Convention Relative to the Protection of Civilian Persons in Time of War, 12 August 1949, 6 UST 3516, T.I.A.S. 3365, 75 UNTS 287.

66. The Nuremberg judgment treated the Hague rules as derived from customary international law, a view widely held by publicists. See Office of United States Chief of Counsel for Prosecution of Axis Criminality, *Nazi Conspiracy and Aggression: Opinion and Judgment* (Washington, D.C.: U.S. Government Printing Office, 1947), pp. 50–51.

    Israel has generally agreed that the 1907 Hague rules on belligerent occupation are binding as a matter of customary international law. See Roberts, "Prolonged Military Occupation," pp. 62–63.

67. United Nations War Crimes Commission, *Law Reports of Trials of War Criminals* (15 vols.; London: United Nations War Crimes Commission/His Majesty's Stationery Office, 1947–49).

68. See Roberts, "Prolonged Military Occupation."

69. For an early judicial decision incorporating this, see *Military Prosecutor v. Halil Muhamad Mahmud Halil Bakhis et al.,* Military Court in Ramallah, June 10, 1968, *International Law Reports,* vol. 47, p. 484 (1974).

    For a careful analysis of Israel's position regarding the applicability of the 1949 Fourth Geneva Convention to the territories, see Roberts, "Prolonged Occupation," pp. 63–66.

70. See U.S. Department of State, *Department of State Bulletin* (July 28, 1969), p. 76; U.N.S.C. Res. 237, June 14, 1967, *Resolutions Adopted and Decisions Taken by the Security Council in 1967,* p. 5; U.N.G.A. Res. 3240, November 29, 1974 in *U.N. Resolutions on Palestine and the Arab-Israeli Conflict,* George Tomeh, ed. (Washington, D.C.: Institute of Palestine Studies, 1988), I: 112–15.

    See Adam Roberts, Boel Joergensen and Frank Newman, *Academic Freedom under Israeli Military Occupation, Report of WCS/ICJ Into Higher Education in the West Bank and Gaza* (London and Geneva: World University Service (UK)/International

Commission of Jurists, 1984), p. 25 and sources cited therein; Gerson, *Israel, the West Bank and International Law,* pp. 11–12.

71. *Military Government in the Territories Administered by Israel, 1967–1980: The Legal Aspects* (Jerusalem: Hebrew University Jerusalem Faculty of Law, Harry Sacher Institute for Legislative Research and Comparative Law, 1982) I: 31–43.

72. Roberts, "Prolonged Military Occupation," pp. 63–64.

73. Ibid., pp. 65–66.

74. Shamgar, *Military Government in the Territories Administered by Israel, 1967–1980,* I; 48–49.

75. Ibid., p. 45.

76. See, for example, National Lawyers Guild, *Treatment of Palestinians in Israeli-Occupied West Bank and Gaza* (New York: National Lawyers Guild, 1978) and *International Human Rights Law and Israel's Efforts to Suppress the Palestinian Uprising* (New York: National Lawyers Guild, 1989); W. Thomas & Sally V. Mallison, *The Palestine Problem in International Law and World Order* (Essex, Longmans, 1986), Ch. 6, pp. 240–75; Shehadeh, *Occupier's Law;* David H. Ott, *Palestine in Perspective: Politics, Human Rights and the West Bank,* (London: Quartet Books, 1980).

77. Roberts, while performing a thorough legal analysis of the Israeli occupation of the territories, asserts that there are other methodologies that must be brought into play, e.g., "those of history and political science, even strategy and arms control." "Prolonged Military Occupation," p. 45.

78. "Rabin Advocates Blows, Not Guns, to Put down Unrest," *Jerusalem Post,* daily edition, [hereinafter, *JDP*], January 20, 1988, p. 1, cols. 1–5; Peretz, *Intifada,* p. 50.

79. Editorial, "Between Brutal and Lethal," *JPD,* January 20, 1988, p. 10; "Rabin: Use of Blows Instills Fear of IDF," ibid., January 26, 1988, p. 1.

80. "Army to Brief Men on Limits of Force," ibid., February 23, 1988.

81. Ibid.

82. "Force Should Never be Used As a Means of Punishment," *JPD,* February 24, 1988, p. 2. Israel emphasized General Shomron's "dispatch" in its January 3, 1990, Response to Amnesty International [hereinafter cited as Israel Foreign Ministry, *Response to AI*]. At the time of General Shomron's policy statement, an incident occurred on February 25, 1988, in which a CBS camera crew filmed IDF soldiers beating two Palestinians brutally. The IDF obtained a copy of the film and ordered officers to watch it as an example of "unacceptable behavior." See "Israeli Officers Ordered to Watch Tape of 4 Soldiers Beating Arabs," *NYT,* February 29, 1988, p. 1, col. 4; p. 15, cols. 1–5.

83. " 'Beating' Orders Defended," *WP,* March 2, 1989, A43, col. 1; Schiff and Ya'ari, *Intifada,* p. 149.

84. U.S. Department of State, *Country Reports on Human Rights Practices for 1988* [hereinafter, *Country Reports, 1988* or *Country Reports, 1989*], p. 1378.

85. "Rabin Advocates Blows, Not Guns, to Put down Unrest," *JPD,* January 20, 1988, p. 1, cols. 1–5; Editorial, "Between Brutal and Lethal," ibid., p. 10, col. 1.

86. "Defense Establishment Still at a Loss on How to Put down the Unrest," *JPD,* January 20, 1988, p. 1, cols. 1–2; p. 2, col. 1.

87. "Rabin: Use of Blows Instills Fear of IDF," *JPD,* January 26, 1988, p. 1, cols. 2–3; p. 10, cols. 1–2.

88. Amnesty International, "Israel and the Occupied Territories: Excessive Force: Beatings to Maintain Law and Order," August 1, 1988, in *Journal of Palestine Studies* 18 (Winter 1989): 176–91, quote on p. 187.

89. " 'Break Bones' Officer to Face Trial; Wife Blames Rabin," *JPI,* January 6, 1990, p. 5, cols. 1–5.

90. See, for instance, Schiff and Ya'ari, *Intifada,* pp. 149–56; Peretz, *Intifada,* pp. 45–52; "History and Anger Turn Israeli Soldiers Violent," *WP,* January 31, 1988, A1, cols. 1–2; A25, cols. 1–6; "Why Beat the Rioters?" *Newsweek,* February 8, 1988, p. 39; "Beatings Victims' Anger Festers," *WP,* February 14, 1988, A1, cols. 4–5; A34, cols. 1–5; see also the reports of Palestinians and an American citizen in al-Haq, *Punishing a Nation,* pp. 27–32.

91. Israel Ministry of Justice, *Response to AI.*

92. Al-Haq, *Punishing a Nation: Human Rights Violations During the Palestinian Uprising, December 1987–December 1988,* pp. 12, 30; Amnesty International, "Israel and the Occupied Territories: the Misuse of Tear Gas by Israeli Army Personnel in the Occupied Territories," June 1, 1988, in *Journal of Palestine Studies* 18 (Autumn 1988): 259–63.

93. Amnesty International, "Israel and the Occupied Territories," p. 259. The American manufacturer which supplied tear gas to the IDF was concerned enough about reports of misuse, and their effect on the company, that it suspended export to Israel. The decision has apparently been reversed following a U.S. government report which found that the misuse was not widespread. See "U.S. Firm Gives in to Pressure, Stops Selling Tear Gas to Israel," *JPD,* May 8, 1988, p. 1, cols. 2–4, and "Report to Congress: Israel Does Not Misuse U.S. Tear Gas," ibid., May 26, 1990, p. 6, col. 1.

94. *Israel's Measures in the Territories and Human Rights* (Washington, D.C.: Embassy of Israel, January 1990), p. 5.

95. U.S. General Accounting Office, "Israel—Use of U.S. Manufactured Tear Gas in the Occupied Territories (Report to Representative Ronald Dellums)," April 1990, pp. 2, 7.

96. Response of Attorney General Harish to Amnesty International, May 17, 1989, mimeo. Others have been unable to substantiate allegations of deaths involving tear gas; see Physicians for Human Rights, *The Casualties of Conflict: Medical Care and Human Rights in the West Bank and Gaza Strip,* (March 30, 1988).

97. "Israel Jails Army Officer Who Tear Gassed Babies," *WP,* June 14, 1990, p. 36, cols. 5–6.

98. Editorial, "The Law and the Intifada," *JPD,* January 24, 1988, p. 24, cols. 1–2.

99. Israel Ministry of Justice, *Response to AI.*

100. Ibid.

101. Human Rights Watch, *The Israeli Army and the Intifada: Policies that Contribute to the Killing,* (NY: Human Rights Watch, 1990), p. 31.

102. Dumdum bullets were prohibited by Hague Declaration IV Concerning Expanding Bullets, of July 29, 1898. See McDougal and Feliciano, *Law and Minimum World Public Order,* p. 620.

103. "Rabin: More Injuries 'Is Precisely Our Aim'," *JPD*, September 28, 1988, p. 1, cols. 5–7.

104. "The Army and the Intifada," *JPI*, p. 1, cols. 3–5; p. 2, cols. 4–5.

105 "ACRI Calls for Guidelines on Use of Plastic Bullets," *JPD*, September 30, 1988, p. 1, cols. 2–3; p. 20, cols. 6–7.

106. State Department Spokesman in "US Protesting Israelis' Use of Plastic Bullets," *NYT*, September 29, 1988, p. 11, cols. 1–4.

107. Editorial, "The Law and the Intifada," *JPD*, January 24, 1988, p. 24, cols. 1–2.

108. Al-Haq, *Punishing a Nation*, p. 18.

109. "Shomron: Force Can't End Uprising," *JPI*, June 24, 1989, p. 1, cols. 1–3; p. 2, cols. 1–2.

110. "Rules of Engagement for Soldiers in the Administered Territories," reproduced from the *Manual of Regulations Concerning Rules of Engagement of the Operational Branch of the IDF* (in Judea and Samaria, Regulations 23 and 26; in the Gaza District, Regulations 22 and 30), Embassy of Israel, Washington, D.C. "Israel's Measures in the Territories and Human Rights," Appendix, pp. 23–29; Israel Ministry of Justice, *Response to AI*. The rules have apparently not changed much over the years; see Meron Benvenisti, *The West Bank Handbook* (Jerusalem: Jerusalem Post, 1986), p. 12.

111. Israel Ministry of Justice, *Response to AI*.

112. "Killings by Israeli Forces," *Focus* (AI newsletter), January 1990.

113. Al-Haq, *Punishing a Nation*, p. 15.

114. Material provided by Yigal Carmon, Advisor to the Prime Minister of Israel for Countering Terrorism.

115. 42 UN SCOR (2781st mtg.), p. 6.

116. "Plastic Bullet Ricochet," *JPI*, October 8, 1988, p. 3, cols. 3–4.

117. 42 UN SCOR (2774th mtg.) pp. 74–75.

118. U.S. Department of State, *Country Reports, 1988*, p. 1377.

119. See n. 112 above.

120. Al-Haq, *Punishing a Nation*, p. 16. The same arguments are asserted in Joost R. Hilterman, "Human Rights and the Mass Movement: The First Year of the Intifada," *Journal of Palestine Studies* 18 (Spring 1989): 128.

121. U.S. Department of State, *Country Reports, 1988*, p. 1377.

122. "Just Wars and Others," interview with Benny Morris, *JPI*, July 8, 1989, pp. 9–10.

123. Thomas Friedman, *From Beirut to Jerusalem*, pp. 76–105.

124. Israel Ministry of Justice, *Response to AI*.

125. *Karp Report: An Israeli Government Inquiry into Settler Violence against Palestinians on the West Bank* (Washington, D.C.: Institute for Palestine Studies, 1984).

126. "Mitzna: Settler Who Shot Soldiers Was Over-reacting," *JPD*, September 2, 1988, p. 1, cols. 2–3; p. 24, cols. 4–6.

127. State Department, *Country Reports, 1989*, p. 1433.

128. Teveth, *Cursed Blessing*, pp. 243–45.

129. Jan Metzger, Martin Orth and Christian Sterzing, *This Land Is Our Land: The West Bank under Israeli Occupation* (London: Zed Books, 1983), p. 69.

130. U.S. Department of State, *Country Reports, 1988*, p. 1381; *Country Reports, 1989*, p. 1437.

131. U.S. Department of State, *Country Reports, 1988*, p. 1381; *Country Reports, 1989*, p. 1437.

132. "Court Curbs Home Demolitions," *JPI*, August 12, 1989, p. 3, cols. 3–4; Embassy of Israel, Washington, D.C., "Israel's Measures in the Territories and Human Rights," p. 11.
    The Israeli Supreme Court sits as High Court of Justice in cases involving "the rights of citizens and residents who have come into conflict with the Government." Marver H. Bernstein, *The Politics of Israel* (Princeton, N.J.: Princeton University Press, 1957), p. 113. See Oscar Kraines, *Government and Politics in Israel* (Boston: Houghton Mifflin, 1961), pp. 157–58; Henry E. Baker, *The Legal System of Israel* (2d ed. rev.; Jerusalem, London and New York: Israel Universities Press, 1968), pp. 199–200.

133. Israeli National Section of the International Commission of Jurists, *The Rule of Law in the Areas Administered by Israel* (Tel Aviv: Tzatz, 1981) [hereinafter, Israeli ICJ, *Rule of Law*], p. 69, citing Pictet, *Commentaries, IV Geneva Convention* (Geneva: ICRC, 1958), p. 302. See Embassy of Israel, Washington, D.C., "Israel's Measures in the Territories and Human Rights." pp. 10–11.

134. Shamgar, "The Observance of International Law in the Administered Territories," in Israeli ICJ, *The Rule of Law*, pp. 69–70.

135. National Lawyers Guild, *Treatment of Palestinians in Israeli Occupied West Bank and Gaza* [hereinafter, NLG, *Treatment*], pp. 64–65, citing Alan Dershowitz, *Israel Yearbook on Human Rights* 1 (1971): 376.

136. Karl Kalshoven, *Belligerent Reprisals* (Leyden: A.W. Sijthoff, 1981), p. 320.

137. See, e.g., NLG, *Treatment*, pp. 65–68; al-Haq, *Punishing a Nation*, p. 225; Metzger et al., *This is Our Land*, p. 69; David H. Ott, *Palestine in Perspective: Politics, Human Rights and the West Bank* (London: Quartet Books, 1980), pp. 53–55.

138. Ott, *Palestine in Perspective*, p. 55.

139. Al-Haq, *Punishing a Nation*, p. 254; Raja Shehadeh, *Occupier's Law: Israel and the West Bank* (Washington, D.C.: Institute for Palestine Studies, 1985), pp. 133–41.

140. Israeli ICJ, *The Rule of Law*, p. 88.

141. Geoffrey Aronson, *Creating Facts*, pp. 197–98.

142. NLG, *Treatment*, pp. 68–69.

143. *Ibid.*, p. 69.

144. Al-Haq, *Punishing a Nation*, pp. 257–58.

145. See "Dealing with a Protracted War of Attrition," *JPI*, June 30, 1990; p. 8, cols. 1–5.

146. By 1983–84, 11,046 students attended six major universities in the territories; with students at smaller colleges counted, the total student population came to about 14,000. See Adam Roberts, Boel Joergensen and Frank Newman, *Academic Freedom under Israeli Occupation*, Report of World University Service and International Commission of Jurists, 1984, p. 39.

147. Al-Haq, *Punishing a Nation*, p. 419.

148. "West Bank Schools Open after 7-Month Closure," *JPI*, July 29, 1989, p. 3, cols. 1–5; "West Bank Schools Re-Opened [after 2-Month Closure]," *WP*, January 11, 1990, p. 28, col. 6.

149. U.S. Department of State, *Country Reports, 1988*, pp. 161–73.

150. "West Bank Schools to Reopen," *JPI*, May 16, 1988, May 18, 1988, p. 1, cols. 2–4; p. 2, col. 4; "Alternative Classes Blocked in West Bank," ibid., September 9, 1988, p. 1, cols. 2–5; p. 12, cols. 3–4; "Rabin Explains School Closure on West Bank," *JPI*, May 27, 1989, p. 2, cols. 1–2.

151. "The Intifada: After 20 Months, Cracks in the Edifice," *JPI*, August 19, 1989, p. 1, col. 1–5; p. 4., cols. 1–3.

152. Al-Haq, *Punishing a Nation*, p. 428.

153. Penny Johnson, "Palestinian Universities under Occupation, 15 August–15 November," *Journal of Palestine Studies* 18 (1989): 92–100.

154. Joost R. Hilterman, "Human Rights Reports Issued during the Palestinian Uprising," *Journal of Palestine Studies* 18 (1989): 132.

155. Al-Haq, *Punishing a Nation*, p. 423.

156. Ibid., p. 212.

157. "1,900 Held without Trial—'Political Echelon out of Control,' " *JPI*, May 28, 1988, p. 5, cols. 1–4.

158. Al-Haq estimated detainees at 3–4,000. *Punishing a Nation*, pp. 346–47. Hilterman estimated 6,000. "Human Rights and the Mass Movement," p. 130. The U.S. State Department reported a peak of 2,600 in September 1988. *Country Reports, 1988*, p. 1379.

159. U.S. Department of State, *Country Reports, 1989*, p. 1433.

160. Gerson, *Israel, the West Bank and International Law*, p. 119.

161. "Israel Doubles Palestinians Prison Terms," *WP*, August 12, 1989, p. 1, col. 1; p. 14, col. 1.

162. NLG, *Treatment*, pp. 80–81.

163. U.S. Department of State, *Country Reports, 1988*, p. 1380.

164. Israeli ICJ, *The Rule of Law*, p. 72.

165. Statement of the Attorney General, quoted in al-Haq, *Punishing a Nation*, pp. 212–13. See also Dowty, *Emergency Powers in Israel*, pp. 10–11; Alan Dershowitz, "Preventive Detention of Citizens During a National Emergency—A Comparison between Israel and the United States," *Israel Yearbook on Human Rights* 1 (1971): p. 303.

166. "Israel Turns to Detentions As Weapon Against Uprising," *WP*, May 11, 1988, A1, cols. 5–6; A30, cols. 1–4.

167. Al-Haq, *Punishing a Nation*, p. 216; see U.S. Department of State, *Country Reports, 1988*, p. 1379.

168. "Israeli Prison in Gaza was 'Finishing School' for Rioters," *WP*, January 3, 1988, A1. cols 5–6, A24, cols, 1–2.

169. Al-Haq, *Punishing a Nation*, pp. 215–16.

170. See the reported complaints of an ICRC representative, al-Haq, *Punishing a Nation*, p. 339.

171. Ibid., pp. 338–41.

172. "The No. 300 Bus to Ashkelon," *JPI*, January 2, 1987, p. 3, cols. 3–5; "Shin Bet: The End of the Affair?" ibid., p. 1, cols. 4–5; p. 3, cols. 3–5.

173. Ibid.

174. "High Court Rejects Detainees' Appeal," *JPI*, November 19, 1988, p. 5, cols. 2–4.

175. U.S. Department of State, *Country Reports, 1988*, p. 1380; Shehadeh, *Occupier's Law*, pp. 147–51.

176. "Army Probing Riots at Detention Camp," *JPI*, August 27, 1988, p. 2, cols. 1–2; "The Ketziot Cauldron," ibid., September 3, 1988, p. 3, cols. 1–4.

177. "Pro-Palestinian Group Accuses Israel," *WP*, September 10, 1987, p. 32, cols. 1–4.

178. "The Ketziot Cauldron," *JPI*, September 3, 1988, p. 3, cols. 1–4. The U.S. State Department reported that "conditions are rigorous and there is over-crowding," and that detainees lived in tents not designed for extended periods; *Country Reports, 1988*, p. 1380.

179. Text of the 1984 Convention in 100th Congress, 2d Session, Senate, Treaty Doc. 100-20, *Message from the President of the United States Transmitting The Convention Against Torture and Other Cruel, Inhuman or Degrading Treatment or Punishment Adopted by Unanimous Agreement of the United Nations General Assembly on December 10, 1984, and Signed by the United States on April 18, 1988* (Washington, D.C.: U.S. Government Printing Office, 1988), p. 19.

180. Al-Haq, *Punishing a Nation*, pp. 352–57. See Amnesty International, *Report on the Treatment of Certain Prisoners under Interrogation in Israel* (1970); NLG, *Treatment*, Chap. XII; London *Sunday Times*, June 19, 1977; U.S. Department of State, *Country Reports, 1977*, p. 39; *Country Reports, 1978*, p. 366; Shehadeh, *Occupier's Law*, pp. 148–51.

181. "Shin Bet Perjury: Terrorists May Seek Retrial," *JPI*, November 7, 1987, p. 1, cols. 1–5; p. 2, cols. 2–3.

182. See National Lawyers Guild, *Israeli Human Rights Law*, Chap. 7; al-Haq, *Punishing a Nation*, pp. 341–45, 351–57.

183. "More Expulsions Despite US Anger," *JPI*, July 8, 1989, p. 1, cols. 4–5.

184. Article 64 of the 1949 Fourth Geneva Convention provides in its second paragraph:

    The Occupying Power may, however, subject the population of the occupied territory to provisions which are essential to enable the Occupying Power to fulfil its obligations under the present Convention, to maintain the orderly government of the territory, and to ensure the security of the Occupying Power, of the members and property of the occupying forces or administration, and likewise of the establishments and lines of communication used by them.

185. "The Case for Deportations," *JPI*, September 3, 1988, p. 2, cols. 3–4.

186. Israeli ICJ, *The Rule of Law*, p. 69, citing *Abu Awad v. the National Commander of Judea and Samaria*, HCJ 97/79, *Piskei Din*, vol. 33, part 3 (1979), p. 309.

187. Netanyahu, 43 UN SCOR (2780th mtg.), January 5, 1988, p. 13. See Yosef Goell, "An Alternative to Shooting," *JPI*, July 8, 1989, p. 6, cols. 1–2.

188. See U.S. Department of State, *Country Reports, 1988,* p. 1379. Regarding more private and strong U.S. protests, see "Israel Defends Deportations," *JPI,* September 3, 1988, p. 1, cols. 3–4.

189. Al-Haq, *Punishing a Nation,* p. 211. See Thomas Friedman, "In Separate Gestures, a Mosaic of Intentions," *NYT,* April 17, 1988, IV: 1, cols. 1–3; IV: 2, cols. 4–5.

190. See Friedman's article, n. 189.

191. "The Army and the Intifada," *JPI,* February 4, 1989, p. 1, cols. 3–5; p. 2, cols. 4–5.

192. "Israeli Army Fights Charges of 'Whitewash' in Deaths," *WP,* April 1, 1989, A1, cols. 4–5; A18, cols. 1–5.

193. "Brigade Commander Suspended for Killing Demonstrator in Areas," *JPI,* August 17, 1988, p. 2, cols. 6–7. In this case, Straschnow recommended court-martial, but Shomron ordered a disciplinary hearing after taking into consideration the officer's previous "good work."

194. See the statement of Brig. Gen. Ehud Gross, IDF chief educational officer, in "Jarring Film Prepares Israeli Troops for Uprising," *WP,* March 3, 1989, A29, cols. 1–3; A34, cols. 1.

195. See above, pp. 231–41.

196. "Civilians Face an Army: The Riot Control Dilemma," *JPI,* November 14, 1987, p. 5, cols. 1–2.

197. See the Karp Report, pp. 38–39; Shehadeh, *Occupier's Law,* p. 238.

198. "Israel Army Fights Charges of 'Whitewash' in Deaths"; al Haq, *Punishing a Nation,* p. 55.

199. See, for example, "Israel's Occupation Accused of Legal Double Standard," *WP,* October 10, 1988, A1, cols. 2–3; A28, cols. 4–6.

200. U.S. Department of State, *Country Reports, 1988,* p. 1378. The language in the 1989 report is essentially identical; see p. 1438.

201. IDF Spokesman, "Soldiers Tried for Offenses Related to the Uprising in Judea, Samaria, and Gaza," June 9, 1990.

Part III

Morality in
Israel's War with the PLO

9

Modern Just War Doctrine

Modern just war doctrine in the West traces its origins to the Roman concepts of just war that were adapted and infused with Christian values by St. Augustine and other early Christian moralists. Although the Christian just war doctrine that subsequently was developed during the Middle Ages had Christian theological bases and expression in Canon Law, it was very largely worked out as a matter of natural law rather than theological ethics, combined, in the case of the war-conduct, *jus in bello,* doctrine, with the customary law of war of the times. Like the international law of war, just war doctrine is divided into a war-decision, *jus ad bellum,* and war-conduct, *just in bello,* law. The emphasis of St. Augustine was very much on the war-decision element, and when St. Thomas Aquinas restated the doctrine in the thirteenth century, his attention was almost entirely focused on the moral issues of the war decision.[1] St. Thomas gave only very partial and passing attention to some particularistic aspects of war conduct. It remained for the late Scholastics such as Francisco de Vitoria and Francisco Suarez in the sixteenth and seventeenth centuries to complete the formulation of classic Western just war doctrine by balancing the war-decision law with a substantial war-conduct law which was much indebted to the customary practice of war and notably to the influence of the chivalric codes that sought to guide and restrain warfare by the knightly class.[2]

As the seventeenth century unfolded, the influence of Christian just war doctrine declined markedly. In a world torn by internecine Christian strife, the Scholastic just war tradition was unacceptable to many because it was Catholic in origin. Moreover, both Catholic and Protestant just war writing was viewed with skepticism when it was applied to contemporary issues in an age of religious wars. Meanwhile, Hugo Grotius's *De Jure Belli ac Pacis* (1625) inspired the development of a European law of nations which, although greatly indebted to the classic just war doctrine, was based on a mixture of secular natural law and customary law. The war-decision element of just war was soon abandoned, all of the states in the Westphalian international system being considered free to go to war as they chose. However, customary war-conduct law flourished in a era of limited wars fought largely by mercenary armies.

From the early seventeenth century the Scholastic scholarship that had developed, among other things, the classic just war doctrine virtually disappeared. In the eighteenth and nineteenth centuries this scholarship was either scorned because of its religious elements or relegated to the status of an archaic relic in the history of ideas. It took two world wars, the Holocaust and the threat of nuclear war to bring about acceptance of a revised just war doctrine which has been developed in the contemporary era.

Although this just war revival was initially associated with the Catholic church and with Catholic scholars such as Fr. John Courtney Murray,[3] it soon profited from the ecumenical spirit of the 1960s that has been preserved to the present day. The leading force in this development was the work of Paul Ramsey, a Methodist and professor of religion at Princeton, who plunged into the task of applying just war doctrine to the moral dilemmas of modern deterrence and war.[4] Other Protestant moralists, notably James Turner Johnson[5] and James Childress,[6] contributed significantly to a growing literature which undertook to develop and refine the classic just war doctrine so that it could be a practical guide for statesmen, military commanders and responsible citizens irrespective of religious associations. Michael Walzer, an eminent secular Jewish scholar, contributed perhaps the most widely read and discussed book on modern jut war, *Just and Unjust Wars*.[7] Meanwhile, just war doctrine was also revived within the Catholic church, notably in the 1983 pastoral *The Challenge of Peace*[8] of the American bishops and the subsequent pastoral letters of the German and French bishops.[9]

Modern just war doctrine, then, can be approached from a number of perspectives. A Catholic can approach it from a theological basis, incorporating the teaching of the church on the morality of war. Some of this teaching is morally binding, more of it is to be treated with respect but subject to debate.[10] Other Christians can develop their own versions of just war doctrine, incorporating Catholic teaching when its concepts and arguments are persuasive. Non-Christians can approach just war doctrine at the level of philosophical ethics or as part of the Western cultural tradition, prescinding it from its theological antecedents. Statesmen, military commanders, responsible citizens can find in just war doctrine a practical guide to decision-making and the conduct of war.

Thus far, the modern just war revival has focused primarily on the awesome issues of nuclear deterrence and defense. Very few just war analyses of contemporary conventional and subconventional wars have been attempted.[11] A major purpose of this book is to apply modern just war doctrine to a war which raises most of the critical issues of contemporary revolutionary/counterinsurgency wars, the kinds of wars that have proliferated while the nuclear balance of terror has prevented major conventional as well as nuclear wars. While Israel's war with the PLO is in many respects unique, it raises a great number of political-military and legal-moral issues which are typical of modern wars and which have not been extensively analyzed.

Modern Just War Doctrine:
War-decision Law

Just war doctrine is based on three concepts: the right of self-defense of a body politic, the presumption against war and the resolution of the tensions between these two concepts through the requirement of conditions that must be met to overcome the presumption against war.[12]

Just war doctrine begins with the conviction, derived from the Aristotelian-Thomistic-Suarezian tradition, that human beings are social and political, that they require political society to live good lives, that these political societies should be protected from internal and external attacks under the inherent right of self-defense. In this tradition, it is not simply the individual human beings and their property that are defended but the political society itself.[13]

However, self-defense requires killing and injuring other human beings. Killing is forbidden by religion and by most ethical perspectives. There is, therefore, a presumption against the killing that is necessarily involved in defense of the political society.[14] The just war doctrine resolves the dilemma by making the right of self-defense conditional. In order to invoke the right of self-defense, a political society must meet a number of conditions before embarking on a war and during it. These conditions constitute just war doctrine.

From the outset, just war doctrine has encountered difficulty over the question of whether a political society is morally entitled to go to war for any reason other than self-defense. In the Augustinian tradition, an offensive just war could be waged on behalf of justice, for the punishment of evil. As will be seen, the trend in modern just war doctrine has been to confine morally permissible recourse to force to self-defense. However, in a world where genocide and other massive assaults on human rights occur, the question of offensive war to terminate such situations may need to be reconsidered. For purposes of this study, however, the just war justification of self-defense will suffice.

The just war conditions that must be met in order to overcome the presumption against recourse to war are numerous. They are somewhat differently organized by different moralists.[15] Following the organization of St. Thomas Aquinas's treatment of the subject, I will discuss them as follows:

(1) Competent Authority
(2) Just Cause
    (a) the substance of the cause
    (b) comparative justice
    (c) the proportionality of probable good to probable evil to result from the war in the light of the probability of success
    (d) Reasonable exhaustion of peaceful means of resolving the conflict
(3) Right Intention

Competent Authority

In medieval times the issue of competent authority was important because the decentralized and sometimes disorganized feudal society was subject to armed clashes that might more closely resemble brigandage than public warfare. Accordingly, a just war had to be ordered by a king or other high official possessed of the legal competence to declare it.

In the modern world, competent authority to wage war is usually a matter of constitutional law and practice in each state. While there have been controversies over competent authority, as in those between the American president and Congress in the Vietnam War and the interventions in Central America and the Middle East, competent authority has not usually been a major issue in modern just war doctrine insofar as states are concerned.[16] However, given the proliferation of revolutionary groups in our times, the issue of competent authority has been a very important one in revolutionary/ counterinsurgency wars.

Currently, the competent authority of Arafat and the PLO to wage a revolutionary war is not altogether clear, given the considerable extent to which the *intifada* seems to be controlled by organizations and leaders indigenous to the West Bank and Gaza, whose relationships with the PLO are unknown to outsiders. There is a need for research into the extent to which contemporary revolutionary movements can be shown really to be representative of the peoples on whose behalf they fight, and the case of the PLO is an interesting one. This is not a subject that can be adequately addressed in this study, however. It will be assumed that the PLO has competent authority to wage revolutionary war against Israel.

Just Cause

The *substance of the just cause* must either be self-defense or some other cause that would warrant an offensive war such as humanitarian intervention. While Israel has sometimes justified interventions in Lebanon in part on the grounds of assistance to Christian elements facing disastrous defeat, it cannot be said that any major Israeli military initiative was mainly justified as humanitarian intervention. Accordingly, the interesting question as to whether just war doctrine ought to recognize the possibility of an offensive war on behalf of justice will not be explored in this study.

The second element in determining the justice of a cause worth fighting for is the *comparative justice* of the contending parties. This is a difficult but unavoidable subject. Just war doctrine is essentially about ends and means. Do the ends sought justify the means employed given the probable costs of a war? The issue comes down to the question: What will happen to the political society contemplating a just war if it is defeated? Since 1949 NATO has been based on the proposition that it is morally inadmissible to permit the Soviet Union and its Warsaw Pact allies to defeat any of the NATO countries. The essence of this proposition is that it is morally inadmissible for the NATO countries to permit a Soviet or Soviet Bloc type of regime to be imposed on any NATO member. The extreme means of nuclear deterrence and defense have been justified not only on the grounds of self-defense against aggression but of the prevention of the forcible imposition on any of the NATO countries of the kind of regimes in power in the Soviet Union and its allies. Recent developments in the Soviet Union and the communist states of Eastern Europe may alter perceptions of both aspects of the threat, i.e., the threat of aggression and the threat of forcible imposition of a communist totalitarian regime. Nevertheless, thus far NATO and the nuclear deterrent/defense system remain in place.

The issue in the Arab-Israeli conflict ultimately comes down to the question of the fate of a defeated party in the conflict. What would it mean to Israel to be defeated? This question must be considered in Chapter 10.

Obviously, the requirement to judge the comparative justice of contending regimes is difficult and controversial. International law avoids this requirement by treating all states as equals, including in their right to self-defense. Just war doctrine cannot avoid the evaluation of the comparative justice of contending regimes.

The heart of the just war doctrine is the calculation of the *proportionality of means to ends in the light of the probability of success.* This calculation requires a thorough estimate of the situation and a projected estimate of the strategies, outcomes and effects of the war. Moreover, it is important to emphasize that this calculation should not occur only prior to or at the beginning of the war. It should continue throughout the war, at all important thresholds. However accurate the original estimates of the situation and of the course of the war, unexpected developments may alter the probability of success. If they do, means that formerly appeared to be proportionate to the end may have become disproportionate. In that case, revision of war aims and/or termination of the war may be required by just war doctrine.

Since the presumption is against war, *peaceful means of settling the conflict must be exhausted.* Prior to the war, all reasonable efforts to avoid it while protecting the just cause should be tried. Once the war has begun, the just belligerent should be open to opportunities to interrupt or terminate it and negotiate a peaceful settlement.

Right Intention

The last requirement of just war-decision law is that the belligerent must have right intention. This requirement has several elements. First, the belligerent must limit its efforts to achieving the just cause. If the belligerent goes beyond that, for example, by pursuing an open-ended imperial course, the war is no longer justified. Second, the just belligerent must recognize the humanity of the enemy, repressing natural feelings of antagonism and hatred. Third, the belligerent must always bear in mind that the ultimate end of the war is a just and lasting peace. Accordingly, actions should be avoided which predictably would produce such long-term hatred and bitterness that such a peace would not be possible. This last requirement is designed not only for the benefit of enemies but for the moral health of the just belligerent.

The requirements of right intention may appear to be unrealistic, particularly in conflicts arising from profound religious, ideological and racial differences. On reflection, however, the requirements of right intention recommend themselves on the grounds of practical utility. Hatred, revenge, vindictiveness are not good qualities to bring into the decision-making and political processes necessary to secure peace with justice for a political society.

Modern Just War Doctrine:
War-conduct Law

The war-conduct law of modern just war doctrine consists essentially of two principles already encountered in international war-conduct law: proportion and discrimination. Most just war scholars rely on the international law of war for the detailed principles and prescriptions governing the conduct of war.

Proportion

Proportion has already been discussed as part of the war-decision law of just war doctrine. That proportion is a kind of grand strategic proportion, looking at the total picture of ends, means and probable costs, outcomes and effects. The proportionality of war-conduct law is strategic and tactical. It is concerned with the proportionality of military means to military ends. In the classic French terms, war-decision proportionality is *raison d'état;* war-conduct proportionality is *raison de guerre.*

The determination of the proportionality of a military means is, in the first instance, a matter of defining true military necessity. A military action must be justified on its military merits. But that is not enough—either as a matter of just conduct of war or as the proper use of the military instrument for political ends. A military action must be proportionate in the context of the grand strategic political and moral ends of the war. An action might be justified in purely military terms at the tactical or strategic level, but not justified as part of a total pattern of behavior when viewed from the standpoint of the grand strategic ends of the war.

For example, it is widely conceded that the U.S. forces in Vietnam used excessive firepower to the detriment of the goals of the war, which included retaining the loyalty of the civilian population. Taken individually, many of the combat incidents producing excessive use of firepower might not appear unreasonable from the standpoint of the tactical proportionality of the means. Yet, multiplied by thousands of such incidents, the overall effect of liberal use of firepower might be judged to have worked against the objectives of the war.

To be sure, commanders at the tactical and strategic levels cannot always be expected to foresee all of the consequences of their acts, and a unit in a fire-fight may not have the luxury of worrying about the big picture. But the overall orders, missions, Rule of Engagement and review of operations should be such that measures that make military sense at the tactical or strategic level but which are harmful to the overall pursuit of the just cause of the war are avoided.

Discrimination

Discrimination or noncombatant immunity is the principle that has been most debated in modern just war doctrine. Essentially this is because discrimination is difficult in every form of modern warfare. Discrimination is obviously very difficult if not impossible in nuclear war. Given the incredible firepower and mobility of modern armies, discrimination is very difficult in any conventional war that is fought in populated areas. Discrimination is also very difficult in most revolutionary/counterinsurgency wars wherein the population is often used by the adversaries, usually the revolutionaries, as a shield that must be attacked along with the military targets behind it.

Beyond the practical difficulties of observing the principle of discrimination in modern warfare, there continue to be debates about its interpretation. The principle prohibits direct intentional attacks against noncombatants and civilian targets. Since the nature of modern weapons and means and of military targets is such that it is often virtually impossible to attack legitimate targets without substantial civilian damage, just war doctrine struggles with the problem of reconciling the principle with the realities of effective modern warfare. A pacifist solution, of course, is to conclude that since all modern warfare involves substantial civilian damage, all modern warfare is immoral. Just war doctrine rejects that solution.

The majority of just war moralists attempt to solve the problem by invoking the principle of double effect. This has an illustrious history going back to St. Thomas Aquinas and was most recently revised by Michael Walzer to meet the difficulties of applying the principle of discrimination. In Walzer's revised version the principle of double effect is presented as follows:

(1) The act is good in itself or at least indifferent, which means for our purposes, that it is a legitimate act of war.
(2) The direct effect is morally acceptable—the destruction of military supplies, for example, or the killing of enemy soldiers.
(3) The intention of the actor is good, that is, he aims narrowly at the acceptable effect; the evil effect is not one of his ends, nor is it a means to his ends, and, aware of the evil involved, he seeks to minimize it, accepting costs to himself.
(4) The good effect is sufficiently good to compensate for allowing the evil effect; it must be justifiable under Sidgwick's proportionality rule.[17]

I find this approach to discrimination unpersuasive. No matter how one understands the concept of intention, dividing it up in various ways, it seems clear to me that the decision to launch a particular type of attack or fire a particular weapon involves the intention to produce the results which normally are produced by the attack or the fire. If a sniper fires at soldiers from a window in a house in a crowded street and they respond with automatic fire, bazooka fire and hand grenades that cause great destruction to the building and a dozen casualties to civilians in the house and its environs, civilians whose relation to the sniper is unknown, I cannot concede that the soldiers did not *intend* the civilian casualties and destruction.

My own approach is to consider the principle of discrimination or noncombatant immunity as relative rather than absolute. In my view, the principle of discrimination requires that *foreseeable* civilian damage be proportionate to the military end of an action. In the example above, the soldiers caused disproportionate civilian damage and their actions were wrong. They should have employed limited fire and maneuver to silence the sniper. In the course of their actions, they would necessarily have risked civilian casualties and damage. If they minimized that damage by their actions, the collateral damage might be considered proportionate to the military end of taking out the sniper. But it is clear to me that even this *undesired* civilian damage was *intended* when the soldiers responded to the sniper's fire in a crowded street. Moreover, with respect to Walzer's condition in proposition 3 that "the evil effect is not one of his ends,"[18] I would contend that foreseeable collateral damage is one of the belligerent's ends if there is no way that he can achieve his legitimate military purpose without causing collateral damage.

My understanding of the principle of discrimination or noncombatant immunity is that it requires a belligerent to intend to be as discriminate as possible, taking serious steps to limit collateral damage so that it is proportionate to the military utility of attacking a legitimate military target that is colocated or intermingled with civilian targets. It may well be that in practice this understanding could produce much the same kind of efforts to limit collateral damage as would be elicited by the approach of those who hold discrimination to be an absolute principle, but mitigate it in operation through the invocation of the rule of double effect.

If it is conceded that in most forms of modern warfare there will predictably be some collateral damage, how does one distinguish discriminate from indiscriminate belligerent actions? There are two sources of evidence. One has to do with evidence of the belligerent's intention. Such evidence can be deduced from missions, target selections, Rules of Engagement, premission briefings and the interventions of superiors in the chain of command during operations. This evidence can also be deduced from actions taken after operations, critiques, reprimands, investigations, and various kinds of courts-martial proceedings. It can also be deduced from statements by commanders and political officials defending or repudiating various policies or particular actions.

The other sources of evidence are the reports of military and civilian casualties, civilian damage and social dislocation caused by operations. In extreme cases civilian casualties and damage may be clearly disproportionate to any plausible military utility. This was true in the British-American air raid on Dresden in World War II. However, there are many cases, at all levels of warfare, where the putative military advantage is hard to define and balance against the civilian casualties and damage. The problem is further complicated when the military purpose is primarily deterrence.

It is impossible to establish a formula for balancing military necessity against the requirement to avoid and/or minimize civilian casualties and damage. As in domestic law, when standards of reasonableness are established by studying and comparing cases, standards for discriminate warfare must be developed by comparative military studies. It is my intention to contribute to this critical but largely neglected part of the law of war by the analyses presented in this study.

The Application of
Just War Doctrine

Just war doctrine requires that all of its conditions be met, of war conduct as well as war decisions. However, this does not mean that failure to meet all conditions fully necessarily renders a war unjust. It is possible for a belligerent to fall below just war standards, particularly in the conduct of the war, and still be considered a just belligerent. In World War II the United Nations forces certainly violated the principles of proportion and discrimination in their countervalue strategic bombing practices, but that war is generally considered to have been just. Much depends upon the just cause, and the cause of defeating the Axis powers was so just that the war has been considered just. This still does not excuse the disproportionate and indiscriminate destruction of whole metropolitan areas. Just war doctrine can be employed to judge the moral permissibility of discrete policies and actions irrespective of the overall justice of a war. Indeed, a critical aspect of just war doctrine is that, unlike many holy war doctrines, it does not take the position that the just end justifies any and all means. On the contrary, just war doctrine insists that in addition to meeting the requirements of war-decision law, the just belligerent must meet the conditions of just conduct.

Just war doctrine, then, serves two functions. First, it provides a comprehensive analytical framework for evaluating the moral permissibility of a war, both in terms of the decisions to initiate, continue and terminate it and of the means used to conduct it. Second, it provides a basis for judging strategies, tactics and individual actions employed during the war. In Chapter 10, Israel's war with the PLO will be evaluated in terms of the requirements of just doctrine.

Just war doctrine is sometimes confused with various holy war doctrines such as those that encouraged the excesses of the Christian religious wars of the sixteenth and seventeenth centuries. It should be clear that the requirements of both just war war-decision and war-conduct law bar the just belligerent from justifying such excesses solely on the basis of a just cause supposedly warranted by divine approbation. However, in the contemporary world there are moral and ideological perspectives that encourage a holy war approach. Two that are particularly relevant to this study are Islamic just war/holy war doctrines and secular doctrines justifying wars of national liberation.

Islamic Just War/Holy War Doctrines and Wars of National Liberation

Although the word *Jihad,* understood as "holy war," is often employed by Arab politicians and moralists, it appears that Islamic just war/holy war doctrines have not been developed in the modern era to the extent that Western just war doctrine has been. Accordingly, it is difficult to write with confidence on Islamic just war/holy war doctrines and their application in contemporary conflicts. Nevertheless, some general characteristics of these doctrines can be discerned.[19]

First, Islamic just war/holy war doctrine is clearly theological in character. It has been observed that Western just war doctrine, although stemming from theological perspectives, is mainly natural law ethics. Those who prefer to evaluate the moral permissibility of war without interjecting theological elements into analysis can do so. Islamic just war/holy war doctrines, on the other hand, are derived from Islamic theological teaching.

Second, given the religious character of Islamic just war/holy war, the issue of competent authority is decisive. In Western just war doctrine, war may be morally permissible if, in the first place, it is ordered by some one who has competent authority to commit the political society to public war. In Islamic just war/holy war doctrine, competent authority is exercised by someone who has God's mandate to wage war for religious purposes. To be sure, selfish political motives may be involved, as they often have been when Western rulers invoked religious causes, but in the Islamic tradition there is a much greater emphasis on war as a means to advance the realm of Islam.

Muslims see the world as divided between the *dar al-Islam,* where the true religion prevails, and the world of the infidels, the *dar al-Harb*. From the time of Mohammed to the fifteenth century, Islamic tribes, states and empires waged *Jihad* against the infidels who were rejecting or even threatening the true religion. While this worldview contemplating a perpetual struggle between the Muslims and non-Muslim worlds has long been modified by the course of history, it appears that there is a perennial propensity in Islamic thought and practice to view relations with the non-Muslim world in adversarial terms.

A consequence of this perspective is that there is an implied justification for denying non-Muslims the protections of war-conduct law. It should be recalled that this was a problem with classic Christian just war doctrine. Christian just war doctrine was for Christians. It did not apply to the "Moors" nor to pagans such as the Indians of the New World. As late as the sixteenth century, Vitoria was attempting to persuade the Spaniards that Indians were human beings made in the image and likeness of God and that they should be treated as such.

In similar fashion, there is a historic temptation in Islamic theory and practice to think of just war/holy war doctrine as primarily concerned with the advancement of Islam and only marginally concerned with limiting the use of force against the enemies of Islam. I will not pursue the difficult subject of wars between Muslims.

In more specific terms, it appears that Islamic just war doctrine is mainly focused on war-decision law. There is an Islamic war-conduct law, but it seems to be much less developed than Western war-conduct law. As a result, there is a tendency of Islamic *Jihad* to be more like a holy war than a just war, with a propensity to hold that any means is justified by the just cause of advancing the realm of Islam. To the extent that this perspective prevails, Islamic attitudes toward Israel would be particularly hostile. Israel is not just any member of the *dar al-Harb*. It is, in Muslim eyes, the usurper of the sacred city of Jerusalem and the state that has pushed back the realm of Islam.

Muslim fundamentalists play an important part in Israel's war with the PLO, Palestinians in the *intifada* and Shiites in Lebanon. Their objectives and means are no doubt strongly influenced by the characteristics of Islamic just war/holy war thought. Even secular Arabs who are not particularly observant may be influenced by the Islamic tradition of war with the infidels. In any case, there is a secular source of "higher law" that is available to the Palestinians and their supporters. Contemporary doctrines of wars of national liberation, most of them Marxist, emphasize the irreconcilable differences between the oppressed and their oppressors. They tend to justify any and all means employed by the oppressed to overthrow the oppressors. If those claiming to fight a war of national liberation even pause to justify conduct that appears immoral by ordinary standards, they usually give the twofold answer that the oppressor deserves whatever he gets and that the achievement of the just cause, the just society, amply justifies any action that advances the just cause.

This view of wars of national liberation is admirably summarized by the Chinese delegate to the UN Security Council, Ambassador Huang, in the debate on S.C. Res. 347 of April 24, 1974. He asserted:

> . . . the violence used by the aggressors and oppressors is injust, while the violence used by the victims of aggression and the oppressed to resist aggression and win liberation is just. . . . The Israeli Zionists have been using reactionary violence to carry out aggression and oppression against the Palestinians and other peoples.[20]

That this endorsement of what might be called "just terror" was typical of perspectives often brought to legal and moral judgments about the PLO's war of national liberation with Israel was demonstrated in the Security Council debates described in Chapter 4.

Notes

1. St. Thomas Aquinas, *Summa theologica, secunda secundae,* 15, Q.40. (Art. 1), in A.P. D'Entreves, ed., *Aquinas: Selected Political Writings,* trans. J.G. Dawson (Oxford: Blackwell, 1948), pp. 159, 161.

2. Alfred Vanderpool, *La doctrine scolastique du droit de guerre* (Paris: Pedone, 1919); James Turner Johnson, *Ideology, Reason and Limitation of War* (Princeton, N.J., Princeton University Press, 1975); idem, *Just War Tradition and the Restraint of War* (Princeton, N.J.: Princeton University Press, 1981).

3. John Courtney Murray, S.J., "Theology and Modern War," *Theological Studies* 20 (1959): 40–61; "The Uses of a Doctrine on the Use of Force: War as a Moral Problem," in *We Hold These Truths,* ed. John Courtney Murray (New York: Sheed & Ward), pp. 249–73.

4. Paul Ramsey, *War and the Christian Conscience: How Shall Modern War Be Conducted Justly?* (Durham, N.C.: Duke University Press, 1961); idem, *The Just War: Force and Political Responsibility* (New York: Scribner's, 1968).

5. Johnson, *Ideology, Reason and the Limitation of War;* idem, *Just War Tradition and the Restraint of War;* idem, *Can Modern War Be Just?* (New Haven, Conn.: Yale University Press, 1984).

6. James F. Childress, "Just War Theories," *Theological Studies* 39 (1978): 427–45; idem, "Just-War Criteria," in *War or Peace: The Search for New Answers,* ed. Thomas A. Shannon (Maryknoll, N.Y.: Orbis, 1980), pp. 40–58.

7. Michael Walzer, *Just and Unjust Wars* (New York: Basic Books, 1977).

8. National Conference of Catholic Bishops, *The Challenge of Peace: God's Promise and Our Response* (Washington, D.C., May 1983).

9. *Out of Justice, Peace,* joint pastoral letter of the West German bishops; *Winning the Peace,* joint pastoral letter of the French bishops, James V. Schall, S.J. (San Francisco: Ignatius Press, 1984).

10. See the U.S. Catholic bishops' *The Challenge of Peace,* paras. 9–12, pp. 4–5.

11. On issues of revolutionary war/counterinsurgency, see Ramsey, *The Just War,* Part 5, "Vietnam and Insurgency Warfare," pp. 427–536. Walzer addresses the subject in two chapters, "Guerrilla War" and "Terrorism," pp. 176–206. Johnson discusses Israel's war with the PLO in *Can Modern War Be Just?* pp. 53–63. I devote three chapters to the subject—"Just War Applied: The United States in Vietnam," "Critical Issues of Just War: The *Jus ad Bellum* of Revolutionary/counterinsurgency War," and "Critical Issues of Just War: The *Jus in Bello* of Revolutionary/Counterinsurgency Wars," in *The Conduct of Just and Limited War* (New York: Praeger, 1981), pp. 91–126, 154–203.

12. See Heinrich A. Rommen, *The State in Catholic Thought* (St. Louis: Herder, 1945), particularly Chaps. IX and X on the origins and nature of the state, and Chap. XXIX on just war doctrine.

13. See Rommen's discussion, ibid., especially pp. 652–54.

14. On the presumption against recourse to war, see St. Thomas Aquinas, *Summa theologica, secunda secundae* 40 (Art. 1) in Vanderpol, *La doctrine scholastique du droit de guerre,* pp. 308–12; Francisco de Vitoria, *De jure belli,* in Vanderpol, *La doctrine scholastique du droit de guerre,* pp. 326–29; Francisco Suarez, *De Bello,* in Vanderpol, *La doctrine scolastique du droit de guerre,* pp. 362–7.

15. The 1983 pastoral letter of the American Catholic bishops organizes just war doctrine as follows: *Jus ad bellum:* Just Cause, Competent Authority, Comparative Justice, Right Intention, Last Resort, Probability of Success and Proportionality; *Jus in bello:* Proportionality and Discrimination. *The Challenge of Peace* (Washington, D.C.: NCCB, May 1983), pp. 28–31. See Johnson, *Can Modern War Be Just?* Chap. 1.

16. On the issue of competent authority, see O'Brien, *Conduct of Just and Limited War,* pp. 17–19, 91–92.

17. Walzer, *Just and Unjust Wars,* pp. 153, 155. (Point 3 is revised by Walzer on p. 155. Sidgwick's rule prohibits excessive harm relative to: 1) the end of victory and 2) the proportionality of the harm done by the evil.

18. Ibid., p. 155.

19. I base my comments on Islamic just/holy war doctrine primarily on what I have learned as part of a continuing seminar on Western and Islamic traditions on war, peace, and statecraft, convened at Rutgers University by Prof. James T. Johnson of Rutgers and John Kelsay of Florida State University, 1988–89. Papers discussed in the seminar are being published in two volumes, the first, John Kelsay and James T. Johnson, *War, Peace and Statecraft in the Western and Islamic Traditions,* will be published by Greenwood Press in 1991.

20. Huang (China), 27 U.N. SCOR (1769th mtg.), p. 26. On the claims and practices of national liberation movements, see Inis L. Claude, "Just Wars: Doctrines and Institutions," *Political Science Quarterly* 95 (1980): 38–96; W. Michael Reisman, "Old Wine in New Bottles: The Reagan and Brezhnev Doctrines in Contemporary International Law," *Yale Journal of International Law* 13 (1988): 87–96; Harris Okun Schoenberg, *Mandate for Terror: The United Nations and the PLO* (New York: Shapolsky, 1989).

10

A Just War Analysis of Israel's War with the PLO

As explained in Chapter 9, modern just war doctrine resembles the international law of war in that it includes separate sections on war-decision law (*jus ad bellum*) and war-conduct law (*jus in bello*). However, just war doctrine differs from the international law of war in that it closely relates war-decision and war-conduct law, combining them in a comprehensive calculus of ends and means. International law, on the other hand, sharply separates the issue of the legal permissibility of recourse to armed force from the issues of war conduct. Indeed, international law attempts to exclude considerations of justice from the law of war since, in a heterogeneous and conflictual international system, it is nearly impossible to obtain consensus on issues of justice most of the time.

Just war doctrine, on the other hand, does not require such consensus. It is directed as the consciences of statesmen, military commanders, military personnel, citizens who must decide what is worth fighting for and how to fight for it—whatever others may think. This, of course, carries an inherent risk of self-serving subjectivity and hypocrisy. The antidote to these risks is to be found in individual consciences and in the collective conscience of nations invoking just war justifications for their use of armed force.

One does not have to study the history of Israel for long to be struck by the extent to which both individual consciences and the national conscience of the Jewish nation play a part in Israeli security policies. To be sure, conscience in Israel is relentlessly tested by the permanent state of emergency in which the country exists. The lure of arguments of "supreme emergency," "self-preservation" and "necessity" is powerful and they are sometimes invoked. Prime Minister Begin, in particular, was given to dismissing all criticism of Israeli security measures with arguments of this kind.

In the end, however, Israel has not succumbed to the temptation to justify any and all means employed in defense of her vital interests or even of

289

her existence. Individual consciences and the national conscience demand persuasive justifications for recourse to armed force and the conduct of military and counterterror operations. With this in mind, I will offer a moral evaluation of Israel's conduct in its war with the PLO from the perspectives of modern just war doctrine as outlined in Chapter 9.

War-decision Law
(jus ad bellum)

Competent authority

War must be waged on behalf of a body politic or political movement on the order of those who have been entrusted with the right and duty to obtain it for the public security and good. In a democratic country such as Israel, competent authority rests with the prime minister and cabinet. However, that authority is subject to the requirement of retaining support of the legislative branch, the Knesset, and, as a practical if not a legal matter, of the people.

Israel's long war with the PLO is not a matter of choice. Some phases of it, such as the 1978 Litani Operation and 1982 Operation Peace for Galilee have been wars—or campaigns—of choice.[1] It could be said that other phases of lower-intensity preventive/attrition counterterror operations—e.g., 1979–81—have been mini-wars, or campaigns, of choice. But the basic conflict is, from Israel's point of view, a defensive one, determined by the extent of the PLO's determination to fight a war of national liberation to the finish. During most of this war the PLO's apparent goals have made a peaceful settlement impossible. The most peaceably inclined Israeli government would have had to take some measures to defend the country against the PLO's pursuit of those goals through terrorism.

Accordingly, there is really no problem about affirming the competent authority of Israel's leaders to defend the country against the PLO's attacks. The problem has been that the more preventive and preemptive forms of defense, particularly when they escalated to full-scale war, have been questioned. It is necessary, then, to consider the issue of competent authority in relation to the principal levels of Israeli response to the PLO's war of national liberation.

I see no evidence that there has been in Israel a substantial disagreement in the Knesset or in the general public with a policy of retaliation for terrorist attacks. Indeed, it is clear that retaliation after a major terrorist attack or an accumulation of such attacks is demanded by the Knesset and the public. As discussed in Chapters 1, 2, 4 and 5, such retaliation has always been justified by Israel to a considerable degree on a rationale of deterrence and prevention. I have the impression that the presumption has almost always been in favor of such counterterror measures. The prime minister and cabinet are expected to take such measures when a major terrorist incident occurs or when the accumulation of attacks becomes intolerable.

It appears that this consensus weakens somewhat when preventive/attrition counterterror operations are not linked with the rationale of retaliation for past attacks, but are more in the nature of what Yaniv calls "sustained operations," such as those initiated under Begin from 1979 to 1981.[2] Nevertheless, it seems clear that a strong consensus continued to give the presumption of military/security necessity to more aggressive counterterror preventive/attrition operations.

The Litani Operation was broadly supported. It was a response to the "Country Club" raid, one of the most destructive and spectacular of the PLO's terrorist attacks. It had from the outset the appearance of a temporary occupation during which the areas from which terrorism was being organized and launched would be cleaned up. The excessive collateral damage involved did not seem to raise great opposition to the operation.

It remained for the 1982 Lebanon War to create sufficient opposition to security measures that competent authority became a clear issue. This was the case more because of Sharon's method of getting Israel into the war and of escalating it than because of doubts about the original announced objectives of Operation Peace For Galilee. The Cabinet, Knesset and the people supported an improved version of the Litani Operation. They understood that the necessity to drive the PLO far away from the border was decisively greater than in 1978, given the PLO's new capabilities to attack Israeli population centers in the north.[3]

Many in the government and most of the public would have little inkling of the extent to which Sharon had deceived and manipulated Begin, the Cabinet and the IDF itself with respect to his real objectives in the campaign. But, as Israeli forces ringed Beirut, week after week, as casualties mounted and condemnations of Israeli attacks on Beirut burgeoned, considerable opposition to the war's aims and conduct arose in the Knesset and in the public.

I would consider that Begin's and Sharon's competent authority for waging the 1982 Lebanon War (I don't include the rest of the Cabinet, since they seemed to have little influence) had become doubtful by August 1982. I think that they had just enough of a political and popular mandate to finish the business of expelling the PLO from Beirut to get them through the hostilities. Of course, after hostilities ended, Begin's and Sharon's actions were so widely condemned as time went on that there was a kind of retrospective withdrawal of competent authority. However, as the war was being conducted, Begin and Sharon, profiting from the underlying presumption in favor of measures to counter PLO terror, had competent authority to wage it. Moreover, despite growing criticism of the risks and costs of the 1982–85 occupation of large parts of Lebanon, the political mandate to continue it remained sufficient.

I conclude that, for most of Israel's war with the PLO, the political leaders have had a strong legal and political mandate to defend the country by preventive/attrition counterterror attacks and, occasionally, by major incursions and even by conventional military campaigns in Lebanon.

Just Cause

I divide the category of just cause into two parts. First, I consider the justice of the cause. Second, I consider the comparative justice of the adversaries in order to estimate the probable consequences of a party having a just cause losing its just war.

The *substance* of Israel's just cause depends upon one's evaluation of the PLO's goals. If they remain those of the Palestinian Covenant, Israel's ultimate just cause is self-preservation. It is certainly self-preservation of the state of Israel. It is, moreover, self-preservation of an independent Jewish society. It may very well be the self-preservation of the Israeli population. A Palestinian/Arab victory would raise the prospect of some form of genocide. At the very least, expulsion of virtually the whole Israeli population from Palestine could be expected if the Covenant goals were operative.

Obviously, neither the PLO nor a Palestinian state in the West Bank and Gaza by themselves pose such an extreme threat to Israel. The threat comes from the prospect that other Arab states with a long record of warfare with and enmity against Israel might join together finally to make it possible for the Palestinians to achieve the goals of the covenant.

If Arafat's avowals of recognition of Israel's permanent right to exist and renunciation of terrorism are credited, Israel's just cause is self-defense against a war of national liberation that threatens to force establishment of Palestinian state in the occupied territories. The war is just, in the first place, since Israel has a right to defend itself against continuing attacks. Deterrence and defense against terrorist and guerrilla attacks are the immediate Israeli just cause. The war may, further, be just in that it rejects relaxation of self-defense measures as long as the possibility exists of a two-phase Palestinian attempt to regain all of Palestine, i.e., of a phase 2, after establishment of a West Bank/Gaza state, in which the Palestinian state becomes the launching pad for attacks by Arab states designed to destroy Israel.

Thus, the just cause for continuing hostilities with the PLO rests to a great extent on estimates of the intentions and future behavior of the PLO, the Palestinians in the territories and the Arab states, especially the most hostile states such as Syria and Iraq. These estimates must include evaluations of trends in the continuing Middle East arms races which are ominous— development of missile delivery systems, chemical warfare and, possibly, nuclear weapons. Obviously, these estimates must include consideration of the extent to which Arafat and his supporters can control the PLO factions and the Palestinians, whether in the territories or in the *diaspora,* and the intentions and futures of the rulers and elites in the Arab states, particularly Syria, Jordan, Iraq, Saudi Arabia and Egypt. Indeed, even if Arafat were absolutely sincere in a claim to settle for a Palestinian state in the territories and end the conflict, Israel could not be sure that his position would prevail.

The element of *comparative justice* has emerged relatively recently in modern just war doctrine. I raised the issue in *The Conduct of Just and Limited War* in 1981.[4] The American Catholic bishops acknowledged its importance in their 1983 pastoral letter, *The Challenge of Peace.*[5] The issue of comparative justice has hitherto been debated, either explicitly or implicitly, mainly in terms of wars involving totalitarian states or revolutionary movements. The issue of comparative justice was debated in the context of the long U.S./NATO v. USSR/Warsaw Pact confrontation, or of Third World wars between communist and anticommunist states or movements, e.g., in Vietnam and Central America.

The events of 1989 will require a major reassessment of the comparative justice of the members of NATO and the Warsaw Pact. Leaving that task to others, I must grapple with a kind of comparative analysis which is more difficult than that involved in assessing communist or other totalitarian threats in the recent past. Before Gorbachev, one could pose the question of comparative justice more or less in this manner: Is it a sufficient just cause to undertake to prevent West Germany and other Western European democracies from being overrun by the Soviet Union and its Eastern Bloc allies and being subjected to the kind of repressive regimes that have existed for so long in the communist states? It was possible to pose the question that way because there was a long record of the ideologies and policies of the opposing blocs on which to base answers to "Better Red than Dead" or "vice versa" positions.

As we have seen, in the case of the PLO we have a national liberation movement that has an ideology—expressed in the Palestinian Covenant—

that may or may not be "caduc." At the least we have the problem of diversity and conflict within the PLO, the Palestinians generally, and the more involved Arab states so that it is not a simple matter to know what life would be like if the Palestinians had their way. However, although the PLO has not had an opportunity really to manage an independent state, it has a record of governance in parts of Jordan and, particularly, Lebanon.

That record has been a disturbing one. Both in Jordan and in Lebanon the PLO has abused the local populations when it controlled enclaves or even the so-called state-within-a-state in Lebanon. In part this behavior may be explained more by the presence within the PLO of rebellions, violent elements unwilling to submit to the direction and discipline of the mainstream organizations. That in itself would be cause for concern. A weak Palestinian regime, struggling to control rebellious elements within, subject to the interventions and manipulations of other Arab states, might be unable to protect the rights of defeated Jews, even if it wanted to. However, there is no certainty that the mainstream PLO elements may not be capable of repressive behavior against a defeated enemy that had long humiliated them.

Beyond speculation about the character of a Palestinian regime finally successful in its war of national liberation—either in phase 1 or 2—there is a problem of the general pattern of government and politics in Arab states. The regimes of Syria and Iraq are very harsh and repressive. Assad plays by what Thomas Friedman calls "Hama rules" under which whole cities of people resisting his authority are simply rubbed out.[6] Iraq is notorious for purges and for slaughtering Kurds with poison gas and other means. As I write, Saddam Hussein has added aggression against Kuwait to his record of crimes against the peace, war crimes and crimes against humanity. Despite its relatively moderate foreign policy, Jordan has been a tightly controlled state that operated under martial law from 1967 to 1990 and banned political parties.[7] Saudi Arabia, another Arab moderate, has a strong authoritarian regime grounded on religious attitudes that are not tolerant of unbelievers. Egypt looks to be a far more moderate and stable polity than states like Syria and Iraq, but the rule is still heavy-handed. Lebanon is a tragic case of the failure of democracy and the rule of law in the Middle East.

There is little in the record of Arab states around Israel that encourages the belief that a Palestinian state would be more moderate, more democratic, more devoted to the rule of law and human rights, more stable and able to control violent elements than its Arab neighbors.

If Israel were subjugated, in one war or several, most of its surviving citizens would probably be expelled. Those permitted to remain would probably lead the existence of a repressed minority, comparable to the status of such minorities in contemporary Arab states.

Thus, it is not unreasonable for the Israelis to believe that a Palestinian/ "Arab Nation" victory would, in the worst case, mean the end of Israel or, in the two-phase version, mean that Israel would have to continue to live as a garrison state operating under a permanent state of emergency from less defensible borders both in terms of conventional and terrorist attacks.

At the level of counterterror deterrence/defense, Israel claims the continuing right of self-defense against terrorist attacks, understanding self-defense as discussed in the preceding chapters.

In summary, Israel has two just causes. The ultimate just cause is preservation of the state, society and people of Israel. The immediate just cause is legitimate self-defense against terrorist and guerrilla attacks, a just cause that is part of a broader right of self-defense against conventional, chemical and nuclear attacks.

At this point Palestinian claims of just cause must be acknowledged. The Palestinians claims, with wide support, a right of self-determination. Taken in the sense of the Palestinian Covenant, this claim demands the extinction of the state of Israel and the removal of most of the Jewish population of that country.[8]

When expressed in less severe terms, as in the form of the binational "secular state," the Palestinian claim still comes down to the drastic alteration of Israeli society and suggests a status for the Jews similar to that of the unfortunate minorities in Lebanon. If the Palestinian claim to self-determination does require that all of Palestine be united in a state dominated by an Arab majority, it collides head-on with the Israeli claim to the right of self-determination.

Some of the Scholastic just war writers acknowledged that there could be cases of simultaneous ostensible justice on both sides in a war.[9] Ostensible justice on both sides can be conceded in this war. However, that is only the beginning of the just war calculus. It is not enough to have a plausible just cause. The other just war conditions must be substantially met. Indeed, if it is possible that both sides may have a just cause, it is also possible that neither side may meet all of the just war conditions in which case they are both fighting an unjust war.

As UN Security Council debates about the Arab-Israeli conflict amply demonstrate, the PLO managed to elevate its claim to the right of self-determination to a very high level, a kind of axiomatic moral imperative.[10] However, no one has sorted out the practical and moral criteria whereby claims of self-determination are to be judged and priorities assigned. The Kurds and Armenians, for example, have long struggled for self-determination without encouragement from the PLO's supporters in the United Nations. Apparently, it is considered that the price of self-determination for the Kurds and Armenians would be so disproportionate to the good of self-determination that the claim is not even seriously entertained.

The right of self-determination, then, must be balanced against other claims of self-determination as well as claims for international stability and peace. The Palestinian claim for self-determination ought to be treated as one of many claims that must be reconciled if there is to be peace with a modicum of justice in the Middle East. If the claim is modified to mean *some* self-determination compatible with the continuation of Israeli self-determination and with peace and stability in the region, then it becomes more acceptable as a just cause.

To be sure, this may be the extent of the present claims of the mainstream PLO. However, this more moderate version was offered only at the end of 1988, twenty-three years after the establishment of the PLO and the commencement of its war with Israel. As discussed in Chapter 1, the partial self-determination claim remains open to the suspicions that it is not the last claim that will be made. Moreover, the testing of PLO intentions goes on in the context of continuing terrorism, albeit mainly from dissident PLO and radical Lebanese elements. That testing also continues in the context of a violent *intifada* in which more and more "moderate" Palestinians are killed and intimidated by the PLO directly or by Palestinians linked to the PLO or to the fundamentalist Hamas organization. Moreover, the increased hostility to Israel displayed by Palestinians after Iraq's aggression in Kuwait, exacerbated by the October 8, 1990 clash on the Temple Mount, does not encourage hopes for peaceful co-existence between Arabs and Jews.

If the PLO could demonstrate that its just cause was now no more than establishment of an independent state on the West Bank and in Gaza in the context of safeguards, acceptable to Israel, that it would not become the base for conventional and terrorist threats and attacks against Israel, the ultimate Israeli just cause of self-preservation would not have to be invoked. How long and what it would take to demonstrate this elimination of the root source of Israel's war with the PLO can hardly be estimated. Many phases might be necessary before peace and stability would be assured. Given internal and external politics in the Middle East, it would take a great deal of goodwill and good luck for that demonstration to take hold. At this writing such a demonstration seems remote, and Israel's war with the PLO goes on.

Throughout this book I have worked on the assumption that the Israeli polity is a good society, eminently worth defending and preserving. It is a good society because it has given Jews scattered around the world a homeland in the very territory that is most sacred to them. It is a good society because it has lived by the values of democracy, the rule of law and human rights enjoined by the Western tradition to which Judaism has contributed so much. Like all societies, Israel is imperfect and throughout its existence the fact that it has been under siege has required it to deny its Arab citizens many of the rights and privileges extended to Jews. However, given the external and internal threats to its security and very existence, Israel has done remarkably well in its relations with its Arab minority. Nevertheless, that minority understandably resents its condition, as events since the outbreak of the *intifada* in the territories have demonstrated.

If ever Israel is relieved of its all-too-real security concerns, it should make major efforts to improve the lot of its Arab citizens and to try to bring them more into the mainstream of Israeli life. Meanwhile, the prospect is for a very tense coexistence of Jews and Arabs in Israel. In the territories Israel has faced extremely difficult challenges. As indicated in Chapter 8, they have not always been met well. Nevertheless, if one compares the Israeli record of military government with the record of the Arab governments in the area, one is obliged to conclude that life under the Israelis has generally been more tolerable than life in most Arab states. The critical difference, of course, has been the denial of the claim of self-determination. The *intifada* shows that this denial outweighs the benefits of Israeli rule in the minds of the Palestinians. In any event, despite its shortcomings, the state of Israel has managed to balance the requirements of democracy, the rule of law and human rights with those of military and security necessity in circumstances of unparalleled and unremitting threats to its very existence. This is a state that deserves the full protection contemplated in just war doctrine.

Proportion—Probability of Success

Even though Israel has a just cause of self-defense in its war with the PLO, its use of force must be proportionate to the necessities of achieving that just cause. Moreover, the proportionality of initial and continuing recourse to force must be judged in the light of the probability of success. As indicated in Chapter 9, evaluation of proportionality is a continuing process that takes account of the course of hostilities and of their broader political context. A belligerent's original estimate of probability of success may, of course, not be borne out by the fortunes of war, and the need for continuing the conflict may not seem as clear as it was at the outset.

Israel's war with the PLO has lasted for over twenty-five years and has gone through many phases. Evaluation of the proportionality of Israel's continued recourse to force against the PLO can be made for the overall conflict and for particular parts of it. I will consider the proportionality of the overall war with the PLO to Israel's just cause of self-defense. Then I will evaluate the proportionality of Israel's strategies of incursions, air raids and naval operations in sanctuary states: Jordan, Syria and Lebanon. I will next assess the proportionality of Israel's escalation of hostilities in July 1981 and the 1982 Lebanon War. Finally, I will attempt to relate Israel's counterinsurgency strategies and tactics during the *intifada* to the overall calculus of proportionality.

The overall Israeli recourse to force against the PLO and the sanctuary states is clearly proportionate to the just cause of self-defense. This, of course, does not mean that every Israeli use of force is proportionate to its intermediate military objective. Israel has no alternative to self-defense measures against terrorist and guerrilla attacks by the PLO which initiated the war. There has always been a high probability of success. Moreover, it should be noted that in just war doctrine, probability of success is not as important in self-defense as it is in a genuine war of choice, e.g., U.S. intervention in Vietnam.

However, the calculus of proportionality becomes difficult with respect to the Israeli strategies of attacking the PLO in sanctuary states. In the first place, such attacks have always consciously risked broadening the war and escalating to conventional hostilities with the sanctuary state, as has occurred in various forms between Israel and Syria. Moreover, these attacks necessarily involved substantial collateral damage, given the PLO practice of intermingling its bases with the civilian population. The Israeli attacks have caused political, economic and social damage and dislocation; indeed, the whole Israeli deterrent strategy was designed to impose unacceptable damage on sanctuary states and the locales from which the PLO operated. Was this strategy a proportionate means to the just end of self-defense?

The Israeli attacks against the PLO in Jordan, 1965–70, responded to a major, continuing threat of terrorist and guerrilla attacks from that country. At times there was substantial support for the PLO from the Jordanian armed forces. Given the colocation of PLO positions and Jordanian civilian centers, there was no way to attack the PLO bases without collateral damage. Given the military balance, the Israeli attacks against the PLO bases in Jordan did not risk conventional war with that country. The probability of success was confirmed by the success of the strategy. Although the PLO's political and military challenge to Hussein's regime brought on its bloody suppression in September 1970 and thereafter, it is clear that the unacceptable damage inflicted on the PLO's East Bank sanctuaries impelled Jordan to remove the PLO, depriving it of its preferred base for terrorist operations against Israel.

Israel's attacks against the PLO in Syria were also proportionate notwithstanding the danger of escalation to conventional hostilities with that country. Syria's hostility toward Israel has been such that conventional war has always been a possibility, and its outbreak would not result from attacks on PLO bases in Syria but from calculated decisions by Syria that the time was right to take on the Israelis again. In any event, the probability of success of the Israeli strategy in this case has, once again, been borne out by events. As discussed in Chapter 2, Syria has refused to risk its own security by permitting the PLO to launch terrorist operations from its territory, particularly since undertaking not to do so in 1974.

The proportionality of Israeli incursions, air raids and naval operations against PLO targets in Lebanon is the most difficult to assess. To judge the proportionality of these measures, one must take into account the magnitude of the PLO presence in Lebanon, leading to the creation of a state-within-a-state, the fact that after September 1970 Lebanon became virtually the sole base for PLO terrorist attacks against Israel, the fact that Beirut became, in effect, the terrorist capital of the world, and the fact that the Lebanese government and, indeed, the state of Lebanon progressively crumbled into virtual anarchy.

Israel developed excellent passive defenses along the border, but they alone would not have sufficed to limit terrorist incursions to tolerable levels. Moreover, the pressures of counterterror attacks could not elicit curbs on PLO activities comparable to those imposed by Jordan and Syria because the Lebanese government never could summon the will and the means to restrain the PLO. In these circumstances, Israel was obliged to wage its war against the PLO in Lebanon, which became a tragic arena for the conflict.

As a general strategy, some kind of policy of attacking the PLO in its Lebanese bases was necessary and proportionate to the legitimate self-defense requirements of Israel. This does not mean that all of the Israeli raids, incursions and extended operations were proportionate to those requirements. However, in my judgment, an overall policy of fighting the PLO where it lived was proportionate.

As long as the PLO's attacks were limited largely to infiltration missions by small groups of *fedayeen*, the probability of success for Israel's strategy of deterrence and defense was good. Although some individual incursions and raids may have been disproportionate, the general pattern appears to have been one of counterforce operations without excessive collateral damage. Again, this judgment is influenced by awareness of the PLO's responsibility for endangering the lives and property of the local population of south Lebanon by operating from its midst.

However, the Litani Operation presents a case where there is a good argument for the proportionality of the campaign in war-decision terms but evidence of a lack of proportionality and discrimination in war-conduct terms. The Litani Operation was a proportionate response to PLO terrorism, given the collapse of the Lebanese state and the PLO's increasing aggressiveness. However, as discussed in Chapter 6, it appears that the Israelis often employed disproportionate and indiscriminate means in rooting out the PLO. Evidence of this is not overwhelming, but on the basis of newspaper reports and the judgments of Ezer Weizman and Michael Walzer, I assume that criticism of the Israeli conduct of the Litani Operation is well founded.[11] If it is, it may be concluded that the operation, a potentially proportionate measure, was not conducted in a sufficiently proportionate and discriminate manner. Ironically, the Litani Operation is widely believed to have failed the test of military utility as well as that of the just war conditions.[12] It did considerable damage to the PLO and led to the introduction of UNIFIL and the establishment of the Security Zone, but it did not prevent the return of the PLO and reestablishment of its state-within-a-state from which it resumed its conventional build-up, leading to the hostilities of 1981 and the 1982 war. The 1982 Lebanon War was of such a magnitude and duration that the question of its proportionality requires consideration separate from the analysis of the overall proportionality of Israel's war with the PLO. At the same time, the 1982 war cannot be properly understood and judged unless it is recognized that it was only one phase, albeit a singularly major one, of the war. Debate over the way that Sharon planned and conducted the 1982 war has tended to overlook the underlying strategic arguments for it, arguments that would have to be considered by any responsible Israeli leadership.

It is widely believed that the 1982 war was for Israel a war of choice.[13] To the extent that this was the case and that there were good reasons not to initiate this war, its proportionality obviously becomes questionable. The issue, then, becomes one of judging the necessity for the war. Its proportionality turns on that judgment.

As recounted in Chapters 1 and 2, Israel's counterterror strategy was based on a combination of passive defense and a deterrence/defense posture that threatened incursions and raids against the PLO in sanctuary states. If the option of making preventive/attrition attacks in sanctuary states were to be greatly restricted, Israel's counterterror strategy would be limited to passive defense. It had always been axiomatic in Israeli strategy at all levels that passive defense was not an adequate basis for survival in a hostile environment.

When the PLO developed its conventional capability in the late 1970s and early 1980s, it challenged this fundamental Israeli counterterror strategy.

The PLO, with artillery and rocket launchers that could bombard Israeli population centers from distances up to seventeen miles, now had its own capability of inflicting "unacceptable damage" on Israel. Israel's response to major terrorist attacks and/or an accumulation of such attacks had always been to hit PLO bases in the sanctuary states. Now the decision to do so was automatically the decision to subject northern Israeli towns and settlements to indiscriminate countervalue bombardments from long-range artillery and missiles.

The prospect, then, after the July 21, 1981, Habib cease-fire, was the following: Any time the PLO decided to resume terrorist attacks on Israel or on Israeli interests abroad, it could assume that the Israelis would be reluctant to respond with their traditional preventive/attrition attacks since those attacks would inevitably trigger the kind of artillery and rocket bombardments on northern Israeli population centers that had paralyzed them in July 1981. The PLO's conventional countervalue capability could provide a deterrent "umbrella" under which the PLO would be free to conduct terrorist operations.

It is true, of course, that the PLO did not attempt many cross-border terrorist operations against Israel from July 21, 1981, to June 1982. It did make many attacks on Major Haddad's forces in the Security Zone and there were numerous acts of international terrorism culminating with the assassination attempt on Ambassador Argov in London. Apparently, Arafat restrained the more aggressive elements in the PLO for fear of eliciting the kind of full-scale invasion that took place in June 1982. However, the PLO retained the capability of resuming terrorist attacks directly against Israel and of offsetting Israel's traditional responses by countervalue attacks on Israeli population centers.

In these circumstances Israel could stand pat and hope for the best, discounting continued attacks on its Christian allies in the Security Zone and international terror attacks on Israelis, other Jews and their interests. The Israelis could, if sufficiently provoked, resume the kind of hostilities conducted in July 1981, when they apparently came close to a significant victory in their efforts to knock out the PLO's conventional capabilities. The price of such an effort would presumably be a renewed ordeal for the population of northern Israel and that price had proved to be too high in July 1981. Israel could have launched a Litani II Operation and cleared south Lebanon of the PLO, but this kind of operation had proved inadequate and ephemeral in 1978. Rejecting the foregoing options, Israel chose to launch a major attack on the PLO that would destroy its infrastructure and drive it far out of range of Israel's northern population centers. This, at least, was the goal which seems to have been approved by Begin and the

Cabinet. Sharon's real goal, however, was to drive the PLO's fighting forces out of Lebanon altogether, or at least to expel them from all of south Lebanon and Beirut. This became the goal of the war.

What was the probability of success? The question must be answered in two ways, related to Sharon's assumptions. Sharon assumed that Bashir Gemayel and his Christian Phalangists would root the PLO out of Beirut. If so, the IDF would not have to enter or long besiege the city. The probability of success of this part of Sharon's plan was manifestly low, as Israeli intelligence and commanders such as Maj. Gen. Drori repeatedly told him.[14] Gemayel aspired to leadership in Lebanon. He could not expect to be accepted as leader by the Lebanese and by the Arab world if he fought, defeated and expelled the PLO.[15] Moreover, it seems clear that he and his forces were not up to the task and had no stomach for it.[16]

Accordingly, the real calculation of probability of success should focus on the prospects for the IDF either in a battle with the PLO in Beirut or in a siege conducted in the fight-and-negotiate mode to achieve the evacuation of the PLO. In terms of military capabilities, the prospects for the IDF's success in a battle pressed into the PLO's West Beirut positions were excellent. However, there were three major reasons for avoiding a direct attack within the city. First, at the point when it would have been most feasible, when the PLO was beaten and off balance in mid-June, Sharon had no mandate to enter the city. Moreover, it had been traditional Israeli policy not to attack an Arab capital city. Second, as was demonstrated when the IDF penetrated into West Beirut in August, the fighting would be difficult and costly in terms of casualties. Israel was extremely reluctant to incur large casualties. Third, a battle in West Beirut would inevitably cause severe collateral damage. The probability of success, then, for an outright attack on the PLO in West Beirut was no better than borderline, and unless such an attack could have been launched and completed successfully in one overwhelming blow, it would probably have been disproportionate.

The siege and the conduct of fight-and-negotiate warfare, on the other hand, gave reasonable promise of success. Israel had the support of the United States in its attempt to force the PLO's evacuation. There was no sign of intervention by other Arab states or the Soviet Union—even the Syrian involvement was more a function of Israeli than Syrian actions. To be sure, the siege was likely to produce collateral damage that might be judged disproportionate. However, as observed in Chapter 7, there is evidence that the Israelis managed to limit collateral damage, particularly in view of the PLO's deliberate tactics of intermingling with the civilian population.

I conclude that the decision to besiege the PLO in West Beirut and force its evacuation was proportionate to the goal of removing the PLO from south Lebanon and depriving it of its Beirut base. This goal was justified as a reasonable self-defense measure in a continuing war with an enemy that had acquired conventional means of conducting terrorist attacks against northern Israeli population centers. The new PLO conventional capabilities combined with its underlying terrorist strategy and tactics altered the balance of forces and challenged Israel's basic counterterror strategy.

Finally, there is the difficult question of assessing the proportionality of Israel's counterinsurgency measures in the occupied territories during the *intifada*. The probability of success for these measures has been good, given the strength of the IDF and Israeli security forces. However, the proportionality of the Israeli counterinsurgency policies should be judged in the light of the prospects for the future of the territories and the role and objectives of the PLO. The goal of the *intifada* is Palestinian self-determination. As discussed in Chapter 1, it is necessary to consider this goal in alternative versions. If Palestinian self-determination means accomplishing the goals of the Palestinian Covenant, presumably by the two-phase route that starts with a Palestinian state in the territories, Israel is fighting for its existence when it fights the *intifada* and its counterinsurgency measures are clearly proportionate. If self-determination means that the Palestinians would be content with a Palestinian state in the territories, existing in the context of mutual security arrangements satisfactory to Israel, the need to hold on to the territories would not be as great and greater restraint in counterinsurgency policies would be in order.

In either case, the proportionality of Israel's counterinsurgency policies also has to be judged in terms of her obligation to maintain law and order as well as in terms of her prerogatives in fighting a low-intensity civil war. So far, with exceptions noted in Chapter 8, Israel's policies to contain the *intifada* have been proportionate and generally successful.

Exhaustion of Peaceful Means

All of the calculations of proportionality must be conducted with awareness of the possibilities to resolve the conflict generally or some aspects of it by peaceful means. There has been much criticism over the years of Israeli reluctance to cooperate with peace initiatives, including the Jarring Mission, the Rogers Plan and even the Sadat initiative which led to the 1978 Camp David Accords and the 1979 Egyptian-Israeli peace treaty. However, insofar as Israel's war with the PLO was concerned, there never was a serious prospect of peace as long as the PLO appeared to adhere to the goals and the means of the Palestinian Covenant. Negotiations with the

PLO would amount, in effect, to negotiations to arrange the forms and stages of Israel's extinction.

Since Arafat's pronouncements of December 1988 and May 1989 following the declaration of the 1988 Algiers summit purporting to establish the state of Palestine, the issue of exhaustion of peaceful means has finally become critical. To the extent that Arafat's pronouncements are to be believed, the worst case version of the Arab threat to Israel's existence recedes. Israelis are deeply divided in their response to Arafat's pronouncements and the PLO's record since them.

Two main issues appear to determine Israel's position on peace negotiations: the role of the PLO and the definition of self-determination. Some conservative elements refuse to consider any role whatsoever for the PLO, continuing to treat it as a mortal enemy and terrorist organization. Some liberals are more open to conceding some role to the PLO, although they would want substantial representation of Palestinians in the territories who are not part of the PLO. The conservatives and many liberals will not accept a sovereign Palestinian state. Their definition of self-determination is a significant degree of Palestinian self-government without sovereignty. Prospects for agreement have been poor. It appears that it is next to impossible to produce a representative Palestinian negotiating team that lacks substantial PLO membership. It also appears that most of the Palestinians want complete self-determination in the form of a sovereign state. How many also aspire to recover all of Palestine is not clear.

Given the uncertainty regarding the ultimate Palestinian goal, the conservative attitude is certainly understandable. On the other hand, the prospect of a continued status quo in which the *intifada* in some form continues is daunting. If the Palestinians could agree to interim arrangements for increased self-government without complete independence, the deadlock might be broken. However, even this kind of solution might not hold up against the pull of sentiments for complete independence.

In my view, Israel met the just war requirement of exhausting peaceful means from 1964 to 1988 because there was virtually no indication that the PLO would renounce either its ends or its terrorist means. Since the end of 1988, Israel has been challenged to give much more serious consideration to the possibilities of negotiated settlements and, because of the internal divisions discussed, has been unable to meet the challenge. This failure has not been so egregious as to deny Israel's claim to be conducting a just war, but it does, in my view, affect future estimates of the proportionality of Israeli military/security strategies. Thus, a major escalation of the war by Israel would not be warranted as long as the main body of the PLO holds to Arafat's pledge to discontinue terrorist activities.

Right Intention

The first requirement of right intention is to limit war aims to what is necessary to achieve the just cause. Israel has done this. In the United Nations and elsewhere, Israel has been accused of imperialist designs, particularly with regard to Lebanon. Speculative comments by the founders of Israel as to what its borders should be have been cited to support the accusations. In fact, however, Israel's operations and occupations beyond its borders have all been manifestly related to its self-defense measures. The Security Zone in south Lebanon exists because of the problems of defending the border against terrorist and guerrilla incursions. Israel is not interested in ruling the area. The Litani Operation, the 1982 war and the 1982–85 occupation demonstrated the difficulties of extended operations in Lebanon. The Sinai was held for strategic reasons and relinquished when politics removed the strategic threat. The Golan was taken primarily for strategic reasons against the background of its past use by Syria for aggression.

The occupation of the West Bank and Gaza is a more complex matter. Part of the reason is self-defense and internal security, but part of it is based upon religious and historic claims and on economic and social considerations. If self-defense and internal security concerns were persuasively met, it is at least conceivable that Israel would relinquish the territories. Finally, Jerusalem presents a seemingly intractable problem in view of its significance for Muslims and Jews, but the Israeli incorporation of the whole city is hardly expansionist. Whatever one's estimate of the prudence of attempting to hold on to the territories, the intention to do so is not a violation of right intention.

Right intention in just war doctrine makes the severe demand that belligerents not succumb to sentiments of hatred and the desire for vengeance. This is a difficult moral challenge in any war. It is particularly difficult in a war in which one side employs terror against the innocent as its principal form of armed coercion and the other is obliged to attack the enemy in civilian locales with inevitable collateral damage. In the Security Council debates over Israeli counterterror actions, the point has frequently been made that the actions were "punitive." There is, admittedly, a rather narrow line between the notion of punishment as a deterrent and a preventive/attrition measure, and the idea of punishment as vengeance for outrageous terrorist actions. Nevertheless, the Israelis have made a good case that their counterterror measures have been functional to the exigencies of deterrence and defense and not simply injuries inflicted from motives of vengeance.

Having said this, it must be observed that the practice of characterizing all PLO members as "terrorists" may encourage attitudes inconsistent with right intention. If peace is ever to come there must be a point where members of the PLO—most of whom obviously have never engaged directly in terrorist activity, since it is the work of a small minority—might be viewed and characterized as something other than "terrorists."

This brings us to the last element in right intention, the requirement that belligerent measures be limited to the extent that they do not unnecessarily impair the possibility of a just and lasting peace. As observed in the discussion of the requirement to exhaust peaceful alternatives to recourse to force, there was little prospect of just and lasting peace between Israel and the PLO as long as that organization refused to accept the permanence of Israel's existence and to renounce terrorism. The issue is really only raised in clear fashion after the 1988 and 1989 Arafat declarations on the subject. However, this element of right intention has been in question throughout the conflict. Belligerent actions may be adequately justified by military/security necessity but still suspect in terms of right intention because they so harden and embitter attitudes between the enemies that any kind of just and lasting peace becomes virtually unattainable.

Whether Israeli counterterror strategies and tactics have had this effect is hard to say. There are very bitter memories on both sides of the conflict. I have the impression that the Israelis have not worried very much about this issue because they did not believe that the Palestinians and their Arab supporters were interested in a just and lasting peace. Accordingly, I am inclined to limit evaluation of the extent to which Israel has complied with this part of the just war requirement of right intention to the period since December 1988. During this time Israel has continued counterterror operations, but they have been mainly directed at dissident, extremist PLO and Shiite Lebanese factions, not the mainstream PLO. I do not underestimate the legacy of over twenty-five years of bitter war, fought against the background of decades of Arab-Jewish conflict in Palestine. However, I cannot find that Israel's counterterror strategies and tactics have rendered impossible the achievement of a just and lasting peace.

War-conduct Law
(jus in bello)

In Chapters 6 and 7, I have examined Israel's conduct in its counterterror operations against the PLO and in the 1982 Lebanon war. The principle of legitimate military necessity employed in these analyses was applied primarily in terms of the basic principles of proportion and discrimination. These same principles comprise the heart of the just war doctrine's war-conduct law (*jus in bello*). Accordingly, the judgments made about Israel's conduct in its war with the PLO in Chapters 6 and 7 may be reiterated in a just war analysis. Nevertheless, the question arises as to whether incidents, campaigns, phases of Israel's war with the PLO have had negative effects in terms of the overall calculus of proportion of war-decision, *jus ad bellum*, just war requirements. Were there actions which, while reasonable in terms of military necessity, failed to contribute proportionately to the achievement of the just cause of self-defense?

In Chapters 6 and 7, I found that some of the Israeli counterterror measures appeared to have been disproportionate and indiscriminate, e.g., the December 1975 air raids linked to PLO political successes; the 1978 Litani Operation; the July 17, 1981, raid on PLO headquarters in Beirut; the land, air and sea attacks on the PLO in Beirut after August 6, 1982, when the Habib plan for the PLO's evacuation was accepted. Doubtless there were many other lesser instances of disproportionate and indiscriminate Israeli attacks. However, as concluded in Chapters 6 and 7, the overall pattern of Israeli conduct conformed to the requirements of proportion and discrimination. That is all that is reasonably required to meet the just war condition that the just cause must be pursued by just means.

However, two perplexing problems remain to be discussed. The first is the question of Israeli intentions with respect to the conduct of counterterror preventive/attrition attacks. Generally, official Israeli statements have emphasized the intention to minimize collateral damage, and my finding is that this intention has generally been borne out by the record. However, in their attempts to deter sanctuary states and local populations from continuing to assist and/or acquiesce in PLO operations, the Israelis have sometimes threatened general devastation of areas harboring PLO bases. Such threats were made to Jordan and to Lebanon. These threats were followed by very heavy attacks on the PLO which caused extensive collateral damage.[17]

In just war terms, it can be said that this collateral damage was not unintended and incidental but fully intended. If one applies Walzer's double effect approach—which I do not—it could not be said that the collateral damage caused by Israeli counterterror strikes in Jordan and Lebanon was unintended and not one of Israel's ends.[18] If the threats of Rabin, Dayan and others are to be taken seriously, one end of the Israeli attacks was to deter and injure the PLO, but another important end of these attacks was to deter the sanctuary state and the local population from continued support or toleration of PLO operations.

The problem should be clearly stated. I am not suggesting that Israel conducted countervalue warfare with the direct intention of attacking non-combatants and civilian targets as such. I am asserting that Israel conducted counterforce warfare with the primary intention of injuring and deterring the PLO but with the concomitant or ancillary intention of injuring and deterring the sanctuary state and the population in areas from which the PLO operated.

If it could be shown that Israel frequently maximized collateral damage in the course of primarily counterforce attacks, the Israelis would have violated war-conduct law sufficiently to put in question their claim to conducting a just war. In this study, however, I have not found evidence to support such a contention. On the contrary, the pattern of Israeli counterterror attacks has been overwhelmingly counterforce. Collateral damage has been substantial but, I believe, proportionate to the legitimate necessities of attacking the PLO, especially in view of the PLO's policy of intermingling with the civilian population.

This still leaves a further problem, namely, evaluation of the effects of an accumulation of counterterror counterforce attacks on mixed PLO/civilian targets. Even if most of the Israeli counterforce attacks on the PLO over the years were proportionate and discriminate, the cumulative effects of so many such attacks should be taken into consideration. This raises much the same problem confronted by the United States in Vietnam. Even if one would grant that the overwhelming number of search and destroy and other U.S./ARVN operations were justified by military necessity, it could be claimed that the total effects of these actions over a period of six years were disproportionate to the goals of the just cause, particularly in light of the declining probability of success.

In the case of Israel's war with the PLO, counterterror attacks on mixed PLO/civilian targets have been going on for over twenty-five years. They have not been of the magnitude of the conventional operations of the U.S. and ARVN forces in Vietnam, but, as described in this study, they have caused a great deal of civilian damage. This was true with respect to the East Bank of the Jordan, but the events of September 1970 put an end to that ordeal. The problem, then, is the problem of the effects on Lebanon, particularly south Lebanon, of Israel's conduct of its war with the PLO.

Civilian casualties, destruction of homes and businesses, fear of being caught in the seemingly endless hostilities between the PLO, Shiite forces, the Christian militia, and the IDF have driven thousands of Lebanese from their homes. These refugees have greatly complicated life in Beirut and other parts of Lebanon. Moreover, factional conflict in Lebanon, already formidable, has been exacerbated and complicated by the repercussions of the PLO's presence and Israeli attack on the PLO. It is fair to say that there have been enough sources of conflict between the Lebanese factions that, with the heavy-handed Syrian interventions, there would have been civil war and the collapse of the Lebanese government and state in any event, even if Israel had largely abstained from attacking the PLO in Lebanon. However, there is no doubt that the conduct of Israel's war against the PLO in Lebanon contributed greatly to that country's collapse into anarchy.

The issue turns on the question whether Israel has a right to rely on active counterterror deterrence/defense measures, or whether, as the Security Council consistently claimed, it should have been limited to passive self-defense against terrorist attacks. In this study I have taken the position that it was reasonable for Israel to adopt active deterrence/defense measures that necessarily were carried out in the territory of states offering sanctuary to the PLO and either supporting or acquiescing in its terrorist operations. There is no question that, as a matter of international law, a state is obliged to prevent its territory from being used as a base for armed bands that are attacking another state. Lebanon not only failed in its duty to do so but, in various agreements, such as the 1969 Cairo Agreement, made provisions for toleration of the PLO's operations. To be sure, at other times the Lebanese Army tried to curb the PLO, but these efforts failed.

With regret for the losses and suffering of the population of south Lebanon, Beirut and other parts of Lebanon, much of which resented the PLO's presence and activities, it is clear that the cumulative damage done to Lebanon by Israel was the price that that country had to pay for failing to prevent the PLO's terrorist activities. These activities became particularly threatening to Israel's security with the conventional build-up of the late 1970s and early 1980s, and in 1981–82 Israel's whole counterterror deterrence/defense strategy was challenged. All of this occurred because the PLO could occupy large parts of Lebanon, create a state-within-a-state and deploy its forces with impunity. In these circumstances it was not unreasonable for Israel to go into Lebanon and remove this growing threat.

It is, moreover, a sad fact that the damage done to Lebanon by Israel in its war with the PLO does not approach the damage done to that country by civil strife and Syrian interventions. At least the Israelis can argue that the damage they inflicted was proportionate to the necessity of removing or greatly inhibiting the PLO terrorist threat. Thus far, most of the Lebanese self-inflicted damage to which the Syrians have also contributed has not brought any visible positive results. On the contrary, Lebanese hostilities have, for many years, been motivated more by hatred and the desire for vengeance than by any plausible argument of military necessity or any reasonable hope of success.

Israel's War with the PLO: A Just War Evaluation

In this chapter I have concluded that, notwithstanding some actions that are questionable, Israel's overall compliance with the conditions both of just war doctrine's war-decision and war-conduct law is sufficient to characterize its war with the PLO as a just war. It has been frequently noted that the main objection to Israel's decision to follow a policy of preventive/ attrition attacks against the PLO in sanctuary states has been the extent of collateral damage, but that this has been inevitable given the PLO's policy of colocating its bases and forces with civilian locales.

However, a judgment that a war is just at any particular point from initiation to termination does not end the task of just war evaluation. At any point in a conflict conditions and prospects may change, altering evaluations as to what is reasonable in terms of the continuation of the hostilities and their conduct.

At this writing (Fall 1990) it is clear that Israel's war with the PLO continues. However, it has taken a different form since the outbreak of the *intifada* in December 1987 than it had during the hostilities from 1964 to that time. For most of this war the main pattern of hostilities has been one of PLO terrorist attacks and Israeli preventive/attrition counterattacks into sanctuary states. Currently, this kind of hostile interaction has greatly abated. The war that counts most is the war of the *intifada* and Israeli counterinsurgency measures.

Israel claims that the PLO fuels violence in the *intifada* by organizing terrorist bands within the occupied territories. These bands have attacked Israeli soldiers, security forces and civilians. To a much greater extent, Palestinian bands have terrorized alleged collaborators and others targeted for reasons ranging from charges of immoral behavior to purely criminal motives of the terrorists. The extent to which these terrorist bands are PLO-controlled is unclear. Some of them are from the fundamentalist Hamas organization. Others are, in effect, independent street gangs.

Meanwhile, neither Israel nor the PLO can agree to proposals to initiate negotiations for increased Palestinian self-determination under U.S.-Egyptian auspices. In these circumstances, how should Israel behave if it wants to continue to wage a just war of self-defense?

As long as the present situation (Fall 1990) obtains, Israel is acting proportionately and discriminately if it carries out preventive/attrition attacks against PLO and Shiite factions in Lebanon who are continuing terrorist attacks on Israel and on the SLA in the Security Zone. Israel has the right and, indeed, the duty to control *intifada* violence. Suggestions have been made in Chapter 8 as to what counterinsurgency means should be employed and what means should be more strictly limited or eliminated. Israel must make reasonable efforts to find peaceful solutions to the Arab-Israeli conflict, starting with a resolution of the Palestinian question that somehow balances maximum feasible Palestinian self-determination with Israeli security.

In this stage of Israel's war with the PLO, intense preventive/attrition, "sustained operations" against the PLO in Lebanon would not be justified. More severe counterinsurgency measures in the occupied territory would not be justified. Overall, Israel should be concentrating seriously on the issue of balancing the perceived need for military/security measures against the requirements for reconciliation or mutual tolerance in any peace settlement, i.e., right intention.

These recommendations are made with full awareness that they may run counter to the policies and attitudes of elements in Israel that aspire to hold the territories forever and to treat the Palestinians and other Arabs as implacable and dangerous enemies. Indeed, it cannot be taken for granted that Israelis with these views are entirely wrong, since the Palestinians and their Arab allies may prove to be *irredentist* enemies who will not be satisfied until Israel is destroyed. Such views are reinforced by Arafat's continued support of Saddam Hussein in his war with the U.S./U.N. coalition. They are further reinforced by the open satisfaction of the Palestinians with Iraq's Scud terror attacks on Tel Aviv and Haifa.

Nevertheless, just war is not holy war. Just war demands more than a plausible just cause. It requires that the just belligerent meet substantially all of the just war conditions: competent authority, substantive just cause, comparative justice, proportionality of means in the light of probability of success, reasonable exhaustion of peaceful alternatives, right intention and compliance with the principles of proportion and discrimination in the conduct of the war. To meet these conditions, the just belligerent must go beyond the apparent political-military utility of its strategies and tactics and temper them with the moral limits of just war doctrine. Despite some violations of those limits in its long war with the PLO, Israel has, by and large, met the just war conditions. However, in what may be the last phase of that war, the challenge of meeting the just war conditions remains, demanding military, but above all political, responses worthy of a just belligerent.

Notes

1. See Efraim Inbar, "The 'No-Choice War' Debate in Israel," *The Journal of Strategic Studies* 12 (1989): 22–37.

2. Avner Yaniv, *Dilemmas of Security* (New York: Oxford University Press, 1987), p. 69.

3. Ze'ev Schiff and Ehyd Ya'ari, *Israel's Lebanon War,* edited and translated by Ina Friedman (New York: Simon & Schuster, 1984), pp. 102–06.

4. William V. O'Brien, *The Conduct of Just and Limited War* (New York: Praeger, 1981), pp. 20–22.

5. *The Challenge of Peace: God's Promise and Our Response, A Pastoral Letter on War and Peace* (National Conference of Catholic Bishops, Washington, D.C., May 3, 1983), paras. 92–94, pp. 29–30.

6. Thomas L. Friedman, *From Beirut to Jerusalem* (New York: Farrar, Straus & Giroux, 1989), pp. 76–105.

7. It was reported on November 28, 1989, that "King Hussein told the new parliament he will legalize political parties and relax martial law, opening the way for more democracy in Jordan after the first national elections in 22 years." "Hussein Political Pledge," *Washington Post,* November 28, 1989, A28, col. 2. These promises were repeated by the new prime minister, Nudar Badran, on January 1, 1990, after he won a vote of confidence in Jordan's revitalized parliament. "New Jordanian Premier Wins Vote of Confidence," ibid., January 2, 1990, A13, cols. 1–2.

8. See Chapter 1 above.

9. See James Turner Johnson, *Ideology, Reason and the Limitation of War* (Princeton, N.J.: Princeton University Press, 1975), pp. 154–59, 169, 178, 185–95. Johnson states that "when neither side can be unqualifiedly certain of the justice of its cause, it is that much more bound to observe scrupulously the limits set in the *jus in bello*." Ibid., p. 98.

10. See Chapter 4 above.

11. See Chapter 7 above.

12. Yaniv, *Dilemmas of Security,* pp. 71–75.

13. Inbar, "The 'No-Choice War' Debate in Israel."

14. Schiff and Ya'ari, *Israel's Lebanon War,* pp. 33–34, 44–47, 49–51.

15. Ibid., p. 50.

16. Ibid., pp. 188–89.

17. On the threat of unacceptable collateral damage to PLO sanctuaries, see, for example, Chief of Staff Yitzhak Rabin's April 1966 warning: "The operation was intended to make it clear to Jordan, and to the population which is collaborating with Fatah, and to Fatah members themselves, that as long as this side of the border will not be quiet, no quiet will prevail on the other side." *Skira Hodsheet* (Monthly Survey), a journal for IDF officers (Hebrew), 13, no. 4 (1966): 91; quoted in Hanan Alon, *Countering Palestinian Terrorism in Israel: Toward a Policy Analysis of Countermeasures* (Santa Monica, Calif.: RAND, August 1980), p. 38.

    Following the April 11, 1974, terrorist attack on Kiryat Shemona, Dayan threatened that if Lebanon did not prevent terrorist attacks on Israel from its territory, Israel would continue its punitive raids until all of southern Lebanon was abandoned. Dayan stated: "The people will find it impossible to live there. Their homes will be destroyed and the whole area will be deserted." Dayan explained that "our objective this time was political, not military," and that the raid (of April 12–13, 1974) was limited in size and damage. "Dayan Says Raids Against Lebanon Will Be Continued," *New York Times,* April 14, 1974, p. 1, col. 8; p. 3, cols. 3–6.

    See Chapter 2, n. 22, for further text of Dayan's warning. This warning was held out as evidence of Israeli policy by Naffah (Lebanon), 29 U.N. SCOR (1766th mtg.), p. 6.

18. Michael Walzer, *Just and Unjust Wars* (New York: Basic Books, 1977), pp. 151–59.

11

Conclusions

In this study political-military strategies and the patterns of hostilities between belligerents have been described before any attempt at legal and moral analyses. Before judging the legal or moral permissibility of any behavior, one should understand as far as possible the reasons for the behavior, whether it be in the fields of medicine, economic-social relations or nuclear deterrence.

Accordingly, Part I outlined the respective strategies of the PLO and Israel and traced the course of the war between them to serve as a basis for legal and moral analysis. This has not been the approach of most legal and moral analyses of war in general and Israel's war with the PLO in particular. As can be seen from Part II, the legal permissibility of Israel's recourse to force and conduct of counterterror operations has almost always been judged in the UN Security Council and other international arenas and by publicists and commentators in terms of legal norms applied without serious efforts to understand or acknowledge the practical context of PLO actions and Israeli responses. The fervor with which these legal norms are applied indicates an underlying substructure of moral absolutes that do not allow for the balancing of competing moral claims. In Part III, I have evaluated the morality of Israel's recourse to force and conduct of operations in its war with the PLO in terms of modern just war doctrine. This doctrine provides a framework for assessing and balancing multiple values rather than establishing a rigid, immutable hierarchy of values. Thus neither war avoidance nor defense of justice are *a priori* supreme values. Their claims to priority, as those of other values, are evaluated in a comprehensive calculus of ends and means that takes fully into account the practical political-military context and realities of a war.

Because I have taken a different approach to the international law of war and reinforced it with an application of modern just war doctrine, I have come to different judgments about the legal and moral issues in Israel's war with the PLO than the Security Council, most of the authoritative decision-makers in the international political/legal system, and the majority of publicists and commentators who have expressed their views on the subject.

Since my legal and moral analyses have always been made in the light of my understanding of political-military necessities, I must begin my conclusions with reflections on the objectives and results of the military means employed by Israel in its war with the PLO.

The Utility of Israel's Strategies in its War with the PLO

Throughout its war with the PLO, Israel has relied primarily on counterterror strategies of deterrence/defense. After maximizing passive defense deployments, Israel has sought to deter terrorist attacks by striking at their source in neighboring sanctuary states with preventive/attrition attacks. Understanding that no counterterror strategy can deter definitively attacks by committed terrorists, Israel has placed a heavy price on the continuation of terrorism—on the terrorists, on the populations in the localities from which the terrorists have operated, on the state that permits its sovereign territory to be a base for terrorist operations.

Evaluating the effectiveness of a deterrent strategy is obviously difficult. One is speculating about what might have happened had the deterrent posture not been maintained. Since, unlike nuclear deterrence to date, the effectiveness of counterterror deterrence is necessarily relative rather than absolute, there is room for different assessments of a counterterror posture such as Israel's. Nevertheless, some evaluation of the utility of Israel's measures must be attempted because it must precede legal and moral judgments of them.[1]

My assessment is that Israel built up a counterterror deterrence/defense posture between 1953 and 1970 which amply demonstrated that it could and would inflict unacceptable damage on localities from which terrorists operated and on states that permitted or encouraged terrorists to operate from their territory. This posture included the threat of escalation to full-scale international conventional war, as in 1956. It took such an escalation to eliminate for a long period the terrorist threat from Gaza and Egypt.

However, even without this degree of escalation, Israel's counterterror deterrence/defense posture was successful in influencing Jordan to drive out the PLO forces altogether in 1970–71. To be sure, Black September 1970 was in great part a showdown between Hussein's regime and the PLO for control of Jordan. However, the long-term effects of Israel's preventive/

attrition attacks against the PLO in Jordan had, in my view, clearly inflicted unacceptable damage on Jordan and vindicated the Israeli counterterror deterrence/defense strategy.

The case of Syria is even more dramatic. Syria has been among the most hostile of Israel's enemies. Yet terrorist operations from that country virtually ceased after Assad's pledge to Kissinger at the time of the Syrian-Israeli disengagement agreement, May 31, 1974. Syria has had a turbulent relationship with the PLO and continues to support and control elements of it. However, Syria has not risked Israeli responses to PLO terrorist operations emanating from its territory.

In Lebanon, of course, the Israeli counterterror deterrence/defense strategy has failed because of the weakness of the Lebanese government before the 1975–76 Civil War and the subsequent lack of anything approaching an effective, representative Lebanese government since then. Because of this failure of the Lebanese polity, the threat and imposition of unacceptable damage on parts of Lebanon serving as PLO operational areas has not been sufficient to prevent aggressive PLO terrorist attacks on Israel. The result has been a long succession of brief, limited IDF forays into south Lebanon, air strikes at PLO positions in many parts of Lebanon, naval attacks on the PLO in coastal bases, the development of the Security Zone and the South Lebanese Army, the longer and more extensive 1978 Litani Operation, and the 1982 Lebanon War.

It should be recognized that it is very unlikely that a Lebanon with governments as strong as those of Hussein in Jordan and Assad in Syria would have tolerated the PLO's creating a state-within-a-state and waging terrorist war against Israel at the cost of unacceptable damage to Lebanon in forms ranging from heavy civilian casualties and damage to the political chaos to which the PLO so greatly contributed. Had there been a strong government in Lebanon, the PLO would have been severely curbed, nothing like the level of Israeli local attacks would have occurred, and there would have been no Litani Operation or 1982 war.

However, given the situation in Lebanon, the Israeli counterterror deterrence/defense measures were necessary. Were they successful? I do not think that one can evaluate the success of Israeli strategies for dealing with the PLO in Lebanon in the same way that commentators have judged the counterterror strategies of earlier periods vis-à-vis *fedayeen* attacks from Jordan and Egypt. First, from 1970, when Lebanon became the main terrorist front, to the present, there has not been a Lebanese government to serve as the target for "coercive diplomacy" to force abatement of the PLO's terrorist operations. Second, the duration and magnitude of this phase of Israel's war with the PLO greatly exceeds that of the earlier phases studied.

Third, these earlier studies either precede or end early in the era of PLO independent initiatives in the terrorist war against Israel.

Accordingly, one must judge in very broad terms the general pattern of PLO terrorist attacks and Israeli responses. To be sure, the IDF has detailed data and analyses relating the patterns of PLO and Israeli operations, including data relating to the PLO operations that were preempted altogether or cut down before they reached their targets. The IDF is not going to share these data and analyses with the outside world. However, an evaluation unsupported by sophisticated behavioral studies can be offered. The Israeli counterterror deterrence/defense strategy from 1970 to 1990 was generally quite effective, greatly limiting the incidence of PLO and other terrorist attempted attacks on Israel and even more greatly limiting the number of attacks that caused casualties and damage.

Where the Israeli counterterror deterrence/defense strategy proved ineffective was in its initial response to the PLO's conventional build-up and the initiating of indiscriminate attacks with long-range artillery and rockets on northern Israeli population centers. It was this major change in PLO capabilities and strategies that brought on the hostilities in July 1981, and it was probably the most important element in determining Israel to launch the 1982 Lebanon War. While there has been great emphasis in Israel on the proposition that this was a "war of choice," I believe that there was not much choice involved in attacking the PLO's conventional countervalue forces—one time or another under one *casus belli* or another. Whether it was necessary to besiege Beirut and force the PLO's evacuation is more controversial. However, given the continuing threat of terrorist attacks on Israel and of international terrorism directed from Beirut by the PLO, the effort to drive the organization out of Beirut altogether was made in pursuit of an objective that was certainly strategically desirable. Whether it was made at proportionate cost is another matter which must be judged in legal and moral terms.

Finally, what can be said of Israel's military necessities in combating the *intifada*? The first step in evaluating these necessities is the recognition that the *intifada* initially took the form of mob violence rather than nonviolent resistance. Although not waged with firearms, the *intifada* was waged with weapons that were potentially lethal and certainly capable of inflicting serious injuries and damage. Moreover, the *intifada* from the outset featured aggressive attacks on Israeli military and police personnel, vehicles and facilities. Particularly when small detachments of Israelis were isolated by mobs, particularly in crowded urban areas, their situation was life-threatening. Finally, it must be recognized that the very strength of the *intifada* was its broad base; whole communities sprang to the barricades.

All of these facts may attest to the general profound attachment of the Palestinian population in the territories and in Jerusalem to the Palestinian cause. This is widely acknowledged by Israelis who had not previously sensed the width and depth of this attachment. The *intifada* is a genuine political, economic, social, racial, religious revolution.

What are the necessities of a state confronted with such a revolution if it refuses to capitulate and accede to the demands of the revolutionaries? This is a particularly difficult question for Israel because there is good reason to believe that a great number of these revolutionaries want more than a Palestinian state in the territories. A great number undoubtedly want the destruction of Israel, however long and whatever it takes.

I have had the necessities of a state facing such a deep-rooted revolutionary challenge in mind when I judged the legal and moral permissibility of Israel's counterinsurgency measures in the *intifada*. With these reminders of the political-military context of Israel's war with the PLO, I undertook analyses of the permissibility of Israel's use of armed force and other forms of coercion in its counterterror preventive/attrition operations, in the 1982 war and its response to the *intifada*.

Israel and the International Law of War

Part II, on the international law of war in Israel's war with the PLO, is the largest portion of this book. This is necessarily the case because Israel operates in an international political and legal system in which value judgments are expressed primarily in terms of law, not morality. I believe it has been important for the reader to learn in some detail what is purported to be the international law regulating recourse to armed force and the conduct of military operations. I have contrasted the law as interpreted by the United Nations, publicists and commentators with the law as it would be interpreted and applied by a belligerent in the predicaments in which Israel has found itself.

I have contended that what is held out in the Security Council, General Assembly and much of the international law literature as binding law for Israel does not take into account the practical realities of the present international political and legal system, much less Israel's self-defense requirements. It is a law largely unsanctioned except by rhetorical condemnations and political discrimination and a law that offers no remedy to the victim of terrorism except self-help measures—which are then denounced if taken.

Law lacking coercive community sanctions may still be effective if it recommends itself to the members of a community as reasonable and if it is supported by some higher legal or moral norm, some "ought." However, the law of the UN Security Council, the General Assembly and much of the literature on war-decision law does not recommend itself to a state faced with the kinds of terrorist threats (in the context of constant greater threats of conventional war) that Israel has confronted throughout its existence. Nor does this law find convincing support in some higher norm. Leaving the supposed state of international law aside, there is no higher norm that denies a state the right or waives the duty to protect its citizens from terrorist attacks and confines a nation to waiting fearfully for the next atrocity being organized in the sanctuary of a neighboring state.

I have sought a way out of the unrealistic and unfair legal straitjackets fashioned by the UN organs and many international-law publicists and commentators by attempting to assess the reasonableness of Israel's exercise of the right of self-defense in the various phases of its war with the PLO. However, there is no question that this goes against the general opinion of those who interpret modern international war-decision law. This means that the PLO and its supporters may easily win legal debates over Israel's recourse to force and collect additional condemnations to flaunt while the international legal system refuses to condemn PLO terrorism. This is harmful to Israel, but it is not so harmful as to encourage that country to abandon effective self-defense measures against terrorism.

I have likewise gone against prevailing legal and popular appraisals of Israel's conduct of military operations ranging from retaliatory raids to the 1982 war to counterinsurgency tactics in the *intifada*. This is because I have not viewed the law of war as a collection of *a priori* prohibitions to be applied rigidly, irrespective of the combat context of belligerent behavior. I have taken the prescriptions derived from the principle of humanity seriously, but I have also taken seriously persuasive claims of military necessity. In my analyses of war-conduct law, I have often found that the question is not whether a particular means or practice is "legal" or "illegal," but whether recourse to a potentially permissible means or practice is reasonable in the light of the sometimes conflicting, sometimes converging claims of military necessity and humanity.

Following this approach, one is struck by the difficulty of generalizing either about the facts of belligerent practice or their legal and moral permissibility. Because Israel is an open society and its wars are fought increasingly on world television and under the scrutiny of the media, it is always possible to obtain evidence of apparently illegal behavior. This evidence is then cited by commissions of inquiry, humanitarian organizations, journalists, legal publicists and other commentators as proof of a general pattern of lawlessness and inhumanity.

However, it would take massive investigations by military experts having access to the archives of the IDF to establish the proportion between clear violations of the laws of war, borderline violations, propaganda claims and disinformation and the generality of troop behavior in the various phases of Israel's war with the PLO. Hays Parks's investigation of IAF bombing practices in the 1982 war is a rare example of an assessment of Israeli practice by a third-party observer possessed of military experience and good access to evidence of the conduct of operations.[2]

All of this means that future development of the law of war should emphasize the need to learn more about war and be less concerned with sophisticated legal issues. The purpose of the law of war is to mitigate the destruction and suffering of war by imposing limits on belligerent actions that are compatible with legitimate military necessities. In order to do this, there must be a much greater appreciation of military necessities than appears in the critiques of Israeli conduct in the war with the PLO.

Israel and Just War Doctrine

This book would have been less difficult to write had I written it entirely from the perspectives of just war doctrine. I attempted to deal with the issues raised in the positive international law of war because they are usually framed in terms of that body of law in international arenas and in scholarly and popular debates. Moreover, I am not so despairing of the future of international law that I would avoid the challenge of demonstrating its faults with respect to war-decision and war-conduct issues and suggesting a different approach. However, while governments must make claims and counterclaims in terms of international law, I suggest that governmental officials, military commanders, ordinary soldiers and citizens can properly evaluate issues of war decision and war conduct from moral perspectives which may or may not coincide closely with those of international law as it is being interpreted by others.

The moral perspectives I have applied to Israel's war with the PLO are those of modern just war, the product of Western civilization to which Judaic religion and culture have made and continue to make the most profound contributions. Applying modern just war doctrine in Chapter 10, I have attempted to show how comprehensive it is in organizing an analytical framework in which to make and evaluate the decisions to have recourse to war, to continue a war, to terminate a war. By comparison, international law tends to treat all international actors as anonymous equals, without distinctive characteristics for good or evil, and to implement a presumption that war avoidance is always the highest normative value to be upheld with a mechanical no-first-use-of-force rule.

Israel fails the test almost every time when it collides with this version of international war-decision law. Moreover, this legal perspective dominates interpretation of war-conduct law, creating a presumption against the legal permissibility of every Israeli belligerent action. If one turns to just war doctrine, Israel does not automatically qualify as a just belligerent in any particular phase of its war with the PLO, but it is assured of a comprehensive evaluation of its claims to a just cause, to comparative justice, to use of proportionate means in the light of probability of success, and to reasonable compliance with the principles of proportion and discrimination in war conduct.

I trust that I have demonstrated that just war doctrine is not holy war. It does not claim that the just end justifies any means. On the contrary, just war doctrine requires an exhaustive and extended analyses of the reasons why a war is being fought and what its consequences should be.

This means that Israel must continue to review its strategies and tactics, particularly in the *intifada*, to make sure that they do indeed conform to the principles of proportion and discrimination. Beyond that, having made my own just war evaluation of Israel's role in its war with the PLO and judged Israel to be engaged in a just war, it remains to emphasize two requirements that should become critical in the future. They are the requirements that a just belligerent must exhaust peaceful alternatives to war, so that war is a last resort, and that a just belligerent must have right intention.

Exhausting peaceful alternatives does not mean taking foolish risks, but it does mean confronting the question whether the costs of war—for the adversaries, for third parties and the international community—may not have become so great as to require extraordinary efforts to find a peaceful resolution to a conflict. Right intention means sticking to the pursuit of the just cause and nothing more, repressing emotions of hatred and vengeance and acting in consonance with the ultimate goal of just war, a just and lasting peace. On its face, this is asking a lot in any war, and it is an especially demanding requirement in Israel's bitter war with the PLO. But the injunctions honestly to seek peaceful alternatives to a just war and to maintain right intention, so that the war may remain just, are not only the prescriptions of just war doctrine. They are the counsels of enlightened self-interest and prudence.

Notes

1. Studies have been made by Barry Blechman as well as Jonathan Shimshoni, tracing the apparent relation between Israeli counterterror operations and the incidence of *fedayeen* terrorist attacks from the 1950s to 1969. Blechman concludes that Israeli reprisals have had some success in compelling Arab states to limit "private" as well as "officially sponsored" *fedayeen* operations. He find that Israeli reprisals did not achieve a further purpose (not considered in my analysis) of eliciting Arab acceptance of Israel and the need for peace. Barry Blechman, "The Consequences of the Israeli Reprisals: An Assessment," Ph.D. diss., Georgetown University, 1971; idem, "The Impact of Israel's Reprisals on Behavior of the Bordering Arab Nations Directed at Israel," *Journal of Conflict Resolution* 16 (1972): 155–81. For Blechman's conclusions, see ibid., pp. 158, 176.

   Shimshoni concludes that Israeli reprisals, which he terms "active-deterrence-by-reprisal," were relatively successful *vis-à-vis* Jordan in 1953–54, but not sufficiently effective *vis-à-vis* Egypt in 1953–56, hence Israel's decision to launch its part of the Suez war. Jonathan Shimshoni, *Israel and Conventional Deterrence: Border Warfare from 1953 to 1970* (Ithaca, N.Y.: Cornell University Press, 1988), pp. 65–68, 119–20.

2. W. Hays Parks, "Air War and the Law of War," *Air Force Law Review* 32 (1990): 1–226.

Bibliography

Yigal Allon, *The Making of Israel's Army* (London: Valentine & Mitchell, 1970).

Hana Alon, *Countering Palestinian Terrorism in Israel: Toward a Policy Analysis of Counter-measures* (Santa Monica, Calif.: RAND, August 1980).

Joseph Alpher and Shai Feldman, *The West Bank and Gaza: Israel's Options for Peace (Report of a JCSS Study Group* (Tel Aviv: Jaffee Center for Strategic Studies, 1989).

Al-Haq, Law in the Service of Man, West Bank Affiliate of the International Commission of Jurists, *Punishing a Nation: Human Rights Violations During the Palestinian Uprising, December 1987—December 1988* (Law in the Service of Man, 1988).

John W. Amos II, *Palestinian Resistance: Organization of a Nationalist Movement* (New York: Pergamon Press, 1980).

St. Thomas Aquinas, *Summa Theologica, secunda secundae,* in A.P. D'Entreves, ed., *Aquinas: Selected Political Writings,* trans. J. G. Dawson (Oxford: Blackwell, 1948).

Geoffrey Aronson, *Creating Facts: Israel, Palestinians and the West Bank* (Washington, D.C.: Institute for Palestine Studies, 1987).

Henry E. Baker, *The Legal System of Israel* (2d ed. rev., Jerusalem, London and New York: Israel Universities Press, 1968).

Yaacov Bar-Siman-Tov, *Israel, the Superpowers and the War in the Middle East* (New York: Praeger, 1987).

Michael Bar-Zohar, *Ben-Gurion: A Biography* (New York Delacorte Press, 1979).

Dan Bavly and Eliahu Salpeter, *Fire in Beirut: Israel's War in Lebanon with the PLO* (New York: Stein & Day, 1984).

Jillian Becker, *The PLO: The Rise and Fall of the Palestine Liberation Organization* (London: Weidenfeld & Nicolson, 1984).

Avi Beker, *The United Nations and Israel* (Lexington, Mass.: Lexington Books, 1988).

Yo'av Ben-Horin and Barry Posen, *Israel's Strategic Doctrine* (Santa Monica, Calif.: Rand, 1981).

Yehuda Ben Mier, *National Decision-Making: The Israeli Case* (Boulder, Colo.: Westview/ JCSS, 1986).

Eliezer Ben-Rafael, *Israel-Palestine: A Guerrilla Conflict in International Politics* (New York: Greenwood, 1987).

323

Meron Benvenisti, *The West Bank Data Base Project: A Survey of Israel's Policies* (Washington, D.C.: American Enterprise Institute, 1984).

————. *The West Bank Handbook* (Jerusalem: Jerusalem Post, 1986).

Uzi Benziman, *Sharon: An Israeli Caesar,* trans. Louis Rousso (New York: Adama Books, 1985).

Marver H. Bernstein, *The Politics of Israel* (Princeton, N.J.: Princeton University Press, 1957).

Geoffrey Best, *Humanity in Warfare* (New York: Columbia University Press, 1980).

William W. Bishop, Jr., *International Law: Cases and Materials* (3d ed., Boston: Little, Brown, 1971).

D. W. Bowett, *Self-Defense in International Law* (New York: Praeger, 1958).

Michael Brecher, *Decisions in Israel's Foreign Policy* (London: Oxford University Press, 1974).

————. *The Foreign Policy System of Israel* (New Haven, Conn.: Yale University Press, 1972).

Michael Brecher, ed., *Studies in International Crisis Behavior* (New Brunswick, N.J.: Transaction, 1979).

J. L. Brierly, *The Law of Nations* (6th ed., Oxford: Oxford University Press, 1963).

Helena Cobban, *The Palestinian Liberation Organization* (Cambridge: Cambridge University Press, 1984).

Inis L. Claude, Jr., *Swords into Plowshares* (4th ed., New York: Random House, 1971).

Moshe Dayan, *Diary of the Sinai Campaign* (London: Weidenfeld & Nicolson, 1966).

Moshe Dayan, *Moshe Dayan: Story of My Life* (New York: Morrow, 1976).

Richard Deacon, *The Israeli Secret Service* (London: Hamilton, 1977).

Yoram Dinstein, *War, Aggression and Self-Defense* (Cambridge: Grotius, 1988).

Christopher Dobson, *Black September* (New York: Macmillan, 1974).

Trevor N. Dupuy and Paul Martell, *Flawed Victory: The Arab-Israeli Conflict and the 1982 War in Lebanon* (Fairfax, Va.: Hero Books, 1986).

Yair Evron, *War and Intervention in Lebanon* (Baltimore, Md.: Johns Hopkins University Press, 1987).

Ernst H. Feilchenfeld, *The International Economic Law of Belligerent Occupation* (Washington, D.C.: Carnegie Endowment for International Peace, 1942).

Thomas L. Friedman, *From Beirut to Jerusalem* (New York: Farrar, Straus & Giroux, 1989).

Wolfgang Friedmann, *The Changing Structure of International Law* (New York: Columbia University Press, 1964).

Richard A. Gabriel, *Operation Peace for Galilee* (New York: Hill & Wang, 1984).

Deborah J. Gerner, *One Land, Two Peoples: The Conflict over Palestine* (Boulder, Colo.: Westview, 1991).

Allan Gerson, *Israel, the West Bank and International Law* (London: Frank Cass, 1978).

Gerhard von Glahn, *The Occupation of Enemy Territory* (Minneapolis: University of Minnesota Press, 1957).

Matti Golan, *The Road to Peace: A Biography of Shimon Peres,* trans. Akiva Ron (New York: Warner, 1989).

Doris Appel Graber, *The Development of the Law of Belligerent Occupation, 1863–1914* (New York: Columbia University Press, 1949).

Kazimierz Grzbowski, *Soviet Public International Law—Doctrines and Diplomatic Practice* (Leyden: Sijthoff, 1970).

Green Haywood Hackworth, *Digest of International Law* (8 vols.; Washington, D.C.: U.S. Government Printing Office, 1941–1944), Vol. 2.

Wadi D. Haddad, *Lebanon: The Politics of Revolving Doors* (New York: Praeger/Center for Strategic and International Studies, 1985).

Alexander M. Haig, *Caveat: Realism, Reagan and Foreign Policy* (New York: Macmillan, 1984).

Beate Hamizrachi, *The Emergence of the South Lebanon Security Zone* (New York: Praeger, 1988).

Michael I. Handel, *Israel's Political-Military Doctrine* (Cambridge, Mass.: Harvard Center for International Affairs, 1973).

Yehoshafat Harkabi, *Israel's Fateful Hour* (New York: Harper & Row, 1988).

———. *Arab Strategies and Israel's Response* (New York: Free Press, 1977).

———. *The Palestinian Covenant and Its Meaning* (London: Vallentine, Mitchell & Co., 1979).

Alan Hart, *Arafat* (Bloomington, Ind.: Indiana University Press, 1984).

Louis Henkin, *How Nations Behave* (2d ed., New York: Council on Foreign Relations/ Columbia University Press, 1979).

Dilip Hiro, *Holy Wars: The Rise of Islamic Fundamentalism* (New York, Routledge, 1989).

David Hirst, *The Gun and the Olive Branch* (London: Faber & Faber, 1984).

Bruce Hoffman, *Recent Trends in Palestinian Terror: II* (Santa Monica, Calif.: RAND, March 1985, P–7076).

Israeli National Section of the International Commission of Jurists, *The Rule of Law in the Areas Administered by Israel* (Tel Aviv: Tzatz, 1981).

Raphael Israeli, ed., *PLO in Lebanon: Selected Documents* (London: Weidenfeld and Nicolson, 1983).

Brian Jenkins, *International Terrorism* (Santa Monica, Calif.: RAND Project Air Force, November 1985).

James Turner Johnson, *Ideology, Reason and Limitation of War* (Princeton, N.J.: Princeton University Press, 1975).

———. *Just War Tradition and the Restraint of War* (Princeton, N.J.: Princeton University Press, 1981).

———. *Can Modern War Be Just?* (New Haven, Conn.: Yale University Press, 1984).

George Jonas, *Vengeance* (New York: Simon & Schuster, 1984).

The Kahan Report (The Commission of Inquiry into the Events at the Refugee Camps in Beirut, Final Report; authorized translation. Jerusalem: Reprinted from the *Jerusalem Post*).

Karl Kalshoven, *Belligerent Reprisals* (Leyden: A.W. Sijthoff, 1981).

Karp Report: An Israeli Government Inquiry into Settler Violence against Palestinians on the West Bank (Washington, D.C.: Institute for Palestine Studies, 1984).

Charles W. Kegley, Jr., ed., *International Terrorism* (New York, St. Martin's, 1990).

Rashid Khalidi, *Under Siege: PLO Decisionmaking During the 1982 War* (New York: Columbia University Press, 1986).

Walid Khalidi, *Conflict and Violence in Lebanon* (Cambridge, Mass.: Harvard Studies in International Affairs, no. 38, 1975).

Fred J. Khouri, *The Arab-Israeli Dilemma* (3d ed. Syracuse, N.Y.: Syracuse University Press, 1985).

Leila Kidd, ed., *Basic Political Documents of the Armed Palestinian Liberation Organization Research Center* (Palestine Books, no. 27, Palestine Liberation Organization Research Center, 1969).

Henry Kissinger, *White House Years* (Boston: Little, Brown, 1979).

Aaron S. Kleiman, *Israel and the World after Forty Years* (Washington, D.C.: Pergamon-Brassy's, 1990).

Oscar Kraines, *Government and Politics in Israel* (Boston: Houghton Mifflin, 1961).

Stephen Krasner, *Structural Conflict* (Berkeley: University of California Press, 1985).

Dan Kurzman, *Ben-Gurion* (New York: Simon & Schuster, 1983).

John Laffin, *The PLO Connections* (London: Corgi, 1982).

Tzvi Lanir, ed., *Israeli Security Planning in the 1980s* (Tel Aviv: Jaffee Center for Strategic Studies, 1985).

————. *War by Choice?* (Tel Aviv: Jaffee Center for Strategic Studies, 1985).

Walter Laqueur, *Terrorism* (Lexington, Mass.: Lexington Books, 1988).

————. *The Terrorist Reader* (New York: New American Library, 1978).

Ann Mosely Lesch, *Political Perceptions of the Palestinians on the West Bank and the Gaza Strip* (Washington, D.C.: Middle East Institute, 1980).

Guenter Lewy, *America in Vietnam* (New York: Oxford University Press, 1978).

Myres S. McDougal et al, *Studies in World Public Order* (New Haven, Conn.: Yale University Press, 1960).

Myres S. McDougal and Florentino P. Feliciano, *Law and Minimum World Public Order* (New Haven, Conn.: Yale University Press, 1961).

W. Thomas and Sally V. Mallison, *The Palestine Problem in International Law and World Order* (London: Longman, 1986).

Moshe Ma'oz, *Palestinian Leadership on the West Bank: The Changing Role of the Arab Mayors Under Jordan and Israel* (London: Frank Cass, 1984).

Moshe Ma'ov and Avner Yaniv, *Syria under Assad* (New York: St. Martin's, 1986).

Yossi Melman, *The Master Terrorist: The True Story Behind Abu Nidal* (New York: Adama, 1986).

Ariel Merari and Shlomi Elad, *The International Dimension of Palestinian Terrorism* (Boulder, Colo.: Westview, JCSS Study no. 6, 1986).

Ariel Merari, ed., *On Terrorism and Combatting Terrorism* (Frederick, Md.: University Publications of America, 1987).

Jan Metzger, Martin Orth and Christian Sterzing, *This Land Is Our Land: The West Bank under Israeli Occupation* (London: Zed Books, 1983).

Aaron David Miller, *The PLO and the Politics of Survival* (Washington, D.C.: CSIS/New York: Praeger, 1983).

Shaul Mishal, *The PLO under Arafat: Between Olive Branch and Gun* (New Haven, Conn.: Yale University Press, 1986).

————. *East Bank, West Bank* (New Haven, Conn.: Yale University Press, 1978).

John Bassett Moore, *A Digest of International Law* (8 vols., Washington, D.C.: Government Printing Office, 1906).

John Norton Moore, ed., *The Arab-Israeli Conflict* (Princeton, N.J.: Princeton University Press, 1975).

National Conference of Catholic Bishops, *The Challenge of Peace: God's Promise and Our Response* (Washington, D.C., May 1983).

National Lawyers Guild, *Treatment of Palestinians in Israeli-Occupied West Bank and Gaza* (New York: National Lawyers Guild, 1978).

————. *International Human Rights Law and Israel's Efforts to Suppress the Palestinian Uprising* (New York: National Lawyers Guild, 1989).

Edgar O'Ballance, *Arab Guerrilla Power, 1967–1972* (Hamden, Conn.: Action Books, 1974).

Conor Cruise O'Brien, *The Siege* (New York: Simon & Schuster, 1986).

William V. O'Brien, *The Conduct of Just and Limited War* (New York: Praeger, 1981).

Bard E. O'Neill, *Armed Struggle in Palestine: A Political-Military Analysis* (Boulder, Colo.: Westview, 1978).

L. Oppenheim, *International Law*, ed. H. Lauterpacht (7th ed., 2 vols., London: Longmans, Green, 1952).

David H. Ott, *Palestine in Perspective: Politics, Human Rights and the West Bank* (London: Quartet Books, 1980).

Bernard Oxman et al. *Law of the Sea: US Policy Dilemmas* (San Francisco, Calif.: ICS Press, 1983).

Alan Peleg, *Begin's Foreign Policy, 1977–1983* (New York: Greenwood, 1987).

Don Peretz, *Intifada* (Boulder, Colo.: Westview, 1990).

Istyan Pogany, *The Security Council and the Arab-Israeli Conflict* (New York: St. Martin's Press, 1984).

William B. Quandt, *Palestinian Nationalism: Its Political and Military Dimension* (Santa Monica, Calif.: RAND, 1971).

William B. Quandt, Fuad Jabber and Ann Mosley Lesch, *The Politics of Palestinian Nationalism* (Berkeley: University of California Press, 1973).

Yitzhak, Rabin, *The Rabin Memoirs* (Boston: Little, Brown, 1976).

Itamar Rabinovitch, *The War for Lebanon, 1970–1983* (Ithaca, N.Y.: Cornell University Press, 1984).

Gideon Rafael, *Destination Peace* (New York: Stein & Day, 1981).

Paul Ramsey, *War and the Christian Conscience: How Shall Modern War Be Conducted Justly?* (Durham, N.C.: Duke University Press, 1961).

————. *The Just War: Force and Political Responsibility* (New York: Charles Scribner's Sons, 1968).

Jonathan C. Randal, *Going All the Way: Christian Warlords, Adventurers and the War in Lebanon* (New York: Viking, 1983).

Bernard Reich, *The United States and Israel* (New York: Praeger, 1984).

Bernard Reich and Gershon R. Kieval, *Israeli National Security Policy* (Westport, Conn.: Greenwood Press, 1988).

Adam Roberts et al., *Academic Freedom under Israeli Occupation* (London: World University Service and International Commission of Jurists, 1984).

Heinrich A. Rommen, *The State in Catholic Thought* (St. Louis, Mo.: Herder, 1945).

Natalino Ronzitti, *Rescuing Nationals Abroad through Military Coercion and Intervention on Grounds of Humanity* (Dordrecht, Boston and Lancaster: Martinus Nijhoff, 1985).

Cheryle Rubenberg, *The Palestine Liberation Organization: Its Institutional Infrastructure* (Belmont, Mass.: Institute of Arab Studies, 1983).

Alvin Z. Rubinstein, ed., *The Arab-Israeli Conflict* (New York: Praeger, 1984).

Howard M. Sachar, *A History of Israel* (2 vols., New York: Knopf, 1976; Oxford University Press, 1987).

Nadav Safran, *Israel: The Embattled Ally* (Cambridge, Mass.: Harvard University Press, 1978).

————. *From War to War, 1948–1967* (New York: Pegasus, 1969).

Emile F. Sahilyeh, *The PLO After the Lebanon War* (Boulder, Co.: Westview, 1986).

James V. Schall, S. J., ed., *German Bishops, "Out of Justice, Peace;" French Bishops, "Winning the Peace"* (San Francisco, Calif.: Ignatius Press, 1984).

Ze'ev Schiff and Ehud Ya'ari, *Israel's Lebanon War* edited and translated by Ina Friedman (New York: Simon & Schuster, 1984).

————. *Intifada,* edited and translated by Ina Friedman (New York: Simon & Schuster, 1990).

Harris A. Schoenberg, *A Mandate for Terror: The United Nations and the PLO* (New York: Shapolsky, 1989).

Ariel Sharon with David Chanoff, *Warrior* (New York: Simon & Schuster, 1989).

Meir Shamgar, *Military Government in the Territories Administered by Israel* (Jerusalem: Hebrew University of Jerusalem, Faculty of Law, Harry Sacher Institute for Legislative Research and Comparative Law, 1982).

Raja Shehadeh, *Occupier's Law: Israel and the West Bank* (Washington, D.C.: Institute for Palestine Studies, 1985).

Jonathan Shimshoni, *Israel and Conventional Deterrence: Border Warfare from 1953 to 1970* (Ithaca, N.Y.: Cornell Univeristy Press, 1988).

Eric Silver, *Begin: The Haunted Prophet* (New York: Random House, 1984).

Steven L. Speigel, *The Other Arab-Israeli Conflict* (Chicago: University of Chicago Press, 1985).

Steward Stevens, *The Spymasters of Israel* (New York: Macmillan, 1980).

Julius Stone, *Israel and Palestine: Assault on the Law of Nations* (Baltimore, Md.: Johns Hopkins University Press, 1981).

————. *Legal Controls of International Conflict* (New York: Rinehart, 1954).

————. *Aggression and World Order* (Berkeley: University of California Press, 1958).

Asher Susser, *In Through the out Door: Jordan's Disengagement and the Middle East Peace Process,* Washington Institute Policy Papers no. 19 (Washington, D.C.: Washington Institute for Near East Policy, 1990).

Shabtai Teveth, *The Cursed Blessing* (London: Weidenfeld & Nicolson, 1970).

Seth Tillman, *The United States in the Middle East* (Bloomington, Ind.: Indiana University Press, 1982).

Saadia Touval, *The Peace Brokers: Mediators in the Arab-Israeli Conflict* (Princeton, N.J.: Princeton University Press, 1982).

G.I. Tunkin, *Theory of International Law* (Cambridge, Mass.: Harvard University Press, 1974).

U.S. Department of the Air Force, *International Law—The Conduct of Armed Conflict and Air Operations, 19 November 1976, AFP 110–31* (Washington, D.C.: Department of the Air Force, 1976).

U.S. Department of State, *Country Reports on Human Rights Practices, 1988* and *1989.*

Alfred Vanderpol, *La doctrine scolastique du droit de guerre* (Paris: Pedone, 1919).

Gerhard von Glahn, *The Occupation of Enemy Territory* (Minneapolis: University of Minnesota Press, 1957).

Michael Walzer, *Just and Unjust War* (New York: Basic Books, 1977).

Ezer Weizman, *The Battle for Peace* (New York: Bantam, 1981).

Avner Yaniv, *Dilemmas of Security* (New York: Oxford University Press, 1987).

————. *Deterrence without the Bomb* (Lexington, Mass.: Lexington Books, 1987).

Ehud Ya'ari, *Strike Terror: The Story of Fatah* (New York: Sabra Books, 1970).

Aryeh Yodfat and Yuval Ohanna-Arnon, *PLO Strategy and Tactics* (London: Croom Helm, 1981).

Articles

Roberto Barsotti, "Armed Reprisals," in A. Cassese, ed., *The Current Legal Regulation of the Use of Force* (Dodrecht: Nijhoff, 1986), pp. 79–110.

Gabriel Ben-Dor, "The Strategy of Terrorism in the Arab-Israeli Conflict: The Case of the Palestinian Guerrillas," in Yair Evron, ed., *International Violence: Terrorism, Surprise and Control* (Jerusalem: Leonard Davis Institute for International Relations, Hebrew University of Jerusalem, 1979), p. 126–64.

Barry M. Blechman, "The Impact of Israel's Reprisals on Behavior of the Bordering Arab Nations directed at Israel," *Journal of Conflict Resolution* 16 (1972): 155–81.

Yehuda Z. Blum, "The Missing Reversioner: Reflections on the Status of Judea and Samaria," in J.N. Moore, *The Arab-Israeli Conflict* (Princeton: Princeton University Press, 1977).

Derek Bowett, "Reprisals Involving Recourse to Armed Force," *American Journal of International Law* 66 (1972): 1–36.

Antonio Cassese, "Sabra and Shatilla," in *Violence and Law in the Modern Age*, Idem. ed., trans. S. J. K. Greensleaves (Cambridge: Polity, 1988). pp. 76–87.

James F. Childress, "Just War Theories," *Theological Studies* 39 (1978).

———. "Just War Criteria," in Thomas Shannon, ed., *War or Peace: The Search for New Answers* (Maryknoll, N.Y.: Orbis, 1980). pp. 40–58.

Inis Claude, "Just Wars: Doctrines and Institutions," *Political Science Quarterly* 95 (1980): 83–96.

Moshe Dayan, "Why Israel Strikes Back," in Donald Robinson, ed., *Under Fire: Israel's 20-Year Struggle for Survival* (New York: Norton, 1968), pp. 122–23.

Alan Dershowitz, "Preventive Detention of Citizens During a National Emergency," *Israel Yearbook on Human Rights* 1 (1971): 295–321.

Alan Dowty, "Emergency Powers in Israel: The Devaluation of Crisis," in Shao-chuan Leng, ed., *Coping with Crises: How Governments Deal with Emergencies* (Lanham, Md.: University Press of America, 1990), pp. 1–43.

Richard A. Falk, "The Beirut Raid and the International Law of Reprisal," *American Journal of International Law* 63 (1979): 415–43.

James E. S. Fawcett, "Intervention in International Law: A Study of Some Recent Cases," Académie de Droit International, *Recueil des cours* 2 (1961): 347–421.

Thomas Franck, "Who Killed Article 2(4)? or, Changing Norms Governing the Use of Force by States," *American Journal of International Law* 64 (1970): 809–37.

Elisa D. Harris, "Sverdlovsk and Yellow Rain: Two Cases of Soviet Noncompliance?" *International Security* 11 (1987): 41–95.

Joost R. Hilterman, "Human Rights and the Mass Movement: The First Year of the Intifada," *Journal of Palestine Studies* 18 (1989): 126–33.

D. Brian Hufford and Robert Malley, "The War in Lebanon," in W. Michael Reisman and Andrew R. Willard, eds., *International Incidents: The Law That Counts in World Politics* (Princeton, N.J.: Princeton University Press, 1988), pp. 144–80.

Efraim Inbar, "The 'No-Choice War' Debate in Israel," *The Journal of Strategic Studies* 12 (1989): 22–37.

Penny Johnson, "Palestinian Universities under Occupation," *Journal of Palestine Studies* 18 (1989): 92–100.

A.F. Kassim, "The Palestine Liberation Organization's Claim to Status: A Juridical Analysis under International Law," *Denver Journal of International Law and Policy* 9 (1980): 1–33.

Major Dan Laish, "Peace for Galilee: Ansar Detention Facility," *IDF Journal* 1 (1982): 38–9.

Barry Levenfeld, "Israeli Counter-Fedayeen Tactics of Lebanon: Self-Defense and Reprisals under Modern International Law," *Columbia Journal of Transnational Law* 21 (1982). 1–48.

Howard S. Levie, "Maltreatment of Prisoners of War in Vietnam," in Richard A. Falk, ed., *The Vietnam War in International Law* (4 vols., Princeton, N.J.: Princeton University Press, 1969–76). 2: 361–97.

Samuel W. Lewis, "Israel: The Peres Era and Its Legacy," *Foreign Affairs* 65 (1987): 582–610.

Richard B. Lillich, "Forcible Self-Help under International Law," *International Law Studies* 62 (1980):

———. "Forcible Help by States to Protect Human Rights," *Iowa Law Review* 53 (1967): 325–51.

———. "Humanitarian Intervention: A Reply to Ian Brownlie and a Plea for Constructive Alternatives," in *Law and Civil War in the Modern World,* ed. J. N. Moore (Baltimore, Md.: Johns Hopkins University Press, 1974): 229–51.

———. "Intervention to Protect Human Rights," *McGill Law Journal* 15 (1969): 205–19.

Myres S. McDougal and W. Michael Reisman, "Rhodesia and the United Nations: The Lawfulness of International Concern," *American Journal of International Law* 62 (1968): 1–19.

Aaron David Miller, "Palestinians and the Intifada: One Year Later," *Current History* 88 (1989): 73–76, 106–07.

Joshua Muravchik, "Misreporting Lebanon," *Policy Review* (Winter 1983): 11–66.

John Courtney Murray, S.J., "Theology and Modern War," *Theological Studies* 20 (1959): 40–61.

———. "The Uses of a Doctrine on the Use of Force: War as a Moral Problem" in *We Hold These Truths* (New York: Sheed & Ward, 1960), pp. 249–73.

William V. O'Brien, "The PLO in International Law," *Boston University International Law Journal* 3 (1984): pp. 349–413.

———. "International Law and the Outbreak of War in the Middle East," *Orbis* 11 (1967): 692–723.

———. "Biological/Chemical Warfare and the International Law of War," *Georgetown Law Journal* 51 (1962): 1–63.

———. "Legitimate Military Necessity in Nuclear War," *World Polity* 2 (1960): 35–120.

———. "The Meaning of 'Military Necessity' in International Law," *World Polity* 1 (1957): 109–76.

W. Hays Parks, "Air War and the Law of War," *The Air Force Law Review* 32 (1990): 1–226.

———. "Crossing the Line," *US Naval Institute Proceedings* 112 (1986): 964–80.

Martin Peretz, "Lebanon Eyewitness," *New Republic,* (August 2, 1982), pp. 15–23.

Paul de la Pradelle, "Le proces des grands criminels de guerre et le développment du droit international," *Nouvelle revue de droit international privé* (Paris: Editions Internationales, 1947), pp. 15–17.

William B. Quandt, "Political and Military Dimensions of Contemporary Palestinian Nationalism," in Quandt, Fuad Jabbar & Ann Mosely Lesch, *The Politics of Palestinian Nationalism* (Berkeley: University of California Press, 1973), pp. 43–153.

W. Michael Reisman, "Criteria for the Lawful Use of Force in International Law," *Yale Journal of International Law* 10 (1985): 279–85.

———. "Old Wine in New Bottles: The Reagan and Brezhnev Doctrines in Contemporary International Law," *Yale Journal of International Law* 13 (1988): 171–198.

Adam Roberts, "Prolonged Military Occupation: The Israeli Occupied Territories Since 1967," *American Journal of International Law* 84 (1990): 44–103.

Romana Sadurska, "Threats of Force," *American Journal of International Law* 82 (1988). pp. 239–68.

Oscar Schacter, "The Right of States to Use Armed Force," *Michigan Law Review* 82 (1984): 1620–45.

Meir Shamgar, "The Observance of International Law in the Administered Territories," in J.N. Moore, *The Arab-Israeli Conflict* (Princeton, N.J.: Princeton University Press, 1977) pp. 489–507.

Ronald Stockton, "Intifada Deaths," *Journal of Palestine Studies* 18 (1989): 101–08.

Robert W. Tucker, "Reprisals, and Self-Defense: the Customary Law," *American Journal of International Law* 66 (1972): 586–95.

Avner Yaniv, "Israel Comes of Age," *Current History* 88 (1989): 69–72, 100–02.

Lt. Col. Yoel Zinger, "Peace for Galilee: The Prisoners," *IDF Journal* 1 (1982): 37–8.

Government Publications and Other Reports

Amnesty International, "Israel and the Occupied Territories: Excessive Force: Beatings to Maintain Law and Order," in *Journal of Palestine Studies* 18 (1989).

———. "Israel and the Occupied Territories: The Misuse of Tear Gas by Israeli Army Personnel in the Occupied Territories," in *Journal of Palestine Studies* 18 (1988).

———. "Israel and the Occupied Territories: Update to the Use of Live Ammunition by Members of the Israeli Defense Force," *Journal of Palestine Studies* 18 (1988).

———. "Killings by Israeli Forces," *Focus* (AI newsletter) 1 (1990).

Foreign and Commonwealth Office (UK), *Background Brief: Palestine Liberation Organisation* (London: September 1989).

Kriegets Lagar: Folkrattsliga Gallande under Krig, neutralitet och occupation, Carl-Ivar Skarstedt, ed. (Stockholm, 1979).

Ministry of Foreign Affairs (Israel), *The PLO: Has It Complied with Its Commitments?* (Jerusalem: May 1990).

Nuremberg International Military Tribunal, *Trial of Major Criminals* (Washington, D.C.: U.S. Government Printing Office, 1949–51).

Office of the U.S. Chief Counsel for Prosecution of Axis Criminality, *Nazi Conspiracy and Aggression—Opinion and Judgment* (Washington, D.C.: U.S. Government Printing Office, 1947).

Overenskomster Vedrorende Krigens Rett Som Norwge Star Tilsluttet (Norwegian Military Manual) (Oslo: Grondahl & Sons Boktrykkeri, 1961).

United Nations, *Security Council Official Records.*

United Nations, *Resolutions and Decisions of the Security Council.*

U.S. Army, *The Law of Landwarfare, FM 27-10* (Washington, D.C.: War Department, 1940, and Department of the Army, 1956).

U.S. Dept of the Air Force, *International Law—The Conduct of Armed Conflict and Air Operations,* AFP 110–31.

U.S. Dept. of the Navy, *The Commander's Handbook For the Law of Naval Operations* (Washington, D.C.: Naval Warfare Pub. 9, 1987).

War Office (U.K.), *The Law of War on Land* (London: Her Majesty's Stationery Office, 1958).

Turgill Wulf, *Handbook i Folkratt: under Krig, neutralitet och ockupation* (Stockholm, 1980).

Newspapers and Newsmagazines

The Jerusalem Post (daily and international editions)

Newsweek

The New York Times

The Washington Post

Other Sources

The Shiloah Center for Middle Eastern and African Studies, Dayan Center, *Middle East Contemporary Survey* (Tel Aviv: Dayan Center, 1978–).

Unpublished Dissertations

Barry Blechman, "The Consequences of the Israeli Reprisals: An Assessment," (Washington, D.C.: Georgetown University, 1971).

Richard Winslow, "American Military Intervention in the Middle East: Its Political Prudence, Military Feasibility and Moral Permissibility—An Analysis of Four Cases" (Washington, D.C.: Georgetown University, 1989).

Epilogue:
After the Gulf War

Israel's war with the PLO continues after the end of the Gulf War. From the outset Arafat aligned himself and the PLO with Saddam Hussein. After the U.S. and coalition forces began their air war against Iraq on January 16/17, 1991 Fatah forces in Lebanon became active. Mainline PLO forces launched rocket attacks against targets in the Israeli Security Zone in south Lebanon. Israel replied with major air strikes against Fatah bases in Lebanon, marking the collapse of a tacit two-year truce.[1] Continuing PLO attacks on Israeli forces and facilities in the Security Zone elicited further Israeli air raids against PLO bases. It is impossible to predict whether these renewed hostilities will continue after Iraq's defeat.

On the political-diplomatic level the Gulf War has been a disaster for Arafat and the PLO. By "standing in the same trench" with Saddam Hussein Arafat foreited the support of Kuwait, Saudi Arabia, Egypt and other Arab members of the UN coalition at a time when the Soviet Union is no longer a source of assistance. The Palestinians may come to terms with Israel without the PLO.[2]

During the Gulf War the Palestinians in Jordan and the Territories openly demonstrated in support of Saddam Hussein. They cheered the Scud attacks on Israeli cities. Naturally this embittered Israelis of virtually all political dispositions. Throughout the period of hostilities the Israeli hold on the Territories became tighter and more onerous to the Palestinians. Even if the PLO is displaced as the sole representative of the Palestinians and the coalition partners generate new and promising approaches to ending the Arab-Israeli conflict, the task will be very difficult. But it is an indispensable task that calls for our prayers as well as for our practical support. Ironically, if the conflict can be resolved without the participation of the PLO, Israel's war with the PLO may end because of events over which the PLO has little or no control.

Under any scenario, optimistic or pessimistic, strong Israeli security postures will remain necessary. In particular, deterrence and defense against terrorism may continue to be important. As indicated in Chapter 3, I am doubtful that the successful UN Security Council enforcement action in the Gulf War marks the beginning of a "new world order." I think that UN enforcement action on behalf of Israel is particularly unlikely. If that proves to be the case, the practical, legal and moral dilemmas of counterterror deterrence/defense discussed in this book may remain with us for some time.

March 1991

Notes

1. "Israel Bombs Fatah Sites in Lebanon," *New York Times,* February 6, 1991, A19, cols. 1–4.
2. Youssef M. Ibrahim, "Arafat, the Survivor, Now Finds Support Vanishing," ibid., February 13, 1991, A16, cols. 1–6.

Index

Palestine Communist Party (PCP) 11
Popular Front for the Liberation of
Palestine (PFLP) 11, 17, 35, 37,
61–62
Popular Front for the Liberation of
Palestine-General Command
(PFLP-GC) 11, 45
Palestine Liberation Front (PLF) 8,
11, 17, 43, 45
Palestine National Council 28–29 n
Algiers (1988) 7, 12, 304
Cairo (1974) 7, 27 n
Palestinian National Front 60, 219
Palestinian Covenant 7, 8, 10, 292,
293, 295
Parks, W. Hays 191, 319
Passive defense 21
PLO
Algiers Summit (1988) 7, 12, 304
armed struggle 13, 54, 56
assassinations 17, 41
belligerent status of 13–14
Cairo Declaration (11/1985) 55, 56
colocation 158, 178, 186, 191, 209
conventional forces 44, 47, 140–41,
300–01
Covenant 7–8, 9, 10, 292, 293–94,
295, 303
declaration of a state (1988) 7, 29
n, 223
diplomatic strategy 13
grand strategy 12–13, 14
guerrilla war 35
hijacking 35–37
international terrorism 35–37
Jordan, relations with, 37
Lebanon front 37–41
objectives 7–10, 12
organization 11–12
political/diplomatic strategy 13–15
renunciation of terror 8, 59–64
tactics 18
terror 13–17, 54, 55, 57
2 Phase Plan 9, 292–93
war of national liberation 7, 34, 121

PLO Attacks
Beaches Raid (5/1990) 63–64
Country Club Raid (3/1978) 42
Kiryat Shemona (4/1974) 39
Munich Olympic Massacre (9/1972)
39
Nahariya (4/1979) 43
Peres, Shimon 220
Pictet, Jean S. 243–44
Poleg, Brig. Gen. Zvi 224
Popular Struggle Front (PSF) 11
preemptive attacks, defined, 24
preventive/attrition, defined, 22, 24
proportion, principle of, 281
"The Purity of Arms" 208–09

Qibya Raid (10/14–15/1953) 101–02

Rabat Arab Summit 40
Rabin, Yitzhak 23, 30 n, 31 n, 166,
222, 223–24, 231, 236–37, 251
Ramsey, Paul 276
Randal, Jonathan 188
Reisman, W. Michael 96 n, 130 n,
142
Reprisals 98 n
"accumulation argument" 102,
108, 118, 120
and deterrence 103, 117–18
Barsotti on 129
Bowett distinguishes from self-
defense 102–04
Critique of Security Council
practice 117–22
Dinstein on 123
Israel's self-defense arguments 112–
14
Israeli types of 105–06
lack of U.N. sanctions for 122
"reasonable reprisals" 104, 117,
122–25
Security Council on Israeli
arguments 104–12
status of in international law 117